Harold G. Koenig, MD, M.

Aging and God: Spiritual Pathways to Mental Health in Midlife and Later Years

Pre-publication
REVIEWS,
COMMENTARIES,
EVALUATIONS . . .

"**H**arold Koenig, in *Aging and God*, has again undertaken the task of identifying how religion affects mental health in adulthood. Building upon his earlier works, this book contains reviews of the most recent research and findings from Koenig's own studies. He provides a historical review of the tension between behavioral science and religious perspectives, especially in the work of Freud. He demonstrates that scientific developments often involve 'preferences' for viewing phenomena and that the religious perspective can complement science when understanding and treating mental distress. In the final analysis, they both call for love, forgiveness, and caring.

The author draws extensively from two North Carolina data sources: 1,000 hospitalized male veterans and 1,300 community-dwelling elders participating in the NIMH Epidemiological Catchment Area study. Considerable case study material is presented along with statistical analyses. The book's focus is on the Judeo-Christian orientation, and Koenig integrates numerous passages from the Talmud and Bible. Readers will find the discussions of religious coping and depression and anxiety most illuminating. The chapter on physician-assisted suicide is masterfully developed.

Koenig is to be commended for probing deeper into the links between spiritual and mental health while considering successful aging. Although he does so from a theoretical and scholarly approach, THE BOOK WILL BE WELCOMED BY PRACTITIONERS FOR ITS PRACTICAL RELEVANCE AND IMPLICATIONS."

Kenneth F. Ferraro, PhD
Associate Professor of Sociology, Purdue University

"This is a masterful successor to the author's *Religion, Health, and Aging*. Solidly based upon medical scholarship, research, and clinical experience, including his own innovative studies and careful documentation of original sources, it is nevertheless easily comprehended by non-medical readers. The whole–person perspective that accentuates the interplay of physical, mental, and spiritual well-being is evident throughout the book. Competent critiques of previous research, of poorly grounded assumptions undergirding psychotherapy, and of Fowler's faith stages are superlative. Clear, perceptive, and sensitive discussions of such topics as the spiritual needs of the physically ill, religion as a means for coping with human problems, neurotic uses of religion, alcoholism, religious conversion, and physician-assisted suicide make this AN OUTSTANDING RESOURCE FOR GERONTOLOGISTS, SOCIAL AND BEHAVIORAL SCIENTISTS, AND THERAPISTS OF ALL KINDS, NOT JUST THOSE IN THE CHAPLAINCY, GERIATRICS, AND OTHER HEALTH-RELATED PROFESSIONS."

David O. Moberg, PhD
Professor Emeritus, Sociology, Marquette University

"**H**arold Koenig's numerous articles and previous publications in mental health, spirituality, and aging place him in the ideal position to offer the book he has completed. *Aging and God* is a thoroughly researched and highly readable summary of the literature in religion, mental health, and aging. It includes a significant amount of work of the findings from research that Koenig and others at Duke University have produced.

The summary of Erickson, Kohlberg, and Fowler on human and faith/religious development constructs is especially valuable for a quick-study of major materials in this area. Koenig's outline of his own theory of later life faith development will be instructive for both students and advanced scholars. In addition, his report on research advances in depression, religious coping, and anxiety should be read by practitioners and graduate students as well as faculty who need to 'catch up' in the field.

An equal strength of the volume is seen in its clinical usefulness and the special populations with whom religion and spiritual care is especially appropriate, i.e., nursing home residents, drug and alcohol abusing persons, bereaved, and terminally ill people. I PREDICT THAT THIS WILL BE A VALUED TEXT AND REFERENCE BOOK FOR YEARS TO COME AMONG PEOPLE WHO UTILIZE SPIRITUAL RESOURCES IN WORKING WITH OLDER PERSONS."

James J. Seeber, PhD
Associate Professor of Sociology,
California Baptist College

"**I**n his book, *Aging and God*, Dr. Harold Koenig explores the problems caused when older adults lose most of the 'natural joys of life,' and what resources are available to help make successful aging a reality. The author deals with the long-time conflict between psychiatry and religion, noting that both disciplines offer parallel positive approaches useful in meeting the spiritual needs in aging; that religion can play a major role in enlivening later years. Religion and spirituality are used interchangeably.

The Haworth Pastoral Press
An Imprint of The Haworth Press, Inc.

Aging and God
Spiritual Pathways to Mental Health in Midlife and Later Years

The Haworth Pastoral Press
Religion, Ministry & Pastoral Care
William M. Clements, PhD
Senior Editor

New, Recent, and Forthcoming Titles:

Growing Up: Pastoral Nurture for the Later Years by Thomas B. Robb

Religion and Family: When God Helps by Laurel Arthur Burton

Victims of Dementia: Services, Support, and Care by Wm. Michael Clemmer

Horrific Traumata: A Pastoral Response to the Post-Traumatic Stress Disorder by N. Duncan Sinclair

Aging and God: Spiritual Pathways to Mental Health in Midlife and Later Years by Harold G. Koenig

Aging and God
Spiritual Pathways
to Mental Health
in Midlife and Later Years

Harold G. Koenig, MD, MHSc

The Haworth Pastoral Press
An Imprint of The Haworth Press, Inc.
New York • London • Norwood (Australia)

Published by

The Haworth Pastoral Press, an imprint of The Haworth Press, Inc., 10 Alice Street, Binghamton, NY 13904-1580

Library of Congress Cataloging-in-Publication Data

Aging and God : spiritual pathways to mental health in midlife and later years / Harold G. Koenig, editor.
   p.   cm.
Includes bibliographical references and index.
ISBN 1-56024-424-0 (alk. paper).
1. Aging–Religious aspects. 2. Mental health–Religious aspects. 3. Psychology and religion. I. Koenig, Harold George.
BV4580.A45   1993
261.8'3426–dc20   92-44916
                                                                       CIP

FTW

AFR 9189

This book is dedicated to Maria and Harold E. Koenig,
my beloved parents, who made it all possible

ABOUT THE AUTHOR

Harold G. Koenig, MD, MHSc, has researched and written on the relationship between religion and mental health for the past ten years. He is Assistant Professor of Psychiatry and of Internal Medicine and Director of the *Program on Religion, Aging, and Health* in the Center for Aging at Duke University Medical Center. Dr. Koenig recently received a 5-year National Institute of Mental Health Academic Award to study depression in medically ill hospitalized older adults. He has given numerous talks and educational seminars on religion, aging, and mental health in the United States and Canada.

CONTENTS

PART III: ADVANCES IN RESEARCH

Foreword

Aging and God is an important book! Two of the most significant concerns of the elderly–spirituality and health–are now addressed in a comprehensive and intelligible way by the author, Harold G. Koenig, MD, a geriatric psychiatrist from the Duke University Medical Center. Specialists in health, religion, and aging should be in dialogue with each other at every routine turning point and crisis in the fourth quarter of life. The information in these pages could turn the "should" (that usually doesn't happen) into a reality that often takes place in hospitals, nursing homes, living rooms, and houses of worship.

Aging and God will be received as a beacon of light illuminating at least three broad areas of knowledge and professional practice: aging, religion, and mental health. Professionals in these areas have often labored in relative isolation from one another–to the detriment of elderly people. With the publication of this book, a reasonable, responsible, and informed dialogue can begin to take place within each profession and between the professions.

While the elderly themselves are vitally concerned about religious faith and health, professional compartmentalization has led us into far too many cul-de-sacs over the years. Persons knowledgeable about one area of the emerging trialogue between mental health, religion, and aging are often uninformed or even misinformed about a second area and perhaps only partially informed about a third. This unfortunate reality has made communication between the professions extremely difficult. Harold Koenig begins to build some extremely important bridges for interprofessional communication in the pages of *Aging and God.* In the coming decades, we will need to walk across these bridges of understanding and enlightenment repeatedly, if not continuously.

Ideally the field of mental health should encompass expertise from many disciplines such as medicine, gerontology, psychology, and religion. In the same fashion, gerontology needs to be cognizant of medicine and religion, as well as many other subjects such as sociology and psychology. No professions work with elderly people day in and day out more frequently than those from religion or health. Unfortunately, the religious professional often lags behind in knowledge appropriate for high level functioning with elderly people, both from a mental health and a gerontological perspective. But if you identify with a health or gerontological profession and are feeling just a little smug at this point, then this book is *especially* important reading for you!

Broad groups of people, mental health professionals and ger-ontologists are buried deep *below* ground zero when it comes to the knowledge (or even the personal openness) necessary to understand the vitally important role and function that religion often plays in the lives of elderly people. Because of the scientific community's iden-tification with what I have referred to as "empirical positivism"[1] health and gerontology tend to ignore religion–at best. When this reality is coupled with the historic separation of church and state, then public institutions tend to miss many of the opportunities to understand and help the elderly–who often hold strong religious and spiritual values. Religious faith and spiritual perspectives that have grown and matured over decades of an individual's life are seem-ingly invisible or at best so marginalized or trivialized that they might as well be invisible. Carefully constructed policies that under-gird public institutions have essentially ignored the one dynamic that could make a difference. Likewise, religious professionals "need to get a handle" on the oftentimes subtle interaction between faith and mental health as well as basic facts about human aging. Dealing with all of these disparate concerns in one book had never taken place before the publication of *Aging and God*.

Because Dr. Koenig writes primarily from the viewpoints and methodologies afforded by empirical positivism, he has marshaled the results from measurable research in ways that are highly relevant

---

1. "Science and Religion: Unlikely Partners in Gerontology?" William M. Clements. Chapter from a forthcoming book entitled, *The Handbook of Religion, Spirituality and Aging*. Edited by Kimble, Ellor, McFadden, and Seeber. To be published by Fortress Press.

to both the scientific and the religious communities. Simultaneously, he manages to successfully sidestep many of the blatantly ideological debates from religion that do not lend themselves to empirical verification, nor is one theological perspective allowed to totally dominate his discussion.

As a result, this book admirably opens the door between science and religion as they relate to human aging. Religious professionals need to know about mental health and aging, just as health professionals need to grow in their understanding of religion and spiritual health. So, while each professional has a different set of strengths to bring to the discussion, each also brings a concomitant set of deficits. Koenig addresses these inadequacies in a very accessible and enlightened fashion. You will not only profit from reading this book, you will also enjoy reading it and discussing it with your colleagues. *Aging and God* is an important book!

William M. Clements, PhD
Edna and Lowell Craig Professor
of Pastoral Care & Counseling,
The School of Theology at Claremont;
Director of Pastoral Counseling Education,
The Clinebell Institute;
Editor, *The Journal of Religious Gerontology*

Preface

Though outwardly we are wasting away,
yet inwardly we are being renewed day by day.

–2 Corinthians 4:16[1]

The premise of this volume is that successful aging is possible for every older person, even in the midst of circumstances that on the surface would appear dismal and hopeless. As people enter the later years of life, many are able to continue experiencing joy, fulfillment, purpose, and meaning. They are financially secure, surrounded by loved ones, physically healthy and capable of pursuing life's pleasures independently and without restrictions. For others, however, the story is different. Things happen which interfere with the ability to experience such satisfactions. Physical health deteriorates, friends and loved ones die, finances dwindle, the meaning and purpose of life become questioned. This book focuses on older adults who, because of changes brought on by aging, have (or at least think they have) lost many of the "natural" joys of life. What resources are available to help make successful aging a reality to these individuals? Religion claims to be one such resource. How true is this?

For the past eight years, my colleagues and I at Duke University's Center for Aging have been studying the relationship between religion and mental health in later life. Much of this work comes from two major projects now completed: (1) a study of over 1000 veterans hospitalized with medical or neurological illnesses and (2) a study of 1300 community-dwelling elders participating in the NIMH Epidemiologic Catchment Area (ECA) program. These in-

---

1. Unless otherwise specified, biblical references throughout the book are from the New International Version.

vestigations, along with recent work by others on community-dwelling and institutionalized elders, have extended the findings of earlier research broadly summarized in our previous book *Religion, Health, and Aging* (1988). While the latter publication primarily concerns an extensive review of previous research conducted over the past 50 years on that topic, this book focuses more on recent findings, theoretical issues, and implications for clinical practice.

In order to understand why religion has been neglected as a potential resource, I examine the relationship between religion and the psychological sciences from a historical and then present-day perspective. Having done this, I then review the major theories of human development and construct a theory of religious faith development particularly applicable to older adults. Recent studies are then reviewed that have attempted to operationalize religious concepts and relate them to common mental health problems such as depression and anxiety. Clinical applications derived from theory and research are then examined in terms of prevention and treatment, emphasizing the roles of the clergy and mental health professionals. Finally, I address a number of urgent problems that older adults must face (disability and dependency in the nursing home, Alzheimer's disease, caregiver stress, alcoholism, sexual dysfunction, bereavement, importance of the family, dying and death, suicide, and assisted-suicide), and examine how religion may help to facilitate successful aging in these areas.

The twenty-two chapters are divided into six major parts. In Part I, I critically evaluate the relationship between religion and the mental health sciences (psychiatry and psychology). My objective is to convey to the reader a better understanding of why religion has been neglected by these professions as a possible mental health resource. Chapter 1 traces the history of religion and medical psychology from prehistoric times to the present, focusing on the uneasy relationship between these two disciplines. Chapter 2 examines the life of Freud, his teachings and impact on attitudes of mental health professionals toward religion. Chapter 3 addresses the views of man taken by members of the mental health profession and Judeo-Christian religion, with an emphasis on differences. Uncertainty in science is stressed, biases in the observation of facts are pointed out, and scientific support for psychoanalysis and related psychotherapies is challenged, as a case is made for the religious approach as a rational alternative. Chapter 4 focuses on similarities and areas of overlap between religion and psychology, explores how religion and the mental sciences may complement and build on the strengths of each other, and speculates on a possible biological basis for religiousness.

In Part II, I address theoretical aspects of human development, focusing on cognitive, moral, and religious faith development. In Chapter 5, I review and discuss the classical theories of human psychological development, touching on the works of Freud, Jung, Piaget, Mahler, Bowlby, Sullivan, Erikson, and others. In Chapter 6, I review and critique Fowler's theory of faith development as it applies to an older population. In Chapter 7, I describe a biopsycho-social-spiritual view of man and elaborate a theory of religious development applicable to older persons, thereby providing a theoretical background for the research to follow.

Part III summarizes recent findings on the relationship between religion and mental health, focusing on the Durham Veterans Administration Mental Health Survey (DVAMHS), Piedmont Epidemiologic Catchment Area (ECA) study, and other investigations such as the Yale Health and Aging project. Chapter 8 presents an overview of the DVAMHS, focusing on the sample and study design; included here are data on the prevalence of depression among hospitalized medical inpatients, most of whom were elderly. Chapter 9 describes the use of religious coping by younger and older patients, and discusses changes in this behavior with aging. Chapter 10 presents a detailed description of the religious coping responses of 13 younger and 69 older patients systematically selected from this population. Chapter 11 addresses the relationship between religion and depression from a cross-sectional and a longitudinal perspective; associations between religious coping, self-rated and observer-rated depressive symptoms, and major depressive disorder are examined. In Chapter 12, I summarize the Duke ECA study findings on the relationships between anxiety disorders and religious denomination, church attendance, Bible reading, prayer, "born again" status, and self-rated religiosity in a large population of community-dwelling older adults. In addition to discussing a number of theories possibly relating religion and anxiety, I also examine the neurotic uses of religion.

Part IV (and Part V to some extent) deals with practical issues relevant to those who work on the front line with older adults. Theoretical considerations and research findings described in previous chapters are now applied to the problem of meeting the spiritual and mental health needs of elders with chronic or acute health problems. Chapter 13 reviews the spiritual needs of physically ill older persons hospitalized with medical illness. Chapter 14 examines the crisis ahead in geriatric psychiatry and the increasing role that community clergy and chaplains will need to play in meeting the mental and spiritual needs of older adults. The chapter also describes interventions that health professionals can make to help ease the psychological burden of chronic illness, severe disability, and terminal illness. Included here is advice about how to approach patients on religious matters without invading privacy or showing disrespect for individual autonomy. Chapter 15 reviews the types of psychotherapy most helpful in older adults, compares them with approaches to mental health taken by religion, and examines how psychotherapy and religion can be integrated.

Part V examines situations and disorders of particular concern to older persons. Here I review the current knowledge on these subjects and examine how religion can be used as a resource. Chapter 16 examines life in the nursing home and how religion can help bring about successful aging even in this setting. Included here is a discussion of the problem of Alzheimer's Disease and other dementing illnesses and how these disorders affect religious faith and its expression. Alcoholism and sexual dysfunction are the topics of Chapter 17. I discuss the findings from the DVAMHS on alcohol use and examine factors which lead to abstinence and its maintenance. Included here are data from a study of elderly men attending a urology clinic for sexual impotence; the effects of religion on the way older men cope with this problem are discussed. Chapter 18 addresses the importance of family to older adults and the role that religion plays in determining family belief systems that impact on health care decisions. Bereavement is also addressed, as is the role of religion in facilitating (and at times, impeding) the grief process. Chapter 19 deals with the issue of religious conversion in later life.

Here, I examine factors in older persons which lead to conversion and discuss the mental health effects that follow. Again, data from the DVAMHS provide a basis for the discussion.

Part VI takes an in-depth look at end of life issues. Chapter 20 examines the topics of death and dying, exploring different attitudes toward death and discussing how religion may ease the process of dying and lead to a "good death." In the final two chapters, I deal with the controversial subjects of geriatric suicide, physician-assisted suicide and euthanasia. The increasing prevalence of elder suicide is examined, risk factors are discussed, and role of religion as a deterrent is considered. In the final chapter, the euthanasia debate is reviewed with a special emphasis on whether or not physician-assisted suicide should be legalized.

This volume is unique in that it is the first publication to comprehensively address the issue of religion and *mental health* in later life. Many nations are looking to the United States for leadership and direction in how to cope with their own aging populations. This book will be of interest to health professionals (physicians, psychologists, nurses, social workers, chaplains, and pastoral counselors) working with older adults who need updated information on the mental health problems that elders face and knowledge about the contributions and limitations of religion as a resource.

Aging and God will be of use to educators in the fields of psychiatry and psychology, medicine, nursing and allied health sciences, social sciences, and religion, who need a text for their classes which takes a critical and comprehensive look at recent research and existing theories concerning the relationship between aging, religion and mental health. Policy-makers will find the text helpful, as they face the enormous task of providing for the mental health needs of older adults in this country, a group whose numbers will double over the next 30 years. Because of a near-epidemic of drug use, depression, and other mental-health problems in the baby-boom cohort (Klerman & Weissman 1989), once this generation reaches old age the costs of mental health services are likely to skyrocket and overwhelm the capacity of the current secular system to provide needed care (Chapter 14). Religious organizations may be called on to help out with this crisis. Until now, there has been no central resource to turn to that summarizes the theory, presents the research, and details applications for clinical practice in a form accessible to both mental health and religious professionals.

At the present time, hospital (and nursing home) chaplains are already providing much of the psychological care to older adults in situations where health care professionals lack the time to do so. They will find this book informative and encouraging. Community clergy, faced with increasingly older congregations (25-30% of many Methodist and Catholic congregations are now over age 65) will find the wide range of topics presented here both interesting and directive. Finally, this text will be of use to many aging persons themselves, as well as their families, as they seek to better adapt to and cope with the very real and difficult problems that old age can bring.

Because of my lack of in-depth knowledge on the subject, I have generally avoided the topic of aging, mental health, and religious faiths outside of the Judeo-Christian tradition. The primary exceptions to this are in Chapter 11, where I briefly address the relationship between other world religions and mental health, and in Chapter 21, where I devote several paragraphs to the topic of suicide and world religions. More information on this topic can be obtained from William Clements' *Religion, Aging, and Health* (1989), which devotes entire chapters to Mohammedism, Buddhism, Confucianism, and Shintoism.

My focus on the Judeo-Christian religions is a practical one, given that over 95% of older Americans are affiliated with this tradition and that most of the systematic research on the topic has been among members of this religious faith. While there are many differences that separate Jews and Christians, they are at least united in the belief in a single supreme God who is objectively real, exists separate and apart from the things created, and has an interest in the human predicament. Jews see evidence for the latter in God's powerful acts to bring the Jewish people out of Egyptian slavery and into the promised land of Israel. Christians, on the other hand, see evidence for God's concern by the act of his becoming a human in Jesus Christ, dying and freeing them from the bondage of sin. Just as clinicians and researchers in the health professions refer to a body of credible scientific data to support their statements, so also do religious professionals base their opinions and advice on what to them is a reliable and credible source—religious scriptures. For this reason, I will be as liberal in quoting scriptural references from the Bible or Talmud[2] as I will in quoting scientific publications.

DEFINITIONS

The terms successful aging, religion, and mental health carry a variety of meanings for different people. It is important, then, to define what I mean by these words and to explain how I will be using them in the text.

Successful Aging

By aging I mean the process of growing older that begins at birth and ends in death and encompasses physical, psychological, and spiritual changes that take place throughout the life cycle. What, then, is successful aging? In 1974, the Duke Center for Aging put together an entire volume to address this issue (Pfeiffer 1974). Included were contributions by renowned experts in the field of aging—Eric Pfeiffer, George Maddox, Bernice Neugarten, Carl Eisdorfer, and Robert Butler, to name but a few. They sought to arrive at a common definition for successful aging. Is it freedom from physical illness or disability, achievement of financial security, and/or maintenance of supportive relationships in later life? Is it the fulfillment of goals and projects initiated in young or middle adulthood? Is it the successful raising of children and launching them into their careers and families? Certainly, successful aging can and often does include all of these. However, I do not believe that it should be limited to one's health or successes in earlier life. If so, then many older adults because of their current health conditions, life situations, or earlier failures would have no hope of ever achieving this end.

---

2. All Talmudic references from Bokser BZ (1989). *The Talmud: Selected Writings.* New York: Paulist Press.

Successful aging, as I see it, involves how an older person feels, thinks, and acts in whatever circumstances he or she finds themselves. Successful aging is defined by crisis. Indeed, success at anything implies a barrier or problems to be overcome. Successful aging involves *how* individuals meet the difficulties they encounter. It is not surprising, then, that much of what it means to successfully age has nothing to do with circumstances. Rather it depends on how older adults perceive and react to events in their lives. This, in turn, depends on how they interpret their experiences in the world and what gives their lives meaning and cohesiveness.

In particular, successful aging involves how older adults see themselves fitting into their world and what purpose, if any, they play. Purpose involves having a goal, a vision, a reason to live, a reason to get up in the morning, a reason to struggle and fight against the forces that would overwhelm and destroy. Older adults, particularly those disabled by chronic illness, need a vision that can sustain them through difficult times, can motivate them onwards in life, can keep hope alive when circumstances indicate otherwise. In this book, I will explore the extent to which religion provides the elder with a world-view that assists in overcoming emotional problems in later life, thus enabling them to age more successfully.

Religion

As I mentioned earlier, the definition of religion used here is one primarily based in the Judeo-Christian tradition. I have intentionally chosen this perspective because of my focus on religion among older persons in a Western society. I use the terms "spiritual" or "spirituality" as synonymous with religion or religiosity. Strictly speaking, however, spirituality is a much broader term than religion, and may or may not include an allegiance to God or a higher power. Faith as used here is closely linked with religion and is meant as the force that organizes and aligns a person's life towards his or her ultimate concern. I am particularly interested in and will focus on the "contents" of one's faith, which according to James Fowler (1981) involves the following:

The operative contents of our faiths—whether explicitly religious or not—shape our perceptions, interpretations, priorities and passions. They constitute our life wages. Our loves and trusts, our values and visions, constitute our characters as persons and communities of faith. Few things could be more important than serious reflection on how we form and commit ourselves to (and through) the *contents* [my italics] of our faiths. (p. 281)

For the purposes of this text, the contents of faith, the focus of ultimate concern, will center on God and on a person's relationship with God (as opposed to faith in self, profession, pleasure, possession, institution or social group). There are, of course, many possible images of God. God may be equated with the universe itself, in which case all things—including humans—are seen as part of God; this view is generally known as pantheism. The other view (the one I am taking) sees God as separate and distinct from the universe; if the universe was destroyed, God would remain. Within the latter view, there is much disagreement over the more specific characteristics of God. He may be seen as distant, impersonal, uninterested—as having created the universe, set it on course, and now wanting to be left alone. Some may see God as interested and concerned, but lacking in power to be of much help. On the other hand, God may be seen as all-powerful, angry, difficult to please, ready to judge and quick to demand retribution—as someone to be feared, respected, and appeased.

Another view, while acknowledging God as all-powerful (omnipotent), always and everywhere present (omnipresent), and all-knowing (omniscient), emphasizes other characteristics such as caring, understanding, forgiving, merciful, and responsive. This view, according to C.S. Lewis (1943), sees the force behind the universe as "more like a mind than it is like anything else we know. That is to say, it is conscious, and has purposes, and prefers one thing to another" (p. 32). Seeing God in this way, as a person, allows for the possibility of relationship. Later, I will look at the impact that these different views of God may have on the elder's mental health and ability to cope with stress.

Mental Health. Mental health as used here indicates a spectrum of mental functioning ranging from illness (primarily depression or anxiety), to "normal" or "ordinary" psychological health, to extraordinarily adaptive and robust mental health (as represented by successful aging). According to Frieda Fromm-Reichman (1950), in *Principles of Intensive Psychotherapy,*

> . . . these therapeutic goals [mental health] will be reached by the growth, maturation, and inner independence of the patient. Accomplishment will be further realized by his potential freedom from fear, anxiety, and the entanglements of greed, envy, and jealousy. This goal will also be actualized by the development of his capacity for self-realization, his ability to form durable relationships of intimacy with others, and to give and accept mature love. I define "mature love" in accordance with E. Fromm and H. S. Sullivan, as the state of interpersonal relatedness in which one is as concerned with the growth, maturation, welfare, and happiness of the beloved person as one is with one's own. This capacity for mature love presupposes the development of a healthy and stable self-respect. (pp. 33,34)

Mental health and psychosocial adjustment are closely related concepts in the elderly. Vaillant and Vaillant (1990) reported on the predictors of psychosocial adjustment in later life among a sample of 173 men followed from age 18 through to age 65. They found that the following four factors were important in this regard: family relationships, maturity of defenses (sublimation, altruism, suppression), absence of alcoholism, and absence of depression. As we shall see, religion impacts each of these factors related to psychosocial adjustment in the later years.

Let us first, however, deal with another issue. Currently, there is great reluctance by many mental health professionals to consider religion a source of help; rather, it is often attributed to psychopathology. We will now take a close look at history to see how the domains of religion and psychiatry have overlapped in the past and try to better understand how the schism between these two disciplines developed. We will then see if there is any hope or reason for reconciliation.

REFERENCES

Clements, W.M. (1989). *Religion, Aging and Health: A Global Perspective*. NY: The Haworth Press.

Fowler, J.W. (1981). *Stages of Faith*. San Francisco: Harper & Row.

Fromm-Reichman, F. (1950). *Principles of Intensive Psychotherapy*. Chicago: University of Chicago Press.

Klerman, G.L., and M.M. Weissman. (1989). Increasing rates of depression. *Journal of the American Medical Association* 261:2229-2235.

Koenig, H.G., M. Smiley, and J.P. Gonzales. (1988). *Religion, Health, and Aging: A Review and Theoretical Integration*. New York: Greenwood Press.

Lewis, C.S. (1943). *Mere Christianity*. New York: Harper & Row.

Pfeiffer, E. (1974). *Successful Aging: A Conference Report*. Duke University, Durham, NC: Center for the Study of Aging and Human Development.

Vaillant, G., and C.O. Vaillant. (1990). Natural history of male psychosocial health, XII: A 45-year study of predictors of successful aging at age 65. *American Journal of Psychiatry* 147:31-37.

PART I:
RELIGION AND THE MENTAL SCIENCES

Chapter 1

The History of Psychiatry and Religion

> The most important of more recent events–that 'God is dead,' that the belief in the Christian God has become unworthy of belief–already begins to cast its first shadows over Europe.
>
> –*Friedrich Nietzsche*

In 1828, Webster's Dictionary defined *psychology* as "A discourse or treatise on the human soul; or the doctrine of the nature and properties of the soul." The separation of medicine and psychiatry from religion has only been a relatively recent phenomenon. Both medicine and the mental health professions have their origins in religion and spiritual practice. The first recorded history of health and illness can be found in the writings of the Mesopotamians and Egyptians almost 5000 years ago. Illness was viewed in religious terms, felt to be connected with sin, and was treated almost exclusively by priests (Kuhn 1988).

PRIMITIVE MAN

In *A History of Medical Psychology*, Gregory Zilboorg and G. W. Henry (1941) plot the evolution of psychiatry/psychology from its origins in primitive man (no gender implied) through the time of Freud and beyond. In the early days of humanity, there was no separation of illness into physical, mental, and spiritual categories–all sickness was spiritual. In old age, people with either physical or mental illness were often killed off, since they interfered with the movements of early tribes (Koty 1934; Simmons 1945; Glascock &

Feinman 1981). As civilization progressed, persons with mental disorder became distinguished from those with physical illness; rather than being pitied, however, they were regarded with fear and imbued with supernatural power. If benign, such persons were revered; if evil, they were endured and placated–the task of the primitive medicine man.

Because the insane were viewed as sacred, there was no attempt to "treat" them. In large part, their illness was kept a mystery from the general public, and revealed only to the priest. Zilboorg and Henry write, "Things of the spirit, of the supernatural, might not be touched by the hand of the earthy, materialistic, herb-brewing and urine-smelling man" (p. 23). Many different spirits populated the world of early man. By 5000 BC, this was the situation in ancient Egypt where artifacts from that period show images of royalty possessed by demons. The first psychiatric treatment was believed to be hypnotism, practiced by shamans in northern Russia, parts of China, and by priests in Malaysia.

EARLY HEBRAIC TIMES

Zilboorg and Henry then jump to early Hebrew times, when monotheism became a dominant form of religious belief (1500-1000 BC). References are made to persons in the Old Testament with mental disorder, including Hannah (mother of Samuel), Saul (first king of Israel), Ezekiel, and David (feigning as a mad man). The first mention of mental illness in the Bible is in Deuteronomy (28:28): "The Lord shall afflict you with madness, blindness and confusion of mind." Of particular interest is the passage in Leviticus (20:27) that became the primary justification for the merciless killings of the Inquisition during the Dark Ages: "A man or woman who is a medium or spiritist among you must be put to death. You are to stone them; their blood will be on their own heads."

In concluding this section, Zilboorg and Henry note that ". . . our civilization from the primitive man to early Hebraic culture contributed almost nothing to our understanding of psychological difficulties" (p. 30). In making this statement, they generally ignore the psychological truths and proscriptions contained in the Old Testament. Yet it is to these that Western civilization owes its very shape and form, as well as its notions of morality. Early Hebrew ideas involving interpersonal relations, concern and care for sick or disabled persons, and treatment of older family members, were new concepts in a day when such persons were killed off or left to die unattended. Although many physical and most mental illnesses were viewed as resulting from spiritual influences, this at least provided a framework by which such diseases could be understood and a method by which they could be treated.

The early Hindus also viewed psychopathology from a religious perspective, where it was dealt with by priestly metaphysics. Like others, Indian scriptures (the Vedas, the Code of Manu, Mahabharata, Ramayana) attributed mental illness to demoniacal possession. The Hindu view of man's psychological makeup was a mystic philosophy, involving a union of religion and psychology, where psychological theory was derived from theology and based on spiritual migration. Zilboorg and Henry conclude, "Mental disease, however, whether viewed with the clouded vision of a very primitive man, through the mystic eyes of Mosaic law, or through the pantheistic glasses of the Hindu, remained a mystery, reprehensible or admirable, which did not seem to belong to medicine" (p. 35).

HIPPOCRATES

It was not until around 500 BC that Greek medicine began to take scientific form with the teachings of Hippocrates. Prior to Hippocrates, the Homeric tradition was dominant, which saw mental illness as originating from influences by mythological gods; for instance, Lyssa, the goddess of night and madness, was felt to have caused Hercules to lose his mind. Hippocrates was the first to describe a number of mental disorders, including post-partum psychosis, phobias, mania, melancholia, paranoia, hysteria, memory disturbances, and delirium, claiming that the brain was the sole cause of mental disease. Despite his genius, Hippocrates' view remained primitive. For instance, he believed that depressive illness was the effect of an excess of black bile, whereas anxiety disorders and nightmares resulted from a sudden influx of bile to the brain. Thus, the Greeks tended to view mental disorder as stemming from physical disorder–physical disorder being a disharmony in the combination of humors.

After Hippocrates, mind and body increasingly came to be seen as distinct entities. Physical illness was viewed as resulting from natural causes, although the forces of nature were felt to have divine origins. In fact, about this time in Greece, a group proclaimed Asclepius as the god of healing, and the Temple of Asclepius became a type of early hospital where the sick came in hopes of being cured. The Aesculapiadae were priests at the temple who had inherited healing secrets. Their job was to stir up the powers of the god of healing through religious ceremonies; the god would then appear to the sick during dreams and produce healing or suggest potions of herbs that may be helpful. About the third century BC, Rome came under the influence of the Greek Asclepian cult, and healing by means of astrology, magic, and herbs became commonplace.

PLATO AND ARISTOTLE

Plato (427-347 BC) was the next influential personage after Hippocrates. His psychology was a mixture of idealistic and mystical elements. Rational and irrational souls which sought union were thought to exist within each person. When severed from each other, madness was felt to result, of which there were three varieties: melancholia, mania, and dementia. He distinguished one form of mania as a gift coming from the gods; this type of mania was felt to be of a higher nature that carried with it prophetic powers. Zilboorg and Henry write that the "medical point of view was thus considerably weakened by Plato" (p. 53), due to his mixture of scientific and mystic elements.

Plato's student Aristotle, however, is said to have "laid the foundation of the science of psychology" (p. 54), although his knowledge of anatomy and physiology was somewhat limited, and he believed that the heart, not the brain, was responsible for emotional disorder. After Aristotle, interest in man's feelings and behavior became the domain of the philosopher, not the physician. From 350 to 250 BC, the Stoic and Epicurian philosophers debated these issues. This group clearly denied the existence of God or a hereafter. Instead, they invested in social and psychological topics, ethics, contemplation, and introspection, setting the stage for "the true development of the psychology of man" (p. 60). Ideas about the origin and nature of mental illness during this period fluctuated back and forth from those focusing on malign supernatural powers, to those emphasizing the role of intense emotion, to those implicating physical factors. Interestingly, these same notions continue to be the focus of vigorous debate in the field of psychiatry today.

THE PSYCHOLOGY OF JESUS

Three hundred years after Plato, the teachings of Jesus focused on the meaning of suffering and on healing of the whole person. He made little distinction between the power to heal the body, mind, or spirit. While early science struggled with the diagnosis and classification of illness (linking different disorders with different types of treatment), Jesus was less concerned with this because his method of healing depended little on the type of illness present. Besides claiming miraculous cures, he stressed some very basic psychological concepts that bear a remarkable resemblance to the "nonspecific factors" which mental health professionals claim are common to all forms of effective psychotherapy (see Chapter 3).

Jesus' major emphasis was on relationships. When asked what the two greatest commandments were, he referred to (1) man's relationship to God and (2) man's relationship to man. Positive regard for others and service to one's neighbor were central in his teachings. These principles aimed at preparing man to live a full and happy life in the human community. Long-term satisfactions, rather than short-term thrills, were emphasized. Forgiveness and mercy were stressed: God forgiving man and man forgiving man. Not only did he talk about the need to forgive, but also provided a method by which forgiveness could be obtained. While traditional psychotherapy can point out that bitterness, resentfulness, and unforgiveness are at the root of many psychological ills, it is not always so successful in enabling patients to let go of these negative emotions/attitudes. Jesus provided the basis for a belief system and rituals which help persons to forgive others and obtain forgiveness for themselves.

Other examples of teachings by Jesus which strengthen interpersonal relations included an emphasis on being compassionate (good samaritan–Luke 10:30-37), expressing unconditional love (prodigal son–Luke 15:11-31), treating others as one wishes to be treated (Matthew 7:12), avoiding counter-transference (mote in the eye–Matthew 7:3-5), monitoring cognitions (Mark 7:20-23), valuing every human being as equally important (Matthew 18:12), maintaining a stable family life (Matthew 5:32), avoiding unnecessary anxiety or worry (Matthew 6:34), and being aware of the dangers of narcissism and hypocrisy (Mark 7:6-9). Some of these ideas were truly revolutionary in Jesus' time. Nevertheless, Zilboorg and Henry make little mention of such contributions. For instance, he notes "Soon the early Christian trends began to make themselves felt, and yet the sum total of the scientific equipment [contributions to psychology] which was at the disposal of the world came from polytheistic, pagan sources" (p. 60).

After Jesus, came a series of Greeks and Romans who further advanced knowledge and understanding in the field of psychology: Asclepiades (objected to the dark cells and dungeons where the mentally ill were kept), Cicero (emphasized the role of the emotions in mental disorder), Plutarch (accurately described depressive illness), Celsus and Aretaeus (provided a description and classification of mental disorder), Solanus (treatment of mania), and Galen (summarized all prior knowledge of mental illness). Galen stands out because of his physiological approach to mental illness. In his writings, he described the brain, the meninges, ventricles, cranial nerves, and attributed all psychic functions to the brain. After Galen's death (200 AD), came the Dark Ages. Says medical historian Paul Diepgen in 1914, "Medical wisdom came to an end with the passing of Galen" (p. 9).

THE DARK AGES

Although Zilboorg and Henry state "One may not lay the responsibility for this retrogressive change at the portals of the Christian Church" (p. 93), much of what they say both before and after implies the opposite–that the decline in scientific advancement and the abuses and inhumane treatments of the mentally ill during the Dark Ages were largely a result of church activities. Again, an emphasis is placed on the negative, not the positive, contributions of religion to the care of the mentally ill. He does admit, however, that the societal forces which brought on the Dark Ages were not exclusively an outgrowth of Christian theology; a major contribution also came from a fusion of expanding monotheism with pagan spiritistic and polytheistic forces. With gnosticism came the idea of a hierarchy of angels between a Christian and his or her God, as well as the notion of saint worship, reflecting the polytheistic tendencies of pre-Christian Rome. Zilboorg and Henry also note that even before Christianity began having an influence, superstition and intolerance were becoming increasingly common in society. After the third century, when Roman emperor Constantine was converted, Christianity spread rapidly throughout much of the known world. A vigorous effort was made to suppress superstition, magic, and occult practices. The teachings of classical science and philosophy were included among the latter, and the study of Plato and Aristotle became forbidden.

DEMONOLOGY

In the fourth century, nearly all physical and mental disorders became viewed as demonic possession. According to Zilboorg and Henry, there developed a

> formidable structure which became known as demonology and which was to rule medical psychology for *sixteen hundred years* [my italics] . . . Religious debates and metaphysical contentions took precedence over the empirical traditions in medicine. (pp. 98-99)

Religion finally achieved a complete victory over scientific progress and then nearly obliterated it over the next thousand years. Hence came a widening of the split between the two disciplines, with each pitted against the other as foes.

What Zilboorg and Henry fail to mention, however, is that at no time did the Church imply that "possession" was the only cause of mental illness. There were a number of Christian physicians who accepted the detailed Greek descriptions and teachings on pathology, but rejected its excessively naturalistic explanations. Unlike their Hellenistic colleagues, they believed that even patients with incurable disease should be treated, even if that consisted of nothing more than loving and caring for them in a manner consistent with Christian teachings. Referring to this, Braceland and Stock (1963) note the following:

> The early Christians also inaugurated regular medical, nursing, and social assistance through their hospitals, and there came to the fore a religious form of psychotherapy which was both therapeutic and consoling. Had Christianity been able to maintain the equilibrium of its early outlook, the history of Western medicine might have been quite different. (p. 29)

Thus, while these were certainly dark times for the relationship between the Church and the natural sciences, there was at least some attempt to integrate the two in certain circles.

Towards the beginning of the fifth century, according to Zilboorg and Henry, "Medical psychology as a legitimate branch of the healing art practically ceased to exist. It was recaptured by the priest and incorporated into this theurgic system" (p. 103). These times marked a universal decline of both medicine and European civilization in general, as the Roman empire collapsed and disintegrated. War, famine, and disease were rampant. There was a destruction of libraries, schools, and universities; the Church had little to do with much of this. As noted above, mental diseases were not as sharply separated from medicine as Zilboorg and Henry indicate. Rather, spiritual, medical, and psychological forces were each felt to play a role, and the Church even became a refuge for many students of Hippocrates, Aristotle, and Galen.

By the beginning of the seventh century, "Psychiatry finally became a study of the ways and means of the devil and his cohorts" (p. 108). The treatment of mental disease was accomplished by application of sainted relics, recitation of magical words, and by exorcism. Emphasis was now placed on early diagnosis and recognition of demon possession, a trend that continued for the next twelve hundred years. Religion and psychology had become nearly fused.

FIRST HOSPITALS

The first hospitals began to appear around the turn of the tenth century. Clergy-operated monasteries were the primary institutions of healing, for both physical and mental (spiritual) diseases, and were the forerunners of hospitals as we know them today. They were especially common in the Holy Land where they were used by pilgrims on their way to Jerusalem. The Knights Hospitalers (equivalent of modern day hospital physicians) evolved from an order of military monks that operated one of these hospitals located in Jerusalem around 1050 AD (Stevens, 1989). In the twelfth century, scientific medicine was under strict control by the Church which controlled the issuing of medical licenses. The treatment of illness could not begin until the patient had confessed their sins to a priest; consequently, most physicians were members of the clergy.

EFFORTS AT PROGRESS

About this time, a monk named Machael Psellus (1020-1105) summarized the current knowledge of medicine and psychiatry. He codified and systematized demonology (the basis upon which psychiatry was practiced in the medieval period). By the twelfth century, patients suffering from mental illness were either considered heretics or "naturally" ill (i.e., from physical causes). In general, however, there was a kind attitude toward the possessed. They were frequently prayed for using power from the tombs of the saints. The Church took an active part in initiating the humane treatment of mental patients in areas such as Gheel, Belgium, where patients were cared for in peoples' homes and included in family life, a tradition which has persisted to this very day. Furthermore, mental patients were admitted to general hospitals set up by Pope Innocent III and provided with humane care (Braceland & Stock 1963). Zilboorg and Henry note, however, that because the population of mentally ill persons was increasing and causing anxiety to the public, torture and execution of the possessed began to occur.

In the thirteenth and fourteenth centuries came a resurgence of learning, greater interest in the arts and sciences, and the start of a number of major European universities. Interest in the philosophy of Aristotle was revived and examined from a Christian perspective by St. Albert the Great and St. Thomas Aquinas. Interestingly, as early as the thirteenth century Thomas Aquinas observed that much about a person's mental functioning might be understood by analyzing their dreams and that there were many intentions and purposes about which men were not conscious (Stock 1958). About this time, a Franciscan monk named Roger Bacon appeared on the scene and questioned whether mental disease might not be "natural" rather than supernatural disease. Nevertheless, witches were still felt to be the cause of diseases like impotence and memory loss, and as the mentally ill became more populous, they came to be feared more and pitied less.

THE INQUISITION

When the Inquisition became established in the fourteenth century, the care of the mentally ill declined further. People with mental disease were expelled from their families and forced to live on the streets. Because of poor hygiene, their physical appearances became disgusting and fed into the superstitions of the time. The psychotic or severely depressed person was placed in the same category as the magician, witch, or heretic. Towards the end of the fifteenth century, a movement to exterminate witches took force, and in 1487 a book entitled *Malleus Maleficarum* ("the Witches' Hammer") was submitted for approval to the faculty of theology at the University of Cologne. It became the textbook for the Inquisition. The book consisted of three parts: first, a section attempting to prove the existence of witches; second, a series of clinical cases; and third, a section for the legal execution of witches (typically burning). According to Zilboorg and Henry, almost all mentally ill persons (many of them elders living alone) were considered witches or sorcerers, and hundreds of thousands of people were burned in a cooperative effort of church and state. This continued in Europe for almost 200 years, and the last witch to be decapitated occurred as late as 1782 in Switzerland.

SEPARATION OF CHURCH AND MEDICINE

In the sixteenth century, a well-educated man from a religious family, Juan Vives, stressed the relationship between psychological factors, emotional illness, and memory. He championed the cause of the mentally ill, encouraging a gentle and humane form of treatment. Paracelsus, who saw man as a psychobiological entity, criticized the prevalent belief in witchcraft of his time. Johann Weyer soon thereafter wrote the book *De Praestigiis Daemonum* (1563) which vigorously attacked the presumed association between mental illness and witchcraft.

It was not however until the late eighteenth century, during the French revolution, that the health care system finally broke free from the control of the Church. In the mid-1700s, Albrecht von Haller did much work to establish the scientific discipline of physiology and thus paved the way for the development of experimental medicine. The advancement of psychiatry, however, did not parallel that of medicine. From a scientific perspective, psychiatry remained virtually weaponless, with an armamentarium consisting primarily of a humane purpose. The mid-19th century found medicine grounded in the rational method and thriving independently of religious institutions. Mental illness was now seen as emanating either from physiological or psychological processes, depending on what branch of science one was in. From the work of John Locke, David Hume, and Paul Broca came the association between certain mental illnesses and disorders in functioning of circumscribed areas of the brain; thus, the relationship between mental and brain disease became stronger and stronger. The pendulum began to swing far away from the idea that mental illness might result from improper conduct or failure to comply with the laws of morality, for which individuals themselves were responsible.

THE BIRTH OF CONTEMPORARY PSYCHOLOGY AND PSYCHIATRY

In the 1800s, a revolution occurred in the way mentally ill patients were treated. Until the beginning of this century, there were no true mental hospitals; instead, the insane were often incarcerated in remote areas, frequently in almshouses, cellars, dungeons, or prisons. Leaders in Paris (Philippe Pinel), Britain (William Tuke), and the United States (Eli Todd) began to call for the "moral treatment" of the mentally ill–a serious effort to provide humane treatment in appropriate hospital settings.

About this time Pinel and Emile Kraeplin began working on the classification of mental illness. Soon after them came Eugene Bleuler, Adolf Meyer, and Sigmund Freud. With the advent of Freud's psychoanalysis came a theory about the operation of the mind that brought with it the notion that mental illnesses could be treated through psychotherapy. Because of the importance of Freud's contribution to the development of psychiatry, and because of his strong ideas concerning religion in particular, his work and contributions will be comprehensively dealt with in the next chapter.

In the early to mid-1900s came the development of true biological psychiatry. In 1938 came the discovery and soon widespread use of electroconvulsive therapy; in 1949, the use of lithium for mania was introduced; in 1952, the first major tranquilizer–chlorpromazine (Thorazine)–revolutionized the treatment of psychosis; in 1958, the first antidepressant (imipramine) appeared on the scene; finally, in 1960, benzodiazepines (Valium) were introduced for the treatment of anxiety. These forms of biological therapy have had an enormous impact on the treatment of mental illness and have enabled many severely ill patients to live productively in the community.

With rapid advances of technology and science in the twentieth century has come the development and refinement of the biomedical model, which seeks to explain the origin and course of all medical illness in terms of altered physiological processes. The field of psychiatry–among the most recent of the medical specialties–has fought hard to rid itself of a mystical reputation. As a discipline, psychiatry has sought to ground itself on a biomedical model in order to achieve credibility in the mainstream of medicine.

Mental processes, however, are amazingly complex, as are the interpersonal interactions and behaviors of humans in general. It is yet to be established that the biomedical model is the only or even most appropriate way of viewing human psychology. One negative outgrowth of the tremendous advances in the biomedical approach to disease has been a view of human behavior and experience, in a rather narrow, reductionistic fashion. With this has come a near complete denial of the existence or relevance of man's soul or spirit.

SUMMARY

A long and arduous struggle has characterized the relationship between religion and the psychological sciences throughout history. There have been atrocities committed on both sides along the way, none of which are excusable except for ignorance. While historians trained in the psychological tradition frequently report in great detail the vulgar acts committed in the name of religion, they tend to gloss over gross errors and inhumane treatments initiated under the banner of medical science. Paracelsus, for instance, thinking that excess heat was the cause for mania, had his patients' toes and fingers "scarified so that fresh air might be let in to reduce the excess heat" (p. 199). Likewise, at one point, Freud believed that his friend Wilhelm Fleiss had made a discovery that unlocked "the mysteries of the universe and of life." This discovery involved a relationship between the nose and the female genitalia, which led Fleiss to attempt to cure neurosis by cauterizing the turbinate bone of the nasal cavity. Freud submitted one of his own patients to this process; when complications developed, Freud attributed these to the patient's neurotic conflict over love and attention (Sulloway 1991, pp. 248-249). Clearly, neither religion nor science is faultless; human error is universal regardless of whose name it is committed in.

Both medicine and psychiatry have their origins deeply rooted in religion, yet both have struggled hard to free themselves of any vestige of its influence. Is it any wonder that the chasm between religion and psychiatry is so deep and the animosity between them so strong? Among the goals of this volume are to identify the strengths and truth in each and to integrate them into a system of care which views and treats older persons as complex physical, psychological, interpersonal, and spiritual entities.

In the next chapter, we will take a look at a man whose influence on modern psychological thought has been second to no one. Although the schism between religion and psychiatry/psychology was well established by the time Freud appeared on the scene, his views have added considerably to the antagonism between the two fields that one finds today.

REFERENCES

Braceland, F.J., and M. Stock. (1963). *Modern Psychiatry.* Garden City, NY: Doubleday & Co.

Diepgen, P. (1914). *Geschichte der Medizine (History of Medicine)*, vol. II. Berlin, Germany.

Glascock, A., and S. Feinman. (1981). Social asset or social burden: An analysis of the treatment of the aged in non-industrial societies. In *Dimensions: Aging, Culture, and Health*, edited by C.I. Fry. NY: Praeger, p. 25.

Koty, J. (1934). *Die Behandlung der Alten und Kranken bei den Naturvokern.* Stuttgart, Germany.

Kuhn, C.C. (1988). A spiritual inventory of the medically ill patient. *Psychiatric Medicine* 6:87-100.

Simmons, L. (1945). *The Role of the Aged in Primitive Society.* New Haven: Yale University Press, pp. 225-228, 235-240.

Stevens, R. (1989). *In Sickness and in Wealth: American Hospitals in the Twentieth Century.* NY: Basic Books.

Stock, M. (1958). Thomistic psychology and Freud's psychoanalysis. *The Thomist* 21(2) April issue.

Sulloway, F. (1991). Reassessing Freud's case histories: The social construction of psychoanalysis. *International Review of the History of Science and Its Cultural Influences (ISIS)* 82:245-275.

Webster, N. (1828). *American Dictionary of the English Language.* Reprinted by The Foundation for American Christian Education, San Francisco, California (3rd ed., 1983).

Zilboorg, G., and G.W. Henry. (1941). *A History of Medical Psychology.* NY: WW Norton Co.

Chapter 2

Sigmund Freud

Religion is an attempt to get control over the sensory world in which we are placed, by means of the wish-world, which we have developed inside us as a result of biological and psychological necessities.

–Sigmund Freud

Freud has become one of the most influential and controversial figures of our time. Many have described him as a genius devoted to the study of the mind, to the discovery of truth, and to the adherence to reason. A brilliant natural observer, a prolific and scholarly writer, and an unparalleled teacher and lecturer, Freud both intellectually and scientifically has been acclaimed a giant. His insights have given modern psychiatry much of its direction. Because his ideas were put forth so strongly and so confidently (and their implications were so far-reaching), Freud has had both many followers and many adversaries. Because of his views on infantile sexuality, Freud was ostracized from the mainstream of psychology and for years worked in isolation; it was then that he developed many of his theories.

Many of Freud's original ideas have undergone intense criticism and have required modification. Perhaps in no other area were his views so adamant (and perhaps so misinformed) as in that of religion. A number of his publications have dealt directly or indirectly with this topic. Both his personal and public views on religion have been considered biased and over-reductionistic (Meissner 1984). Nevertheless, Braceland and Stock (1963) rightly admonish that "it is wise to know exactly what a man has said before venturing an opinion about his theories . . ." (p. 54). Let us do so.

VIEWS ON RELIGION

In the process of establishing a rationalistic perspective on human behavior grounded in drive theory, Freud attempted to discredit the religious view of man prevalent in his time. In 1927, at the age of 70, he convincingly argued that religion was becoming outmoded in a technologically sophisticated, scientifically oriented world. Freud believed that man's rational intellect would eventually replace religion as a more powerful tool in dealing with the fears and uncertainties of his or her existence. In *Future of an Illusion* (1927), Freud wrote the following:

> Our God, Logos, will fulfill whichever of these wishes nature outside us allows, but will do it very gradually, only in the unforeseeable future, and for a new generation of man. He promises noncompensation for us, who suffer grievously from life. On the way to this distant goal your religious doctrines will have to be discarded, no matter whether the first attempts fail, or whether the first substitutes prove untenable. And you know why: in the long run nothing can withstand reason and experience, and the contradiction which religion offers to both is all too palpable. (p. 54)

In Webster's Dictionary (1980), the ancient Greek definition of *Logos* is *reason*–"the controlling principle of the universe . . ." (p. 832). Traditional religion was viewed by Freud as a neurotic and primitive approach to controlling human drives which would ultimately fail to allay anxiety and fear in a healthy way. Freud did not accept the underlying assumptions of religion; consequently, he found little that was logical or reasonable about it. Because he could not come to religion through reason, Freud rejected it for himself and tried to convince others to do the same. Thus, he embarked on the task of systematically discrediting religion through the process of reductionism–breaking it up into its component parts and explaining them away.

> The psychoanalysis of individual human beings, however, teaches us with quite special insistence that the god of each of them is formed in the likeness of his father, that his personal

relation to God depends on his relation to his father in the flesh and oscillates and changes along with that relation, and that at bottom God is nothing other than an exalted father.[1] (Freud 1913, p. 147)

As an alternative to religion, Freud provided another way of looking at the world which has since been adopted by many of those in psychology and psychiatry. The tenets of classical psychoanalytic theory are the "laws" by which this new worldview or *Weltanschauung* operated. Mental health and pathology became explained in terms of conscious and unconscious forces, drives, defense mechanisms, conflict, and compromise formation. These principles are logically and rationally connected together by psychoanalytic theory, and provide a relatively cohesive set of explanations for human behaviors and experiences. In many ways psychoanalytic theory as a philosophy represented a new religion with its own belief system, sacred writings, rituals and magical auras (the mystique of the couch, hypnosis, etc.), shrines (psychiatrist's office, hospital), and tithes (fees). Thus, Freud hoped that his religion, supposedly based on scientific principles, was to replace the old, outdated religion of his time, based on grace and faith.

Freud's antagonistic view towards religion spread fast in the psychoanalytic community. Traditional religious beliefs and practices became viewed as neurotic. Originating from oedipal conflict, a belief in God served no healthy purpose and could be dispensed with. Although Freud himself claimed that psychoanalysis would not interfere with one's belief in God or with the relationship between man and God, in practice this was not always the case.

---

1. Freud explains man's notion of God as originating from feelings toward one's parents (father or mother), and that God really represents an all-powerful parental image that was submerged into the unconscious during early childhood and then resurfaces later during later childhood and adulthood as God. However, one might look at it in the opposite way just as well. God's unconditional love for human's may have been instilled as the "natural" love that parents have for their children (for instance, a mother's love for her baby). Thus, man's experience of an all-powerful and loving parent in childhood may actually represent God's own love for that person. Hence, rather than man's image of God coming from the natural father, the image of the natural father may in fact come from God.

Discussing the technique of analysis, Fenichel (1941) notes the following:

> It has been said that religious people in analysis remain uninfluenced in their religious philosophies since analysis itself is supposed to be philosophically neutral. I consider this not to be correct. Repeatedly I have seen that with the analysis of the sexual anxieties and with maturing of the personality, the attachment to religion has ended. (p. 89)

Classical psychoanalytic theory, then, involves concepts and ideas foreign to, and at times, inimical to a traditional religious worldview. Indeed, it includes a philosophy about life, human behavior and motivation, which acts in many instances as a replacement for religion. We should be careful, however, not to confuse the philosophy with the technique itself. Addressing this issue, widely respected philosopher Jacques Maritain (1956) has distinguished psychoanalysis as *a method of psychological investigation* from Freudianism as *a way of looking at the world.* He divides psychoanalysis into three parts: (1) psychoanalytic methods, (2) Freudian psychology, and (3) Freudian philosophy. In his development of the psychoanalytic method, Freud is seen by Maritain as a brilliant observer and scientific genius. As a psychologist, Freud is viewed as admirable, penetrating, and possessing an instinct for discovery, but as one whose ideas have been "spoiled by radical empiricism and an erroneous metaphysics that is unaware of itself." With regard to Freudian philosophy, Maritain observes that Freud "seems like a man obsessed." Thus, according to this philosopher, Freud's contributions to the development of a method of inquiry into the origin of psychic conflict and a technique for its possible resolution, should be highly respected and applauded. His worldview and ideas concerning philosophy and religion, on the other hand, must be viewed with skepticism.

The criticism of Freud, however, goes beyond this. There is even some justification for suspecting the validity of Freud's scientific theories. Although I will develop this point at length in Chapter 3, some discussion is appropriate here. Frank Sulloway, at the Massachusetts Institute of Technology Program in Science, has examined closely the scientific basis for Freud's theories and notes the following:

> In this connection I have argued that many of Freud's most essential psychoanalytic concepts were based upon erroneous and now outmoded assumptions from nineteenth-century biology . . . *bad biology ultimately spawned bad psychology* [my italics]. Freud erected his psychoanalytic edifice on a kind of intellectual quicksand, a circumstance that consequently doomed many of his most important theoretical conclusions from the outset. (Sulloway 1991, p. 245)

For now, it is sufficient to say that the scientific basis for Freud's psychoanalytic methods and psychology may be as questionable as is his philosophy about man and God.

FREUD'S EXPERIENCE WITH RELIGION

If not based entirely on unbiased observation and logical reasoning, where might Freud's ideas about religion have originated? Zilboorg (1958) has noted that Freud's antagonistic views toward religion were not entirely based on his resolute allegiance to science, but rather on a lifelong inner conflict concerning religion. Although a self-professed agnostic ("godless Jew"), Freud was somewhat paradoxically preoccupied with the subject of religion, as reflected in his writings from 1913 (*Totem and Taboo*) to his death in 1939 (*Moses and Monotheism*). Harvard psychoanalyst, William Meissner, thoroughly reviews Freud's early experiences with religion in his book *Psychoanalysis and Religious Experience* (1984).

Freud was raised in a Jewish home. While his family engaged in some of the usual religious practices, they were basically nonreligious. His father, Jakob Freud, had been a devout student of the Torah and Talmud, although later he turned towards a more secular life-style. As a member of the Haskala, Jakob Freud viewed Judaism as a rational philosophy about life rather than as a religion. Sigmund himself recalls that his upbringing was un-Jewish, and that his mother was even less religiously oriented than was his father.

Freud had several negative experiences with Christianity during his early years. Until the age of two-and-a-half, he was cared for by a devout Catholic nanny who took him to church frequently and provided vigorous counseling concerning the salvation of the good and damnation of the wicked. To his disillusionment, she was caught for stealing and summarily dismissed from the family's service. The impact of such an event on the impressionable mind of a child may have been considerable (Zilboorg 1958). Another event may have affected Freud's views toward religion as a young boy. He was walking with his father along the road when a Christian man knocked his father's cap off, in a gesture of ridicule. His father's failure to retaliate upset Freud and, according to Meissner, may have contributed to his boyhood identification with Hannibal as the conqueror of Rome. Hannibal was the great Carthaginian general who led Spain's forces over the alps to defeat Roman forces during the Punic Wars. By pretending to be Hannibal as a young child, Freud may have been acting out his unresolved anger toward the Christian religion (symbolized by Rome) that was aroused during the incident between his father and the man described above.

While opposing traditional religion, Freud at the same time had an extraordinary tendency towards superstition. This tendency was apparently lifelong, and could be traced from his boyhood days, through his marriage to his wife Martha, to his death. Freud was preoccupied with numbers as a way of predicting good luck (the number 17, in particular) and of foretelling the date of his own death (about which he was quite obsessed). After he lived past his predicted age of death (age 62), Freud seemed to turn more towards telepathy and the occult. In declining an invitation to join the advisory council of the American Psychical Institute in 1921, Freud notes the following: "If I were at the beginning of a scientific career, instead of, as now, at its end, I would perhaps choose no other field of work [than parapsychology] in spite of all the difficulties" (quote from Wallace, 1978, p. 210).

It is clear, then, that there were certain mystical tendencies in Freud which, after his rejection of traditional religion, found their expression in these superstitious leanings. Meissner sums up Freud's experience with religion in the following passage:

. . . Freud simply had little experience with the broad spectrum of religious involvement. His own religious experience was highly colored by dynamic inputs from his own childhood, and his attempts to educate himself about religious phenomena tended to emphasize the occult, superstitious, or relatively primitive forms of religious experience. (p. 137)

Thus, personal biases may have clouded Freud's thinking about religion and influenced his writings on the subject. Although he wished to establish Logos (reason) as a god to replace traditional religion, this god was apparently insufficient to meet even his own needs in this area. Instead, Freud turned to the occult and parapsychology. Certainly, there was little evidence of his rational intellect in these superstitious ventures.

Freud's notions about religion, then, strayed even further from an experimental base than did his other writings. Although these concepts were colored by his own personal biases, they were probably reinforced in his dealings with mental patients who frequently expressed primitive religious views. To generalize the role and function of religion as manifested in psychotic or severely neurotic individuals to a general population of healthy persons, however, was premature and hardly "scientific."

IMPACT OF FREUD'S VIEWS

It is difficult to estimate the extent to which Freud's influence widened the gap between religion and the mental health sciences. Nevertheless, because of his enormous influence on the development of psychiatry, these views probably had and continue to have negative effects on psychiatry's attitudes toward religion. This may have contributed to the relative neglect of religion by psychiatric investigators (Larson et al. 1986), many of whom may never have considered the possibility that religion might have a positive impact on mental health (particularly in the elderly). Instead, as noted earlier, many of Freud's followers have made the practice of psychoanalysis and its philosophical tenets their personal religion, adhering to and defending its concepts with typical religious zeal

(Weisz 1975). Referring to this, Sulloway (1991) notes the following:

> The training methods that Freud ultimately sanctioned were therefore highly influential in removing psychoanalysis from the mainstream of academic science and medicine. As a result, the discipline of psychoanalysis, which has always tapped considerable religious fervor among its adherents, has increasingly come to resemble a religion in its social organization. (p. 246)

Because of the human need to believe in and worship something, once traditional religion is done away with, other objects of devotion are quickly sought to take its place. To demonstrate this point and to show the extent to which Freud has actually become idolized by some in the field, I refer to an advertisement recently circulated through the department of psychiatry at Duke University. "Insightful gifts from FreudToy, Inc." was the title of the flier. Included among the items for sale were a 13-inch doll of Freud, a 50-minute watch with Freud's picture on the dial, and note pads with Freud's bust in the corner.

FREUD'S PREDICTIONS CONCERNING RELIGION

The inaccuracy of Freud's predictions about the inevitable demise of religion is clear from societal trends over the past 50 years since his death. Despite a dramatic increase in the advancement of technology, science, and understanding of human behavior since the 1920s and 1930s, there is no solid evidence of any significant decline of interest or activity in religion among the American public. Gallup surveys indicate that the proportion of Americans who believe in God and who attend church on a weekly basis has changed little over the past 50 years (Princeton Religion Research Center 1985). In fact, a report to the American Academy of Religion by sociologists Wade Clark Roof and David Roozen recently indicated that many baby-boomers born since World War II are now turning back to religion as they begin to raise families and search for meaning in their own lives (Newsweek 1990). There appears to be a human need for religion that "the rational operation of the intellect" simply cannot satisfy.

In the next chapter, I will examine the divergent views of man's nature held by religion and the mental health sciences, discuss their possible impact on the treatment of psychological problems, and explore the scientific evidence that undergirds current psychological approaches. My purpose is to remove some of the barriers which cloud the recognition of religion's value in the treatment and prevention of mental health problems in later life.

REFERENCES

Braceland, F.J., and M. Stock. (1963). *Modern Psychiatry.* Garden City, NY: Doubleday & Co.

Fenichel, O. (1941). *Problems of Psychoanalytic Technique.* NY: Psychoanalytic Quarterly.

Freud, S. (1913). *Totem and Taboo.* Standard Edition (vol. 13), London: Hogarth Press, 1962.

Freud, S. (1927). *The Future of an Illusion.* Standard Edition (vol. 21), London: Hogarth Press, 1962.

Freud, S. (1939). *Moses and Monotheism.* Standard Edition (vol. 23:3-141), London: Hogarth Press, 1962.

Larson, D.B., D.G. Blazer, E.M. Pattison, D.G. Omran, and B.H. Kaplan. (1986). Systematic analysis of research on religious variables in four major psychiatric journals. *American Journal of Psychiatry* 143:329-334.

Maritain, J. (1956). Freudianism and psychoanalysis. *Cross Currents* 6(4):307.

Meissner, W.W. (1984). *Psychoanalysis and Religious Experience.* New Haven: Yale University Press.

Newsweek. (1990). And the children shall lead them: Young Americans turn back to God. (December 17):50-56.

Princeton Religion Research Center. (1985). Religion in America. Princeton: Gallup Poll.

Sulloway, F.J. (1991). Reassessing Freud's case histories: The social construction of psychoanalysis. *International Review of the History of Science and Its Cultural Influences (ISIS)* 82:245-275.

Wallace, E.R. (1978). Freud's mysticism and its psychodynamic determinants. *Bulletin of the Menninger Clinic* 42:203-222.

Webster's New World Dictionary (1980). 2nd college edition (D.B. Guralnik, ed.). NY: Simon & Schuster.

Weisz, G. (1975). Scientists and sectarians: The case of psychoanalysis. *Journal of the History of the Behavioral Sciences* 11:350-364.

Zilboorg, G. (1958). *Freud and Religion, a Restatement of an Old Controversy.* Westminster, MD: Newman Press.

Chapter 3

Conflicting Approaches to Mental Health

Das Höchste wäre zu erkennen: das alle Fakitsche schon Theorie ist.
(The ultimate to know: that all fact is already theory.)

–Goethe

In the next two chapters, I will distinguish and properly relate religion and the mental health sciences, with the goal of achieving a better understanding of the contributions and limits of biology, psychology, and religion. In this chapter, I will (1) compare and contrast the different approaches taken by psychology and religion towards understanding human behavior and treating neurotic illness; (2) discuss the scientific process and demonstrate how every "objective" fact depends heavily on the perspective of the observer; (3) show how both science and religion make different assumptions based on their own facts, but then proceed with these facts in a remarkably similar manner; and (4) review the scientific evidence supporting the validity of specific psychological techniques, especially classical psychoanalysis.

Psychology and religion understand and explain human behavior, thought, and emotion in fundamentally different ways. The mental health professions see humans as highly evolved organisms made up of biological, psychological, and social elements. Secular psychotherapy seeks to free the individual from exaggerated fears and needless limitations, in order to more effectively get their needs met. Self-reliance and independence is encouraged. The emphasis is on the self and the self's needs. Biological therapies, in turn, are used to correct deficits or excesses in brain chemicals which are believed to underlie certain mental illnesses.

Religion, on the other hand, while not denying man's biological nature, psychological makeup, and social strivings, emphasizes a fourth influence–the spirit or suprapersonal. The latter is seen as strongly affecting, and perhaps being affected by, the other elements. Figure 3.1 illustrates this relationship. The spirit is what distinguishes man from animals; it provides the capacity to seek and to know God (Suprapersonal). Consequently, religion takes a different approach from the psychological sciences in treating the anxieties, fears, restrictions, and addictions that disable humans. Religion concentrates first on man's relationship with God, then on relationships with others (Interpersonal) and with oneself (Self). Religion presumes that individuals already love themselves quite dearly and, in fact, are overconcerned with their own neurotic needs, frequently using and manipulating others to meet those needs. Religion says that there are higher values operative in the world that supercede man's Self-centered personal wants and desires.

Take, for example, adultery. Some interpret the Judeo-Christian scriptures as indicating the existence of a "natural law" which is set into motion when a person commits adultery. Somebody is invariably going to get hurt. Damage is going to be done–either to the characters and consciences of persons committing the act or to their families. Many mental health professionals would disagree, saying that this is simply morality and not natural law. Sometimes it is appropriate to commit adultery in order to get one's needs met; sometimes one must hurt others to satisfy oneself.

Religion presents a different solution to meeting man's most basic needs. At times, personal wants and desires have to be sacrificed for a higher cause, for the good of others alone. Religion proclaims that such sacrifices build character and in the end really are the best way for individuals to meet their ultimate needs. In a strange and somewhat paradoxical fashion, religion calls humans to stop striving so hard to meet their own needs, and instead to depend primarily on God (rather than on themselves or on others) to do so. Having these primary needs met by God, the person's compulsions and conflicts in these areas will diminish and they will become free to love and relate with others in a healthy way. "Love," in this case, does not mean a neurotic need for or dependence on another person as the solution to one's problems; rather, it means a free giving of

FIGURE 3.1

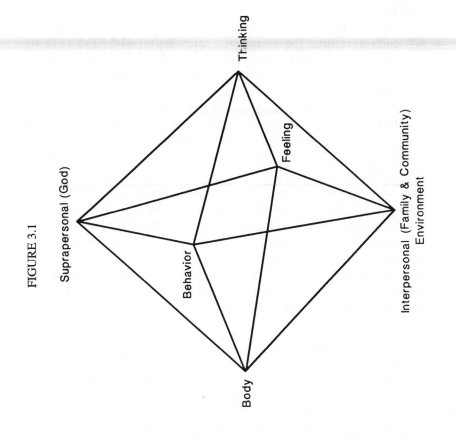

Thinking

Feeling

Interpersonal (Family & Community)
Environment

Suprapersonal (God)

Behavior

Body

S E L F

oneself in a relationship where both persons' needs are considered equally important. Hence, fundamental differences exist between the solutions proscribed by religion and secular psychology to the less severe but troublesome neurotic conflicts which plague most of humanity.

It is easy to understand why mental health professionals have difficulty accepting the notion of a relationship with God as being the primary source of personal fulfillment. Because the existence of God cannot be objectively proven, this idea is viewed with skepticism and categorized as nonsense, fantasy, or neurotic compensation. In the Judeo-Christian religion, the basis for belief is a personal encounter with God initiated by God and involving "revealed truth"–a concept that to men and women of science is vague, difficult to define, and unverifiable by the methods at their disposal. While the reductionistic techniques of the natural sciences work well with simple biological systems that can be isolated and carefully controlled, they lose power when dealing with more complex, interacting systems that require a holistic perspective. Consider the intricacies of human behavior and interpersonal relationships. Add to that influences from religious or spiritual factors based on intuition and faith, and this level of complexity reaches almost astronomical proportions. Thus, at these higher levels, the reductionistic techniques of science are less useful.

BASIS FOR RELIGIOUS TRUTH

Contrary to some claims, the Judeo-Christian religion does make use of rational, logical reasoning in its worldview and its attempts to predict and explain (Acts 17:2,16). Indeed, this tradition's high degree of coherence has enabled it to endure for thousands of years, spread throughout the world, and be understood by people from many different cultures and educational levels. Just as the sciences of physics and mathematics have assumptions that underlie their own theorems and proofs, religion also requires basic assumptions– that a God with certain characteristics exists and is interested in mankind.

The truth of religious assumptions, however, does not rest on human logic or reason. If it did, persons could have easily been dissuaded from these beliefs in the past by clever arguments perhaps based on misinformation or incomplete information. The survival of this religious tradition may be attributed to the fact that it is based on faith, on sometimes believing in spite of apparent evidence to the contrary. While being rational is important, inflexible rationality is clearly a hindrance. Religious scriptures have long emphasized this point. Consider the following passages:

> . . . the wisdom of the wise will perish, the intelligence of the intelligent will vanish. (Isaiah 29:14)

> Where is the wise man? Where is the scholar? Where is the philosopher of this age? Has not God made foolish the wisdom of the world? For since in the wisdom of God *the world through its wisdom did not know Him* [my italics], God was pleased through the foolishness of what was preached to save those who believe." (1 Corinthians 1:20-21)

> Do not deceive yourselves. If any one of you thinks he is wise by the standards of this age, he should become a "fool" so that he may become wise. For the wisdom of this world is foolishness in God's sight. As it is written: "He catches the wise in their craftiness"; and again, "The Lord knows that the thoughts of the wise are futile" (Psalm 94:11) . . .

> Now about food sacrificed to idols: We know that we all possess knowledge. Knowledge puffs up, but love builds up. The man who thinks he knows something does not yet know as he ought to know. (1 Corinthians 3:18-20, 8:1-2)

The argument is that humans simply do not possess sufficient information about the supernatural realm to operate solely in a rational mode; furthermore, some of the facts at man's disposal in the natural realm may be perceived incorrectly. Those who assume that truth and knowledge can only be obtained through deductive logic may be seen as narrow-minded in their view and as somewhat prideful, thinking that they possess the only acceptable method of acquiring information.

Madeline L'Engle (1991), renowned philosopher and writer, uses the following anecdote in her talks to stress the importance of "unprovable truth." One day a woman took her children to an animal park. Upon leaving the park, she found out from a ranger that her red Volkswagen bug had been dented by an elephant who had been trained to sit on red buckets. Relieved that the damage would be covered by insurance, she left for home with her children. On the way, she was detained by a minor accident in the road, but was able to carefully snake around the cars involved in the accident and continue on her way. Soon she was pulled over by a policeman who scolded her for leaving the scene of the accident. She protested to the policeman that she had merely driven around it. He then inquired about the damage to her car. When the lady explained about the elephant, the policeman thought she was intoxicated and brought her to the police station. The point of the story is that even though her explanation sounded totally irrational, it was nevertheless true.

UNCERTAINTY IN SCIENCE

Many scientists recognize the limits of their knowledge and the uncertainty that characterizes the world around them. For instance, the uncertainty of movements of subatomic particles has been incorporated into a law of physics, called the Heisenberg Uncertainty Principle. Furthermore, a recent article in *Nature* and its accompanying editorial describes observations for which there is no present scientific explanation or physical basis (Davenas et al. 1988). This article shows that it is possible to dilute an aqueous solution of an antibody virtually indefinitely without losing biological activity. Eventually, an explanation for this phenomenon will probably be discovered. Nevertheless, it makes the point that there is much that scientists still have to learn. The naturalistic laws of science are constantly being refined and sometimes discarded. All scientific knowledge is, to a certain extent, based upon assumptions, perspective, and theory—each of which require redefinition as new observations are made.

From Francis Bacon comes the philosophy of science known as *logical positivism*. In this system, only things which can be directly observed and measured are of any importance. Such observable facts or data are the building blocks upon which hypotheses and propositions are constructed, theory is developed, laws are derived and confirmed. The general notion is that a correct application of the empirical method will establish scientific truth once and for all, to stand forever. Such final truths are claimed to be free of all uncertainty. This Baconian doctrine strives to stay as close to the data as possible and minimize or eliminate presupposition, inference, unnecessary theorizing, and high level abstraction in order to establish science based on facts and unbiased observation. The closer one comes to this goal, the closer one is to the truth.

Some argue, however, that this is an impossible goal. All scientific knowledge is based on experience and may be overturned at any time that further experience becomes available. Scientific laws which are formulated as universal propositions cannot be verified beyond doubt given any finite set of observations (Brown 1977).

Logical empiricism, a moderate version of logical positivism, challenges the notion that scientific laws can be conclusively verified. The cornerstone upon which logical empiricism rests is that there is a

> fundamental distinction between uninterpreted scientific theories and the body of perceptual experience which confers meaning on our theories and determines which ones are to be accepted . . . it is the empirical facts which are known independently of any theory that guarantee the objectivity of science. (Brown 1977, p. 81)

Perception, however, does not provide us with pure facts; instead, it is the *knowledge, experiences, beliefs and theories we already hold* that play the primary role in determining what is perceived. Much of what is perceived is based on information that we have learned (often unknowingly) during socialization in our particular culture and during training for the profession we practice.

The following quotes demonstrate a convergence of thought by authorities in the philosophy of science:

> One cannot have a fact without having a prior theory. To see this, consider the following bald instruction: Observe carefully and write down every fact you see. It is clear that the instruc-

tion cannot be carried out–for one does not know what, if any, "observation" constitutes a "fact." Observation is a skill over and above the passive reception of the raw data . . . Facts are not picturable, observable entities; instead they are wholly conceptual in nature. (Weimer 1979, p. 21)

Our views as to the reliability of data, and even to some extent how the data are interpreted, depend upon the theory that is held by the investigator. There is no such thing as pure data. (Harre 1972, p. 11)

Fact is inseparable from theory. It is an hypothesis, a conjecture germinated in theory, which guides the scientist in his search for evidence. What kind of world one finds is determined by what kind of structure the world is assumed to have. . . . Thus the world is no longer flat, nor does the sun revolve about the earth, nor do objects in motion seek their natural position. Yet each of these at some time was the fact of observant men. There are innumerable examples wherein a new conceptual-factual context introduces a different excursion into reality. (Turner 1967, p. 15)

In the old system of science, a theory was tested against observations of nature; when discrepancies arose, the theory was modified to fit the data. According to Faust and Miner (1986), the current method of science involves a competition of theories, "worldviews" or "paradigms" against each other:

They [worldviews] come with not only theoretical assumptions but also broad models of nature and with guidelines regarding what problems are most worthy of study and how to study them. Scientists adhering to one or another paradigm attempt to make the best case possible and to *convert* [my italics] scientists holding differing paradigms to their way of seeing and studying nature . . . Attempts to bolster one's view and to convert others to it do include considerable data, but because data cannot be theory neutral they are rarely if ever decisive. The process is essentially one of *persuasion* [my italics], and data play a role, but so do numerous other considerations . . . This process is not "objective" in the strict sense, but it is not irrational or "subjective" either. Exactly how this process of persuasion operates and the mechanisms by which it effectively promotes scientific progress and the growth of knowledge remain a central puzzle. (Faust and Miner 1986, pp. 964-965)

Thus, there is no reality that scientists can know for certain independent of the observer. Objectivity is an illusion. Even if a large group of people agree, that does not ensure a greater validity or truth to a given observation. The growth of scientific knowledge (particularly in the area of man's nature and psychological development), then, is not a clear-cut, unambiguous process; rather, it involves public debate between competing theoretical systems or paradigms and depends on "persuasion" as well as upon "objective" data. When a person is deeply immersed in a particular paradigm, however, it is difficult to see an alternative viewpoint.

RELIGION AND SCIENCE

From the above discussion, we see that religion and science have more in common than might be expected. In both areas, much is unknown and contradictions appear to exist. How is the religious community and its method of observation and "fact" collection so different from the scientific community? Judeo-Christian religion is based upon a general theory about human origins and the world in which we exist. According to this theory, a powerful, purposeful, and personal force exists outside and apart from the universe. This force or Person created the universe, as well as all of the physical laws that maintain it, and has a will and purpose for the future in which man plays a vital part.

These ideas came about through man's observation of and intuition about the surrounding world—the order and beauty of the universe, the unexplained and uncontrollable forces in nature, and the foreknowledge of eventual death. Most convincing, however, was man's direct experience of a powerful, good, and personal God and the active response by this God when requests were made of him. Such observations and experiences, then, make up the "facts" upon which the Judeo-Christian religious paradigm is built. These facts were collected and documented by credible and respected "experts," many with firsthand knowledge, into a comprehensive and cohesive worldview.

One might argue that science differs from religion because it involves a community of individuals who freely disagree with one another and debate openly concerning the truth. This is not true. Religious truths have received far more open debate over the past 3000 years than any scientific or psychological theories have had during the past one or two hundred years. The number of denominations with differing views in the Christian religion today demonstrates this fact. Despite many disagreements between Christian groups, most adhere to a set of fundamental concepts that have withstood assault by skeptics for thousands of years with little variation in substance. Disagreement and debate over religious truths flourish in American society today, as each religious group attempts to persuade others towards their viewpoint on some nuance of doctrine. Indeed, religious persons collect and use "theory-laden" facts and observations in the same way that scientists do in their efforts to convince others of the truth of their claims.

When a member of a religious group attempts to disagree with that group's doctrine, the person is often either pressured to conform or ostracized. The situation is not greatly different in the scientific community. Throughout the history of science, most great scientific discoveries were initially rejected by the majority because the new idea went against the contemporary trends of scientific thought. As noted earlier, Freud himself was ostracized from his peers for almost 10 years when his ideas about infantile sexuality were rejected by the scientific community. Once his psychoanalytic theories rose in prominence and respectability, however, anyone who disagreed with his views or that of his small group were quickly discredited (Sulloway 1991). In order to shield his theories from too close scrutiny by the scientific community at large, Freud moved psychoanalytic training out of the university and into small, private institutes over which he and his group had better control (a tradition which continues today). The manner in which many scientists defend or rationalize their theories against the intrusion of new data or discoveries, then, is not greatly different from the behavior of religious persons.

Thus, while the differences between religious and scientific communities cannot be denied, the similarities are also quite striking. Each depends on theory-laden observations and facts gathered by reliable and reputable persons in their respective communities. The facts that religion deals with are often the same facts that science must address. While there cannot be a contradiction between the actual facts themselves, interpretations of the facts frequently differ because of the different theoretical systems in which they are observed.

The Judeo-Christian religion, however, does make a claim that good scientists do not and cannot make. As science looks in on itself, it finds *relativism* (truth dependent on point of observation). As Judeo-Christianity looks in on itself, it finds *the absolute* (truth not dependent on point of observation). The latter type of truth is one that must be based on faith. That faith, however, is not without justification; rather it is based on an experience which God initiates and man receives (see Chapter 7).

Personal Bias and Single-Mindedness

There are other issues, besides rational ones, which separate mental health and religious professionals from understanding and appreciating each others views. Religious professionals, many without scientific training, may perceive psychiatrists or psychologists as a threat, misunderstanding the contributions that medications or electroconvulsive therapy can make to relieving suffering. Psychologists and psychiatrists, on the other hand, are less likely than the general public or members of other professional disciplines to believe in God or participate in religious activities (Lehman and Witty 1931; Leuba 1934; American Psychiatric Association 1975; Ragan, Malony, and Beit-Hallahmi 1980). In fact, medical students who choose psychiatry as their specialty are less interested in religion than their peers (Eagle & Marcos 1980).

More recently, we examined the prevalence of religious belief and behavior among 130 physicians in nine specialties at Duke Hospital; psychiatrists were among the lowest (bottom one-third) in frequency of belief in God, church attendance, and reliance on religion as a coping behavior (Koenig et al. 1991). Furthermore, psychiatrists referred fewer patients to chaplains than any other medical specialty (less than 25% referred one or more patients in the past six months). The clergy, in turn, may be reluctant to refer members of their congregations to psychiatrists because of their lack of sympathy for religious causes.

Religious persons are frequently pictured by mental health professionals as being uneducated, emotional, superstitious, and relying on a primitive style of coping; they are contrasted with the more refined, educated, rational and objective individual who uses calm, clear, rational logic in dealing with others and the world around them. The devoutly religious are often portrayed as being unwilling to consider explanations inconsistent with their beliefs, unwilling to doubt, unwilling to be self-critical–in essence, as being "single-minded." As I have noted earlier, however, many scientists and mental health professionals may be equally single-minded in their own views. How willing and open are they to consider phenomena outside of the natural order? How willing are they to consider the possibility of revealed truth that appears to go against their own logic and rational conclusions? A greater willingness on both sides to consider and integrate alternative views, then, is necessary for deeper understanding and cooperation.

CONFLICT WITHIN THE PSYCHOLOGICAL SCIENCES

I will now overview approaches to mental illness taken by the psychological sciences, focusing on divisions within the field and examining the scientific evidence that supports the different points of view. Several schools of thought exist on the origins of mental illnesses and the best ways to manage them. In recent years, psychology (as distinct from psychiatry) has come to emphasize *cognitive* and *behavioral* approaches based on learning theory; a significant minority, however, continues to espouse and practice more classical *psychoanalytic* techniques. Psychiatry, while absorbing and integrating some of psychology's techniques, has emphasized psychodynamic explanations for human behavior and proscribed methods of treatment along these lines. *Metapsychologists* follow the teachings of Freud and his descendants in a more classical approach to psychoanalysis. *Anti-metapsychologists*, on the other hand, directly oppose and seek to discredit the views of the meta-psychologists. Finally, *self-psychologists*, *interpersonalists*, and *object-relationists* have tried to preserve Freud's teachings, yet have modified and extended them along their own lines of thought.

Thus, psychiatrists differ widely in their approaches to psychotherapy, some being predominantly behavioralists, some cognitive therapists, some interpersonalists, and some psychoanalysts. Others rely very little on "talk" therapy, and instead emphasize the biological origins of mental illness, treating patients primarily with medications and/or electroconvulsive therapy (*biological psychiatrists*). Most mental health professionals, however, are eclectic in their approach, using bits and pieces from a number of different psychotherapeutic methods, along with medications and other biological therapies when indicated. Thus, unlike traditional medicine where there is usually a well-defined and accepted treatment for every illness, there is little agreement among mental health professionals concerning the best therapy for many persons with neurotic conflicts or even the more severe mental disorders.

In recent years, psychiatrists have taken an increasingly biological view of mental illness. This is nowhere more evident than in the treatment of psychiatric disorders in the elderly, where physical illness predominates and organic etiologies for mental conditions are prevalent. This changing view, however, may also be a reaction to the somewhat disappointing therapeutic results from classical psychoanalysis and related psychotherapies. It may also reflect an attempt to cleanse the field of its ambiguity and align psychiatry more closely with the more traditional approach of medicine. Biological psychiatrists tend to de-emphasize the role of environment, learning, and experience, and instead stress organic deficits and/or genetic aberrations. This movement has received particular impetus from funding sources which see this aspect of psychiatry as more scientifically rigorous and, as mentioned earlier, operating on the more familiar medical model of disease.

Whatever its motivations, scientific progress in biological psychiatry over the past 50 years has been dramatic, particularly in the area of psychopharmacology. The development of drugs like chlorpromazine for the treatment of psychoses, lithium for bipolar disorder, tricyclics for depressive illness, and benzodiazepines for anxiety disorders, have revolutionized the treatment of these conditions. Thus, hope has arisen that greater precision in diagnosis and treatment may eventually lead to biological treatments for all psychiatric illness. One of the clinical ramifications of this movement (and current reimbursement policy) is that many psychiatrists now perform less psychotherapy and rely more heavily on drugs for treatment of mental disorders (especially in the elderly).

The biological approach to psychiatry, however, has paid a cost in terms of reductionism. Man's thoughts, moods, motivations, behaviors, and interpersonal interactions arise from biological processes that are far from simple. In order to study these processes, they must be broken down into their component parts and isolated from outside influences. Whenever a whole is broken down in such a way, however, something of the whole is lost. An example of such reductionism is the current system of classification of mental disorders (Diagnostic and Statistical Manual of Mental Disorders, Third Edition, Revised) (DSM-III-R 1987). Most mental disorders exist naturally on a continuum from wellness to neurosis to severe psychosis (Mirowsky & Ross 1989). Categorizations, then, can be quite arbitrary. There are limitations to pigeon-holing patients with mental illness into discrete categories of disease in order to match them with specific biological treatments. Furthermore, there are questions about the safety and efficacy of psychotropic medications which restrict their use especially among older patients (Koenig & Breitner 1990).

The aim of the previous discussion was to stress a point. A number of distinct currents oppose each other within the psychological sciences today, with behavioralists, analysts, and biological psychiatrists, each moving strongly in their own direction, defending their views and criticizing those who oppose them. Let us now examine the scientific evidence supporting the efficacy of psychological therapies (that compete with the religious approach) and examine therapeutic factors common to them all.

SCIENTIFIC BASIS FOR SECULAR APPROACHES

Through the years mental health professionals have sought to validate their diverse methods by use of the scientific method. This has involved attempts at unbiased observation and careful measurement, hypothesis formulation, and hypothesis validation through experimental testing. The application of the scientific method to the study of psychological phenomena has been most successful in behavioral psychology and biological psychiatry using animal models; in a similar fashion, these disciplines have been able to isolate and study simple behaviors and biological processes in humans. This method, however, is less suited for the validation of psychotherapies which deal with the whole person, as well as interpersonal interactions and influences from the environment, culture, and society which are not easily controlled (Hine, Werman, and Simpson 1982). Nevertheless, the major advantage of the scientific method is that it prevents useless or false ideas, theories or treatments from being perpetuated on the basis of the personal (and possibly biased) experience and authority of a small group of influential leaders in a field.

Psychoanalysis

Unlike behavioral or biological approaches, psychoanalysis has had little scientific verification for its claims. Based upon his extensive clinical experience with mentally disturbed patients, and drawing from the writings of the Greek philosopher Plato, Freud developed the principles and technique of psychoanalysis. As noted earlier, Freud was a brilliant thinker, masterful writer, and strategic planner. His goal was to free man of any hindrance that might prevent him or her from reaching their full human potential. Although the field of psychiatry has moved away from some of Freud's original ideas, the profession's basic view of man and psychotherapeutic methods still rests heavily on his psychodynamic formulations.

While psychoanalytic theory appears to be useful for identifying problem areas in patients' life histories (such as frustrated early needs or unconscious conflicts), its success in treatment and cure has been disappointing. Once the conflict or problem is identified, the power to resolve it is often lacking. Consequently, not only has the efficacy of classical psychoanalysis been challenged, but also the validity of psychoanalytic theory itself.

Albert Ellis (1950) has been particularly vocal in this regard. Consider the following reference to Ellis from Rachman and Costello's (1961, p. 98) classic review of the etiology and treatment of childhood phobias:

> More generally Ellis argues that "the vague, suppositional and multi-interpretive terms in which the theoretical framework of orthodox analysis is usually stated make it almost impossible to test its concepts by normal psychological methods of investigation (Ellis 1950, p. 156)." And we may add, it also makes it almost impossible to appraise the internal consistency and logic of psychoanalytic theory–as a theory. Ellis has criticized the unscientific nature of psychoanalysis and emphasizes the inadequacies and confusion of the theory, the unreliability of the supportive evidence, the failure to submit any part of the theory or practice of psychoanalysis to acceptable scientific test. One of Ellis's most insistent complaints is against the rampant speculation so common in psychoanalysis. As we hope to demonstrate, one of Ellis's comments on a passage of Freud's writings seems in fact to be applicable to a large body of psychoanalytic literature. He remarks that, "the ratio of speculative statements to empirically adduced facts . . . is slightly overpowering." (Ellis, 1950, p. 189)

The technique of psychoanalysis has received critical review not only by those in the fields of cognitive and behavioral psychology, but also by leaders within the psychoanalytic community itself. In 1961, at the World Congress of Psychiatry, psychoanalyst Jules Masserman announced concern over a lack of therapeutic efficacy: "Patients treated by any of our current rituals may show temporary spurts of improvement but retain no discernible advantage after five years over those diagnostically matched, but left untreated" (Masserman 1961).

An example of an unproven construct in psychoanalytic theory is the Oedipal complex, often used as an underlying explanation for neurotic conflict. While perhaps having some truth, this construct is simply too narrow and limited in scope; it represents a special case of the more general issue of competitiveness or rivalry over personal space, involves other interpersonal dynamics, and has ramifications far beyond sexual activity. The whole idea that psychopathology largely emanates from genital drives represents an overgeneralization. Genital issues are seldom primary, but frequently become involved as a secondary issue–as a part of other conflicts and fears concerning trust, submission, dependence, and so forth.

Others argue that psychoanalysis, while beneficial for treating some disorders, is ineffective and impractical for others. It has been argued that because of the enormous amount of time and effort involved in psychoanalytic training, analytic therapists become too narrow in their therapeutic approach, applying their method in a "one hammer–one nail" fashion to cases where other techniques or multimodal tactics would be more appropriate.

The Evidence

Let us now examine the scientific data that exist to prove whether or not psychotherapy (psychoanalytic therapy, in particular) actually works. Luborsky and colleagues (1975) reviewed psychotherapy research since the 1950s. They concluded that most forms of psychotherapy produced changes in a number of patients; these changes, however, were often but not always greater than changes observed in control patients without treatment. Much of the research involved brief psychotherapies and behavioral therapies, rather than Freud's classical long-term analysis; nevertheless, in the studies that compared brief therapies with time-unlimited or long-term therapy, the brief psychotherapies tended to be more effective.

A review by Patterson and colleagues (1977) indicated that a very large percentage of psychotherapy patients returned to treatment within one year of completing a course of therapy; 60% of patients involved in brief psychodynamic or brief behavioral therapy returned for additional treatment within a year of psychotherapy cessation. Even more striking is that 60% of these patients had had therapy prior to entry into that study, reflecting the short-lived effects of treatment. Examining the lives of psychotherapists, Henry (1971) found that many of the therapists had undergone five or more courses of multi-year therapy themselves. So impressed was H.J. Eysenck by this fact that he wrote on two occasions that psychotherapy often produced no greater changes in emotionally disturbed individuals than did no therapy at all or naturally occurring life experiences (Eysenck 1952; 1965).

Reviewing 25 years of research on psychotherapy at Johns Hopkins, Jerome Frank (1974) described studies of patients receiving formal psychotherapy compared with control patients receiving a placebo pill or minimal intervention. Short-term and long-term improvements seen in both treated and control groups were not greatly different. In reference to these findings, Frank makes the following remarks:

> Psychotherapy has become a major, lucrative American industry catering to the needs of millions of consumers. It is crowded with entrepreneurs, each of whom proclaims the unique virtues of his product while largely ignoring those of his rivals, and backs his claims with speculative pronouncements supported by a few case reports. Solidly based objective information as to the nature and efficacy of the product is, by contrast, sadly lacking. (p. 325)

Thus, there is little scientific evidence to support the unique effectiveness of any one type of psychotherapy over another; however, there *is* concern over the efficacy and practical utility of classical psychoanalysis. The old system in psychiatry relied heavily upon the clinical expertise and teachings of its founders, rather than upon the unbiased, cold eye of science. Just because an idea makes sense or is rational, does not necessarily indicate its truth. Human beings often do not behave like rational creatures, especially when emotional issues are involved. When assumptions go unchecked and are passed from generation to generation based on the fame and prestige of those who generated them, this encourages a perpetuation of false ideas. In his psychotherapy review, Strupp (1978) responds exactly to this point: "the history of science amply demonstrates that humanity's capacity for self-deception is so great that misconceptions (such as the geocentric view of the universe) may persist for centuries" (p. 7).

SUMMARY

The Judeo-Christian religion and secular psychology approach the human condition in fundamentally different ways. On careful examination, we find that psychological approaches and the theories of human nature upon which they are based, have little more scientific support than does the religious approach which emphasizes faith and interpersonal relationships. Each of these disparate views provides a relatively cohesive system by which psychological phenomena can be explained and methods by which aberrations may be treated. We have seen that what is sometimes presented as scientific truth is in reality only a "preference" or one way of looking at things. Because both secular and religious views offer a way of *structuring experience*, they have the potential to positively impact mental health. Which is more accurate, however, is yet to be established.

REFERENCES

American Psychiatric Association. (1975). *Psychiatrists' viewpoints on religion and their services to religious institutions and the ministry.* Task Force Report 10, Washington DC: APA.

Brown, H.I. (1977). *Perception, Theory, and Commitment: The New Philosophy of Science.* Chicago: University of Chicago Press, pp. 22-29, 81-91.

Davenas, E., F. Beauvais, J. Amara, M. Oberbaum, B. Robinzon, A. Miadonna, A. Tedeschi, B. Pomeranz, P. Fortner, P. Belon, J. Sainte-Laudy, B. Poitevin, and J. Benveniste. (1988). Human basophil degranulation triggered by very dilute antiserum against IgE. *Nature* 333:816-818. (Also see Editorial: When to believe the unbelievable, p. 787.)

DSM-III-R. (1987). Diagnostic and Statistical Manual of Mental Disorders, 3rd ed., revised. Washington, DC: American Psychiatric Association Press.

Eagle, P.F., and L.R. Marcos. (1980). Factors in medical students' choice of psychiatry. *American Journal of Psychiatry* 137:423-427.

Ellis, A. (1950). An introduction to the principles of scientific psychoanalysis. *Genetic Psychology Monographs* 41:147-212.

Eysenck, H.J. (1952). The effects of psychotherapy: An evaluation. *Journal of Consulting Psychology* 16:319-324.

Eysenck, H.J. (1965). The effects of psychotherapy. *International Journal of Psychiatry* 1:97-178.

Faust, D., and R.A. Miner. (1986). The empiricist and his new clothes: DSM-III in perspective. *American Journal of Psychiatry* 143:962-67.

Frank, J.D. (1974). Therapeutic components of psychotherapy: A 25 year report of research. *Journal of Nervous & Mental Disease* 159:325-342.

Harre, R. (1972). *The Philosophies of Science.* London: Oxford University Press.

Henry, W.E., J.H. Sims, and S.L. Spray. (1971). In *The Fifth Profession*, San Francisco: Jossey-Bass.

Hine, F.R., D.S. Werman, and D.M. Simpson. (1982). Effectiveness of psychotherapy: Problems of research on complex phenomena. *American Journal of Psychiatry* 139:204-208.

Koenig, H.G. and J.C. Breitner. (1990). Use of antidepressants in medically ill older patients. *Psychosomatics* 31:22-32.

Koenig, H.G., M. Hover, L.B. Bearon, and J.L. Travis. (1991). Religious perspectives of doctors, nurses, patients, and families. *Journal of Pastoral Care* 45:254-267.

Lehman, H.C., and P.A. Witty. (1931). Certain attitudes of present-day physicists and psychologists. *American Journal of Psychology* 43:664-678.

L'Engle, M. (1991). Untitled talk given at Duke University, Durham, NC, during Winter/Spring session. The talk referred to her book, *The Glorious Impossible*. New York: Simon & Schuster, 1990.

Leuba, J.H. (1934). Religious beliefs of American scientists. *Harper's* 169 (August):291- 300.

Luborsky, L., B. Singer, and L. Luborsky. (1975). Comparative studies of psychotherapies: Is it true that "Everybody has won and all must have prizes"? *Archives of General Psychiatry*, 32:995-1008.

Masserman, J. (1961). The contributions of experimental psychiatry to the art of healing. *World Congress of Psychiatry* 1:25.

Mirowsky, J., and C.E. Ross. (1989). Psychiatric diagnosis as reified measurement. *Journal of Health and Social Behavior* 30:11-25.

Patterson, V., H. Levene, and L. Breger. (1977). A one year follow-up study of two forms of brief psychotherapy. *American Journal of Psychotherapy* 31:76-82.

Rachman, S., and C.G. Costello. (1961). The etiology and treatment of children's phobias: A review. *American Journal of Psychiatry* 118:97-105.

Ragan, C., H.N. Malony, and B. Beit-Hallahmi. (1980). Psychologist and religion: professional factors and personal belief. *Review of Religious Research* 21: 208-217.

Strupp, H.H. (1978). Psychotherapy research and practice: An overview. In *Handbook of Psychotherapy and Behavior Change*, 2nd ed., edited by S.L. Garfield and A.E. Bergin. New York: John Wiley and Sons, pp. 3-22.

Sulloway, F.J. (1991). Reassessing Freud's case histories: The social construction of psychoanalysis. *Isis* 82:245-275.

Turner, M.B. (1967). *Psychology and the Philosophy of Science*. NY: Appleton-Century-Crofts.

Weimer, W.B. (1979). *Notes on the Methodology of Scientific Research*. Hillsdale, NJ: Lawrence Erlbaum Associates.

Chapter 4

Overlap and Complementarity

If the head and body are to be well, you must begin by curing the soul, that is the first thing. . . . The great error of our day is that physicians separate the soul and body, when they treat the body.

–Plato

Although one cannot deny the existence of fundamental differences in approach taken by religion and psychology, their overall goals are similar: to relieve mental pain and suffering, to free individuals to love and to accept love, to facilitate the development of human potential, and to enhance character maturation–in other words, *to enable persons to live as fully as possible given their circumstances*. It is unfortunate, as we have seen, that these two disciplines often see each other as adversaries. With a contemporary movement in psychiatry and psychology away from classical psychoanalysis and towards a greater emphasis on behavioral, cognitive, and interpersonal therapies, a potential for greater harmony between religion and the mental sciences has developed. These two disciplines not only overlap in many areas, they also complement and extend the work of the other, with each offering something unique the other cannot provide. This is especially true in the area of geriatric mental health care.

AREAS OF OVERLAP

While the specific techniques may differ depending on the type of secular or religious psychotherapeutic approach, their effec-

tiveness in relieving emotional distress may depend on certain underlying common factors. In an overview of psychotherapy research published in the *Handbook of Psychotherapy and Behavior
Change*, Hans H. Strupp (1978) concluded that "There is as yet
limited evidence that specific techniques [of psychotherapy] are
uniquely effective apart from 'nonspecific factors'" (p. 16). He
describes those nonspecific factors as follows:

> Primary ingredients of these common "nonspecific factors"
> include: understanding, respect, interest, encouragement, ac-
> ceptance, forgiveness–in short, the kinds of human qualities
> that since times immemorial have been considered effective in
> buoying the human spirit. . . . Consequently, any benign hu-
> man influence is likely to boost his morale, which in turn is
> registered as "improvement". . . In any event, it is clear that
> the problem has important ramifications for research and prac-
> tice. For example, if further evidence can be adduced that
> techniques contribute less to good therapy outcomes than has
> been claimed, greater effort might have to be expended in
> selecting and training therapists who are able to provide the
> "nonspecific factors" mentioned earlier. (pp. 12, 13)

Carl Rogers (1957) has similarly emphasized the importance of
nonspecific factors (which he calls 'facilitative conditions') such as
accurate empathy, genuineness, and unconditional positive regard.
Irving Yalom (1970) has reviewed the therapeutic factors active in
individual and group therapy; these are noted in the left hand column of Table 4.1. In the right-hand column of the table, for comparison I have included parallel concepts proscribed by the Judeo-
Christian religion.

Jerome Frank (1974) succinctly and eloquently elaborates the
essence of psychotherapy using an interpersonal perspective in the
following paragraph taken from his classic work *Persuasion and
Healing*:

> For many decades the field was dominated by dyadic inter-
> view therapies, differing to be sure in their conceptualizations,
> but all relying primarily on conversations between patient and
> therapist aimed at uncovering difficulties in adjustment, reex-

TABLE 4.1. Therapeutic Factors in Psychotherapy Compared with Those Stressed by Religion

Factors in Psychotherapy (Yalom)	Factors in Religion
Instillation of hope	Instillation of hope[1]
Universality (others have similar problems)	All persons have sinned (fallen short)[2]
Provide information (i.e. diagnosis & course)	Biblical explanations for distress[3]
Altruism (doing good for another person)	Love and serve your neighbor[4]
Transference (strong feelings toward therapist)	Feelings toward God[5]
Socialization	Religious community involvement[6]
Imitation (modeling of behavior)	Biblical figures as role models[7]
Interpersonal/Intrapsychic learning (insight)	Recognize unforgiveness and sin[8]
Relationship (man to man)	God to man, then man to man[9]
Catharsis (self-disclosure)	Confession of sins and repentance[10]
Existential factors (meaning in life)	Man's purpose in the Divine plan[11]

Other Therapeutic Factors	
Nonpossessive warmth	Love, expecting nothing in return[12]
Congruency (dependable and consistent)	God is unchanging, ever present[13]
Unconditional positive regard	Unconditional love from God and others[14]
Respect for the patient	Man created in God's image[15]
Privacy	Private devotions[16]
Listening	Help carry neighbor's burden[17]
Empathy	Empathy[18]
Specialness	Man "fearfully and wonderfully made"[19]
Recapitulation of family experiences	Giving and receiving forgiveness[20]
Boundaries, limits, structure setting	Commandments, laws[21]

[1]Romans 15:3; [2]Romans 3:23; [3]Matthew 17:20; [4]Luke 10:33; [5]Exodus 20:3-6, Deuteronomy 6:5, Matthew 22:37; [6]Acts 2:46; [7]John 8:12, Romans 4:12, 1 John 2:6; [8]Matthew 6:15, Colossians 3:13; [9]Matthew 22:37-39; [10]Romans 10:9, James 5:16, 1 John 1:9; Jeremiah 15:19, Luke 17:4, Acts 3:19; [11]Job 36:5, Proverbs 19:21, Isaiah 46:10-11, Jeremiah 15:11, Romans 8:28; [12]Matthew 5:44, Luke 6:35; [13]Malachi 3:6, James 1:17; [14]Luke 6:35, 1 John 4:20-21; [15]Genesis 1:27, 5:1; [16]Matthew 6:6; [17]Genesis 4:9, 1 John 3:17; [18]Isaiah 63:9, Hebrews 2:18; [19]Psalm 139:14; [20]Matthew 6:12-14, 18:35, Luke 17:3-4; [21]Exodus 18:20, Leviticus 25:18, John 14:23, 15:10

periencing crippling emotions such as anger and fear in the
therapeutic setting to thereby resolve them, and relieving the
symptoms for which the patient sought help. Violent debates
raged among adherents of Freud, Jung, Adler, Rank, and others, but these were concerned mainly with what the topics of
the therapeutic conversation should be, not the method itself.
(p. 201)

Thus, the simple concept of a relationship established between two
humans, with one intending to help the other, may be more important than the specifics of the communication or therapeutic technique. The therapeutic effect, then, may not require much logical
analysis or explanation on the part of the therapist; instead, it may
rely primarily on the quality of the relationship (therapeutic alliance). Such an approach contrasts with the distant professionalism
of the classical insight-oriented psychoanalyst who, avoiding any
emotional involvement with the patient, instead focuses on observation and rational interpretations.

Because of the cost, time, and unproven superior efficacy of
classical psychoanalysis, many mental health professionals have
turned to other strategies. There is a trend among psychodynamic
therapists to see man's personality and behavior as evolving from
relationship-seeking patterns that are enriched and developed by the
responses they call forth from people in their environment. Behavioral, cognitive, and interpersonal psychotherapies have thus become more common and efforts have been made to integrate these
with psychodynamic approaches (Wachtell 1977). The resulting
psychodynamic-cognitive-behavioral technique refuses to allow
persons to abdicate responsibility for their own contributions to
their illness; this contrasts with earlier therapies that often unduly
placed the blame for the patient's behavior, attitude, and circumstances outside of him or herself (in other words, on inherited
biological drives or on parents). Here, there is an emphasis on the
person's current behavior and on the effects which these behaviors
have on others and self.

This refocus of attention on the quality of interpersonal relationships and individual responsibility for behavior, moves the mental
health sciences in a direction that parallels Judeo-Christian teach-

ings. Relational activities such as listening, empathy, genuineness, unconditional love, forgiveness, encouraging and building up, are behaviors long advocated by this tradition. Thus, as we learn more and more about the essential therapeutic elements at the core of psychotherapy, the overlap between secular and religious techniques becomes increasingly evident.

UNIQUE CONTRIBUTIONS

Religion

Besides considerable overlap, there are also unique benefits that each discipline contributes on its own which complement and extend those of the other. Dynamic and developmental principles in psychology help with the analysis of the problem and the identification of conflicts and deficiencies that need attention. Often, however, the power to heal, cure, or effectively change behavior is lacking with purely secular techniques. If a severely neurotic 75-year-old man discovers that his conflict over depending on others results from inadequate mothering during a particular phase of his early childhood development, how much good does this knowledge do him now? If a depressed 80-year-old woman with a lifelong hatred for men finds out that her feelings stem from being raped by her father when she was eight years old, simply making her aware of this connection does not ensure a resolution of the conflict.

Indeed, analysts will be the first to acknowledge that a mere intellectual understanding is not sufficient for change to occur; experiential factors (emotional understanding and release) are important for healing to occur and relearning to take place. Establishing a transference, collecting memories and making associations, and consciously working through conflicts with the therapist to the point of emotional understanding typically takes a great deal of time (and money), requires "psychological mindedness," and employs concepts based upon a psychodynamic worldview that is unfamiliar to many older persons. Perhaps this is why only about 2% to 4% of patients seen in psychiatric outpatient clinics are age 65 or over and why only 5% of an American psychiatrist's time is spent with elderly persons (Eisdorfer and Stotsky 1977).

Therapists may find elders easier to work with if they understand and perhaps even utilize the patient's religious belief system during treatment. Intrapsychic conflict is frequently expressed in religious terms. Draper and colleagues (1965) examined the value of patients' religious thoughts in facilitating psychodynamic formulation. They make the following comment:

> A number of patients who might be called "unpsychologically minded" whose communications in the psychiatric interviews were stilted and guarded, talked with interest, eagerness, and enlivened affect of their philosophical or religious views. Elderly patients especially talked revealingly of their conflicts in religious terms . . . ." (p. 205)

For example, a *non*-psychotic elderly woman from a fundamentalist religious tradition believes that demons are the cause of her chronic depression. Given her cultural and educational background, this explanation makes more sense to her than psychodynamic formulations based on intrapsychic conflict or early childhood trauma. Using her belief system, the therapist might explain that demonic forces affect a person in childhood because of negative interactions with parents or other caretakers during this vulnerable time; however, by altering her current attitudes, cognitions, and interpersonal behaviors, she can free herself of these influences. Thus, the therapist engages the religious elder into cooperating with therapy in a way that might have been resisted if a more traditional tack had been taken.

Older persons are more likely to understand and accept concepts such as forgiveness, release, and replacement–*forgiveness* of a hurt, *release* of bitterness, *replacement* with a will to love. Religion provides a cognitive framework and formalized rituals (such as confession) that can facilitate the healing process. Because of the belief that God transcends both time and space (2 Peter 3:8), unresolved conflicts with persons who live far away (children, for instance) or are deceased (parents, siblings, spouses) may be worked out using religious methods. The belief in time transcendence facilitates the re-experience of the earlier conflict, catharsis, and resolution (from a psychodynamic view). Finally, the religious community may provide the love and concern needed to compensate for deficits that are inherited or acquired during childhood or adult life as a consequence of illness.

Secular Psychotherapy

Severe neurotic illness, however, may be resistant to religious approaches alone. This is especially true in cases where there is a deeply ingrained fear of affiliation or fear of trusting others (Guntrip 1971); such persons may be so damaged from early life experiences that they have great difficulty accepting love from others (including God), despite a deep inner need for such love. "Borderline" and "antisocial" personality disorders are diagnostic labels given to such patients. As the relationship gets closer, the patient's fear is aroused and he or she strikes out at the therapist in order to reestablish distance. If armed only with good will, such therapists can become easily frustrated. These trust-fear conflicts may be very resistant to psychotherapy; in such instances, the best approach may be one that combines religious and secular therapies along with exposure to a supportive, nurturing religious community or similar group, such as Alcoholic Anonymous (Vaillant 1976).

Psychodynamic techniques can also help differentiate behaviors by religious elders that are motivated out of devotion to God from those that are motivated by neurotic conflict. Some individuals claim to be carrying out God's command to love others and to consider others' needs before their own, when in reality they are not doing this out of love for God, but rather because *they are free to do nothing else*. A case from my clinical practice illustrates this point. Mrs. Thomas (fictitious name) was a 46-year-old woman who came into therapy because of depression and anxiety that was related to her being overburdened and stressed out from caring for an overly dependent 23-year-old daughter, an alcoholic and adulterous husband, and her sick elderly mother. Mrs. Thomas claimed that the reason for her taking on all these responsibilities was out of religious obligation to help others. As we reviewed her childhood, however, the real motivation behind her exaggerated caregiver activities emerged. Mrs. Thomas grew up in a home with three younger siblings and an alcoholic father who could not hold down a job; in order to support the family, her mother worked long hours outside the home. Consequently, Mrs. Thomas had to care for her younger siblings and, at times, for her alcoholic father. At a very young age, then, she had been designated the family caregiver, a role which she had been unable to shake off and which compelled her to assume exaggerated caregiving responsibilities even as an adult.

Unfortunate individuals like Mrs. Thomas, because of absent or mentally impaired parents, are thrust into a premature role as caretaker to siblings and sometimes to parents themselves. They were never allowed to be children and thus go through the normal developmental phases. These persons then carry a psychological need to care for others into their adult life. While on the surface this behavior seems commendable, such individuals often become frustrated and resentful over trying to cope with these excessive responsibilities and eventually present to mental health professionals with complaints of depression, anxiety, and/or relationship problems. Our task then is to free the individual from their neurotic need to serve others so that he or she can meet their own psychological needs. Once no longer trapped into meeting others' needs, such a person can then make a truly free and autonomous choice to serve others in response to God's command to do so, rather than in response to an *inability* to do otherwise.

BIOLOGICAL THERAPIES

Thus far, I have been talking primarily about religion and psychological therapies. Much of the medical discipline of psychiatry, however, involves the prescription of medications and the use of other biological therapies such as electroconvulsive therapy. Such treatments may be viewed negatively by religious professionals. Given the role of stress in spiritual growth and maturation, some religious therapists might question the use of medications that relieve psychiatric symptoms (valium for anxiety), when such symptoms might motivate persons to change negative behavior patterns and thus facilitate their advance in faith development. Indeed, secular psychotherapists often complain that relief of anxiety symptoms may diminish the patient's motivation to remain in therapy and work at altering their behavior. Perhaps by relieving symptoms of depression with antidepressants or electroconvulsive therapy, the elder may be deprived of the experience of God's direct healing power that might lead to a strengthening of faith or even to religious conversion.

On the other hand, how many elders refuse to take antibiotics for pneumonia or insulin for diabetes, in the hope of a spontaneous, miraculous remission that might increase their faith? Not many, I believe. Likewise, few religious therapists or clergy would discourage the use of medication for this purpose. The situation is not greatly different in elders with mental health problems such as anxiety or depression. Physical diseases of the brain are as likely to occur as physical diseases of the heart, lungs, or kidneys. The only difference is that diseases of the brain give rise to psychological symptoms (depression, anxiety, personality changes, psychoses).

A stroke or other neurological illness like Parkinson's disease may devastate even the most devoutly religious person, impairing those parts of the brain that regulate emotion and/or intellectual functioning. A biological depression–resulting from a genetic predisposition, from side-effects of medication, or from overwhelming situational stressors–may worsen to the point that it paralyzes the elder's will, impairs cognitive function, and destroys their ability to engage in meaningful activity. In such cases, biological interventions are often life-saving and may return the elder to a mental state where he or she can once again become involved in life.

A recent case of mine illustrates this point. I was asked to consult on a 72-year-old woman with severe chronic lung disease who had recently moved to the nursing home. Mrs. Jones (fictitious name) could hardly move about her room without becoming exhausted and out of breath. There was nothing more the medical doctors could do to improve her lung condition. Only six months previously she had lived at home, been active in her church, and frequently volunteered time at a local hospital. All this activity stopped, however, after several bouts of pneumonia and a rapid deterioration of her lung function. As her condition worsened, Mrs. Jones had to sell her home and move into the nursing home where she had lived for two months when I saw her. At that time, she could not even go out to dinner with her family because of the severe shortness of breath she developed by just walking across the parking lot. For this reason, she stayed in her room most of the time. Mrs. Jones was lonely, felt abandoned, and became very depressed.

I tried various psychotherapeutic approaches over the next several weeks–supportive therapy, cognitive therapy, behavioral therapy–and suggested several practical ways to make new friends and increase her socialization. Since she was a religious person, I encouraged her to pray and read the Psalms or other inspiring religious literature. Mrs. Jones reported to me that she had already been doing all this on her own initiative long before I had begun seeing her. I sat with her; I listened; I showed compassion; I was empathetic. She only got worse–more tearful, more socially withdrawn, more unhappy. Finally, I started her on 10 mg. of nortriptyline (a very low dose of antidepressant). After three days, her crying spells lessened, her socialization increased, and her mood significantly improved; even breathing became easier as the distress from her mental illness lessened. Her prayer time and Bible reading became more fulfilling as well.

I have had many elderly patients improve dramatically when started on antidepressants or given electroconvulsive therapy, after failing to respond to psychotherapeutic and/or religious approaches. Psychotropic medications, however, are seldom so effective that they can cure mental illness or totally relieve all symptoms of distress. Rather, they often diminish stress to the point that it is tolerable. The person can then more fully engage in psychological or religious therapies which have the potential for inducing real changes in attitude, behavior, and personality that will enhance and maintain psychological health in the future.

Religious professionals should be aware that symptoms of mental disorder can markedly interfere with a person's ability to relate to God. For example, alterations in consciousness, as seen in chronic dementia or acute delirium, can disrupt the concentration necessary for prayer or scripture reading. A severe retarded depression can so immobilize a person that neither private nor social religious activity can be engaged in. Psychotic disorders such as schizophrenia can interrupt thought processes to such a degree that it is impossible for a person to relate meaningfully to either God or man. The appropriate use of antidepressants, antianxiety agents, antipsychotics, and electroconvulsive therapy (ECT), then, can free a person so that they can resume making personal choices and continue on their faith journey. These treatments may be viewed as coming from God, who desires to reduce the much needless suffering that is unrelated to human choices; such suffering does not enhance the development of moral character, but rather interferes with it.

Limitations of Biological Therapies

On the other hand, overmedication or adverse side-effects of ECT can also interfere with consciousness so that religious participation and experience become impossible. The issue of inappropriate use of psychotropic medication is of particular importance in older persons, especially those having physical illnesses or taking other medications which interfere with psychotropic drug metabolism (Koenig et al. 1989). Many elders simply cannot tolerate the side-effects of these medications, even at low doses. The vast majority of emotional disorders that occur in later life are of the mild variety that do not require the use of medications or ECT, and may be treated more effectively and safely by psychotherapy. Minor depressions, adjustment disorders, mild anxiety states, and drug or alcohol abuse problems are disorders in this category. Thus, biological therapies play a vital role in the treatment of mental disorders in later life, but they must be used cautiously and only when clearly indicated; as improvement occurs, psychological, spiritual, and/or social therapies should follow (Koenig 1991).

DISEASE, HEREDITY, AND DEVELOPMENT

The remainder of this chapter deals with a potpourri of ideas and hypotheses relating biological and developmental factors to mental illness and religion. The influences of disease, heredity, and environment on mental health, moral development, and religiousness are exceedingly complex. Those who have survived into later life are more likely than younger persons to have been affected by physical disease, heredity (through genetic expression), injuries and other environmental influences. The impact of such factors on religious development are poorly understood and there is virtually no systematic research on the subject. Thus, much of this discussion is admittedly highly speculative.

As science advances, we are learning more and more about the origins of mental disorder. It is becoming increasingly difficult to "judge" one another. Many behavioral disorders in children, such as attention deficit disorder and certain conduct disorders, rather than being due to "bad parenting" or "bad children" (from a moral perspective), are now known to occur as a result of structural brain abnormalities present since birth that interfere with normal growth and development (as occurs in the mentally retarded). It is also becoming clearer and clearer that mental illness in adulthood, particularly severe depressions and psychotic illnesses (schizophrenia, delusional disorders, bipolar disorder) may likewise have biological or genetic origins, independent of patterns of moral decision making related to spiritual or religious development. In theological terms, biological illnesses result from *original sin* (as do all physical illness and natural disasters not related to man's own willful actions). However, just as religion may help persons cope with pain or disability from physical illness, it may also help those with mental illnesses better cope with their conditions (and, in some cases, heal through supernatural intervention–see Chapter 7).

Granted, it is seldom easy to distinguish illnesses of true biological origin from those resulting from irresponsible decision making (Szasz 1961). Often, both elements are present to some degree. People can use their biological illness to manipulate others and thus serve their own interests (Bonime 1960); likewise, irresponsible or immoral decisions can lead to psychological symptoms or their worsening. The latter may even evolve into a biological illness, as a situational depression deepens to the point that levels of neurotransmitters (or receptor sensitivity) in the brain are adversely affected.

It is also interesting to speculate on why certain persons gravitate towards religion and others do not. The high prevalence of religiosity among elders today may be partly attributable to the historical period in which they were raised (when religion was perhaps more of a societal force than it is today). As will be discussed later, aging itself may influence a person's turning to religion as he or she faces physical illness, loss of loved ones, and the prospect of approaching death. Besides cohort, period, or aging effects, however, biological or genetic factors may also be influential.

Certain temperaments, genetically determined and present at birth, may predispose persons to seek out and accept a religious view of the world or to adhere more tenaciously to moral standards. For instance, the more irritable, easily upset or frightened infant may bring these traits into adulthood and then be motivated by them to seek relief through religious cognitions and behaviors. The more relaxed, sanguine, confident, optimistic individual, on the other hand, may have little reason to seek comfort in religion. This person may quite successfully deny or dismiss fears about his/her eventual mortality or other existential concerns.

While temperament defines the basic equipment that a person has to work with in life, the fit between temperament and early childhood environment is of crucial importance in determining personality type. Certain personality types, in turn, may gravitate towards religion or "feel more comfortable" with a religious worldview. For instance, the more conservative personality type may feel more relaxed in a religious group which espouses conservative values. Or the person with obsessive-compulsive traits may find great solace in the structured, ordered life style and rituals of a religious community. Thus, personality type–determined by both temperament and environment–may influence the likelihood of religious involvement, independent of an individual or free choice to pursue this course.

TOWARDS A BIOLOGY OF RELIGIOUS EXPERIENCE

Cloninger (1987) has developed a personality theory that links personality traits with levels of biogenic amines and other chemicals in the brain. Cloninger describes his personality types as existing along three spectrums: (1) low to high "novelty seeking" (dopamine mediated), (2) low to high "reward dependence" (norepinephrine mediated), and (3) low to high "harm avoidance" (serotonin and acetylcholine mediated). Using this system, the antisocial personality type would be categorized as having high novelty-seeking, but low reward-dependence and low harm-avoidance traits (reflecting an imbalance in brain chemicals). Mentally healthy individuals are described as falling in the mid-range of these spectrums. The biological processes responsible for these traits are reported to reinforce each other. For instance, serotonin tends to both increase norepinephrine and decrease dopamine; thus, the biological mechanisms motivating individuals with high harm avoidance would strengthen reward dependence and reduce novelty-seeking tendencies. This may possibly explain why certain individuals tend toward greater religiousness, while others tend in the opposite direction.

One could speculate that the individual with low novelty seeking (the conservative), high reward dependence (the socially gregarious), and high harm avoidance (the fearful and anxious) may have a greater aptitude for religion than would the high novelty seeking (the liberal), low reward dependence (the independent and socially aloof), and low harm avoidance (the contented and relaxed) individual. Religious tendencies, then, may in part be mediated by a particular balance of brain chemicals (biogenic amines) that is genetically determined and can be influenced by disease processes that affect the brain.

While it may seem strange and a bit discomforting for some to try to identify a biological basis for religious behaviors and cognitions, I do not believe this detracts from the meaning, importance, and truth of religious ideas. Because humans are biological organisms, all religious ideas, beliefs, behaviors or other phenomena a person experiences are necessarily biologically mediated. It is doubtful that there are any psychological experiences that do not involve biological processes–otherwise, they could not be experienced. Although some persons with near-death experiences do relate profound religious experiences, it is not clear that all brain function was absent in these individuals at the time of their experiences. No one knows whether a person in deep coma with no brain activity on EEG is capable of having religious experience, although my professional opinion is that he or she is not. In this case, biological structures in the brain necessary to mediate religious experience are not functioning. On the other hand, of course, spiritual and supernatural processes may be independent of biological processes, and thus not require a functioning brain.

Another interesting but highly speculative area is the possible biological basis for intensely euphoric religious phenomena such as the "born again" or conversion experience. If the above reasoning is correct, apart from supernatural processes, all religious and spiritual experiences are psychological phenomena and result from biological processes within the brain. One would then expect that biological processes would likewise mediate even the most profound of religious experiences. Are there certain parts of the brain that are especially active during religious experience? No one knows.

At one time, it was thought that religious experience was more common in patients with temporal lobe seizures, particularly those with a left temporal focus (Dewhurst and Beard 1970; Waxman and Geschwind 1975; Bear and Fedio 1977; Bear et al. 1982; Persinger 1983). This idea has since been seriously challenged by a number of reputable investigators who have failed to replicate these findings (Nielsen and Kristensen 1981; Mungas 1982; Rodin and Schmaltz 1984; Hermann and Whitman 1984; Master, Toone, and Scott 1984; Tucker, Novelly, and Walker 1987). Some investigators have even argued that both St. Paul and Muhammad the Prophet of Islam had seizure disorders that led to their ecstatic experiences (Freemon 1976; Landsborough 1987). In my opinion, these latter claims are highly contrived. While temporal lobe seizures may be associated with strange, vague, mystical, difficult to describe experiences, they are infrequently accompanied by specific and detailed religious knowledge that consequently affects an individual for the rest of his or her life.

Another biological disorder in which religious experience tends to be heightened is in the manic phase of bipolar disorder (manic-depressive illness). Bizarre, grandiose religious delusions are frequently seen, and are sometimes used in the diagnosis of this syndrome. Could pathological processes operating in a particular part of the brain give rise to this type of distorted religious experience? There is some evidence that bipolar disorder may actually arise from epileptiform activity deep within the brain (like the amygdala); indeed, anticonvulsants like carbamazapine and valproic acid are frequently used to treat this disorder. No systemic research has examined the effect of such treatments on the religious fervor that sometimes accompanies this illness.

Observations of patients with stroke and stimulation of areas of

the brain during surgery have led to discoveries about the functioning of different parts of the brain. Work has especially centered
around separating functions of the right and left halves of the brain
(Luria 1973). The left brain has been shown to be the center of
speech, language and verbal abilities, rational thinking, and mathe-
matical abilities. The right brain, on the other hand, is more a center
for visual-spacial orientation, artistic ability, and even perhaps the
location of the intuitive sense; this part of the brain deals more with
patterns and general schemas. Although purely speculative, perhaps
religious experiences are mediated through processes occurring in
the right brain. Arguing against this idea, however, are the findings
of Bear and Fedio (1977) from their study of interictal behaviors in
temporal lobe epileptics; they found religious thoughts and ideas
more common in *left* temporal lobe epileptics.

It is my opinion that religious experience, if biologically based, is
a more general brain phenomenon that is not localized to any particular anatomical part. Future research exploring the religious experiences of patients with stroke and other localized brain injuries are
needed to help further our understanding of the complex neurobio-
logical basis for religious experience.

SUMMARY

While there are fundamental differences in the views of mental
health and religious professionals concerning the origin and treatment of humanity's psychological ills, there is also much that is
common between these disciplines. Furthermore, each has a unique
contribution to the treatment of mental illness in later life which
complements and extends the benefits achieved by either one separately. Psychodynamic techniques may be used to identify conflicts
and their origins; religious rituals and prayer, integrated with more
traditional insight-oriented, cognitive-behavioral, or interpersonal
methods, may facilitate their resolution.

Given (1) the high prevalence of religious belief and behavior
among the elderly, (2) the many physical, social, and economic
stresses that affect this age group, and (3) the high likelihood of
many psychological symptoms having a biological origin, treatment
approaches which combine and integrate the strengths of both

religion and the mental sciences would seem most useful. Each discipline may then serve to keep the other in check, avoiding excesses and ensuring adequate attention to areas of neglect–religion's neglect of biological factors in mental illness and psychology/psychiatry's neglect of spiritual factors.

In Section II, we will review the classical theories of psychological, social, cognitive, moral, and faith development. I will then present a biopsychosocial-spiritual view of man and discuss a theory of religious faith development based on that view, emphasizing religious change throughout the life cycle but especially in later life.

REFERENCES

Bear, D.M., and P. Fedio. (1977). Quantitative analysis of interictal behavior in temporal lobe epilepsy. *Archives of Neurology* 34:454-467.

Bear, D.M., K. Levin, D. Blumer, D. Chetham, and J. Ryder. (1982). Interictal behavior in temporal lobe epilepsy. Relationship to idiopathic psychiatric syndromes. *Journal of Neurology, Neurosurgery, and Psychiatry* 45:481-488.

Bonime, W. (1960). Depression as a practice: Dynamic and psychotherapeutic considerations. *Comprehensive Psychiatry* 1:194-198.

Cloninger, C.R. (1987). A systematic method for clinical description and classification of personality. *Archives of General Psychiatry* 44:573-588.

Dewhurst, K., and A.W. Beard. (1970). Sudden religious conversions in temporal lobe epilepsy. *British Journal of Psychiatry* 117:497-507.

Draper, E., G.G. Meyer, Z. Parzen, and G. Samuelson. (1965). On the diagnostic value of religious ideation. *Archives of General Psychiatry* 13:202-207.

Eisdorfer, C., and B.A. Stotsky. (1977). Intervention, treatment and rehabilitation of psychiatric disorders. In *The Handbook of the Psychology of Aging*, edited by J.E. Birren and K.W. Schaie. NY: Van Nostrand Reinhold.

Frank, J.D. (1974). *Persuasion and Healing*. Baltimore: Johns Hopkins Press.

Freemon, F.R. (1976). A differential diagnosis of the inspirational spells of Muhammad, the Prophet of Islam. *Epilepsia* 17:423-427.

Guntrip, H. (1971). *Psychoanalytic Theory, Therapy, and the Self*. NY: Basic Books.

Hermann, B.P., and S. Whitman. (1984). Behavioral and personality correlates of epilepsy: A review, methodological critique, and conceptual model. *Psychological Bulletin* 95:451-497.

Koenig, H.G. (1991). Treatment considerations for the depressed geriatric medical patient. *Drugs & Aging* 1:266-278.

Koenig, H.G., V. Goli, F. Shelp, H.S. Kudler, H.J. Cohen, K.G. Meador, and D.G. Blazer. (1989). Antidepressant use in older medically ill inpatients: Lessons from an attempted clinical trial. *Journal of General Internal Medicine* 4:498-505.

Landsborough, D. (1987). St. Paul and temporal lobe epilepsy. *Journal of Neurology, Neurosurgery, and Psychiatry* 50:659-664.

Luria, A.R. (1973). *The Working Brain.* NY: Basic Books

Master, D.R., B.K. Toone, and D.F. Scott. (1984). Interictal behavior in temporal lobe epilepsy. In *Advances in Epileptology*, edited by R.F. Porter, R.J. Porter, R.H. Mattson, A.A. Ward, and M. Dam. The XVth Epilepsy International Symposium. NY: Raven Press, pp. 557-565.

Mungas, D. (1982). Interictal behavioral abnormality in temporal lobe epilepsy: A specific syndrome or non-specific psychopathology? *Archives of General Psychiatry* 39:108-111.

Nielsen, H., and O. Kristensen. (1981). Personality correlates of sphenoidal EEG-foci in temporal lobe epilepsy. *Acta Neurologica Scandinavia* 64:289-300.

Persinger, M.A. (1983). Religious and mystical experiences as artifacts of temporal lobe function: A general hypothesis. *Perceptual and Motor Skills* 57: 1255-1262.

Rodin, E., and S. Schmaltz. (1984). The Bear-Fedio personality inventory and temporal lobe epilepsy. *Neurology* 34:591-596.

Rogers, C.R. (1957). The necessary and sufficient conditions of therapeutic personality change. *Journal of Consulting Psychology* 21:95-103.

Strupp, H.H. (1978). Psychotherapy research and practice: An overview. In *Handbook of Psychotherapy and Behavior Change*, 2nd ed., edited by S.L. Garfield and A.E. Bergin. NY: John Wiley and Sons, pp. 3-22.

Szasz, T. (1961). *Myth of Mental Illness.* NY: Hoeber-Harper.

Tucker, D.M., R.A. Novelly, and P.J. Walker. (1987). Hyperreligiosity in temporal lobe epilepsy: Redefining the relationship. *Journal of Nervous and Mental Disease* 175:181-184.

Vaillant, G.E. (1976). Sociopathy as a human process. *Archives of General Psychiatry* 32:173-183.

Wachtell, P. (1977). *Psychoanalysis and Behavioral Therapy: Toward an Integration.* NY: Basic Books.

Waxman, S.G., and N. Geschwind. (1975). The interictal behavior syndrome of temporal lobe epilepsy. *Archives of General Psychiatry* 32:1580-1586.

Yalom, I.D. (1970). *The Theory and Practice of Group Psychotherapy.* NY: Basic Books.

PART II:
THEORETICAL ISSUES

Chapter 5

Theories of Human Development

Man is the product of causes which had no prevision of the end they were achieving; his origin, his growth, his hopes and fears, his loves and his beliefs are but the outcome of accidental collocations of atoms.

–Bertrand Russell

Secular theories of normal human development seek to account for and predict patterns of human behavior and thought as they evolve throughout the life cycle from birth through childhood, adulthood, and into old age. Gergen (1977, 1980) has divided developmental theories into three major categories: the stability account, the ordered change account, and the aleatoric account. The *stability account* emphasizes behavioral constancy, focusing on biological and social influences in early childhood that establish an enduring pattern of behavior that remains generally stable throughout adult life. Exemplifying this approach is Freud's view of psychological development as occurring in discrete psychosexual stages that are nearly completed by the age of six. This approach, however, tends to neglect important changes that occur in later life.

The *ordered change account*, a view that has predominated for the past 30 to 40 years, sees development as occurring in systematic and predictable ways as the individual passes through successive stages beginning in infancy and extending into the adult years and then later life. Erikson's psychosocial theory of development falls into this category, as do the accounts of Piaget, Kohlberg, and Buhler. The individual is seen as playing a different role in each stage of life which is associated with a primary developmental task which must be completed for smooth and successful progress into the next stage. Remnants of uncompleted tasks from previous stages may hinder completion of tasks in later stages. For instance, the failure to establish trust in infancy may interfere with the development of autonomy during toddlerhood as well as the development of intimacy during the teen years.

Finally, the *aleatoric account* emphasizes the flexibility and variability of developmental patterns, their lack of universal application, and their heavy influence by culture and historical setting. This approach sees the person as an active agent in his or her own development at all points throughout the life cycle; humans are seen as *active* rather than *reactive* in responses to their environment. Included in this perspective are theorists such as Jung, Sullivan, Maslow, and Allport. The aleatoric account allows for a view of aging that sees losses as providing the opportunity for new, creative developments in one's personality. This view is of particular interest because it most closely harmonizes with the religious account, in which man is seen as influencing his or her character growth and development throughout life by decisions and choices made in response to internal drives and environmental circumstances.

None of these theories of human psychological development are scientifically proven; rather, each is based on observation and clinical experience from a particular viewpoint. Among the major theorists, only Erikson and Jung specifically address development in later life. Let us now more closely examine the major classical theories and the people who developed them. This review is quite elementary and is not intended to be comprehensive; nevertheless, I believe it will provide a background against which the religious account may be viewed.

PSYCHOANALYTIC THEORY

Freud's ideas were instrumental in the genesis and development of classical psychoanalytic theory, also known as drive psychology. By 1900, he had almost single-handedly developed a field of investigation, a method of inquiry, and a psychotherapeutic strategy (Strachey 1953-1974). Freud developed these ideas in three major theories: libido theory, the topographical theory (conscious, preconscious, and unconscious), and the structural theory (id, ego, super-ego). He viewed human psychological development as occurring in five major psychosexual stages: oral (birth to 1 year), anal (1 to 3 years), phallic (3 to 5 years), latency (5 to 11 years), and adolescence (puberty to young adulthood). Freud's developmental theory focuses on attachments to parental figures and their resolution; behavioral states are understandable in terms of fixation and/or regression. Emphasis is primarily on expression of innate sexual or aggressive drives, with a relative downplay of environmental and caretaker influences.

Early psychoanalytic theory, then, concentrated on the biologically driven natural unfolding of the psyche. This approach was at least in part an outgrowth of early attempts to conform ideas about the mind to the prevailing views of the time in the neurological sciences, the area in which Freud did most of his early research and training. Freud was culture-bound, carrying over into his psychological views those of his mentor, Helmholtz. Man was viewed as a biological organism whose psychological development followed certain predictable laws, in the same way that physical events did in the natural sciences.

As noted in Chapter 2, this application of the laws of genetics and physiology to the development of mental processes has been criticized as unnecessarily reductionistic and overly biological. However, psychiatry's drive to become an acceptable medical science tended to perpetuate these views. The unfolding of the psyche was seen as so internally controlled and genetically regulated that influences from the environment were deemphasized. Human relationships and life experiences were regarded as having only secondary effects on early psychological development. The notion of an internally regulated, biological determination of personality development reached its most extreme statement in the work of Melanie Klein (1964), who implied that a growing infant or toddler developed patterns of dealing with others independent of the particular parent he or she happened to have. This trend, while consistent with some of Freud's early and mid-period thoughts, did contrast with his later ideas that focused more on the importance of unfavorable childhood experiences.

Ego psychology evolved from Freud's structural theory of the mind. In his final theories, the ego comprised that group of psychological functions which mediated between internal drives or instincts and the outside world. Heinz Hartmann (1964) expanded Freud's concepts by describing a group of ego functions that developed independent of instincts or drives, called primary autonomous ego functions; in this category were such functions as perception, thinking, language, and intelligence. Although they developed independent of id drives, they could become involved in conflict between these drives and other ego functions (an example being aggression that interferes with learning). Anna Freud (1936) contributed to the development of ego psychology by classifying defense mechanisms by whether they controlled sexual or aggressive impulses, and by associating them with different stages of development. For instance, immature defenses used primarily during the oral phase of development were denial, projection, introjection, and regression. Other defense mechanisms were attributed to the anal and phallic stages in a similar fashion.

This overly biological view of man's psychological development was challenged by investigators who emphasized the importance of human relationships and interactions to normal growth and development ("object relations") (see Greenberg and Mitchell 1983 for a review). Systematic observation and followup of young infants and children in the 1940s and 1950s by investigators such as Margaret Mahler, John Bowlby, and Rene Spitz documented the importance of interaction between mother and baby on development and the severe psychological impairments that resulted when such interaction was missing.

Mahler (1975) is best known for her ideas on the stages of separation and individuation of the toddler. She linked difficulties at this stage with predictable effects on later personality development. Bowlby (1969) is known for his theory of attachment and research involving the emotional tone between the developing child and mother dyad. His studies, along with those of Rene Spitz (1965), documented long-term personality deficits in those infants separated from their mothers or inadequately stimulated because of hospitalization or social reasons. Edith Jacobsen (1964), Otto Kernberg (1976), and Heinz Kohut (1971) (self psychology) also made significant contributions toward a psychoanalytic theory that focused on early human relationships. The implications of this work for adults in later life has yet to be addressed, although personality deficits acquired early in life may later affect willingness and ability to rely on others when physical illness or advancing age forces dependency.

The *interpersonal psychologists* (also known as Neo-Freudians) were an offshoot from the traditional psychoanalytic school. They extended the ideas of the object-relationists into later childhood and adult development, challenging many of Freud's earlier ideas, particularly those that placed sexual and aggressive drives at the core of all human behavior. Included in this group were Alfred Adler (1956) (individual psychology), Carl Jung (1975) (analytic psychology), Karen Horney (1945), and Harry Stack Sullivan (1953) (interpersonal psychology). These analysts strongly emphasized the impact of environment, interpersonal relations, and other psychosocial forces on human behavior and psychological development. This group departed from classical psychoanalysis by their focus on learning and by their willingness to include behavioral techniques in their approach. They highlighted the ill effects of *over*-socialization that resulted in a repression of the real self and emergence of a false self based on compliance (Winnicott 1965).

Sullivan (1953) led the field of interpersonal psychologists and developed a theory of human growth based entirely on interpersonal interaction. He divided the life cycle into six stages: (1) infancy (birth to beginning of language, 18 months to 2 years), (2) childhood (onset of language to time when interaction with peers increased in importance, ages 2 to 5), (3) juvenile era (beginning of school to preadolescence, ages 5 to 9), (4) preadolescence (capacity of intimate relationships with same sex to full genital maturity, ages 9 to 12), (5) adolescence (beginning of genital sexuality to an established pattern of sexual intimacy, ages 12 to 20), and (6) maturity (establishment of fully human and mature interpersonal relationships, self-respect, and collaboration). Sullivan's ideas have strongly influenced the field of psychoanalysis, in that they represented a starting point for a psychodynamic formulation of adult development.

Since Sullivan, a number of other theorists have developed psychodynamic schemas of adult development. Vaillant (1977) examined development in terms of a maturing of defenses and coping mechanisms. Among mature adult defenses, he included sublimation, suppression, humor, and altruism; in the immature category of defenses he placed reaction formation, displacement, and repression. Gould (1978) focused on the evolution of and redefinition of the self in adulthood, with the relinquishment of phantasies of ultimate safety. Levinson (1978) described development in terms of sociocultural life tasks (leaving home, taking on a vocation, raising a family, and so forth). Mann (1985) summarizes and relates these and other psychodynamic theories of adult development. Space does not allow their further consideration here.

LEARNING THEORY

As the techniques of psychoanalysis evolved, another group of mental health specialists (primarily experimental psychologists) came up with a different approach to understanding human behavior and development. This group included individuals such as Harry Harlow (Harlow and Zimmerman 1959) (social development), Ivan Pavlov (1928) (classical conditioning), Konrad Lorenz (1957) (imprinting), and BF Skinner (1959) (operant conditioning). Out of this work came *behavioral theory.* Rather than resulting from an unfolding of innate biological drives, behavior was viewed as being *learned* from experiences in the environment. If behavior was learned, they reasoned, it could be unlearned or relearned. Thus, behavioral therapy was born. Techniques such as reinforcement, progressive relaxation, desensitization, exposure, skills training, and assertiveness training were developed to help change maladaptive behaviors and learn healthier ones.

Cognitive theory also evolved from learning models. Unpleasant emotions were seen as resulting from negative thoughts generated from dysfunctional attitudes learned from interactions with powerful significant others during early development. Albert Ellis (1962) ("rational emotive therapy") and Albert Bandura (1977) ("social learning theory") made significant early contributions to this theory. Synthesizing these ideas with those of his own, Aaron Beck (1963, 1976) developed a method of treating patients with depression (and other emotional disorders) that focused on making the patient aware of their negative thinking (catastrophizing, overgeneralization, personalization), exploring dysfunctional assumptions that generated negative cognitions, and then altering those assumptions and associated thoughts to better reflect reality (and thus reduce emotional distress).

THEORIES OF COGNITIVE AND MORAL DEVELOPMENT

Jean Piaget (1950;1972) formulated a theory of cognitive and intellectual development composed of four discrete and nonoverlapping stages which describe how children think and acquire knowledge: (1) *sensorimotor* (awareness characterized by schemas or elementary concepts; beginning use of mental symbols) (birth to 2 years), (2) *preoperational thought* (learns without use of reason; thinks intuitively and egocentrically; events linked by juxtaposition, not logic) (2 to 7 years), (3) *concrete operations* (beginning use of logic; attends more to information outside of self; able to empathize with others; beginning understanding of moral dilemmas) (7 to 11 years), and (4) *formal operations* (thinks abstractly; reasons deductively) (11 years and over). This theory adheres to the concept of epigenesis, as did Erikson's psychosocial stages of development— one stage building on another in a universal and invariable sequence. Piaget's theory is of value in constructing a model of faith development (next chapter), where it is important to identify the age at which a child becomes intellectually capable of understanding spiritual matters.

Just as the ability to think and intellectualize develops over time, so does the sense of morality and capacity to be moral. Following closely the developmental models of Erikson and Piaget, Lawrence Kohlberg (1971,1973,1979) delineated seven stages of moral development: (1) *punishment and obedience* orientation (ages 1-6), (2) *instrumental relativist* orientation (naive egotism, ages 7-12), (3) *interpersonal concordance* orientation (approval and pleasing others, early adolescence), (4) *law and order* orientation (doing one's duty for its own sake, late adolescence), (5) *social-contract legalistic* orientation (recognition of the arbitrary element in rules), (6) *universal ethical principle* orientation (operating by conscience above and beyond social rules), and (7) *cosmic* orientation. The last three stages deal primarily with moral development in adulthood. In constructing these stages, Kohlberg argued that moral reasoning developed through a succession of stages which were universal and invariant (following the epigenetic structuralist model of Piaget). Higher stages are portrayed as more adequate and mature. This model primarily concerns how humans construct and take into account the social perspectives of other persons. Moral development is closely related to, but not synonymous with, religious faith development.

The extent to which advanced aging or disease (such as Alzheimer's disease) reverses cognitive and moral development along the Piagetian schema has been examined. Studies show consistent problems for elders on tasks of both concrete and formal operations. Deficits are most pronounced among the institutionalized elderly and those with chronic brain syndromes; they are least evident among elders who are well-educated and possess high verbal ability (Papalia & Bielby 1974). Until at least the age of 50, moral development appears to parallel that of intellectual performance (Kuhn et al. 1977).

Coming from a different viewpoint, Riegel and Thomae (1975) argue against using the Piagetian framework for understanding cognitive development in adulthood and later life, stressing that the acceptance of contradiction and the ability to operate at any given Piagetian level as the situation demands is most characteristic of mature adult thought.

PSYCHOLOGICAL DEVELOPMENT IN LATER LIFE

As noted earlier, among classical psychoanalysts only Erikson and Jung discussed a stage devoted exclusively to later life. The contributions of these individuals will be reviewed here along with views on elder development held by more recent thinkers.

Erik Erickson

Erikson (1950) was a contemporary of Sullivan's and the similarities between their theories are many. Erikson also focused on the influence of interpersonal relationships and social forces on psychological development, describing eight stages of psychosocial development, each characterized by a central life-task that needed completion for smooth movement into subsequent stages (principle of epigenesis): (1) *oral-sensory* stage (trust vs. mistrust) (birth to 1 year), (2) *muscular-anal* stage (autonomy vs. shame and doubt) (1 to 3 years), (3) *locomotor-genital* stage (initiative vs. guilt) (3 to 5 years), (4) *latency* (industry vs. inferiority) (6 to 11 years), (5) *adolescence* (ego identity vs. role confusion) (11 to 19 years), (6) *young adulthood* (intimacy vs. self-absorption or isolation) (20 to 40 years), (7) *adulthood* (generativity vs. stagnation) (40 to 65 years), and (8) *maturity* (integrity vs. despair). This description of the life cycle corresponds to Freudian concepts of development through adolescence (Rutter and Hersov 1985).

Erikson is given major credit for focusing attention on development in adulthood (intimacy, generativity, and integrity). Although he devoted only three pages to the final life stage in his seminal contribution *Childhood and Society* (1950), Erikson refocussed his work in the 1970s and 1980s on the developmental potentials of aging (Erikson 1978, 1982, 1984; Erikson, Erikson, and Kivnick 1986). Erikson's eighth stage of psychosocial development is that of maturity, with the primary developmental task being the attainment of *integrity* over *despair*. Erikson (1950) defines integrity as (1) an assurance of life's order and meaning, (2) a love of the human ego (not of the self) that conveys "some world order and spiritual sense," and (3) an "acceptance of one's one and only life cycle as something that, by necessity, permitted no substitutions" (p. 232). To Erikson, integrity reflected an emotional integration that allowed one to be a follower or a leader, depending on the demand of the moment. Despair, on the other hand, indicated a lack or loss of ego integration as manifested by a fear of death, a rejection of the contents of one's life, and a feeling "that the time is short, too short to start another life and to try out alternative roads to integrity" (p. 232).

When physical illness intervenes to limit independence or prompt hospitalization, the struggle between integrity and despair heightens. This is particularly true in situations of increasing disability, decreasing social, financial, and cognitive resources, and increasing awareness of one's own frailty and mortality. Ill health can adversely affect integrity by interfering with a person's ability to experience hope, meaning, and purpose in life; it can impair one's sense of feeling loved; it can make one feel as though one is being punished for some unforgiven sin. These forces can and often do lead to despair, depression, and an increasing sense of worthlessness and hopelessness. Our studies in North Carolina and reports from elsewhere indicate that nearly 40% of hospitalized patients age 70 or over have some type of depressive disorder, and over 10% experience a severe clinical depression that is strongly related to physical health (Koenig et al. 1991).

According to the epigenetic model developed by Erikson, the achievement of integrity depends largely on the successful negotiation of earlier developmental tasks. This point is underscored in Kaplan and Sadock's (1988) textbook of psychiatry:

> However, there is no peace or contentment in old age unless one has achieved intimacy and generativity. Without generativity, there is no sense of purpose and no conviction that one's life has been purposeful. Without that conviction, there is fear of death and a sense of despair. (p. 49)

Because of illness, accidents, or other misfortunes in life, many elders may not have successfully completed earlier developmental tasks. What then? Are these persons doomed to experience despair in their final years when much of their life has already been marginal? Strict adherence to the concept of epigenesis would suggest so. Even Erikson (1976) in recent times has departed from a strictly epigenetic model to take into account the reworking of issues and the impact of accrued experiences.

There may be other ways to achieve integrity in spite of earlier failures in life. One way is perhaps through religion, which provides an orderly view of the world, meaning in life, a continuity between this life and the next, and a schema by which errors in one's past can be forgiven and a new life begun. Erikson himself saw the potential contributions from religion (the "numinous") in achieving integrity at this time (1958;1969;1981;1982).

Carl Jung

Jung (1933) was perhaps first among the psychoanalysts to formally address psychological development in later life. He divided the life-span into four quarters. The first quarter was largely made up of childhood when humans were seen as creating a problem for others but not yet conscious of their own problems. The second and third quarters of life constituted stages when persons dealt with conscious problems of life. The final quarter of life was described as a time when regardless of one's state of consciousness, he or she again became somewhat of a problem to others.

More optimistically, Jung argued that personality development was not fixed by early childhood experiences. He believed that development occurred throughout life, with external factors playing an important role in growth of the person. Jung's ideas were unique in several respects. First, as noted above, he was almost alone among psychoanalysts (except Erikson) to include later life and old age in a theory of human development. In one of his works, *Stages of Life*, (1933) Jung presents in detail his view of old age as a time when the person withdraws from outer life and begins to focus more on him or herself:

> Ageing people should know that their lives are not mounting and expanding, but that an inexorable inner process enforces the contraction of life. For a young person it is almost a sin, or at least a danger, to be too preoccupied with himself; but for the ageing person it is a duty and a necessity to devote serious attention to himself. After having lavished its light upon the world, the sun withdraws its rays in order to illuminate itself. Instead of doing likewise, many old people prefer to be hypochondriacs, niggards, pedants, applauders of the past or else eternal adolescents—all lamentable substitutes for the illumination of self, but inevitable consequences of the delusion that the second half of life must be governed by the principles of the first. (p. 17)

Jung believed that later life had a significance all its own, separate from that in young or middle adulthood. He hypothesized that "culture" was the meaning and purpose of the second half of life:

In primitive tribes we observe that the old people are almost always the guardians of the mysteries and the laws, and it is in these that the cultural heritage of the tribe is expressed. How does the matter stand with us? Where is the wisdom of our old people, where are their precious secrets and visions? For the most part our old people try to compete with the young. In the United States it is almost an ideal for a father to be the brother of his sons, and for the mother to be if possible the younger sister of her daughter. (p. 18)

Jung also saw religious or spiritual factors as important and necessary influences on human development. He suggested a role for religion in supplying life with meaning and hope and in providing a psychologically healthy view of death:

As a doctor I am convinced that it is hygienic–if I may use the word–to discover in death a goal towards which one can strive, and that shrinking away from it is something unhealthy and abnormal which robs the second half of life of its purpose. I therefore consider that all religions with a supramundance goal are eminently reasonable from the point of view of psychic hygiene. When I live in a house which I know will fall about my head within the next two weeks, all my vital functions will be impaired by this thought; but if on the contrary I feel myself to be safe, I can dwell there in a normal and comfortable way. From the standpoint of psychotherapy it would therefore be desirable to think of death as only a transition, as part of a life process whose extent and duration are beyond our knowledge. . . . Before the nineteenth century the thyroid was regarded as a meaningless organ merely because it was not understood. It would be equally shortsighted of us today to call the primordial images senseless. For me these images are something like psychic organs, and I treat them with the greatest of respect. It happens sometimes that I must say to an older patient: "Your picture of God or your idea of immortality is atrophied, consequently your psychic metabolism is out of gear." (pp. 20-22)

Buhler, Kuhlen, and Peck

Besides Erikson and Jung, several other prominent figures have addressed the topic of human development in later life. C. Buhler (1935) used biographies and clinical cases to study motives and goals of individuals during different parts of the life cycle, including old age. R. G. Kuhlen (1964) building on the work of Buhler, concluded that growth and expansion were the primary motives during the first half of life, while conservation and constriction characterized the second half; these tendencies were based on the elder's responses to increasing threats. Kuhlen's ideas were similar to those of Jung, both supporting the disengagement hypothesis of Cumming and Henry (1961) (to be discussed further below).

Robert Peck (1968) further expands the challenges of Erikson's final life stage into three developmental tasks: (1) ego differentiation vs. work-role preoccupation, (2) body transcendence vs. body preoccupation, and (3) ego transcendence vs. ego preoccupation. Ego differentiation indicates a shift in value system by which the elder appraises or defines his or her self-worth; the individual's task is to obtain his or her sense of self-esteem from sources other than productivity and accomplishment associated with work or child-rearing. According to this theory, successful aging requires that one develop a foundation for self-esteem independent of work and engage in a variety of valued activities so that one might have several possible bases for self-worth and satisfaction in later life.

Body transcendence becomes necessary when physical illness causes pain and discomforts that could steal joy from living. According to Peck, redefining happiness and fulfillment in terms of satisfying human relationships, rather than physical comforts and independence, would establish firmer grounds for living. While physical function might decline, new opportunities for mental and social function might actually increase. Finally, Peck uses the term ego transcendence to indicate the ability to rise above the self and face the prospect of death with peace and contentment. One might accomplish this as follows:

> To live so generously and unselfishly that the prospect of personal death–the night of the ego, it might be called–looks and feels less important than the secure knowledge that one

has built for a broader, longer future than any one ego ever could encompass . . . it requires deep active effort to make life more secure, more meaningful, or happier for the people who will go on after one dies. (p. 91)

The capacity to live in such a manner, however, requires a relatively high level of emotional stability and a firm ego integrity *to begin with*. What about the elder who is still struggling with past conflicts, feeling perhaps abandoned by family or society, and, with good reason, questioning his or her identity as social and work roles change and health deteriorates? The idea of transcending the self by devoting oneself to ensuring the happiness of one's children and society is an attractive one; nevertheless, I suspect that many elders may find it difficult to maintain this optimistic view as losses mount and tragedies strike.

Life-Span Theory

Among secular theories of human development, the life-span perspective gives most credit to possibilities for change and growth in later life. Baltes and Nesselroade (1979) summarize this psychological theory of development over the life span, emphasizing concepts such as multidimensionality and multidirectionality. In contrast to Erikson and Piaget, this model suggests that behavioral change processes can emerge throughout life and that only a limited number of behaviors exhibit continuity and cumulation. Development in later life is described as a process of mastering a loosely connected series of age-related tasks. The attractiveness of this theory is that it allows for plasticity in later life and places the elder in an active role capable of affecting their own development (Brandtstadter 1984; Baltes and Reese 1984). This perspective exemplifies the aleatoric account of human development and, as I have noted before, is generally consistent with the religious approach.

Disengagement and Activity Theories

A discussion of psychological development in later life would be incomplete without some mention of "disengagement" and "activity" theories. *Disengagement* indicates a withdrawal from roles or activities and a decreasing level of involvement with others. Cumming and Henry (1961) argued that older persons naturally withdraw from social roles and become more preoccupied with their selves. Society is seen as contributing to this by its withdrawal of opportunities from older persons and its lack of interest in their contributions. According to Robert Atchley, disengagement may have been the case in the 1950s when elders were in a particularly adverse situation; however, since 1965 (social security and Medicare) this has not been the case. Atchley (1971) and others (Roman and Taietz 1967; Carp 1968) have shown that disengagement is neither natural nor inevitable, but instead results mostly from a *lack of opportunity* for involvement.

Successful aging, instead of reflecting disengagement, has today become synonymous with staying active and involved (*activity theory*) (Havighurst 1963; Havighurst, Neugarten, and Tobin 1963). This theory emphasizes (like Peck) a need to find substitutes for activities that because of health, financial or social losses are no longer possible. Critics point out, however, that activity theory is too simplistic. Substitutes are often simply unavailable or cannot be engaged in because of physical or cognitive impairments. Furthermore, many elders do not want to find substitutes for previous activities or roles (retired persons, for instance, may not wish a substitute job). Well-being is not so much determined by the number of activities or number of social involvements, but rather by the level of social integration and quality of relationships (Liang et al. 1980).

SUMMARY

In this chapter I have reviewed the major secular theories of human development, with a focus on those theories which have included a stage devoted to adulthood and later life. Developmental theories were divided into three categories: the stability account, the ordered change account, and the aleatoric account. Freud's psychoanalytic theory was described as a prototype for the stability account which holds that psychological development is biologically driven and achieves near completion in childhood, after which stability is the rule. Erikson's eight psychosocial stages of development exemplify the ordered change account which relies heavily on the concept of epigenesis, where each stage depends on the successful resolution of prior life-tasks. Jung's developmental theory and Baltes' life-span theory were discussed as examples of the third category, the aleatoric account, which emphasizes the flexibility and variability of developmental patterns and includes the possibility that even in old age persons may affect their own development and, in some instances, even make dramatic changes in life course.

It is the premise of this book that the key to successful aging lies in the elder's ability to change and adapt successfully to health, social, and financial losses; such change demands the flexibility that the aleatoric account of human development allows. Because religion both advocates and enables such adaptability and change–regardless of prior life experiences–herein lies its link with successful aging. In the next chapter, I will examine James Fowler's theory of faith development–a perspective that relies heavily on the theories of psychosocial, cognitive, and moral development described in this chapter.

REFERENCES

Adler, A. (1956). In *The Individual Psychology of Alfred Adler: A Systematic Presentation in Selections from His Writings*, edited by H.L. Ansbacher and R.R. Ansbacher. NY: Basic Books.

Atchley, R.C. (1971). Disengagement among professors. *Journal of Gerontology* 26:476-480.

Baltes, P.B. and J.R. Nesselroade. (1979). Paradigm lost and paradigm regained: Critique of Dannefer's portrayal of life-span developmental psychology. *American Sociological Review* 49:841-847.

Baltes, P.B.and H.W. Reese. (1984). The life-span perspective in developmental psychology. In *Developmental Psychology: An Advanced Textbook*, edited by M.H. Bornstein and M.E. Lab. Hillsdale NJ: Erlbaum.

Bandura, A. (1977). *Social learning theory.* Englewood Cliffs, NJ: Prentice Hall.

Beck, A.T. (1963). Thinking and depression. *Archives of General Psychiatry* 9:324-333.

Beck, A.T. (1976). *Cognitive Therapy and Emotional Disorders*. NY: International Universities Press.

Bowlby, J. (1969). *Attachment and Loss*. New York: Basic Books.

Brandtstadter, J. (1984). Personal and social control over development: Some implications of an action perspective in life-span developmental psychology. In *Life-span Development and Behavior*, vol. 6 edited by P.B. Baltes and O.G. Brim. (pp. 1-32). NY: Academic Press.

Buhler, C. (1935). The curve of life as studies in biographies. *Journal of Applied Psychology* 19:405-409.

Carp, F.M. (1968). Some components of disengagement. *Journal of Gerontology* 23:382-386.

Cumming, E. and W.E. Henry, (1961), *Growing Old*, NY: Basic Books.

Ellis, A. (1962). *Reason and Emotion in Psychotherapy*. NY: Lyle Stuart.

Erikson, E.H. (1950). *Childhood and Society*. NY: W.W. Norton Co.

_____ (1958). *Young Man Luther*. NY: W.W. Norton Co.

_____ (1969). *Gandhi's Truth*. NY: W.W. Norton Co.

_____ (1976). Reflection on Dr. Borg's life cycle. *Daedalus* 105:1-28.

_____ (1978). *Adulthood*. NY: W.W. Norton Co.

_____(1981). The Galilean sayings and the sense of "I". *Yale Review* 70:322-362.

_____ (1982). *The Life Cycle Completed: A Review*. NY: W.W. Norton.

_____ (1984). Reflections on the last stage–and the first. *Psychoanalytic Study of the Child* 39:155-165.

Erikson, E.H., J. Erikson, and H. Kivnick. (1986). *Vital Involvement in Old Age*. NY: W.W. Norton.

Freud, A. (1936). *The Ego and the Mechanisms of Defense*. NY: International Universities Press.

Gergen, K.J. (1977). Stability, change, and chance in understanding human development. In *Life-Span Development Psychology*, edited by N. Datan and H. Reese. NY: Academic Press, pp. 135-158.

Gergen, K.J. (1980). The emergency crisis in life-span developmental theory. In *Life-Span Development and Behavior*, vol. 3, edited by P.B. Baltes and O.G. Brim. NY: Academic Press, pp. 31-63.

Gould, R. (1978). *Transformations*. NY: Simon & Schuster.

Greenberg, J.R., and S.A. Mitchell. (1983). *Object Relations in Psychoanalytic Theory*. Cambridge, MA: Harvard University Press.

Harlow, H.F., and R.R. Zimmerman. (1959). Affectional response in the infant monkey. *Science* 130:421-432.

Hartmann, H. (1964). *Essays on Ego Psychology*. NY: International Universities Press.

Havighurst, R.J. (1963). Successful aging. In *Processes of Aging, Social and Psychological Perspectives*, Vol. I, edited by R.H. Williams, C. Tibbitts and W. Donohue. NY: Atherton, pp. 299-320.

Havighurst, R.J., B.L. Neugarten, and S.S. Tobin. (1963). Disengagement, personality and life satisfaction in the later years. In *Age with a Future*, edited by P. Hansen. Copenhagen: Munksgoard, pp. 419-425.

Horney, K. (1945). *Our Inner Conflicts*. NY: W.W. Norton Co.

Jacobson, E. (1964). *The Self and the Object World*. NY: International Universities Press.

Jung, C.G. (1933). The stages of life. In *The Portable Jung*, edited by J. Campbell. NY: The Viking Press, 1971, pp. 3-22.

_____ (1975). *Critique of Psychoanalysis*. Princeton NY: Princeton University Press.

Kaplan, H.I., and B.J. Sadock. (1988). Synopsis of Psychiatry, 5th edition. Baltimore, MD: Williams and Wilkins.

Kernberg, O. (1976). *Object Relations Theory and Clinical Psychoanalysis*. NY: Jason Aronson.

Klein, M. (1964). *Contributions to Psychoanalysis, 1921-1945*. NY: McGraw-Hill.

Koenig, H.G., K.G. Meador, F. Shelp, V. Goli, H.J. Cohen, and D.G. Blazer. (1991). Major depressive disorder in hospitalized medically ill patients: An examination of young and elderly male veterans. *Journal of the American Geriatrics Society* 39:881-890.

Kohlberg, L. (1971). Moral stages and moralization: The cognitive developmental approach. In *Moral Development and Epistemology*, edited by T. Lakona. NY: Academic Press.

_____ (1973). Stages and aging in moral development–some speculations. *The Gerontologist* (Winter Issue):497-502.

_____ (1979). *Measuring Moral Judgement*. Worcester, MA: Clark University Press.

Kohut, H. (1971). *Analysis of the Self*. NY: International Universities Press.

Kuhlen, R.G. (1964). Personality changes with age. In *Personality Change*, edited by P. Worchel and D. Byrne. NY: John Wiley, pp. 524-555.

Kuhn, D., J. Langer, L. Kohlberg, and N.S. Haan. (1977). The development of formal operation in logical and moral judgement. *Genetic Psychology Monographs* 95:97-188.

Levinson, D. (1978). *The Seasons of a Man's Life*. NY: Alfred A. Knopf.

Liang, J., L. Dworkin, E. Kahana, and F. Maziau. (1980). Social integration and morale: A reexamination. *Journal of Gerontology* 35:746-757.

Lorenz, K. (1957). The nature of instinct, 1937. Reprinted in *Instinctive Behavior*, edited by C.H. Schiller. NY: International Universities Press.

Mahler, M. (1975). *The Psychological Birth of the Human Infant*. NY: Basic Books.

Mann, C.H. (1985). Adult development. *Contemporary Psychoanalysis* 21: 284-296.

Papalia, D.E., and D.D.V. Bielby. (1974). Cognitive functioning in middle and old age adults: A review of research based on Piaget's theory. *Human Development* 17:424-443.

Pavlov, I.D. (1928). *Lectures on Conditioned Reflexes*, vol. 1. NY: International Publishers.

Peck, R.C. (1968). Psychological developments in the second half of life. In *Middle Age and Aging*, edited by B.L. Neugarten. Chicago: University of Chicago Press, pp. 88-92.

Piaget, J. (1950). *The Psychology of Intelligence*. London: Routledge & Kegan Paul.

_____ (1972). *The Principles of Genetic Epistemology*. NY: Basic Books.

Riegel, K.F., and H. Thomae. (1975). The development of dialectical operations. *Human Development* 18:1-238.

Roman, P., and P. Taietz. (1967). Organizational structure and disengagement: The emeritus professor. *The Gerontologist* 7:147-152.

Rutter, M., and L. Hersov. (1985). *Child and Adolescent Psychiatry*, 2nd ed. Oxford: Blackwell, pp. 206-211.

Skinner, B.F. (1959). *Cumulative Record*. NY: Appleton-Century-Crofts.

Spitz, R. (1965). *The First Year of Life*. NY: International Universities Press.

Strachey, J. (1953-1974). *The Standard Edition of the Complete Psychological Works of Sigmund Freud*, volumes 1-24. London: Hogarth Press.

Sullivan, H.S. (1953). *The Interpersonal Theory of Psychiatry*. NY: Norton.

Vaillant, G. (1977). *Adaption to Life*. Boston: Brown & Co.

Winnicott, D.W. (1965). *The Maturational Process and the Facilitating Environment*. NY: International Universities Press.

Chapter 6

Fowler's Stages of Faith Development

Nothing in life is more wonderful than faith–the one great moving force which we can neither weigh in the balance nor test in the crucible.

–William Osler

In the last chapter, I reviewed the developmental theories of Freud (drive), Erikson (psychosocial), Sullivan (interpersonal), Piaget (cognitive), and Kohlberg (moral). Just as drives, relationships, and capacities to think and act morally develop and mature throughout life in somewhat predictable stages, so too might one's religious faith. Just as with other lines of development, however, fixation at one stage or another might hinder continuing growth and maturity. Likewise, as development proceeds, there may be regressions to earlier stages during times of stress (or complacency). Alternatively, emotional stress may act as a stimulating factor that leads to new insights and greater levels of maturity. Fowler (1981) has masterfully integrated the developmental theories of Erikson, Piaget, and Kohlberg into a structuralist theory of faith development. Because of the rich insights which this paradigm provides and the scientific base upon which it rests, I will summarize Fowler's ideas and then critique them on their relevance to faith development in later life.

STAGES OF FAITH

An ordained minister in the United Church of Christ, James Fowler received his bachelor's degree from Duke University and a

PhD from Harvard. He taught in the Divinity School at Harvard for several years before moving to Boston College, and now teaches at the Candler School of Theology at Emory University. It was at Boston College in 1981 that he published a book entitled *Stages of Faith*. In it he outlined six stages of faith development. His ideas are firmly grounded in the prior work of developmental theorists Piaget, Erikson, and Kohlberg. The data upon which Fowler's stages are based came from semistructured interviews with persons of all ages from a variety of religious and non-religious backgrounds. This scholarly work has in the past decade become a fundamental text for many divinity schools around the country. Fowler's paradigm, however, has had only limited application to faith development in older adults (Shulik 1988).

Borrowing a definition from Paul Tillich, Fowler describes faith in the following manner:

> Wherever we properly speak of faith it involves people's shaping or testing their lives' defining directions and relationships with others in accordance with coordinates of value and power recognized as ultimate. (p. 93)

"Coordinates of value and power" may refer to God, self, money, job position, or family. Fowler meant this definition of faith, and the stages he describes, to be all encompassing and universally applicable to all religious and nonreligious faiths, both in this culture and others.

> That ultimate concern may center finally in our own ego or its extensions–work, prestige and recognition, power and influence, wealth. One's ultimate concern may be invested in family, university, nation, or church. Love, sex and a loved partner might be the passionate center of one's ultimate concern . . . faith involves an alignment of the heart or will, a commitment of loyalty and trust . . . faith is our way of discerning and committing ourselves to centers of value and power that exert ordering force in our lives . . . faith, as imagination, grasps the ultimate conditions of our existence, unifying them into a comprehensive image in light of which we shape our responses and initiatives. (pp. 4-5, 24-25)

Fowler is careful to differentiate "structure" from "content" in this regard. What he proposes is a universal structure of faith in which the contents (objects of ultimate value or concern) may vary. For example, stage 3 ("synthetic-conventional faith") is the stage at which persons adhere to outside authority or to the general social convention of the times; the particular belief, loyalty, or ultimate concern, however, may be God, Buddha, Mohammed, science, technology, or whatever other object the social group or culture authorizes as worthy of such concern. Thus, the structure is universal–only the object of concern (or content) changes. Following the lead of other developmental theorists, Fowler defines separate and distinct levels of faith that he believes meet the strict structural developmental criteria for stages. By "stages," he means the following:

> They provide generalizable, formal descriptions of integrated sets of operations of knowing and valuing. These stagelike positions are related in a sequence we believe to be *invariant* (my italics). Each new stage integrates and carries forward the operations of all previous stages. (pp. 99-100)

Fowler depicts changes from one faith stage to another as coming about through an interaction between a dynamic, innovative subject and a active, changing environment. Growth in faith occurs as the person faces life crises, challenges, difficulties, and other disruptions through a process that "that theologians call revelation." The disequilibrium thus brought about, forces persons to change their values and way of viewing the world (in other words, to displace previous objects of ultimate concern).

I will now present a brief description of each of the six stages, emphasizing links to the theories of Erikson, Piaget, and Kohlberg in their respective areas of psychosocial, cognitive, and moral development. Although I have included ages along with each stage, these should be viewed as approximations.

Stage 0. Infancy and Undifferentiated Faith (Ages 0-2)

This is equivalent to Erikson's "trust vs. mistrust" psychosocial stage and Piaget's "sensorimotor" cognitive stage. It is a preliminary stage of faith development during which "pre-images" of God are formed through interaction with parents. This is a crucial time for the child, prior to the development of language and symbol formation, during which a basic sense of faith (faith that his needs will be met by powerful others) is established. It is upon this foundation that all ensuing stages will be built.

Stage 1. Intuitive-Projective Faith (Ages 2-7)

Psychosocially, the child is struggling with issues of autonomy (vs. shame) and initiative (vs. guilt). Cognitive development is immature; there is confusion between cause and effect. Thinking is pre-operational, fluid, magical; imagination and fantasy, unlimited by logical thought, are the rule. This is the stage when the child first begins to experience self-awareness. He or she sees the world as revolving primarily around him or herself (cognitive egocentrism). According to Kohlberg, children at this stage of moral development (preconventional) are incapable of seeing things from another's point of view (lacking in the ability to take perspective); he or she is oriented more toward punishment and obedience—rather than understanding and empathy. In this first stage of faith development, through a blend of imagination and intuition, the child is beginning to form pictures of God, of heaven, and of hell. The vehicle for these images is frequently stories. Although the child becomes aware of God during this stage, he or she cannot differentiate God's point of view from his or her own (or from that of parents).

Stage 2. Mythic-Literal Faith (Ages 7-12)

This time corresponds to grades two through seven in elementary school and parallels Erikson's "industry vs. inferiority" stage. Cognitively, the child performs on a level Piaget describes as "concrete operations." He or she is now beginning to use logic, sorting out real from make-believe, and binding experiences into complex stories. The child interprets meanings in a literal or concrete fashion, since he or she cannot abstract or generalize yet. Perspective taking also becomes possible during this stage; others' perspectives on him or herself, however, are still impersonal. Identity is seen in terms of relationships and roles. It is a time in moral development characterized by Kohlberg as "fairness of instrumental exchange." The world operates on the undefiable rule of reciprocity, as exemplified in an "eye for an eye and tooth for a tooth" philosophy. In terms of faith development, the child's image of God takes on characteristics specified by the culture of one's family. The child can now take into account God's perspective on things, and can understand that God takes into consideration one's intentions and struggles. Because of the supremacy of the principle of instrumental exchange, however, God is seen primarily in terms of reciprocity–he gives bad things to bad people, good things to good people.

Stage 3. Synthetic-Conventional Faith (Adolescence Onward)

At this time, an emerging identity is beginning to form that is separate from family, and the opinions of peers begin to dominate. A major change in cognitive development now occurs with the capacity for "formal operations." The child-young adult can now philosophize, conceive of ideals, and begin to take an interpersonal perspective from a third person's view. Because relationships with others are so important, there also arises a need for a more personal relationship with God, a God who "knows, accepts, and confirms the self deeply" (p. 153). Authority, however, is located outside of the self in the "they" (often peer group). Characteristic of this faith stage is an acceptance of faith without critical examination (synthetic) and an adherence to group norms (conventional); there is no view of faith taken independent of the community or family. Fowler notes that most of church life in America works best when members are at this faith stage, and that many persons even in adulthood may not advance much past here (perhaps only 50%).

Stage 4. Individuative-Reflective Faith (Early to Mid-20s or Beyond)

A transition to the "post-conventional" stages is said to occur at this time. Psychosocial tasks now involve a completion of the "intimacy vs. isolation" struggle and a movement onto the "generativity vs. stagnation" conflict. Transitions from faith stage 3 to 4 are often said to take place during an upheaval (like a divorce, change in health, or other stressful event). At this faith stage there is an interruption in reliance upon external authority, a relocation of authority in the self, and a break in the need for sanction and approval by the community. This begins Kohlberg's stage III of moral development characterized by a "clear effort to define moral values and principles which have validity and application apart from the authority of the groups and persons holding these principles . . . " (Kohlberg 1973, p. 499). Faith and ideology are now inspected critically and objectively. The individual must now reconstruct an ideology or belief system of his or her own. Fowler notes that St. Paul after his conversion appears to have been in this stage, as evidenced by much of his early writings; in later New Testament writings, he appears to have made a stage-5 transition according to Fowler.

Stage 5. Conjunctive Faith (Midlife and Beyond)

At this time in life, the major psychosocial issue is the task of achieving generativity over stagnation. It is a faith stage characterized by paradox, depth of understanding and acceptance, and intergenerational responsibility for the world. There comes a disillusionment with the overdependence on logic and rational understanding seen in faith stage 4 and perhaps with some of the faith compromises that were made during that time. The limits of human reason become more apparent. There is a radical openness to the truth that requires the person to rework the past and reintegrate aspects of faith held in childhood. A more open attitude is seen towards other religious traditions besides one's own, and a new "commitment to justice freed from the confines of tribe, class, religious community or nation" (p. 198). Nevertheless, persons in stage 5 remain divided, with the self caught between the need to preserve its own being and fulfill its own needs, and a more universal concern that is willing to lay down one's life for others.

Stage 6. Universalizing Faith (Late Life)

This stage of faith is the final and the ultimate one. There is a readiness to fellowship with persons regardless of faith stage or religious tradition. There is a total commitment of the self to a vision, a willingness to give up oneself and one's life for justice and a transformed world, in order to make the Kingdom of God actual on this earth. As examples of persons in this faith stage, Fowler includes Martin Luther King, Gandhi, Dag Hammarskjold, Abraham Heschel, Thomas Merton, and Mother Teresa for their "radical acts of identification with persons and circumstances where futurity of being is being crushed, blocked or exploited" (p. 203). Included here is the idea of "radical monotheism" borrowed from Richard Niebuhr, with Jesus as the "pioneering embodiment of radical monotheistic faith, the 'pioneer and perfecter' of the faith to which we are called" (p. 206). Fowler emphasizes, however, that the "absoluteness of the divine character can come to expression in different forms and in different contexts with each of these instances bearing the full weight of ultimacy" (p. 209).

CRITIQUE OF FOWLER'S FAITH STAGES

It is a difficult task to critique Fowler's articulately presented, intuitively reasonable, scientifically based, and socially-conscious theory of faith development. Nevertheless, certain comments are in order. Fowler's goal is to unfold a theory of faith development that is separate and distinct from a theory of religious or spiritual development (Shulik 1988). His effort to focus on the structure of faith and avoid content–while a worthy goal in itself and necessary for universality–is restrictive when applying the paradigm to individual cases. This becomes especially evident in his case-examples where he often blurs content and structure. A second concern is inherent in the structural-developmentalist paradigm and is particularly troublesome in matters of faith. There is an implication that higher faith stages are of greater value and contain more truth than lower stages. A third concern, related to the second, is Fowler's heavy reliance on cognitive and intellectual development in his assignment of faith stages. A fourth issue involves the need to recapitulate and reintegrate the past in order to advance in faith development. Fifth, I am troubled by Fowler's claim that post-conventional faith stages are associated with higher levels of intrinsic religiosity (after claiming that this was not a theory of religious or spiritual development).

Finally, I have concern over Fowler's use of data to support his theory. A discussion of these issues now follows.

Difficulties in Application

The operationalization of Fowler's paradigm for determining faith stage in individual cases is not always clear. In discussing Mary's pilgrimage through life (pp. 214-268), Fowler describes her conversion at the age of 22 as a "lateral movement" in stage 3 synthetic-conventional faith, not as an advance in faith stage. Mary had been raised in the United Church of Christ (a traditional, Protestant denomination). After conversion, she took on a new, personal faith in Christ, which required her to move laboriously in a counterculture direction in order to live according to that faith as she understood it. In fact much of what appeared to be dependent behavior on her part, may have been an individual and independent decision to adhere to the doctrine of obedience espoused by the Bible itself. At times, her efforts at self-sacrifice appear quite exemplary.

Fowler then contrasts Mary's case with that of a man named Jack, who was raised in a Catholic home but later also rejected his parents's religion and was "converted" to a counterculture group, the Black Panther organization. On returning to his neighborhood, Jack was rejected by his old friends when they found out about his new political affiliation. Consequently, he sought out groups of people who shared his views. Jack is labeled as being in faith stage 4, ahead of Mary. In her conversion experience, however, it is quite likely that Mary was rejected by her old friends when they found out that she had changed and was no longer willing to live or act as she had previously. Pursuing the same course as Jack, Mary then sought out groups of people with a similar orientation. This she found in an evangelical-fundamentalist religious group, with whom she became actively involved, just as Jack committed himself to the Black Panther organization and other counterculture groups. It is not at all clear to me why Jack is at a more advanced faith stage and portrayed as more self-sacrificing than Mary.

Motivations are often difficult to determine from external appearances. As noted earlier, scripture heavily emphasizes the role of submissiveness, obedience, and service in the religious life. While it is understandable that persons with neurotic tendencies toward overdependence may easily fall into conventional modes of faith, one should not mistake manifestations of more advanced faith as expressed in submissiveness, obedience to authority, or determination towards service, as evidence for a less mature faith. Nor should one mistake a person with a dependence-fear conflict, stemming from lack of trust and exaggerated need for independence, who rejects conventional values and stakes out on a more radical, non-conformist life-style, as having a more mature, post-conventional faith.

Devaluation of Simple Faith

Problems in assignment of faith stage are especially relevant here because of the inherent implication in structural developmental models that progression to higher stages indicates growth, advancement, greater maturity, closer approximation to one's ego-ideal, and so forth. This point is underscored by Fowler's reference to work that connects the concept of intrinsic religiosity (the extent to which faith represents the "master motivator" in life and thus represents true religiosity) with persons who fall in the post-conventional stages of faith (stages 4 through 6):

> As John Chirban's doctoral dissertation has shown, the further one moves beyond a Synthetic-Conventional structuring of faith, the more likely one is to exhibit increased commitment in faith. Using the distinction between intrinsic and extrinsic forms of religious motivation, Chirban found that at stage 4 and beyond, the incidence of extrinsic motivation (utilitarian commitments to religion which really serves other interests one has) virtually disappears. Intrinsic motivation (loyalty and commitment to one's world view as true, regardless of whether it brings benefits or blame) characterizes postconventional faith. (pp. 300-301)

The extent to which post-conventional faith actually relates to intrinsic religiosity will be discussed more in a later section. However, using such a paradigm, it is easy to go the next step and see persons with more simple, childlike, and accepting faith as being somehow underdeveloped. Such an idea is difficult to reconcile, given statements by Jesus himself indicating who and who would not enter the Kingdom of God (Matthew 18:3; Mark 10:15; Luke 10:21, 18:17). As I understand it from Fowler's description, Mary's childlike faith in God and determination to do his will (high level of intrinsic religiosity) kept her going despite many adverse circumstances. Mary's complete recovery and further success in life depended not so much on advances in faith stage, but rather on her persistence in completing her education and changing her circumstances. This determination, to begin with, may have been largely fueled by her spiritual rebirth. Thus, one should not underestimate the powerful effects that a simple, accepting, and unquestioning faith may have.

Overemphasis on Cognitive Development

A related concern involves Fowler's tendency to overassociate Piaget's ideas on cognitive development with faith development. Many adults, because of educational deficiencies or socioeconomic circumstances, never develop cognitively beyond Piaget's stage of concrete operations (Kaplan and Sadock 1988, p. 83). This limitation of cognitive development is commonly encountered when attempting to use dynamic or cognitive forms of psychotherapy in persons with little education, cultural exposure, or intellectual development. These persons may have impaired psychological insight and perform poorly on formal tests of abstraction and generalization.

Using Fowler's paradigm, individuals with impaired cognitive development would be forever prevented from advancing beyond the second or third faith stage, regardless of intensity of devotion or degree to which they conformed their lives to scriptural principles. This overemphasis placed on the intellectual understanding and critical examination of faith is exemplified in Fowler's description of stage 4. Here there is an interruption of reliance on external authority and a recentering of that authority in the self. However, many scriptures warn the believer to "not rely on one's own wisdom" (Isaiah 29:14; 1 Corinthians 1:18-31, 2:5,14) and to "seek many counselor's" (Proverbs 11:14, 13:10, 19:20). The reason for their doing so is understandable. No one person has access to all the information needed to come to a complete rational comprehension of their faith; everyone has gaps in their knowledge that prevent this. Much requires simple acceptance, without proof or understanding. Indeed, the definition of faith provided in scripture involves belief *without seeing* (Hebrews 11:1); even this belief is a gift of grace and not due to our own doing (Romans 11:6; 12:3; Ephesians 2:8).

Thus, there is danger that Fowler's paradigm may relegate higher stages of faith development to the more intellectually sophisticated and cognitively advanced, leaving the simple, devout and obedient (but less introspective) fellow at more primitive levels. This aspect of Fowler's theory is worrisome in its application to older adults whose abstract reasoning may be impaired due to disease or to the aging process itself (Poon 1985). The potential to acquire mature faith should be equally accessible to all and be more dependent on one's will and personal decisions than on biologically-determined intellectual capacities. The opportunity to advance in faith, rather than being procurable only by a select few, should be available even to a small child, a retarded adult, or an elderly person with a stroke or slowly advancing organic brain syndrome.

Case #67 in Chapter 10 illustrates this point. A 75-year-old man with colon cancer was readmitted 18 months after his initial evaluation with extensive metastases involving his liver, lungs, and kidneys. During his final five months of life, I was in contact with him anywhere from one to three times per week. During this time, his mental status fluctuated on and off during chemotherapy, blood infections, and severe pain. His simple trust in God to heal him of his cancer never wavered–even though his intellectual and cognitive capacity became severely compromised. Presbyterian minister Robert Davis (1989) reflects on the value and power of such innocent faith:

> During the hundreds of funerals I have conducted, I have often heard little children become the messengers of faith. For instance, I do not know how many times I have heard a little child innocently say, "I can't understand why everyone is crying. After all, grandpa is happy with Jesus in heaven, and pretty soon we will all be happy in heaven with Jesus. Just as

soon as we get there, grandpa will be there to hug us."
(pp. 129-130)

Although I will develop this point further in the next chapter, the
faith that carries persons through the tough times and does not
fluctuate in either triumph or tragedy, this is mature faith. The
extent to which such faith involves advanced cognitive faculties or
deep introspection is debatable in my estimation.

Need to Recapitulate the Past

In keeping with the requirements for progression to faith stage 4,
Fowler emphasizes the need for Mary to return to her past, reintegrate and recapitulate her early experiences. While understanding
the past is important for determining the nature of underlying conflicts and identifying origins of maladaptive patterns of behavior, it
is a mistake to excessively focus on past rather than present events.
Much dissension between behavioral psychologists and classical
psychoanalysts stems precisely from this issue (Wachtell 1977). It is
quite clear that unearthing the past is not the only or even the best
way to work with patients in therapy. Behavioral therapists, cognitive therapists, and interpersonal psychoanalysts (Paul Wachtell,
Walter Bonime, Karen Horney, Fred Hine) all argue against focusing on the past, given the faulty reconstructions, contortions, and
misremembering that may occur; rather, they emphasize present
events, *current decisions*, ongoing patterns of behavior and ways of
relating to others. Wachtell (1977) underscores Karen Horney's
insistence that:

> meaningful change [in the individual personality] could best
> be approached through understanding of how the person was
> currently living his life, and her view that concern with history
> often entailed an unwitting collusion on the part of the thera-
> pist with the patient's resistances, enabling him to keep con-
> cealed the current significance of some pattern in his life.
> (p. 67)

The Biblical approach is likewise heavily behavioralistic and
present-day oriented in its proscriptions on matters of faith (Mat-

thew 7:24-27; Luke 7:46-49; John 14:23-24). While heredity and environment are not ignored, most of the emphasis is placed on current decisions. Rather than dwelling on the past, the believer is encouraged to act differently in the here and now:

> Forget the former things; do not dwell on the past. See, I am doing a new thing! (Isaiah 43:18-19)

> Forgetting what is behind and straining toward what is ahead, I press on toward the goal to win the prize . . . (Philippians 3:13-14)

Many–perhaps most–prominent figures in scripture had life histories that were marked by failure, mistakes and problems; nevertheless, these persons are portrayed as accomplishing great things after they began obeying God and following him in the present (1 Corinthians 1:26-28). The notion that God forgives the past (Psalm 86:5; 103:2-3; Matthew 6:14-15) is one of the most powerful, therapeutic, and liberating teachings of the Judeo-Christian religion.

Hence, I see little need to spend too much time in the past in order to advance either emotional or faith development. In saying this, I do not undervalue the importance of reminiscence (Butler 1963) or disregard the need for persons to reexamine and put in perspective past conflicts that are affecting present functioning. It is necessary, at times, to show that current behavior is a consequence of past learning experiences. Nevertheless, my point is that an overemphasis on the past often shifts the burden of responsibility away from the person and onto others (blaming of parents, for instance), rather than focusing energy on what *he or she can do now* to change attitudes and behaviors that are perpetuating the difficulties in the present.

Relationship with Intrinsic Religiosity

As noted earlier, Fowler attempts to make a connection between faith stages (more specifically, post-conventional stages) and intrinsic religiosity. In order to assess the face validity of this claim, let us examine some of the questions which are commonly used to measure intrinsic religiosity and see how answers line up with the definitions of Fowler's last three faith stages. For this purpose I will present items from the Hoge Intrinsic Religiosity Scale (Hoge 1972), an instrument frequently used in epidemiological studies to measure this construct. High scores on this scale have been associated with psychological well-being in later life (Koenig, Kvale, and Ferrel 1988a).

Extrinsic Items:

1. It doesn't matter so much what I believe so long as I lead a moral life.
2. Although I believe in religion, I feel there are many more important things in life.
3. Although I am a religious person, I refuse to let religious considerations influence my everyday affairs.

Intrinsic Items:

1. I try hard to carry my religion over into all my other dealings in life.
2. Quite often I have been keenly aware of the presence of God or the Divine Being.
3. My religious beliefs are what really lie behind my whole approach to life.

Consider again the characteristics of stage 4 (individuative-reflective faith): interruption of reliance on external source of authority; relocation of authority within the self; objective, critical reflection. Consider now stage 5 (conjunctive faith): readiness for faith encounters with other traditions; new commitment to justice freed from the confines of tribe, class, religious community or nation; "detachment"–allowing reality to speak its word, regardless of impact on security or self-esteem. Finally, consider stage 6 (universalizing faith): commitment of one's whole being to justice and love, with a selfless passion for a transformed world; commitment to radical monotheism, so that the reality of God exerts a transforming impact on the structures of life and faith. While it is relatively easy to see how stage 6 reflects intrinsic religiosity, it is less clear how stages 4 and 5 do so.

Evidence Supporting the Theory

The scientific basis for Fowler's theory rests on information obtained during interviews with 356 persons. This sample was not randomly selected using a predetermined sampling method. Rather, interviews were conducted with paid volunteers who were conveniently located in and around academic communities (i.e., Boston, Toronto, Atlanta). Only age, race, sex, and religious orientation of participants is given in Fowler's text; educational level is not included. This sample, then, may have differed from the general population in terms of educational level and intellectual capacity (and may explain Fowler's heavy emphasis on cognitive development). Further bias may have been introduced by the choice of cases to be presented in the text to justify the various faith stages. Rather than data driving the theory, it appears here that the theory may have driven the data. Given these potential sampling biases, one might challenge the claims of universal applicability.

We are also told that there was high reliability between raters in the categorization of different individuals into faith stages (85-90% agreement). Reliability (the ability to reproduce results), however, is completely different from validity (the degree to which the results correspond to the true state of affairs). Mistakes may be repeated with great accuracy, yet still remain mistakes. Two other ways of determining the validity of a method are (1) to demonstrate a close correlation with other valid measures of the same construct, based on the logic that instruments that measure a similar variable should correlate highly (concurrent validity), and (2) to demonstrate an ability to predict outcomes like well-being or adjustment that would be expected on theoretical grounds (predictive validity).

In an attempt to establish concurrent validity, Fowler refers to a possible correlation between his faith stages and intrinsic religiosity, citing the 1980 doctoral dissertation of John Chirban (later published in a book, Chirban 1981). Because intrinsic religiosity has been validated as a measure of religious motivation in prior studies (Hoge 1972; Koenig, Smiley, and Gonzales 1988b), an association with Fowler's paradigm would provide evidence for concurrent validity. This, of course, would depend on whether intrinsic religiosity was measured in an acceptable manner and whether a clinically significant correlation with faith stages was obtained. However, a review of the data upon which the acclaimed relationship between faith stages and intrinsic religiosity is based, raises uncertainty in this regard.

An analysis of Chirban's methods (1981) reveals that no live patients were interviewed; instead, interviews conducted by Fowler or his associates were retrospectively reviewed to determine the number of intrinsic (I), extrinsic (E), and ambivalent (A) statements in the interview transcripts. An established I-E scale to measure religious motivation (Allport and Ross 1967; Hoge 1972; Feagin 1965) could not be used because the data had already been collected. Instead, a method of determining I, E, and A statements was devised by the investigators, using their own definitions of I, E, and A concepts. Concurrent validity of this method was then established not against a previously validated I-E scale, but instead against Loevinger and Wessler's (1970) stages of ego development (that on the surface seem to correspond better with Fowler's stages than to I-E concepts). Raters were then trained to distinguish I, E, and A statements by practicing on examples taken from Fowler transcripts. In the main study (n = 50), transcripts were "selected" by Fowler himself to give good examples of the various faith stages.

This method of research is highly circular, with a potential for bias present at nearly every step. Although Chirban reports significantly more intrinsic statements among transcripts of persons with higher faith stages, it is not at all clear what this means, given the concepts of I-E used, the method of selecting transcripts, and the ratings themselves. In addition, transcripts were reviewed for only two persons over age 40 and no one was over age 60. Based on these results, then, the association between intrinsic religiosity and Fowler faith stages–especially among older adults–remains unestablished. Consequently, the validity of Fowler's theory rests primarily on its questionable face validity and on results from interviews with a relatively young and possibly unrepresentative sample.

Applicability to Older Adults

The generalizability of Fowler's theory to older adults is especially concerning given that only four (1%) of his subjects were over 60 years of age. Using Fowler's interview, Shulik (1988) presents additional data on 20 elderly men and 20 elderly women, concluding that Fowler's faith development paradigm could make a meaningful contribution to gerontology. Even this conclusion, however, is somewhat dubious. First, there is again no evidence that elders chosen for Shulik's interviews were randomly sampled, and may have represented a sample of convenience. Second, the small sample (n = 40) limits statistical comparisons, requiring that results be reported in a subjective rather than objective fashion. Finally, none of Shulik's older adults had chronic illnesses, making them a rather atypical population, given that 80% of persons age 65 or older, according to a report by the U.S. Senate Committee on Aging (1987-1988), have at least one chronic illness.

Aside from basic methodological concerns, Shulik's study did uncover some interesting points. First, he found that subjects in the intermediate stages of faith (not the higher stages) demonstrated the lowest level of depression, and thus, the best adaptation. Second, he reported a relationship between increasing intelligence and increasing faith development, a concern I mentioned earlier. Thus, given our previous discussion, these data provide little support for applying Fowler's paradigm of faith development to a general population of older adults, particularly those with chronic health problems.

SUMMARY

Fowler's stages of faith represent an important advance in our understanding of faith development across the life cycle. It is articulately presented, rationally based, and firmly grounded in the classical developmental theories of Erikson, Piaget, and Kohlberg. I have reviewed the stages here and have presented a critique. My criticisms, especially of the scientific basis for this theory, have been rigorous and may be viewed as unnecessarily harsh. Nevertheless, the points I have raised are important and draw attention to aspects of Fowler's theory that may require reformulation. The greatest overall concern is that these stages represent an intellectualized version of faith that may not be relevant for the uneducated, cognitively impaired, or psychologically unsophisticated. I raise this concern with special reference to the elderly who may have limited education and are likely to have some degree of chronic physical illness and/or cognitive dysfunction. Thus, I question the wisdom of applying a cognitively-based paradigm as a measure of faith development in older adults.

In the next chapter, I will develop a theory of religious faith development that is applicable to older adults and considers the physical and mental conditions they are likely to face.

REFERENCES

Allport, G.W., and J.M. Ross. (1967). Personal religious orientation and prejudice. *Journal of Personality & Social Psychology* 5:432-443.

Butler, R.N. (1963). The life-review: An interpretation of reminiscence in the aged. *Psychiatry* 26:65-76.

Chirban, J. (1980). Intrinsic and extrinsic religious motivation and stages of faith. ThD dissertation, Harvard Divinity School.

Chirban, J. (1981). *Human Growth and Faith: Intrinsic and Extrinsic Motivation in Human Development*. Washington, DC: University Press of America.

Davis, R. (1989). My Journey into Alzheimer's Disease. Wheaton, IL: Tyndale House.

Feagin, J. (1965). Prejudice and religious types: A focused study of Southern Fundamentalists. *Journal for the Scientific Study of Religion* 4:3-13.

Fowler, J.W. (1981). *Stages of Faith*. San Francisco: Harper & Row Publishers.

Hoge, D.R. (1972). A validated intrinsic religiosity motivation scale. *Journal for the Scientific Study of Religion* 11:369-376.

Kaplan, H.I., and B.J. Sadock. (1988). Synopsis of Psychiatry, 5th edition. Baltimore, MD: Williams & Wilkins.

Koenig, H.G., J.N. Kvale, and C. Ferrel. (1988a). Religion and well-being in later life. *The Gerontologist* 28:18-28.

Koenig, H.G., M. Smiley, and J.P. Gonzales. (1988b). *Religion, Health, and Aging*. Westport, CT: Greenwood Press.

Kohlberg, L. (1973). Stages and aging in moral development–some speculations. *The Gerontologist* 13:497-502.

Loevinger, J., and R. Wessler. (1970). *Measuring Ego Development*, Vol. 1. San Francisco: Jossey-Bass, Inc. Publishers.

Poon, L. (1985). Differences in human memory with aging: Nature, causes, and clinical implications. In *Handbook of the Psychology of Aging* (2nd ed.), edited by J.E. Birren and K.W. Schaie. NY: Van Nostrand Reinhold, pp. 427-462.

Shulik, R.N. (1988). Faith development in older adults. *Educational Gerontology* 14:291-301.

Senate Committee on Aging. (1987-1988). *U.S. Senate Special Committee on Aging: Aging America–Trends and Projections*. Washington, DC: U.S. Department of Health and Human Services.

Wachtell, P.L. (1977). *Psychoanalysis and Behavior Therapy: Toward an Integration*. NY: Basic Books.

Chapter 7

A Theory of Religious Faith Development

> Be completely humble and gentle;
> be patient, bearing with one another in love.
>
> *–Ephesians 4:2*

This chapter contains an organized collection of comments, thoughts, and reflections on religious faith development across the lifespan. Unlike Fowler's theory, these ideas are not meant to be universally applicable to all persons regardless of religious orientation or belief system; rather, they are intended for a specific audience: persons who affiliate themselves with the Judeo-Christian religious tradition. While these ideas have their clearest and primary application to Christians, they may also have relevance to many Jews and Moslems. In any case, monotheists from any tradition should not be offended by these views. My primary intent is to examine the growth and maturation of faith in adulthood, especially among elders with chronic health problems.

In contrast to Fowler's theory which claims to deal with the "structure" of faith, the present account focuses more on content issues. I have chosen this orientation because I hypothesize that it is the content of the Judeo-Christian religion that is the most important aspect of this tradition that impacts on mental health. The content of belief is what determines attitude and behavior which, in turn, influence the emotional state. Because I will be dealing with the content of religious faith, this discussion necessarily includes a good deal of theology. The theology presented here, however, should not be new, unfamiliar, or couched in terms that are difficult to understand. I will attempt to follow traditional Judeo-Christian scriptures as closely as possible, quoting original sources as I proceed. I will also draw on the research and writings of William Meissner and William James, as well as on Fowler, Kohlberg, Piaget, and others. Let us begin by examining a view of man (no gender implied) which expands the conventional biopsychosocial model to include a spiritual dimension.

THE NATURE OF MAN

The biopsychosocial-spiritual model has been formulated by a number of different authors at different times, although perhaps not exactly along the lines that I propose. This model is useful because it is simple, comprehensive, and fits in relatively well with contemporary views in biology and psychology. Likewise, the model includes a spiritual dimension of man that is consistent with traditional Judeo-Christian scriptures.

Figure 7.1 presents a schematic representation of man's triune nature. Man is seen as having three separate and distinct natures that overlap and influence each other: Body (physical), Mind (psychosocial), and Spirit (soul). The Body includes all biological processes of the physical body and the brain which enable humans to exist and function on this physical plane; inherited or genetic influences are included here. The Mind includes all psychological processes such as emotion, thought, memory, all physical sensations (pain, touch, temperature, vision, hearing, taste), motivation, the will, and social drives which are presumed to result from biological processes occurring in the brain; included here are the effects of childhood and adult social and environmental influences on the personality. The Spirit is viewed as existing separate and distinct from the Body and the Mind. The Spirit[1] is considered to be that supernatural, rela-

---

1. The terms "spirit" and "soul" are used interchangeably here. However, some theologians use the term *soul* to indicate a combination of both man's psychological and spiritual natures. Although the differentiation of spiritual from psychological processes may be difficult (perhaps impossible), I believe this is necessary because various diseases of the brain can have a profound effect on psychological function, yet have no permanent effect on man's spirit (which is influenced by the choices that human's make). Judeo-Christian scriptures indicate that the soul (mind) and spirit can be separated, suggesting that they are indeed distinct entities (Hebrews 4:12).

FIGURE 7.1

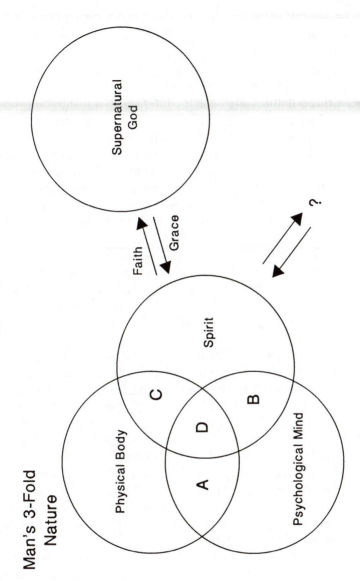

Man's 3-Fold Nature

Physical Body

Psychological Mind

Spirit

Supernatural God

Faith

Grace

A

B

C

D

?

tively constant part of man that endures after death of the physical body (Psalm 31:5; Luke 23:46). The existence of the Spirit is scientifically unproven and unprovable. The only empirical evidence of its existence comes from its impact on man's biological and psychosocial natures. Other evidence of the Spirit is testimonial, experiential, and revelational (see Moberg 1967a;1967b).

These three natures are seen as interacting and affecting each other in a dynamic fashion. The relationship of the natures to each other would probably best be represented by completely superimposing one on the other; however, because of the two-dimensional construction of Figure 7.1, a partial overlap will be used to indicate areas of interaction (areas A-D). The Body is seen as influencing the Mind during disease (area A); examples include such states as hypothyroidism causing depression, Alzheimer's disease or multiple strokes affecting memory and personality function, or severe systemic infection causing delirium. The Mind, on the other hand, may influence the Body through psychosomatic processes; for instance, chronic psychosocial stress causing peptic ulcer disease, severe depression causing dysfunction of the immune system, or extreme fright or shock precipitating cardiac arrhythmias or sudden death (again, area A).

The Spirit is seen as the medium through which God can affect both Mind and Body. Spiritual forces in this way may influence emotions, motivations, and all cognitive processes (area B), as well as influence the Body either directly (and supernaturally) (area C) or indirectly via the Mind (psychosomatic healings) (area D). The Spirit is the more constant part of man's triune nature, given that death of the Body and Mind do not threaten its existence. Whether and to what extent the Body and Mind can affect the Spirit is not entirely clear to me; nevertheless, Judeo-Christian scriptures indicate that moral and ethical choices (psychological processes involving the will) do have an impact on man's Spirit that has consequences both in this life and the next.

Consistent with the Judeo-Christian view, God is placed outside and apart from man or the universe. This view is distinct from that of pantheism, which does not distinguish God from creation. Scripture describes God as "great, mighty, and awesome" (Deuteronomy 10:17), as one to be revered and worshiped (Tractate Shabbat

30b-31b). Although God is separated from man, scriptures indicate that he loves and cares about man, and desires a special relationship with him or her (Genesis 50:24; Exodus 4:31, 19:4-6, 29:45; Leviticus 26:12; Numbers 35:34; Deuteronomy 4:37-38, 7:8-9, 14:2, 23:5, 32:10-12, 33:3; Psalm 36:7-8; Isaiah 43:1-4, 49:14-15; Jeremiah 31:3; Hosea 1:1 through 14:9; see also Tractate Avot, ch. III, sec. 18). This relationship is initiated by God, who reaches out to man through grace ("We love because He first loved us"–1 John 4:19). Through an act of faith, man responds to this divine initiative by reaching toward God, thus opening him or herself up to divine influence. This concept is perhaps nowhere more beautifully illustrated than on the ceiling of the Sistine Chapel in a fresco by Michelangelo. In this timeless art, man and God both reach out, straining to touch each other's outstretched hand, with their finger tips barely touching at the very center and highest point of the chapel's ceiling (Figure 7.2).

According to this paradigm, man's faith makes it possible for God to affect man's physical and psychological natures through his or her spirit. The role of faith, then, is central. Faith determines whether or not the channel is open between God and man's spirit. Not only does it largely determine the possibility of divine influence, it may also define the magnitude of that influence. Scripture (primarily the gospels) is replete with examples of the role of faith in divine healing (Matthew 8:2-3, 5-20, 25-26; 9:1-7, 18-19, 20-22, 28-30; 14:31; 15:28, 17:19-21, 20:33-34; Mark 1:40-41; 2:3-12; 5:22-24, 34; 7:24-30; 8:22; 9:17-25; 10:47-52; Luke 5:17-20, 7:3-9, 8:40-42, 8:48, 9:37-41; John 4:47-53, 11:1-44). In the 32 accounts of healing performed by Jesus in the New Testament, faith is directly mentioned in 16 (50%) and implied in another nine (23%); faith is not mentioned or implied in only seven accounts. Thus, in the vast majority of cases, God does not interfere with the human situation unless his invitation is accepted. There are instances, however, where God does act in a sovereign fashion–but not usually and probably never against a person's will.

Because of its controversial nature, I have presented evil (Satan or the Devil) as a question mark (?) in Figure 7.1. Nevertheless, given its emphasis in both Christianity and Judaism (Genesis 3:1; 1 Chronicles 21:1; Job 1:6; Isaiah 14:12-17; Tractate Berakhot

FIGURE 7.2

The Vatican Museums, Copyright 1972
SCALA, Instituto Fotografico Editoriale, Firenze, Rome, Italy

16b-17a), this less popular aspect of human nature cannot be ignored. Evil is viewed here as a force or a spirit, separate and distinct from man or God, which can affect man's biological and psychological natures through his or her spirit nature in the same way that God does. Alternatively, or perhaps in addition, evil may be viewed as originating from within man's psychological and/or biological natures. Scriptures emphasize man's "sinful nature" as coming from wrong desires and motivations (the Mind) and/or the "flesh" (Body) (Romans 8:9, 7:17-18, 8:3-4, 8:12, Galatians 5:19-21). Thus, while there is debate about whether to place evil outside or inside of man (or both), there is little doubt that it needs inclusion.

Both mental health professionals and philosophers have underscored the importance of dealing with evil (James 1902; Buber 1953; Fromm 1964; Menninger 1973; Peck 1983). American psychologist and philosopher William James (1902) wrote that to exclude man's darker side, destructive urges, or capacity for evil from any general view of man, is to present an incomplete, unrealistic picture of human nature. Even Freud, in *Beyond the Pleasure Principle*, recognized a part of man called the "death instinct," or a destructive force within the person which Freud could not explain by his theory in terms of sexual or generative drives (Freud 1920).

In the paradigm I have described, all humans have a spiritual nature, whether they believe in God or not. God reaches out through grace to relate to man, who must decide whether or not to respond to God. The decision pivots on faith. It is reasonable to argue that God never overrides a person's free will in this regard; if God did, man would be little more than a puppet and the relationship would have little meaning. Instead, God draws people to himself through experiences in life (frequently traumatic) which call for a response.

God may also at times influence a person in response to prayer from another individual (e.g., a mother praying for a wayward son). With regard to physical healings, scripture indicates that God responds to requests by family members (Matthew 9:18-19; 15:28; Mark 5:22-24; 7:24-30; 9:17-25; Luke 8:40-42; John 4:47-53), by friends (Matthew 9:1-7; Mark 2:3-12; 8:22; Luke 5:17-20), by employers (Luke 7:3-9), or by the healer (Matthew 17:19-20). There is a difference, however, between requests for physical or mental healing and requests for bringing about another's conversion. As I see it, God can and does influence a person in response to others' prayers by drawing that person to him (through life events or the actions of other people), but does not directly override the individual's free will.

Using this simplified schema, then, we can examine the effects of a traumatic physical event on the whole person. An elderly man has a stroke or develops Alzheimer's disease that affects his physical nature, which then causes a loss of any one of several psychological functions: memory may be affected, personality may change, thinking may be altered, a deep depression may occur (due to disruption of neurologic pathways or chemical substances in the brain), the ability to speak and understand speech may change, motivation and drive may be severely affected. Nevertheless, the elder's spiritual nature remains generally unaffected, since it is not inextricably linked to his physical or mental natures. Through this spiritual nature, then, God can influence both psychological and physical states, facilitating adjustment and return to a maximum state of health within the physical limits imposed by an illness. Alternatively, he may supernaturally heal the basic disease process. Thus, by believing and trusting in God, a person allows him to act through their spiritual nature to either directly and miraculously reverse biological changes (rare, in my opinion) or give psychological stability and strength to cope with the changes that have resulted (most often, in my opinion). This schema also allows for the therapeutic effects of prayer by family members or friends–through either the experience of support and love from another person or through divine intervention in healing the physical illness.

The reader should be aware that the biopsychosocial-spiritual model represents a gross over-simplification of an enormously complex process which is difficult to understand and to communicate in terms of rational constructs. Rather than attempting to establish theological truth, the usefulness of this schema lies primarily in providing a background for discussing and examining issues of faith development. In general, however, this view should be acceptable to many Protestant and Catholic Christians and to a significant but smaller number of Jews and Moslems. While there are some parallels with Eastern religions, the pantheistic concept of God is different from the perspective here which sees God as distinct and separate from both man and the rest of creation. There are also similarities between man's spiritual nature and Jung's "collective unconscious," however my understanding is that Jung (1934) believed the collective unconsciousness was inherited in a genetic sense from generation to generation; this is quite different from a spiritual nature that is exclusively of supernatural origin, without a biological or hereditary basis. We shall now move onto the main task of this chapter, that is, to discuss religious faith development across the life span.

RELIGIOUS FAITH DEVELOPMENT

Religious faith is defined here as more than just belief; rather, it is believing, experiencing, and acting (Hebrews 11:1-12:2). Faith involves the receiving of a promise (by grace) and the entering into a relationship. Religious faith development is a process during which persons' relationship with God (or Jesus, for the Christian) becomes their ultimate concern and primary motivation in life (Romans 6:16). These definitions follow Fowler's structure of faith (ultimate concern) and include specific references to content (i.e., relating to God).

Every person follows a unique path of faith development. Such development seldom if ever occurs in a single, predictable, progressive fashion, as different parts of the physical body or parts of the psyche might grow and mature. Faith development often pushes forward and regresses backward. The novice may be closest to the greatest of all religious truths soon after conversion, while the seasoned practitioner may find him or herself locked into a dry routine and meaningless habit with few fresh insights or experiences.

Both age and cognitive development influence the expression of religious faith and its level of maturation. Mature faith in a child is expressed differently than that in an adult. Likewise, mature faith in an intellectually gifted person is manifested differently than that in a cognitively impaired individual. Mature faith involves maximizing whatever level of faith is possible given one's emotional and intellectual abilities. Just as there are differences, however, there are also similarities that transcend both age and intellectual function. Before proceeding to examine specific stages of religious faith development, let us explore the common and dissimilar characteristics of mature faith at different ages and intellectual capacities.

Faith of the Child

Although Judeo-Christian scriptures give general instructions on the raising of children and on appropriate attitudes of children toward parents, they give little specific information concerning the development of religious faith during childhood. This may be taken to mean that the more important principles of faith development are common to all ages. Scripture makes quite clear that a small child is capable of a certain type of faith; in fact, this brand of faith is even used as a gold standard for faith in adulthood.

> I tell you the truth, anyone who will not receive the kingdom of God like a little child will never enter it. (Mark 10:15; Luke 18:17)

> I tell you the truth, unless you change and become like little children, you will never enter the kingdom of heaven. Therefore, whoever humbles himself like this child is the greatest in the kingdom of heaven. (Matthew 18:3-4)

Recall from our biopsychosocial-spiritual model that God initiates the communication between man and himself. Man, however, must respond. In other words, he or she must receive or accept the invitation to come into relationship ("receive the kingdom of God"). This involves a humbling, a revealing, an opening up that is possible only if one has trust–unqualified trust like that exhibited by a child–trust that God exists, that he cares, and that he has a plan and good purpose for a person's life. Having received the kingdom of God in this way, man then begins his or her faith journey–or at least moves to a different level on that journey.

The idea that even a small child is capable of possessing the most important and basic element of faith is comforting. The picture of God presented by the Judeo-Christian scriptures is that of a just and fair God. It would make little sense if such a God made the benefits of religious faith available only to those who had reached a certain age or level of cognitive development–or made such faith unaccessible to children, the retarded, or the cognitively impaired elderly. Freeing religious faith of age and cognitive restraints, then, makes it available to all people, regardless of heredity, age, background, education, or intellectual capacity. Indeed, the ability to trust and enter into relationship is one of the first psychosocial developments in the human infant.

The intellectual comprehension of profound religious truths is less important in terms of faith development than is the willingness to trust God, set aside pride and selfishness, and act on truths that can be understood. In cases where cognitive function and other intellectual capacities diminish in later life, simple religious truths– such as God's care and promise to never leave one's side–remain within the elder's grasp long after other functions have left. Even in advanced stages of dementia, as long as consciousness is preserved and some form of relating to others and God is possible, then religious faith may continue to mature and relationship with God strengthen (see Chapter 16).

Transition to an Internalized Faith

As children move into adolescence and young adulthood, they develop new cognitive and moral capacities. As these psychological powers mature, the types of relationships with others also expand. As the child becomes able to see and appreciate another person's perspective, he/she becomes able to relate in a less self-centered fashion. As psychological, cognitive, and social functioning mature, the person's relationship with God is expected to change as well. What was a fully appropriate relationship with God as a child with a child's capacity, may be necessary but no longer sufficient as an adult. "When I was a child, I talked like a child, I thought as a child, I reasoned like a child. When I became a man, I put childish ways behind me" (1 Corinthians 13:11).

As intellectual abilities mature, there arises a need to establish a new basis for faith. Even small children have a reason for trusting and seldom do so without justification. For a child, faith in God is usually based on the instruction and example given by parents or teachers–individuals whom he or she has found to be trustworthy. Thus, the child's trust and acceptance of God is based on a source outside of him or herself (i.e., parents). This is not to deny that in some instances, God may give a revelation of himself directly to a child, thus giving him or her a more personal basis for faith. It is my impression, however, that in the majority of cases the parents provide this for their children, especially for small children. When the child moves into adolescence and adulthood, however, the basis for (or locus of) faith must change from external to internal.

This point is also made by Fowler who emphasizes a transition from conventional faith (faith based primarily on the faith of parents, powerful others, or peers) and individuative faith (based on a reworking and reintegration of earlier beliefs). Around puberty there often occurs a separation from or rejection of parents' moral teachings and religious convictions; this is necessary for the young adult to individuate and take on religious beliefs and values that he or she can call their own. The establishment of such a faith often involves a personal experience of God independent of family or teachers (although the form this experience takes may be heavily dependent on prior teachings). The movement towards a more personal faith based on internal standards that is not dependent on family's or even society's approval, then, represents a significant step forward in faith development. The timing of this change is highly individualized. It may occur during or soon after adolescence, or it may not occur until later life, if it occurs at all. Once this transition occurs, however, one's relationship with God takes on greater meaning and depth. Religious motivations and strivings now become centered within the person (intrinsic faith). Once acquired, however, this faith must be maintained, nurtured, and integrated with all other goals and drives in life (the difficult part).

The transition to a personalized faith, while depending on a certain basic level of cognitive maturity, does not require a highly developed intellect. At times, as I mentioned earlier, it may even be seen in a child. More important than intellect, as noted earlier, it requires an open mind that allows for experiences with God that are personally meaningful. The psychological turmoil associated with adolescence may facilitate this openness, as the youth struggles with their identity and seeks answers (Starbuck 1899; James 1902). If not occurring during adolescence, transitions in faith may not take place until a future life crisis shakes one's values and priorities and causes one to question. Whatever had consumed one's energies as the ultimate concern must be displaced in order for God to move in.

Regardless of when this transition occurs, it can take on a variety of forms. It may happen suddenly with little forethought, or come about only gradually after much pondering and deep reflection. The transition may be referred to by many names and given different emphases depending on the person's particular religious background. Among Catholics and some Protestants, the Sacrament of Confirmation symbolically represents the time of transition to a more adult form of religious faith. Having a "salvation" experience represents this transition in other Protestant faiths. The "born again" experience noted in scripture refers to the same thing (John 1:12-13; 3:3-8; 6:63; 2 Corinthians 5:17; 1 Peter 1:3, 23). When such a transition occurs suddenly and dramatically, it may be labeled a conversion experience; the process, however, is often more subtle. Whether sudden and dramatic or gradual and stepwise, the basic change is that religious faith now becomes personally meaningful and one's relationship with God evolves to a more intimate level.

Certain characterological traits, and even perhaps biological influences (Chapter 4), may affect the likelihood of such a transition. While highly developed intellectual capacities may enhance religious faith, they can also detract from it. According to William James (1902),

> Some persons, for instance, never are, and possibly never under any circumstances could be, converted. Religious ideas cannot become the center of their spiritual energy. They may be excellent persons, servants of God in practical ways, but they are not children of his kingdom. They are either incapable of imagining the invisible; or else, in the language of devotion, they are life-long subjects of "barrenness" and "dryness." Such inaptitude for religious faith may in some cases be *intellectual* [my italics] in its origin. (p. 168)

Indeed, great intellectual effort may be required to advance to the point where intellect (and pride) can be laid aside so that simple truths can be accepted humbly and whole-heartedly without objective incontrovertible proof or verification. British professor and

Christian apologist C.S. Lewis (1943) has remarked that the truths of religion are really very, very simple until one begins to intellectually delve into them–it is only then that they become exceedingly complex. Scriptures provide reasons for the difficulty which the intellect has in grasping spiritual truths: "so that no one may boast before him [God]" (1 Corinthians 1:29) and "so that your faith might not rest on men's wisdom, but on God's power" (1 Corinthians 2:5). The conflict between pride and faith appears ever present.

SPECIFIC STAGES OF DEVELOPMENT

Having this general background, let us now proceed to examine five specific stages of religious faith development that may occur between infancy and old age. The first four stages usually take place before the transition to a personal faith and thus tend to follow the general lines of cognitive and moral development. In describing pretransition faith development, then, I will adhere to a structuralist developmental approach that closely parallels Fowler's early faith stages. In stage 5 (post-transition faith), which covers the maturation of personal faith during adulthood and later life, I will depart from a structural perspective and instead view faith development along a continuum of increasing maturity and integration.

Stage 1: Early Childhood (Ages 0-2)

In general, parents reflect God. According to Harvard psychiatrist and theologian, William Meissner (1984), "mirroring" occurs in the interaction between mother and infant that provides a basis for the concept of God; if mother is seen as a loving and caring presence, then chances are that God will be seen in this way too. This stage corresponds to Fowler's Stage 0 when "pre-images" of God begin to form and a sense of trust, acceptance, and security is established. The trust relationship developed between infant and mother lays down an important pattern upon which the ability to trust in God may later depend. At the toddler stage, imitation is the primary form of religious expression. At this time, there is little sense of God as separate from mother or self, since individuation of the self does not take place until between ages two and three years (Mahler, Pine, and Bergman 1975).

Stage 2: Middle Childhood (Ages 2-6)

This stage corresponds to Fowler's "intuitive-projective" period (Stage 1). The notion of God begins to form around an internalized, idealized maternal imago. Ideas and experiences concerning God depend on instruction and example by parents or significant others, and are heavily influenced by fantasy. Religious expression remains primarily imitative, as the child attempts to please parents. He or she begins now to internalize values and beliefs of parents, although the egocentricity and lack of perspective-taking characteristic of this pre-operational period of cognitive development (Kohlberg 1971; Piaget 1950), make it difficult if not impossible for child to make personal decisions about whether to accept or reject God independent of influences by parents or other powerful figures in their environment. At the age of three or four, children may have little difficulty imagining a God, but the picture is heavily colored by fantasy in a way not greatly different from a fairy tale (Meissner 1984). Ages four to six are a critical time for developing a more stable image of God as being either loving and benevolent or harsh and judgemental. Relationships with parental figures, as in the infant and toddler period, play a heavy role in the formation of this image. With the resolution of oedipal concerns around the age of six, the child becomes more and more aware of the distinction between his or her parents (who are increasingly seen as less omnipotent and more fallible) and God (who is seen as all powerful and perfect). By the age of five or six, the child may be capable of either accepting or rejecting the concept of God (Dobson 1988), but the stability of such a decision is debatable.

Stage 3: Late Childhood (Ages 6-12)

This stage corresponds to Fowler's mythic-literal period (Stage 2). Sometime in the latter part of stage 2 or the early portion of stage 3, the notion of evil becomes crystallized in the form of the Devil, who may become a source of anxiety to the child. Because the child is now capable of taking perspective, he or she can begin to independently explore what God is like as an entity outside of him or herself. The child's views of God are still heavily influenced by parents, teachers, and increasingly by peers; however, the child is coming to know God as a person or powerful figure in his own right, with requests and demands that may differ from the child's own desires or even those of his or her parents. At the age of six or seven, God becomes increasingly more real to the child and consequently a relationship with God may begin to form. Personal prayer becomes more meaningful as the child comes to recognize that God listens and answers him or her. Towards the end of this stage, the child develops the cognitive capacity to reflect on religious themes and may decide to accept or reject previous notions of God, the Devil, and other supernatural beings. This decision, however, because of the continued strong influence of parents and other authority figures, still does not yet represent a well-thought out, free and independent decision that can be claimed as their own and upon which their life can be structured.

Between the ages of nine and thirteen, children of both Christian and Jewish traditions frequently undergo rituals in which they formally announce (or reaffirm) a decision to follow God (or Jesus). In Catholic and many Protestant traditions, confirmation serves this purpose by bestowing on children the gift of the Holy Spirit to strengthen their faith; this is the equivalent of the baptism of the Holy Spirit in evangelical and fundamentalist traditions. Confirmation among Jews is a relatively modern rite dating from 1810; this resembles the Bar Mitzvah, but provides for the consecration of Jewish girls as well as boys (Encyclopedia Britannica 1949).

Stage 4: Adolescence and Young Adulthood (Ages 12-21)

Major psychological and physical changes begin to occur about this time. With the development of formal operations (Piaget 1950) along with the capacity for mutual and third-person perspective-taking (Kohlberg 1971), the adolescent can now form a much more complex and personal image of God. At this stage, called in psychodynamic language "the second individuation" (Harrison and McDermott 1972), the youth may reject earlier notions of God, repel moral and ethical values taught by parents, and seek a religious identity of his or her own (or none at all). This stage of moving away from parents and authority figures is normative. In fact, the absence of such strivings should be viewed with concern, since it suggests the persistence of an immature psychic organization.

Undeniably, this is a difficult time for the youth, who under a pressure to reject authority may experience considerable doubt about God and spend much time obsessing over God's existence and its meaning for him or her. On the other hand, some teens may give little thought to such matters and instead direct their energy towards peer relationships or career goals. Peers and idealized adult figures may heavily influence the formation of a religious identity and level of commitment in this regard. Because of the importance of intimacy to adolescents and young adults, they may picture God in highly personal and affective terms–as a loving, caring, relating God, and/or as a judging, obedience-demanding, fear-inducing God.

From here onward, religious faith can take several different paths, depending on whether a transition in locus of faith has occurred and the direction in which it has occurred. Decisions are now made which project the youth on a course that either (1) establishes a conventional faith (passively following a pattern of religious thought and action acceptable and condoned by parents, social or cultural group), (2) rejects all previous religious teachings and abandons further development in this area, or (3) proceeds to a post-transition faith (actively struggling to establish a relationship with God that has meaning and value in a personal and individual way, independent of–although not necessarily different from–that of parents or peers).

Any decision that establishes a lifelong meaningful relationship with God is difficult to make prior to the establishment of a stable personal identity and a certain degree of emotional maturity. According to Vergote (1969), this may not be fully possible until some time after adolescence:

> Man does not acquire true religious faith, that is, a really personal faith recognized in its transcendent finality, before

the age of thirty years. Experience has shown that after adolescence the whole religious formation apparently has to undergo revision–not because the child or adolescent has not hitherto been authentically religious, but because man does not acquire sufficient maturity to make a real personal choice and to recognize reality, before he has become an adult. (p. 300)

In these first four stages of religious development, I have closely followed Fowler's stages of faith. I have done so because of the impact that cognitive, moral, and psychosocial development have on these early stages of faith development. The rapid physical and psychological changes during this time affect a person's capacity to relate to and experience God in a stable and meaningful way. Having said this, I must again reaffirm that it is unwise to say that children (or mentally retarded adults), because of their developmental limitations, are prevented from entering into a deep, personally meaningful and satisfying relationship with God. A young child may have a personal encounter with God which allows for a far deeper relationship with him than could occur with a psychologically mature, closed-minded adult without such an experience. Thus, I tread cautiously here wishing to avoid the same mistake made by Jesus's disciples when they tried to chase the children away from him (Matthew 19:13-15). It may be that the purpose of maturing, experiencing, and developing in religious faith is to eventually help us to overcome the intellectual blocks that prevent us from seeing the most simple and basic truth known instinctively even to a small child: the importance and power of trust as the essential and irreplaceable factor upon which a relationship with God is based.

Stage 5: Adulthood and Later Life

All developmental models imply a spectrum of increasing maturity from an undeveloped, juvenile condition to a fully mature and seasoned state. As far as religious faith is concerned, determining where a particular adult falls on the spectrum of maturity is more difficult than for other developmental lines. Where a person stands in this regard is dependent on an enormous number of complex and not easily defined factors, including genetic, environmental, cultural, and interpersonal influences. It is probably true that no individual has sufficient knowledge and insight about another person to enable him or her to assess all these factors accurately enough to make a judgement about that person's level of faith. Indeed, the most heinous criminal (born with a degree of mental retardation, rejected and/or abused as a child) who performs the smallest, most insignificant kindness towards another criminal, may in fact be demonstrating greater religious maturity than the intellectually gifted, financially secure, socially prominent leader who neglects his or her family or other responsibilities. To him who is given much, much is expected (Luke 12:48).

Religious faith is also expressed differently by members of different religious traditions, even within Christianity. Without recognizing these differences, one might fail to distinguish the structure of faith from its content (a criticism I have of Fowler's theory). Indeed, what may seem like a silly ritual or even idol worship to a Protestant, may be the expression of deepest devotion and worship by a Catholic. Likewise, a behavior like "prophecy" or "speaking in tongues" may seem bizarre and even irreverent to a traditional Catholic, while a fundamentalist Protestant would find these activities elemental to their worship of God. Failure to recognize the value of different perspectives and faith expressions has fostered divisions within Christianity since its inception. Bearing these considerations in mind, let us proceed with a discussion of mature religious faith as it occurs and evolves during adulthood and later life.

MATURE RELIGIOUS FAITH

The first step on the path that leads to a mature adult religious faith occurs when a person makes a decision to believe in God and enters into a personally meaningful relationship with him. For such a relationship to develop, it cannot be commanded, demanded, or inherited; instead, it must be freely and willfully entered into. Emphasis is often placed on "repentance" as preliminary to such transitions (1 Samuel 7:3; Psalm 51:10-13; Ezekial 18:30-31; Acts 26:20). William James (1902) actually describes the conversion process as a "struggle away from sin rather than a striving towards righteousness" (p. 172). The act of a sincere repentance indicates a willingness to change direction, to remove whatever was at the center of ultimate concern in the past, and to replace it with God. According to both James (1902) and Starbuck (1899) this invariably involves a type of "self-surrender." This then begins the post-transitional period. It represents only a first step, and by itself does not indicate religious maturity. Entering into such a relationship with God is by no means irreversible. In fact, the post-transitional period is frequently characterized by a waxing and waning in the quality and intensity of commitment to this relationship. The average person may fall away for a while and then later rededicate his or her life back to God; this may occur several times in a lifetime. As faith matures, however, greater stability should come about (Ephesians 4:1-3).

Focus of Ultimate Concern

Central to the message conveyed by Judeo-Christian scriptures is the notion that mature faith involves a deep, intimate, stable and exclusive relationship with God. In the Old Testament, the first commandment given to Moses on Mount Sinai was "I am the Lord thy God, who brought you out of Egypt, out of the land of slavery. You shall have no other gods before me" (Exodus 20:2-3). In other words, no one and no thing is to take the place of God as the center of man's ultimate concern. In the New Testament, Jesus was asked a question concerning how a person could get to heaven. His immediate response was the following: "Love the Lord your God with all your heart and with all your soul and with all your mind" (Matthew 22:37). In this matter, then, both Old and New Testaments agree that placing God at the center of one's concern is *the* essential component of religious faith, and comes even before the social commandments (i.e., not to steal or kill, and to love neighbor as self).

In Greek, the term "Lord" indicates one who possesses supreme authority. The religious man or woman is to turn control of his or her life over to God and serve only him. This service includes both commitment and obedience. *Commitment* involves loving God "with all your heart [emotions] and with all your soul [motivation or will], and with all your mind [thoughts and intellect]" (Matthew

22:37; also see Exodus 20:3-6, Deuteronomy 6:5, Matthew 4:10, Mishnah 9:5, Yerushalmi 1:5 (3c), and Tractate Berakhot 61b). Loving God involves *obedience*: "This is love for God: to obey his commands" (1 John 5:3). Obedience involves following the laws governing both attitude and behavior set forth in scripture (Leviticus 18:26-30; 26:3-6; Psalm 119; Luke 6:46-49).

A depiction of mature faith as involving commitment, obedience, and the surrendering of one's will to the will of God, is not likely to be popular in a society where individual autonomy is highly valued. Nevertheless, popular or not, this is the central message of the Judeo-Christian scriptures and is (paradoxically) immensely freeing in itself (Isaiah 61:1; John 8:32; Romans 7:25; Galatians 5:1; Hebrews 2:15; see also Tractate Avot, ch. III, sec. 6). Scriptures indicate that man is a slave to whatever masters him or her, whatever directs his or her path, whatever resides at the place of ultimate concern in his or her life (2 Peter 2:19, Romans 7:25; John 8:34), and that the burden which God places on a person is light in comparison to that associated with other addictions (Matthew 11:30; Romans 8:15; 1 John 5:3).

Mature religious faith, however, depends not only on placing God at the center of one's ultimate concern but also on keeping him there. The "worries of this life" and "deceitfulness of wealth" (Matthew 13:22) are forces which compete with God for the focus of one's concern. Likewise, the process of conforming attitudes and behaviors to those which are consistent with a God-centered life is often prolonged and arduous. The exact form the process takes in a person's life is variable and depends on the person's perception of what God's will is for him or her. Both the direction to take and the power to accomplish this proceeds out of relationship with God. Just like any relationship, however, time must be spent together in order to preserve and nurture it. Time regularly spent with God in private prayer (Proverbs 8:34; Luke 18:1), scripture reading (Joshua 1:8), public worship (1 Chronicles 16:29), and other forms of devotion, serves this purpose.

Trusting Without Doubt

Mature religious faith involves a complete and whole-hearted trust in God, regardless of circumstances, believing that he is in control, knows best, and will remain by one's side: "Now faith is being sure of what we hope for and certain of what we do not see" (Hebrews 11:1). It is out of this devout, unquestioning, undoubting faith that peace and strength is derived. While some writers have suggested that mature faith involves keeping an open mind and being ready to be convinced otherwise, scripture does not indicate this–at least in matters of basic doctrine. In fact, those who questioned or doubted are portrayed as losing the power that unswerving belief conveyed (Matthew 14:31, 17:19-21, 22:21; Mark 11:22; James 1:6-8). Mature faith involves such a trust and dependence on God that it determines how one thinks about and acts towards oneself and others in daily life. This attitude enables a person to transcend negative life events, maintain a sense of meaning, hope, and purpose even in the most dismal of circumstances, and function on the highest possible level (physically, socially, and emotionally) given available resources.

Religious faith of this type seldom develops in the absence of hardship or suffering, and it requires the personal experience of having one's faith successfully carry one through a difficult time. Such a faith, then, is not inherited or taught; instead, it is often born out of adversity. For some persons, this level of adversity is not experienced until later life, when the ravages of old age strike. Before full religious maturity can be achieved, other objects of ultimate concern–such as physical or mental abilities, accomplishments or possessions, financial successes, friends, and even family members–must be replaced by God. This may involve the natural loss of objects or persons that previously occupied this place of concern. While this concept may appear radical to some, it is the key to being able to transcend losses and changes associated with aging.

Action and Faith

If God is at the center of ultimate concern, then a person's life–their attitudes and behaviors–should reflect this. Belief by itself is insufficient (James 2:17,19; Tractate Berakhot 17a). Scriptures indicate that mature faith involves action. St. Paul underscores this point in his letter to the Hebrews: "By faith Abraham . . . *obeyed* and *went . . . made* his home . . . *lived . . . look*[ed] forward . . .

offered Isaac as a sacrifice" (Hebrews 11:8-17). These are words of action. Abraham's faith was demonstrated and proven by what he did. There are many circumstances in adulthood and later life that require action based on faith in the absence of evidence, and sometimes, even contrary to evidence. The bereaved elder may be unable to see how he or she can manage their home and begin socializing again now that their spouse is gone. Faith involves mobilizing whatever resources persons have (contacting other family members, social service agencies, self-help groups), based on a trust that God will assist them and make these efforts successful. Another example might be that of an older person who because of progressive, crippling arthritis becomes a heavy burden on family or nursing home staff. Faith involves believing that persons are worthwhile, important, and of value, even if helpless and dependent on others, because God cares about and values every human being, regardless of their capacity to produce for society.

Mature faith involves putting on positive attitudes and/or taking steps toward constructive action despite feelings to the contrary. The action of loving is the most important command in the Judeo-Christian scriptures (Leviticus 19:18; Deuteronomy 6:5; Proverbs 10:12; Matthew 22:39; Corinthians 13:1-13; Ephesians 3:17-19; 1 John 4:7). Not only is one encouraged to love God and neighbor, but even to love his or her enemies (be they an inconsiderate caregiver or a thankless patient). Such faith comes about only through action–stepping out, taking risks, believing that God will help.

IDENTIFYING MATURE FAITH

Mature faith is best identified by its fruits (Matthew 7:16; Galatians 5:22-23; Ephesians 4:32; Colossians 3:12-14; James 3:17). For example, how does a person's faith serve him or her during success and tragedy? Does it bolster self-esteem and thus enable him or her to withstand the experiences of failure, desertion, loneliness, pain? Does it sustain morale in the face of death–either their own or that of loved ones? Does it provide meaning and purpose in life despite changes in physical appearance and function, social position, and other transformations associated with aging? Do persons have more "love, joy, peace, patience, kindness, goodness, faithfulness, gentleness, and self control" (Galatians 5:22-23) because of their faith? Maturity indicates consequences in the emotional realm: "For the kingdom of God is not a matter of eating and drinking, but of righteousness, peace and joy in the Holy Spirit" (Romans 14:17).

Psychological Consequences

It is clear that many of the "fruits" of faith are psychological in nature. The emphasis on *relationship* is central to these effects–relationship with God and relationship with man. As the interpersonal psychotherapists have pointed out, the basis for much of intrapsychic life, particularly emotion, rests on current and past relationships. Because of man's long period of dependency and helplessness as an infant and child, he or she carries into adulthood a need to feel cared for, protected, loved and valued; these psychological needs are filled during the process of communication and interaction. It is seldom that persons are anxious or depressed apart from some real or imagined conflict in their interactions with significant others. If emotional wounds frequently take place in the context of relationship, then so does psychological healing. The relationship that heals may be with a therapist, with a friend or family member, or directly with God.

By reading scripture or other aids to devotion, spending time in personal prayer and meditation, and worshiping within a community of believers, persons nurture their relationship with God, which may then help to meet the psychological needs described above. Scripture communicates that God loves and cares for his people, promises to protect them, and reaffirms their importance and value to him. Times of private prayer may involve an experience of God's response to requests for aid and assistance with difficult problems in life. During worship service, God's presence may be sensed and associated with feelings of safety and belonging as part of a community. Thus, a relationship with God begins to form and strengthen. A distant, impartial, unconcerned God with whom there is little or no interaction, who is only to be revered or feared–such a God has little, if any, positive impact on a person's ability to adapt and age in a lonely and harsh world.

The mental health effects of mature faith also result from the alignment of a person's will or drive with that of the divine will. Jesus said, "For where your treasure is [i.e., ultimate concern], there your heart [emotions, motivations] will be also" (Luke 12:34). If a person's mind is centered on God and his or her motivations are directed toward serving God (both privately and in relationships with others), then it will be easier for that person to tolerate changes in other areas of their life, since these changes have little affect on his or her ultimate source of happiness. Consequently, the older adult with mature religious faith may find it easier (although not easy) to transcend losses of health, social position, family and friends.

Social Consequences

In addition to the positive psychological consequences of a close, personal relationship with God, there are also social consequences that should be evident. Does one's faith contribute to the betterment of life for others–both their immediate family and larger society? The second part of the great commandment (to love others as self) would suggest so. Scriptures indicate that love for others is the clearest and most obvious evidence that God is at the focus of one's ultimate concern:

> We know that we have passed from death to life, because we love our brothers. Anyone who does not love remains in death. Anyone who hates his brother is a murderer, and you know that no murderer has eternal life in him. . . . Whoever does not love does not know God, because God is love. . . . If anyone says "I love God," yet hates his brother, he is a liar. *For anyone who does not love his brother, whom he has seen, cannot love God, whom he has not seen* [my italics]. And he has given us this command: Whoever loves God must also love his brother. (1 John 3:14-15; 4:8, 20-21)

THREATS TO FAITH

Once mature religious faith is established, it tends to resist permanent reversals. Nevertheless, negative experiences and various physical and mental disturbances can temporarily disrupt even the most devout faith. A stroke or degenerative brain disease can and often does cause biological changes that result in depression, paranoia, or other personality changes. This can impair a person's ability to concentrate during prayer or scripture reading. It may even seriously interfere with the experience of God's immediate presence, and may cause confusion and arouse guilt in a religiously devout person.

The process (or at least form) of faith maturation may be affected by mental impairments at birth or acquired developmentally. Some individuals experience paranoia and fear of other persons as a result of biochemical abnormalities in the brain. Appropriate medical and psychiatric help are needed to help correct these deficits and so optimize the ability to trust and relate to God in a meaningful fashion. Other persons suffer early childhood traumas that precluded an adequate initial development of trust as an infant; the unconditional love they never received as a child, then, must somehow be acquired during adulthood or later life. In addition to timely and competent psychiatric and medical care, these individuals need the support and reassurance of family and/or members of their religious community during such times. Members of the faith community are called to provide the unconditional love that these unfortunate persons lack and so desperately need in their lives (Matthew 25:35-40).

AGE AND MATURE FAITH

To what extent is older age associated with mature faith? As I have noted, older persons are more likely to have had experiences in life that have tested their faith. In addition, chances are greater that elders have faced the type of adversity out of which faith arises (situations involving a loss of control, feelings of helplessness and desperation). Few studies, however, have examined religious experience and change across the life span to plot the course of religiousness with increasing age. It is well known that church attendance declines after age 70 as functional disability prevents active participation in the religious community. With the decline in church attendance, however, is an increase in frequency and importance of prayer and other nonorganizational religious activities, particularly among those in poor health (Koenig, Smiley, and Gonzales 1988a). Because of the few longitudinal studies that have examined this question, however, it is difficult to say for certain whether this is due to aging, cohort, or period effects.

In the Durham VA Mental Health Survey (to be discussed in the next chapter), we asked younger and older men whether their religious faith had become more important, less important, or stayed the same as they had grown older. The majority of respondents indicated that religion had increased in importance with aging. In order to show definitively that the development of mature religious faith is age-related, however, one would have to prospectively follow a group of persons in middle age into later life periodically assessing their level of faith. This study has not yet been done.

MEASURING MATURE FAITH

Because of the different expressions of religiousness, as well as the variety of paths by which faith matures, such a construct is predictably difficult to measure. The concept of "intrinsic religiosity" perhaps best approximates the type of mature faith I have been discussing. Intrinsic religiosity is particularly useful because it is not contaminated with indicators of well-being or items confounded by physical health, and thus can be used to explore associations between mature faith and mental health. Below is a sample of items contained in the intrinsic scales of Gordon Allport (Allport and Ross 1967) and Dean Hoge (1972):

- "My faith involves all of my life."
- "In my life, I experience the presence of the Divine (i.e., God)."
- "Nothing is as important to me as serving God as best as I know how."
- "My religious beliefs are what really lie behind my whole approach to life."
- "I try hard to carry my religion over into all my other dealings in life."
- "One should seek God's guidance when making every important decision."

These items seek to identify a religious faith where God is at the center of ultimate concern. A first-hand experience of God, a desire to serve him, an integration of faith into other areas of life, a relationship with God that provides direction and guidance–these are essential elements of mature faith. These items not only have "face" validity, but have also been validated by community pastors' ratings (Hoge 1972; Koenig, Smiley, and Gonzales 1988a). Because of the expected mental health consequences of religious faith, one would anticipate a positive correlation between well-being or life-satisfaction and measures that purport to assess mature faith–in this case, intrinsic religiosity. This has, in fact, been documented in samples of older adults (Koenig, Kvale, and Ferrel 1988b).

Religious Coping and Intrinsic Religiosity. As our research group at Duke has examined the relationship between religion and mental health over the past several years, we have focused on how religion is used to cope with the stress of declining health and physical illness. Questions about religious coping have been found to be unintrusive and readily acceptable to older adults. Although not identical concepts, religious coping and intrinsic religiosity appear to be closely related. Elders who have God at the center of their ultimate concern are likely to depend on God and their relationship with him during threats to health and encounters with death. We have now completed several studies that demonstrate this fact.

In a study of 87 older adults (mean age 74) attending a geriatric medicine outpatient clinic, a statement indicating use of religion to cope ("I rely very little upon my religious beliefs when I deal with tension in my life") was strongly related to intrinsic religiosity ($r = -.44$, $p < .0001$) as measured by the Hoge scale. Likewise, in a study of 707 community-dwelling older adults (mean age 73), a significant relationship was found between intrinsic religiosity (Hoge) and the statement "While dealing with difficult times in my life, I don't get much personal strength and support from God" ($r = -.33$, $p < .0001$). We repeated these questions in a small sample of nursing home patients ($n = 27$, mean age 83) and again found high correlations of these constructs ($r = -.57$, $p < .01$ and $r = -.47$, $p < .01$, respectively) with intrinsic religiosity. In these studies, religious coping items were stated in the "negative" in order to elicit more valid and thoughtful responses from participants. In the chapters ahead, I will review recent research on depression, religious coping, and their interaction in younger and older persons hospitalized with medical illness.

SUMMARY

Religious faith is defined in terms of relationship with God. In mature faith, this relationship lies at the focus of ultimate concern. A simple, whole-hearted belief and trust in God are primary and basic prerequisites for the growth of mature religious faith, regardless of age or psychosocial stage of development; its expression, however, may differ depending on one's cognitive abilities. Such an attitude makes further faith development possible. During childhood, growth in religious faith tends to follow cognitive and moral lines of development. At some time, usually after puberty, a period of emotional unrest may stimulate greater scrutiny of the meaning of religion and its personal significance. By this time, cognitive function has developed and identity stabilized to the point where a relatively permanent decision can be made regarding the role that religion will play in life. If the decision is to place God at the center of ultimate concern, then religious faith takes on a personal meaning that is vastly different from the meaning of faith associated with an imitation of others or a conformation to expectations of family or society.

When religious motivations take on an intrinsic quality, mature adult faith becomes possible. Persons are then faced with the task of reorienting and reorganizing their view of the world to bring it into line with these motivations. Individuals must now integrate their faith into new ways of living, reacting, and interacting with others. Repeated experience of the successful resolution of problems through reliance on God strengthens and matures faith. A personal history develops that can be looked back on during future trials to give hope and confidence for a good outcome.

Mature faith, then, is born out of adversity and involves action. It cannot be inherited or taught. This type of faith is generally stable and may act as a source of strength, peace, and hope for persons in later life as they face the trials of aging. While many persons may never reach this level of faith, it is an ideal worth shooting for and is potentially accessible to a wide variety of persons regardless of social class, intellectual level, or physical condition. Even with advancing cognitive impairment, the ability to participate in relationship with God is one of the last human capacities to be lost before consciousness itself ceases.

In the next section, I will examine research that supports an association between religiousness and mental health, beginning with a review of the Durham VA Mental Health Survey.

REFERENCES

Allport, G.W., and J.M. Ross. (1967). Personal religious orientation and prejudice. *Journal of Personality & Social Psychology* 5:432-443.

Buber, M. (1953). *Good and Evil*. NY: Charles Scribner & Sons.

Dobson, J. (1988). *Dobson Answers Your Questions*. Wheaton, IL: Tyndale House Publishers, p. 37.

Encyclopedia Britannica. (1949). Confirmation. Vol. 6. Chicago: Encyclopedia Britannica, Inc., pp. 232-233.

Freud, S. (1920). Beyond the Pleasure Principle. In *Standard edition of the complete psychological works, 1953-74*, Vol. 18. London: Hogarth.

Fromm, E. (1964). *The Heart of Man: Its Genius for Good and Evil*. NY: Harper & Row.

Harrison, S.I., and J.F. McDermott. (1972). *Childhood Psychopathology*. NY: International Universities Press, pp. 231-232.

Hoge, D.R. (1972). A validated intrinsic religious motivation scale. *Journal for the Scientific Study of Religion* 11:369-376.

James, W. (1902). *Varieties of Religious Experience: A Study of Human Nature*. NY: Longmans, Green, & Co.

Jung, C.G. (1934). *The Archetypes and the Collective Unconscious*. NY: Random House.

Koenig, H.G., J.N. Kvale, and C. Ferrel. (1988b). Religion and well-being in later life. *Gerontologist* 28:11-24.

Koenig, H.G., M. Smiley, and J.P. Gonzales. (1988a). *Religion, Health, and Aging*. NY: Greenwood Press.

Kohlberg, L. (1971). Moral stages and moralization: The cognitive developmental approach. In *Moral Development and Epistemology*, edited by T. Lakona. NY: Academic Press.

Lewis, C.S. (1943). *Mere Christianity*. NY: Macmillan.

Mahler, M.S., F. Pine, and A. Bergman. (1975). *The Psychological Birth of the Human Infant*. NY: Basic Books.

Meissner, W.W. (1984). Psychoanalysis and Religious Experience. New Haven: Yale University Press.

Menninger, K. (1973). *What Ever Became of Sin.* NY: Hawthorn Books.
Moberg, D.O. (1967a). Science and the spiritual nature of man. *Journal of the American Scientific Affiliation* 19(1):12-17.
Moberg, D.O. (1967b). The encounter of scientific and religious values pertinent to man's spiritual nature. *Scociological Analysis* 28(1):22-33.
Peck, M.S. (1983). *People of the Lie.* NY: Simon & Schuster, Inc.
Piaget, J. (1950). *The Psychology of Intelligence.* London: Routledge & Kegan Paul.
Starbuck, E.D. (1899). *The Psychology of Religion.* NY: Charles Scribner & Sons.
Vergote, J. (1969). *The Religious Man.* Dayton, OH: Pflaum.

PART III:
ADVANCES IN RESEARCH

Chapter 8

Depression and Medical Illness

A merry heart doeth good like a medicine:
but a broken spirit drieth the bones.

–Proverbs 17:22[1]

In July, Mr. Williams, at the age of 77, was hospitalized for the second time that year for symptoms of fatigue, weakness, and shortness of breath, all indicative of worsening congestive heart failure. He was treated in intensive care for five days and then spent the remaining 20 days on a general medical ward while his medications were regulated and cardiac function optimized. Mr. Williams had end-stage heart disease. He had suffered two myocardial infarctions (heart attacks), repeated episodes of ventricular tachycardia (rapid heart beat with loss of consciousness), and during that admission had to be resuscitated after experiencing a cardiac arrest. After the July hospitalization, things never returned to normal for Mr. Williams. He took eight different medications to regulate his heart, treat his congestive heart failure, and ease his constipation. He had become so weak that he could no longer hunt in the fields as he had been accustomed to doing for 60 years, care for the chickens and cows on his ranch, tend the garden, or even walk out to the mailbox to get the mail. His condition worsened so that he was forced to go from using a cane, to using a walker, to finally getting about in a wheelchair; soon, he had to also stop driving because of failing vision and poor hearing.

---

1. King James Version

Along with his deteriorating physical condition, Mr. Williams experienced crying spells, lost interest in his usual activities, and became more irritable and less sociable. His sleep was poor, in part because he had to get up every two hours to urinate because of the diuretics (water pills) he was taking and because of prostate problems. He no longer enjoyed eating and soon began to lose weight. Life had lost all meaning for Mr. Williams. He could no longer do the things he enjoyed doing, and he had decided that there was nothing he could do that would give him pleasure. He felt that he was a burden on his family and that they would be better off if he was out of the way. Mr. Williams began thinking of ways to end his terrible existence. Before he had time to act, however, his heart failure suddenly worsened, prompting another admission to the hospital.

In the emergency room, he asked the doctor to just let him die and get it over with. He was made a "no code" and "Do Not Resuscitate" was written on his chart. After a few days, the nurses noticed that he was not eating or sleeping, was hopeless and discouraged, and made little effort in his own rehabilitation. Despite improving heart activity in response to medical therapy, he remained dysphoric, negative, and hopeless. The nurses notified his physician, who gave him a trial of an antidepressant and arranged for a therapist to provide supportive counseling and cognitive therapy. The hospital chaplain was also notified and stopped by frequently to encourage and pray with him.

By the time of his discharge three weeks later, Mr. William's sleep had improved somewhat, his appetite had picked up, and he had gained a couple of pounds back. While he remained weak and became easily fatigued with even minor exertion, his mood gradually improved and he was able to see the important role that he played in his wife's life and the lives of his four grandchildren. When he got home, his family assisted him in getting out into the garden and planting a few seeds that spring. He also resumed playing checkers with a neighbor friend and watching ball games on TV, activities he had stopped completely over the past six months as the depression had worsened. Mr. Williams continued to take the antidepressant and to see a counselor on a weekly basis. While depressive symptoms returned to some degree each time his physical condition worsened, he did not have a recurrence of severe depression and was able to enjoy a number of pleasures in the two years of life he had remaining.

Mr. Williams had experienced a serious clinical depression (major depressive episode) as a reaction to the many losses he had to cope with as he struggled against a progressive, disabling physical illness. Fortunately for him, his symptoms were recognized as potentially treatable and were called to the attention of his doctor, who then instituted appropriate psychotherapy and pharmacotherapy. Along with the chaplain's spiritual support, these treatments eventually led to a significant improvement in his symptoms. Physical illness is stressful for most elders for at least eight reasons (Strain and Grossman 1975): threat to efficacy, threat of separation, threat of loss of love, threat of loss of bodily function, threat of loss of bodily parts, threat of loss of rationality, and threat of pain.

Physical illness interferes with effective functioning in the home, at work, and in social relations; elders are simply less effective in their world when they are sick. Physical illness separates elders from their loved ones, and many fear that their sickness will make them unattractive to friends or loved ones and thus lead to their abandonment by others. Illness often threatens to impair bodily functions such as urinary or bowel continence, and elders frequently become embarrassed and humiliated over the loss of these abilities. Because physical illness (and medications) can impair cognitive functioning, especially in the setting of a recent hospitalization, many elders fear that they are losing their minds, a feeling that generates much anxiety and contributes to dysfunction. Finally, elders fear that illness (or diagnostic procedures) will bring with it pain or other symptoms that are unbearable. These many fears can exhaust the patient and lead to depression, discouragement, and negative thinking.

In this chapter, I will review the results of a study undertaken at the Durham Veterans Administration Hospital which examined depressive illness in the acute hospital setting and the psychosocial and health factors associated with its occurrence. This study was designed to examine the mental and physical health of over 1000 younger and older men consecutively admitted to the medical and neurological wards of the hospital during a 21-month period. While our primary goal was to determine how common depression was among hospitalized patients, we were also interested in studying the relationship between this mental disorder and cognitive impairment, inability to perform activities of daily living (disability), and demographic, social and religious factors. Before proceeding with a description of our study and results, however, let's examine the *illness* of depression a little further.

DEPRESSIVE ILLNESS

Depression is the most common reversible mental health problem in older hospitalized patients. This is a disorder of emotion that commonly develops when persons are overwhelmed by their problems or situations; at times, it can also be caused by physiological changes in the brain due to physical diseases or side-effects from medications. While everyone has mood fluctuations often described as "good days" and "bad days," true depression is something entirely different. When clinically significant, this disorder is associated with protracted feelings of low mood, loss of interest and pleasure in life, difficulties with sleep, loss of appetite, feelings of hopelessness, discouragement, guilt, being a burden on others, and loss of the will to live. Pulitzer Prize winner William Styron (1990) describes vividly his own experience with depression in his book *Darkness Visible: A Memoir of Madness*. A perusal of that volume will provide the reader with a subjective understanding of the intense feelings of distress that come with this disorder. Take, for instance, the following passage:

> . . . the pain of severe depression is quite unimaginable to those who have not suffered it, and it kills in many instances because its anguish can no longer be borne. The prevention of many suicides will continue to be hindered until there is a general awareness of the nature of this pain. Through the

healing process of time and through medical intervention or hospitalization in many cases–most people survive depression, which may be its only blessing; but to the tragic legion who are compelled to destroy themselves there should be no more reproof attached than to the victims of terminal cancer. (p. 35)

Major depression, the most serious type of depressive disorder, has now been documented in anywhere from 5 to 45% of hospitalized older patients (Kitchell et al. 1982; O'Riordan et al. 1989; Rapp, Parisi, and Walsh 1988; Koenig et al. 1988a). The rates of major depression in this population are far higher than those reported in community-dwelling elders, where recent NIMH Epidemiologic Catchment Area studies indicate that less than 3% experience this severe type of depression (Weissman et al. 1988). The high rate of depressive disorder in older persons with acute and chronic health problems is of particular concern given its impact on health care outcomes. In patients with this disorder, recovery from physical illness is much slower (Hesse, Campion, and Karamouz 1984; Mossey, Knott, and Craik 1990; Parikh et al. 1990), death rates are higher (Abram, Moore, and Westervelt 1971; Murphy et al. 1988; Koenig et al. 1989a; Rovner et al. 1991), compliance with medical therapy is lower (Stoudmire and Thompson 1983; Strain 1978; Rodin et al. 1981), and consumption of health resources is greater (Waxman, Carner, and Blum 1983; Koenig et al. 1989a).

Furthermore, it has been demonstrated that these depressions do not quickly resolve once the patient leaves the hospital; over 60% persist without improvement for many months after discharge (Schleifer et al. 1989; Koenig et al. 1991a). Even depressions that are considered only minor in severity have been shown to significantly impair function and ability to care for self (Broadhead et al. 1990). Thus, depression in medically ill older persons represents a serious psychiatric illness that can interfere with both emotional and physical well-being and survival.

For the past six years, we have been studying the problem of depression in hospitalized veterans. In our initial study conducted in 1987, we found a relatively high rate of major depression and other depressive disorders in 130 older men consecutively admitted to the medical and neurological services of the Durham VA Medical Center (Koenig et al. 1988a,b,c). All patients were age 70 or over. For every ten patients admitted, one was diagnosed with a major depressive disorder and two or three others with less severe, but clinically worrisome depression. Only 20% of these depressions were detected by house staff, suggesting that many older patients with coping and adjustment problems were not being recognized or receiving proper treatment. These disturbing results spurred us on to conduct a larger comprehensive study of depression in older patients; this time, however, we included a sample of men under the age of 40 for comparison. Thus, the Durham VA Mental Health Survey (DVAMHS) was born.

THE DURHAM VA MENTAL HEALTH SURVEY

Outcomes from the DVAMHS have been reported elsewhere and interested readers may refer to these sources for more detailed information (Koenig et al. 1989a,b,c; Koenig et al. 1991a,b; Koenig et al. 1992a,b; Koenig, Cohen, and Blazer (1992c); Koenig, Westlund, and Meador (1992d); Koenig, Meador, and Westlund (1992e)). Participants in this study were men acutely hospitalized with either medical or neurological illness between September 1987 and May 1989 at a VA Medical Center in Durham, North Carolina, located across the street from Duke University Medical Center. This VA is a referral center for Federal District 8 which covers most of North Carolina and parts of Virginia, South Carolina, Tennessee, and Kentucky. Because one objective was to study age differences in rates of depression, we included men under age 40 (primarily Vietnam veterans) and men over age 65 (primarily World War II veterans). Men age 40 to 64 were excluded from the study.

A computerized list of all admissions each day was examined for men in the age ranges specified. Patients were typically seen within 48 hours of admission by either a master's degree level social worker and/or by myself (at that time a geriatric medicine fellow). The study was explained to the patient, a consent form was signed, and approval was obtained from his medical physician. Both new patients (cross-sectional study) and readmitted patients (longitudinal study) were evaluated.

Cross-Sectional Phase

Our baseline sample consisted of consecutive new admissions from September 1987 through January 1989. Patients were eligible if they were male, in the age ranges specified, able to communicate during a psychological interview, and scored 15 or higher on the Mini-Mental State Exam (Folstein, Folstein, and McHugh 1975); the latter criterion was chosen because this level of cognitive function (memory and concentration) was felt to be necessary in order to give meaningful responses to interview questions.

All participants received a battery of psychological tests and were asked questions about race, marital status, living situation, retirement status, occupational status, education, income, past psychiatric history, family psychiatric history, alcohol use, admitting medical diagnosis, and religious coping (to be described in later chapters). Social support was measured using a three-item index that explored size of the social network, frequency of interaction, and satisfaction with received support (Blazer 1982; Blake and McKay 1986). Cognitive status was measured using the 30-item Mini-Mental Status Exam (MMSE). Level of physical function was determined by assessing ability to perform activities of daily living (ADLs); a six-item physical ADL scale (Katz et al. 1970) and a five-item instrumental ADL scale (Fillenbaum 1985) were used for this purpose. Severity of medical illness was rated using the five-level American Society of Anesthesiologists' severity of illness scale (ASA 1963).

Depressive symptoms were assessed in all participants using two self-rated scales completed by the patient: the Geriatric Depression Scale (GDS) (Yesavage et al. 1983) and the Brief Carroll Depression Rating Scale (BCDRS) (Duke Depression Evaluation Schedule 1986). Both of these scales had been previously validated for use in medical inpatients (Koenig et al. 1988b). All men who scored 14 or higher on the GDS were also evaluated onsite by a psychiatrist who determined the presence or absence of a depressive disorder using a DSM-III-R (Diagnostic and Statistical Manual, 3rd ed., revised) checklist (DSM-III-R, 1987). Finally, all men under age 40 or over age 70 underwent a structured psychiatric interview. During this 45-60 minute evaluation, patients were given the mood disorders section of the Diagnostic Interview Schedule (DIS) (Robins et al. 1981). Depressive symptoms were also rated in severity by the examiner using two observer-rated scales, the Hamilton Depression Rating Scale (HRS) (Hamilton 1967) and the Montgomery-Asberg Depression Rating Scale (MADRS) (Montgomery and Asberg 1979).

During the cross-sectional study, we screened 1303 consecutively admitted men in the age ranges specified above. Of these, 147 patients scored less than 15 on the MMSE and were excluded. Communication problems such as aphasia, tracheostomy, or severe deafness interfered with evaluation of 27 other patients. Thirty patients were excluded because of the severity of their medical illness or because they were transferred to other hospital services before we could evaluate them. Finally, 88 patients did not participate because they refused, were discharged before evaluation, or did not complete the survey for other reasons. Hence, complete evaluations were obtained on 1011 men who represented our baseline sample.

Age of participants ranged from 20 to 39 and 65 to 102. Sixteen percent of the sample were under age 40, 51% were age 65 to 69, and 33% were age 70 or over. Race was unevenly distributed between young and older men; 53% of young men were Black, compared with 28% of men age 65 or older. Compared with men age 65 or over, men under age 40 were better educated (13 vs. 9 years of schooling), less likely to be married (47% vs. 68%), less likely to be retired (11% vs. 69%), less likely to have severe medical illness (19% vs. 53%), more likely to have a history of psychiatric problems (42% vs. 26%), more likely to have a family history of psychiatric problems (22% vs. 9%), and more likely to use alcohol (47% vs. 18%). Medical diagnoses also differed by age. Younger men were less likely to have cancer (9% vs. 22%) and more likely to have neurological illnesses (30% vs. 14%). Occupational status (40% unskilled) and level of social support did not vary by age. Compared with similar aged patients discharged from VA hospitals in District 8 (covering most of North Carolina and parts of South Carolina, Tennessee, and Virginia), our participants differed little in race, marital status, or medical diagnoses; the only exceptions were a higher proportion of Blacks (52% vs. 38%) and patients with neurological disorders (31% vs. 12%) among our younger participants.

Longitudinal Study

During the 16-month study period and in the five months thereafter, 306 participants in the cross-sectional study (30%) were readmitted one or more times to the Durham VA hospital. Of these, we completed follow up evaluations during readmission on 214 patients (70%). Follow up evaluations were not completed on the other 30% because of severity of illness (6%), impaired cognition (6%), refusal (5%), discharge before being seen (7%), or other miscellaneous reasons (7%). If patients were readmitted more than once during the study period, their last contact was chosen to represent the follow up evaluation for analysis purposes. The longitudinal sample, then, included 211 men evaluated at baseline during the cross-sectional study and then again on readmission; the mean time interval separating these two evaluations was six months.

As in the baseline evaluation, readmitted patients were generally seen within 48 hours of admission. The follow up evaluation was briefer than at baseline, but included an assessment of cognitive status, functional status, religious coping, and depression status. Depressive symptoms were measured using only self-rated scales. The scores thus obtained on the GDS and BCDRS were summed to create an overall depression index.

Characteristics of readmitted patients at baseline were similar to those of participants in the overall cross-sectional sample in terms of social support, depression, functional and cognitive status, and history of psychiatric problems. However, there were fewer younger patients (8% vs. 16%) and more patients with a diagnosis of cancer (34% vs. 20%) among readmits.

RESULTS

Cross-Sectional Study

Table 8.1 summarizes findings on the prevalence of depression. Both depressive symptoms and depressive disorders were common,

TABLE 8.1. Prevalence of depressive symptoms and disorders (n = 1011)

Measure	Young	Elderly
Symptoms		
Geriatric Depression Scale (11 or higher)	33%	22%
Carroll Depression Scale (5 or higher)	23%	20%
Hamilton Rating Scale * (15 or higher)	28%	15%
Montgomery-Asberg Scale * (15 or higher)	33%	28%
Disorders		
Major Depression	22.4%	13.3%
Dysthymia	3.4%	1.8%
Organic Mood Syndrome	0%	0.9%
Bereavement	0%	0.3%
Adjustment Disorder	14.7%	26.2%
Total	40.5%	42.5%

* Includes men age 70 or over

indicating widespread difficulties in adjustment and coping. One out of four (24%) patients scored 11 or higher on the self-rated GDS, suggesting significant depressive symptomatology. One finding, however, was not expected. Depressive symptoms were more common in younger than older men–despite more severe medical illness among elders. The proportion of young white men with depression scores 11 or above on the GDS was 40%, over double the rate in older blacks (19%); scores for older whites and younger blacks fell in the intermediate range (23% and 27%, respectively) (Koenig et al. 1991b). Besides age and race, other characteristics distinguished patients who were having problems coping. These included retirement status (being retired for five years or more), having a personal or family history of prior psychiatric problems (young men in particular), having a low level of social support (again, especially in younger men), having more severe medical illness or being functionally disabled (older men in particular), and having a diagnosis of respiratory disorder (pneumonia, chronic obstructive pulmonary disease).

Depressive disorders, diagnosed during the structured psychiatric interview, were also more common in younger patients (Koenig et al. 1991a). Among men age 70 or over, 13% were diagnosed with a major depressive disorder and 29% with minor depressions. In men under age 40, on the other hand, major depression was diagnosed in 22% of participants while minor depressions were present in 18%. Besides age, the strongest cross-sectional predictors of major depression were low social support, severe medical illness (or impaired functional status), and a history of past psychiatric problems.

The characteristics of major depression in younger and older men also differed. Depression in younger men was more severe (Hamilton Scale Score = 22 vs. 18, $p < .01$), longer in duration (13 months vs. 10 months), and more likely to be associated with suicidal thoughts (58% vs. 46%). Older men were more likely than younger men to be experiencing their first episode of serious depression (31% vs. 13%), and over half of depressed elders (51%) reported that they had never had a depression in their lives until they reached the age of 60 years. Among older men, depression was frequently reactive to physical health problems, whereas in younger men it was most often related to prior psychiatric problems.

Longitudinal Study

Change in depression ratings between admission and readmission (on average six months later) was small for the group as a whole. There was a mean change of only 1.3 points on the depression index (whose possible range was from 0 to 42). However, change scores for individual patients were often quite large. Characteristics of patients at baseline which predicted high readmission depression scores were baseline depression score (how depressed they were initially), prior history of psychiatric problems, low social support, poor functional status, and a diagnosis of renal disease. When these and other variables were included in a regression model to control for confounding, only three characteristics independently predicted outcome depression score: baseline depression score, diagnosis of cancer, and diagnosis of renal disease (religious coping was not examined in this model but will be included and discussed in Chapter 11). Thus, when other factors were controlled, age, level of social support, and functional status did not significantly impact on outcome.

These findings make sense. Patients who are already depressed are more likely to have difficulty coping and adjusting over time. Those with kidney disease, especially if on renal dialysis, and patients with cancer have long been known to suffer increased problems with depression as their conditions progress (Israel 1986; Hinrichsen et al. 1989; De-Nour 1982; Bukberg, Penman, and Holland 1984; Evans et al. 1986).

DISCUSSION

We found serious problems with adjustment common in both younger and older patients. In our earlier VA studies and now in this one, we found rates of major depression exceeding 10% in men age 70 or over (Koenig et al. 1988a; 1991b). Given that rates of depression among older men in the community are less than one percent (measured using the same diagnostic instrument as used here, i.e., the DIS) (Weissman et al. 1988), this raises concern that many older persons hospitalized with chronic and acute health problems are having significant difficulty coping with their illness. Note also that the rates of depression reported here are only for men. Unfortunately, the number of hospitalized elderly women included in studies of this type have been too small to determine stable rates. Nevertheless, community studies indicate that the rate of depression among elderly women is at least double that present in elderly men (Weissman et al. 1988), suggesting that depressive illness in samples of hospitalized patients that include women may be even more common than in our all male sample.

It is not clear that these patients are receiving needed psychological or pharmacological treatment (or that their depression is even being recognized by their physicians) (Koenig et al. 1992a). Given our aging American population and increasing numbers of survivors with chronic illness (especially women), depression in the medically ill elderly is likely to become a serious public health problem in the future. Given depression's adverse effects on recovery rates from hip fracture and stroke (Mossey, Knott, and Craik 1990; Parikh et al. 1990) and its tendency to nearly double inpatient hospital stays (Koenig et al. 1989a), the impact of rising depression rates in this population bids ill tidings for health economists up ahead.

TREATING DEPRESSION

While antidepressants have been shown to be helpful in managing depression in elders with physical illness (Lipsey, Robinson, and Pearlson 1984; Lakshmanan, Mion, and Frengley 1986; Katz et al. 1990), there are still serious concerns about the safety and efficacy of drug therapy in frail elders with multiple medical problems (Koenig and Breitner 1990). In an earlier study, we found that 87% of older medical inpatients with major depression had relative or absolute contraindications to antidepressants (Koenig et al. 1988c). Likewise, in the DVAMHS we found that medical contraindications prevented the enrollment or completion of more than 80% of depressed elders recruited for a clinical trial to examine antidepressant efficacy (Koenig et al. 1989b). Thus, other strategies besides drugs are needed to treat the vast majority of older inpatients who have

trouble adjusting to the life-style changes that medical and neurological illness can bring about (Koenig 1991).

Risk Factors and Alternative Treatment Strategies

Knowledge about risk factors for depression is essential for designing treatment or prevention strategies. The relationship between
severity of the medical illness (or level of functional disability) and
depression is most important. Investigators have long noted physical illness to be a central factor in the genesis of late-onset depressions (Alexopoulos et al. 1988). In fact, this idea was proposed over
35 years ago by Roth and Kay (1956) who argued that physical
illness played a greater role in depressions occurring after age 60
than either genetic or early childhood influences. Most depressions
among older inpatients in the DVAMHS appeared attributable to the
stress of functional disability induced by medical illness, rather than
to biological or genetic factors.

Helping elders with chronic illness to cope better with disabling
conditions may either prevent the development of depression or
prevent its progression. Many of these patients have become ar-
rested in the process of grieving over their multiple losses. Some are
unable to come to terms with the fact that things will never again be
the way they were. They are simply unable to accept anything less
than their previous state of health or home situation. Some have
convinced themselves that nothing in life will ever again bring them
meaning or satisfaction. While there may be an element of reality to
their situation that does limit pleasure to some extent, frequently
there is a *second layer* of exaggerated negativity and unrealistic
pessimism. An attitude like "one is not worth anything and life is
not worth living unless one is producing, independent, and in control" must be challenged by the therapist. These are not absolute
patterns in the universe, but rules that the patient him or herself has
established and that unnecessarily limit their pleasure. The losses
brought on by physical illness do cause realistic sadness and grief;
however, much excessive unhappiness results from exaggerated
emotional responses, catastrophising, and "holding out" for or being purposely dissatisfied with anything less than their previous life
situation before illness intervened. These patients need help in giving up their expectation of a return to a previous nonillness condi-

tion, and in learning to be satisfied with and to obtain pleasure from activities and experiences that are not dependent on physical abilities no longer present and unlikely to be recovered.

Besides the use of cognitive techniques described above, mobilization of social resources is important to provide the emotional support that distressed elders need during these times of adjustment and change. The fact that low social support was the strongest cross-sectional correlate of major depression in the DVAMHS suggests that psychosocial factors play a major role in the etiology and perhaps maintenance of depressions in this setting. There are numerous reasons, then, why psychotherapy–supportive, cognitive, and interpersonal–represents a potentially efficacious and safe treatment (especially when compared with more risky pharmacotherapy).

Psychotherapy

Despite its theoretical advantages, psychotherapy in this setting is surprisingly uncommon. It is perhaps employed in 15% or fewer cases (Koenig et al. 1992a). Financial disincentives may be partly at fault. Nevertheless, cognitive-behavioral or supportive techniques are ideally suited for helping elders better cope with functional disability and dwindling social networks that often fuel such depressions. Researchers have already demonstrated the effectiveness of psychosocial strategies in increasing coping skills and decreasing depression in cancer patients (Fawzy et al. 1990). Such techniques avoid the risk of side-effects in frail elderly patients and open up a viable therapeutic option for the more than 50% of such patients who have medical contraindications to antidepressant drug therapy (Koenig et al. 1989a).

Much theoretical groundwork has already been laid (Lindemann 1944; Kimball 1973; Kohle and Simons 1975; Freyberger 1975). Nevertheless, little systematic research has addressed the effectiveness of the cognitive/supportive techniques described above and other forms of "talk" therapy. Besides the Fawzy et al. (1990) study, only a few case reports have been published on the efficacy of psychotherapeutic techniques in depressed medical patients (Stein, Murdaugh, and Macleoid 1969; Rodin 1984; Yalom and

Greaves 1977), and there has not been a single study examining this issue in hospitalized elderly patients.

In designing psychotherapy that is efficacious, acceptable, and affordable to older patients, information is needed about coping strategies that elders use and find helpful in dealing with health problems and related losses. I have already alluded to the importance of social support in facilitating such adjustment. Cognitive and behavioral coping strategies also need to be explored. As we will see in the next few chapters, religion is another important resource that hospitalized patients frequently turn to for help.

SUMMARY

Depression is common among both younger and older persons with health problems and is associated with increased morbidity (e.g., likelihood of medical complications and worsening physical illness) and mortality (e.g., likelihood of death). The high rate of depression among elders is concerning because they compose the majority of patients hospitalized with medical illness and are a group that is rapidly increasing in size as the American population ages and improved health care extends the life span.

Depression among older patients in the DVAMHS most often resulted from their being overwhelmed by the stress of severe physical illness, on top of other psychosocial losses. Unlike in younger men, these depressions were infrequently associated with prior psychiatric problems, major intrapsychic conflict stemming from childhood, or unresolved developmental tasks. There was also little evidence that most depressions in this setting were a result of organic factors, toxins from physical illness, or side-effects from medications. Rather these depressions were most often situational–due to the realistic stresses of the environment.

In cases where symptoms are mild or antidepressants are contraindicated or unsafe (the majority of cases), then, treatment should be directed at relieving the situation. This can be accomplished by treating reversible medical illness or by providing direct assistance for solvable psychosocial problems. If the situation cannot be changed, then efforts need to be directed at helping the elder adjust better to their difficult circumstances. This may be done through a variety of supportive and cognitive-behavioral techniques. Knowledge of coping behaviors that elders use and find particularly helpful is needed in order to design effective, acceptable, and affordable treatment strategies. The importance of social support in helping elders to cope with health and social problems was underscored by its strong inverse relationship with depression in the DVAMHS. Although I have thus far avoided any discussion of religious coping, the next three chapters will address this issue. Such considerations may have an impact on who provides supportive care or psychotherapy to depressed elders and what therapeutic approach should be taken.

REFERENCES

Abram, H.S., G.L. Moore, and F.B. Westervelt, Jr. (1971). Suicidal behavior in chronic dialysis patients. *American Journal of Psychiatry* 127:1199-1204.

Alexopoulos, G.S., R.C. Young, B.S. Meyers, R.C. Abrams, and C.A. Shamoian. (1988). Late-onset depression. *Psychiatric Clinics of North America* 11: 101-116.

American Society of Anesthesiologists. (1963). New classification of physical status. *Anesthesiology* 24:191-8.

Blake, R.L., and D.A. McKay. (1986). A single-item measure of social supports as a predictor of morbidity. *Journal of Family Practice* 22:82-84.

Blazer, D.G. (1982). Social support and mortality in an elderly community population. *American Journal of Epidemiology* 115:684-694.

Broadhead, W.E., D.G. Blazer, L.K. George, and C.K. Tse. (1990). Depression, disability days, and days lost from work in a prospective epidemiological survey. *Journal of the American Medical Association* 264:2524-2528.

Bukberg, J., D. Penman, and J.C. Holland. (1984). Depression in hospitalized cancer patients. *Psychosomatic Medicine* 46:199-212.

De-Nour, A.K. (1982). Social adjustment of chronic dialysis patients. *American Journal of Psychiatry* 139:97-100.

Diagnostic and Statistical Manual of Mental Disorders. (1987). Third Edition, Revised. Washington, DC: American Psychiatric Association.

Evans, D.L., C.F. McCartney, C.B. Nemeroff, D. Raft, D. Quade, R.N. Golden, J.J. Haggerty, V. Holmes, J.S. Simon, M. Droba, G.A. Mason, and W.C. Fowler. (1986). Depression in women treated for gynecological cancer: clinical and neuroendocrine assessment. *American Journal of Psychiatry* 143: 447-452.

Fawzy, F.I., N. Cousins, N.W. Fawzy, M.E. Kemeny, R. Elashoff, and D. Morton. (1990). A structure psychiatric intervention for cancer patients: I. Changes over time in methods of coping and affective disturbance. *Archives of General Psychiatry* 47:720-725.

Fillenbaum, G.G. (1985). Screening the elderly: A brief instrumental activities of daily living measure. *Journal of the American Geriatrics Society* 33:698-705.

Folstein, M.F., S.E. Folstein, and P.R. McHugh. (1975). "Mini-Mental State": A practical method for grading cognitive state of patients for the clinician. *Journal of Psychiatric Research* 12:189-196.

Freyberger, H. (1975). Psychotherapeutic possibilities in medically extreme situations. *Psychotherapy and Psychosomatics* 26:337-343.

Hamilton, M. (1967). Development of a rating scale for primary depressive illness. *British Journal of Social and Clinical Psychiatry* 6:278-286.

Hesse, K.A., E.W. Campion, and N. Karamouz. (1984). Attitudinal stumbling blocks to geriatric rehabilitation. *Journal of the American Geriatrics Society* 32:747-749.

Hinrichsen, G.A., J.A. Lieberman, S. Pollack, and H. Steinberg. (1989). Depression in hemodialysis patients. *Psychosomatics* 30:284-289.

Israel, M. (1986). Depression in dialysis patients: A review of psychological factors. *Canadian Journal of Psychiatry* 31:445-451.

Katz, S., T.D. Downs, H.R. Cash, and R.C. Grotz. (1970). Progress in development of the index of ADL. *Gerontologist* 10:20-30.

Katz, I.R., G.M. Simpson, S.M. Curlik, P.A. Parmelee, and C. Muhly. (1990). Pharmacologic treatment of major depression for elderly patients in residential care settings. *Journal of Clinical Psychiatry* 51(7)(suppl.):41-47.

Kimball, C.P. (1973). Medical psychotherapy. *Psychotherapy and Psychosomatics* 25:193-200.

Kitchell, M.A., R.F. Barnes, R.C. Veith, J.T. Okimoto, and M.A. Raskind. (1982). Screening for depression in hospitalized geriatric medical patients. *Journal of the American Geriatrics Society* 30:174-177.

Koenig, H.G. (1991). Treatment considerations for the depressed geriatric patient. *Drugs and Aging* 1:266-278.

Koenig, H.G., and J.C.S. Breitner. (1990). Use of antidepressants in medically ill older patients. A review and commentary. *Psychosomatics* 31:22-32.

Koenig, H.G., H.J. Cohen, and D.G. Blazer. (1992c). The Mini-Mental State Exam and assessment of mild to moderate cognitive dysfunction in hospitalized medically ill patients. *Journal of General Internal Medicine* (in submission).

Koenig, H.G., K.G. Meador, and R. Westlund. (1992e). Health care utilization and survival of religious and non-religious copers hospitalized with medical illness. *Journal of Religious Gerontology* (in submission).

Koenig, H.G., R.E. Westlund, and K.G. Meador. (1992d). Functional status and predictors of change hospitalized older adults. *Archives of Physical Medicine and Rehabilitation* (in submission).

Koenig, H.G., K.G. Meador, H.J. Cohen, and D.G. Blazer. (1988a). Depression in elderly hospitalized patients with medical illness. *Archives of Internal Medicine* 148:1929-1936.

_____ (1988b). Self-rated depression scales and screening for major depression in the older hospitalized patient with medical illness. *Journal of the American Geriatrics Society* 36:699-706.

———— (1988c). Detection and treatment of major depression in the older hospitalized patient with medical illness. *International Journal of Psychiatry in Medicine* 18:17-31.

Koenig, H.G., V. Goli, F. Shelp, K.G. Meador, and D.G. Blazer. (1989c). Major depression and the NIMH Diagnostic Interview Schedule: Validation in medically ill hospitalized patients. *International Journal of Psychiatry in Medicine* 19:123-132.

Koenig, H.G., F. Shelp, V. Goli, H.J. Cohen, and D.G. Blazer. (1989a). Survival and healthcare utilization in elderly medical inpatients with major depression. *Journal of the American Geriatrics Society* 37:599-606.

Koenig, H.G., V. Goli, F. Shelp, H.S. Kudler, H.J. Cohen, and D.G. Blazer. (1992a). Major depression in hospitalized medically ill men: Documentation, treatment, and prognosis. *International Journal of Geriatric Psychiatry* 7:25-34.

Koenig, H.G., K.G. Meador, V. Goli, F. Shelp, H.J. Cohen, and D.G. Blazer. (1991b). Self-rated depressive symptoms in medical inpatients. *International Journal of Psychiatry in Medicine* 12:409-429.

Koenig, H.G., K.G. Meador, F. Shelp, V. Goli, H.J. Cohen, and D.G. Blazer. (1991a). Major depressive disorder in hospitalized medically ill patients: An examination of young and elderly male veterans. *Journal of the American Geriatrics Society* 39:881-890.

Koenig, H.G., V. Goli, F. Shelp, H.S. Kudler, H.J. Cohen, K.G. Meador, and D.G. Blazer. (1989b). Antidepressant use in elderly medical inpatients: Lessons from an attempted clinical trial. *Journal of General Internal Medicine* 4:498-505.

Koenig, H.G., H.J. Cohen, D.G. Blazer, C. Pieper, K.G. Meador, F. Shelp, V. Goli, and R. DiPasquale. (1992b). Religious coping and depression in elderly hospitalized medically ill men. *American Journal of Psychiatry* 149:1693-1700.

Kohle, K. and C. Simons. (1975). Integration of the psychosomatic approach into the management of the severely and fatally ill. *Psychotherapy and Psychosomatics* 26:357-363.

Lakshmanan, M., L.C. Mion, and J.D. Frengley. (1986). Effective low dose tricyclic antidepressant treatment for depressed geriatric rehabilitation patients. *Journal of the American Geriatrics Society* 34:421-426.

Lindemann, E. (1944). Symptomatology and management of acute grief. *American Journal of Psychiatry* 101:141-148.

Lipsey, J.R., R.G. Robinson, and G.D. Pearlson. (1984). Nortriptyline treatment of post-stroke depression: A double-blind study. *Lancet* i:297-300.

Montgomery, S.A., and M. Asberg. (1979). A new depression scale designed to be sensitive to change. *British Journal of Psychiatry* 134:382-389.

Mossey, J.M., K. Knott, and R. Craik. (1990): The effects of persistent depressive symptoms on hip fracture recovery. *Journal of Gerontology* 45:M163-M168.

Murphy, E., R. Smith, J. Lindesay, and J. Slatter. (1988). Increased mortality rates in late-life depression. *British Journal of Psychiatry* 152:347-353.

O'Riordan, T.G., J.P. Hayes, R. Shelley, D. O'Neill, J.B. Walsh, and D. Coakley. (1989). The prevalence of depression in an acute geriatric medical assessment unit. *International Journal of Geriatric Psychiatry* 4:17-21.

Parikh, R.M., R.G. Robinson, J.R. Lipsey, S.E. Starkstein, J.P. Fedoroff, and T.R. Price. (1990). The impact of poststroke depression on recovery in activities of daily living over a 2-year follow up. *Archives of Neurology* 47:785-789.

Rapp, S.R., S.A. Parisi, and D.A. Walsh. (1988). Psychological dysfunction and physical health among elderly medical inpatients. *Journal of Consulting and Clinical Psychology* 56:851-855.

Robins, L., J. Helzer, J. Croughan, J. Williams, and R. Spitzer. (1981). National Institute of Mental Health Diagnostic Interview Schedule: History characteristics, validity. *Archives of General Psychiatry* 38:381-389.

Rodin, G. (1984). Expressive psychotherapy in the medically ill: Resistance and possibilities. *International Journal of Psychiatry in Medicine* 14:99-108.

Rodin, G.M., J. Chmara, J. Ennis, S. Fenton, H. Locking, and K. Steinhouse. (1981). Stopping life-sustaining medical treatment: Psychiatric considerations in the termination of renal dialysis. *Canadian Journal of Psychiatry* 26: 540-544.

Roth, M. and D.W.K. Kay. (1956). Affective disorders arising in the senium. II. Physical disability as an aetiological factor. *Journal of Mental Sciences* 102:141-150.

Rovner, B.W., P.S. German, L.J. Brant, R. Clark, L. Burton, and M.F. Folstein. (1991). Depression and mortality in nursing homes. *Journal of the American Medical Association* 265:993-996.

Schleifer, S.J., M.M. Macari-Hinson, D.A. Coyle, W.R. Slater, M. Kahn, R. Gorlin, and H.D. Zucker. (1989). The nature and course of depression following myocardial infarction. *Archives of Internal Medicine* 149:1785-1789.

Stein, E.H., J. Murdaugh, and. J.A. Macleoid. (1969). Brief psychotherapy of psychiatric reactions to physical illness. *American Journal of Psychiatry* 125:76-83.

Stoudmire, A., and T.L. Thompson. (1983). Medication noncompliance: systematic approaches to evaluation and intervention. *General Hospital Psychiatry* 5:233-239.

Strain, J.J. (1978). Noncompliance. In: *Psychological Interventions in Medical Practice*. NY: Appleton-Century-Crofts.

Strain, J.J., and S. Grossman. (1975). Psychological reactions to medical illness and hospitalization. In *Psychological Care of the Medically Ill: A Primer in Liaison Psychiatry*, edited by J.J. Strain and S. Grossman. NY: Appleton, p. 23.

Styron, W. (1990). *Darkness Visible: A Memoir of Madness*. NY: Random House.

Waxman, H.M., E.A. Carner, and A. Blum. (1983). Depressive symptoms and health service utilization among the community elderly. *Journal of American Geriatrics Society* 31:417.

Weissman, M.M., P.J. Leaf, G.L. Tischler, D.G. Blazer, M. Karno, M.L. Bruce, and L.P. Florio. (1988). Affective disorders in five United States communities. *Psychological Medicine* 18:141-153.

Yalom, I.D., and C. Greaves. (1977). Group therapy with the terminally ill. *American Journal of Psychiatry* 134, 396-400.

Yesavage, J.A., R.L. Rink, T.L. Rose, D. Lum, V. Huang, M. Adey, and V.O. Leirer. (1983). Development and validation of a geriatric depression screening scale: A preliminary report. *Journal of Psychiatric Research* 17:37-49.

Chapter 9

Using Religion to Cope

I came to the swift, raging river,
And the roar held the echo of fear;
'Oh, Lord, give me wings to fly over,
If You are, as You promised, quite near.'

But He said, 'Trust the grace I am giving,
All-pervasive, sufficient for you.
Take My hand—we will face this together;
But My plan is—not over, but through.'

–Lee Webber

The onset or exacerbation of medical illness that requires hospitalization is an acute stressor for many younger and older persons. The high prevalence of depression among medical patients testifies to this fact (see Chapter 8). When faced with the stress of physical illness, particularly when other psychosocial and economic resources are limited, the person's ability to cope may be overwhelmed. Religion represents one source of comfort for such patients (Swanson aand Harter 1971; Rosen 1982; Conway 1985; Manfredi and Pickett 1987; Baldree, Murphy, and Powers 1982; Koenig, Moberg, and Kvale 1988a). The term "religious coping" refers to the dependence on religious belief or activity to help manage emotional stress or physical discomfort.

Studies which have examined the prevalence of religious coping have often been fraught with problems. Sample size has typically been small (rarely exceeding 100); method of sample selection has often been biased (religious persons are more likely than nonreligious to become involved); measurement of religious coping has seldom been rigorous; and only a small proportion of participants have been men. Studies of religious behaviors in male medical inpatients are almost nonexistent, and the characteristics of hospitalized patients more likely to use religion as a coping resource are unknown. Knowledge of how religion enables some people to cope, but perhaps interferes with coping in others, is needed by clinicians who would hope to reinforce healthy behaviors and discourage illness-provoking ones. As alluded to in the last chapter, information about types of religious cognitions used by physically ill patients, and how they help with coping, is needed in designing psychotherapeutic strategies to bolster coping efforts.

Finally, almost nothing is known about changes in religious coping over time in patients with ongoing medical illness. Fluctuations in illness and stress level may cause persons to turn towards religion. How commonly does this occur and what effects do age and prior coping behaviors have on this decision? On the other hand, some individuals respond to tragedies and suffering in life with anger and defiance towards God. Why me? How could a loving God allow this to happen? Am I being punished? They feel distant from God and experience feelings of abandonment. How common is this reaction?

THE DURHAM VA MENTAL HEALTH SURVEY

Information about religious coping collected during the DVAMHS has provided at least preliminary answers to some of these questions. Recall from Chapter 8 that this study consisted of cross-sectional and longitudinal phases. Religious coping was measured both on admission and on readmission. The intensity of religious coping was measured using a three-item index (to be described). Several other questions examined (1) duration and type of religious coping, (2) experiences that caused significant changes in feelings about religion, (3) whether importance of religion had changed as participants had grown older, and (4) religiosity of parents or early caretakers. As noted in the last chapter, patients were assessed using standardized measures of medical illness severity, functional status, cognitive status, social support, and other psychosocial variables. Cross-sectional correlates and longitudinal predictors of religious coping were assessed using statistical modeling techniques.

Religious Coping Index

General details concerning methodology and sampling techniques used in the DVAMHS were presented in the last chapter; here I will describe the *Religious Coping Index* (RCI) (Figure 9.1) and other questions pertaining to religion asked during the survey (Koenig et al. 1992). All inquiries about religion were asked at the end of the evaluation, after mental health data had been collected. The RCI consisted of three items. In item I, the patient was asked an open-ended question on how he coped with his illness. If the spontaneous response given by the patient was a religious one (e.g., strength from God, prayer, faith, church) the patient received a score of 10; if the response was one other than religious (family, stay busy, and so forth), he received a score of 0. In item II, the patient was asked to rate on a visual analogue scale the extent to which he found religious beliefs or activities helpful in coping with his situation. The scale was numbered from 0 to 10, where 0 indicated "not much or not at all" and 10 indicated "the most important thing that keeps me going."[1]

Finally, in item III the interviewer rated the patient on a scale from 0 to 10 based on their overall assessment of the extent to which the patient relied on religion to cope. This latter judgement was based on further spontaneous elaboration by the patient concerning their use of and dependence on religion. Discussion was initiated by asking other related questions on this topic (i.e., how religion was helpful, how long it had been so, and so forth). The scores from these three items were then summed to create an index ranging from 0 to 30. The reliability of this index was demonstrated in a sample of 188 consecutively admitted men in whom the RCI was administered by two separate raters approximately 24 hours apart; the correlation between scores obtained by the two raters was acceptable (0.81). Other questions asked about religious coping were the following:

---

1. An alternative method of scaling the visual analogue scale is to use a range from 0 (not much or not at all important) to 100 (the most important things that keep me going); if this is done, then the score will need to be divided by 10 before combining it with the other two items in the RCI (to ensure equal weight per item). This was the method used in the DVAMHS.

FIGURE 9.1. Religious Coping Index

Item I. Spontaneous Religious Coping (Unelicited)

How do you manage to cope with your situation? In other words, how do you keep yourself from getting depressed, sad, or discouraged, despite your physical illness and disability?

[Spontaneous response scored as 0 for non-religious or 10 for religious]

Item II. Self-Rated Religious Coping

Do your religious beliefs or activities help you at all to cope with or handle your situation? [lead-in question]

Here is a scale ranging from 0 to 10 (showing them the scale), where 0 indicates that religion is not at all helpful and 10 indicates that it is the most important thing that keeps you going. Please mark on this scale the extent to which your religious beliefs or activities help you to cope with or handle your situation?

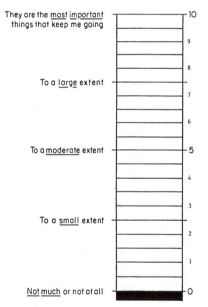

Item III. Observer-Rated Religiosity

Based upon additional comments made by subject to above questions and questions exploring how religion has been a help to them, rate on a scale from 0 to 10 the extent to which the person uses their religious belief or activity to help them to cope with their situation.

Add scores for items I–III to obtain score for RCI that ranges from 0 to 30

1. How many years have you used religion to cope?
2. How does religion help you to cope?
3. Have you ever experienced a distinct change in your feelings about religion that resulted in either a strengthening or a weakening of your religious faith?
4. If yes, how old were you then?
5. Can you describe what that was like? (positive or negative change, and what were the circumstances)
6. As you have grown older, has religion become more important, less important, or stayed the same?*
7. Were your parents religious people?*
8. Who was more religious, your mother or your father? (other caretaker?)*

(* asked only of men under age 40 or over age 70)

Statistical analysis was performed using Pearson correlations, T-tests, and analysis of variance for continuous data; for categorical data, the likelihood-ratio chi-square statistic was used. Cross-sectional correlates of religious coping (RCI) were examined using a general linear regression model; variables were eliminated from the model using a backward technique. Longitudinal predictors of religious coping (Time2 RCI score) were examined using residualized change analysis, where baseline religious coping (Time1 RCI score) was added to the model first and then other variables thereafter; again a backward variable elimination technique was used.

Findings

Here I will summarize the findings for the entire sample of younger and older patients (n = 1011).[2] More than 42 different religious denominations, all based in the Judeo-Christian tradition, were represented in the sample. Denominations were categorized into nine general religious groupings based on a schema provided by Roof and McKinney (1987) (See Table 9.1). There were a disproportion-

---

2. We have already reported elsewhere findings for older patients (n = 850) and the reader is referred to that source for more detailed information specifically for elderly men (Koenig et al. 1992).

TABLE 9.1. Distribution of religious affiliations in the sample compared with their distribution in the United States.

Religious Group	Sample	USA
Liberal Protestants (Episcopal, United Ch of Christ, Presbyter)	7.1%	8.7%
Moderate Protestants (Methodists, Lutherans, Discip of Christ, Reform)	11.9%	19.9%
Conservative Protestants (White Baptists, Ch of Christ, Nazaren, 7th Day Adv)	37.9%	11.3%
Black Protestants (Methodists, Baptists)	25.0%	5.8%
Fundamentalist/Evangel (Pentecostals, Holiness, Assemblies, Ch of God)	5.5%	4.5%
Protestant (unspecified)	2.9%	–
Catholics	2.8%	25.0%
Jews	0%	2.3%
Miscellaneous (Mormons, Jeh Witn, Chr Scien, Unitarian)	3.3%	8.0%
No Religious Preference	3.6%	6.9%

TABLE ADAPTED FROM Koenig et al (1992). Used with permission.

ate number of men from conservative White protestant (38% vs. 11%) and Black protestant (25% vs. 6%) denominations in the sample compared with the United States as a whole.

Religious coping was spontaneously mentioned by 20% of young men, 17% of the young elderly (age 65 to 69), and 24% of men age 70 and over. Self-rated religious coping ranged from 0 to 10, with a mean score of 6.4 for the overall sample; 56% rated themselves 7.5 or higher and 20% rated themselves 10 at the top of the scale. Men over age 70 were more likely (24%) than either the young elderly (18%) or the young (15%) to rate themselves at 10. Mean observer-rated religious coping for the entire sample ranged from 0 to 10 with a mean of 5.6; again, lowest mean ratings were among young men (4.8). Scores for the RCI ranged from 0 to 30 with an overall mean for the sample of 14; scores differed by age group: 12.3 in the young, 14.0 in men aged 65 to 69, and 14.5 in those aged 70 years or over. Degree of religious coping was highest among fundamentalist/ evangelicals, Black protestants, and those from nontraditional Christian groups. It was lowest among Catholics, liberal protestants, and those affiliated with no religious denomination.

Responses to questions about religion and its use in coping were as follows. How long had religion been used in coping? Ten percent of the overall sample reported that they had found religion helpful only within the past five years, especially younger men (31%). Almost half of participants (46%) noted that religion had been used in coping throughout their lives (35% of the young, 52% of those over age 70). Religious coping was strongest in those reporting its use in the past 10 to 25 years (RCI score = 18.1) and lowest among those finding religion helpful only within the past five years (RCI = 14.5) (p < .01).

How many patients experienced a distinct change in feelings about religion at some time in their lives? Thirty-six percent of the sample said that they had, with the overwhelming majority (84%) of this group reporting experiences that strengthened their faith. Younger men were more likely than older men to report a distinct change in faith (54% vs. 33%). The age at which such experiences occurred differed between younger and older men. Among the younger men, the mean age at occurrence was 26 years (range 6 to 39); for men aged 65 to 69, it was 46 years (range 9 to 68); and for men over age 70, it was 40 years (range 5 to 82). Among men over 65 with such an experience, 14% reported that it occurred after the age of 65 and 42% after the age of 50.

Religious coping was strongest in men who reported a distinct change in their feelings about religion, compared to those not experiencing such a change (RCI = 18.9 vs. 13.3, p < .01); among men reporting a change, religious coping was strongest for those experiencing the change between the ages of 40 and 64 (RCI = 20.2) and lowest in those reporting the change before age 21 (RCI = 17.1).

To what extent had the importance of religion in men's lives increased, decreased, or stayed the same with aging? The majority (60%) reported that religion's importance had increased with aging, while 35% said it had stayed the same and 5% said it had decreased. Age of respondent had little effect on these proportions (in the young, 54% increased, 40% remained the same, 6% decreased). Current religious coping was highest among those for whom religion had increased (RCI = 18.1 for increased, 8.7 for stayed the same, 4.9 for decreased, p < .01). Of interest is that depression scores were lower among those reporting an increase in religion's importance with aging, compared with those indicating a decrease (Hamilton Depression Score = 8 vs. 14, p < .01; Geriatric Depression Score 7 vs. 12, p < .01).

To what extent did religiosity of parents affect whether or not men used religion to cope? The distribution of parental religiosity for the sample was as follows: only mother religious (25%), only father religious (2%), both parents equally religious (38%), both parents equal but mother more than father (15%), both parents equal but father more than mother (5%), neither parent religious (14%), only grandparent religious (2%). Overall, current religious coping was strongest among men reporting that both parents were equally religious (RCI = 16.3) and weakest among those reporting neither parent so (RCI = 11.0, p < .05).

Among men under 40, those reporting only their father as being religious or neither parent religious achieved the lowest RCI scores. In contrast, religiosity of the father was a more important influence on current religious coping among men age 70 or over. Those reporting only their father religious or both parents equally religious achieved the highest scores on current religious coping, whereas those reporting only their mother religious or neither parent religious scored the lowest. These differences were statistically significant only among older men.

Health characteristics of patients also impacted on the likelihood of their using religion to cope. Using the American Society of Anesthesiologists' (1963) severity of illness scale (ASA), we rated patients' medical illness severity from 1 to 5 (1 indicating healthy, 5 indicating extreme sickness). Among those who were rated as normal and healthy (ASA = 1), religious coping was the lowest (RCI = 11.5); among those with severe, systemic life-threatening disease (ASA = 4 or 5), religious coping was the highest (RCI = 16.3, p < .05). Functional status of patients was also examined, using activities of daily living (ADLs) as a measure (range 0 to 17). Again those with the most severe impairments in function (ADL score 0-4) were the strongest religious copers (RCI = 16.0).

We next examined the sociodemographic and health correlates of religious coping controlling for the effects of other variables using regression analysis (Table 9.2). Eliminated from the model because of lack of relationship were education, income, employment and occupational status, family history of psychiatric problems, type of medical diagnosis, and six religious groups. Religious coping was more common among older men, Blacks, married men, those living alone, those reporting a higher level of social support, those who were more disabled or severely ill, those with better cognitive function, abstainers from alcohol, those with a history of psychiatric problems, and those with lower depression scores. After controlling for the effects of other variables in the model, religious coping remained strongest in men from fundamentalist or evangelical religious traditions and weakest in those with no religious affiliation. Two interactions were significant in the model. Younger patients who lived alone were more likely to employ religious coping than older persons who lived alone (age by living situation interaction), and patients (all ages) with low social support and poor health status were more likely to use religion to cope (functional status by social support interaction). No specific medical diagnosis was more likely than another to be associated with religious coping.

TABLE 9.2. Sociodemographic and health correlates of religious coping

Variable	b (SE)	p
Age	+0.05 (.02)	<.05
Race (Black)	+3.77 (.59)	<.0001
Marital Status (Married)	+1.43 (.71)	<.05
Living Situation (Alone)	+2.01 (.86)	<.01
Social Support	+0.38 (.16)	<.05
Functional Status (ADLs)	−0.17 (.08)	<.05
Mini-Mental State Exam	+0.30 (.11)	<.01
Alcohol Use	−3.03 (.64)	<.0001
History of Psychiatric Problems	+2.11 (.61)	<.001
Geriatric Depression Scale	−0.24 (.05)	<.0001
No Religious Denomination	−6.73 (1.41)	<.0001
Fundamentalists/Evangelicals	+6.54 (1.12)	<.0001
Age X Living Situation	−5.45 (2.02)	<.01
Functional Status X Social Support	−0.13 (.07)	<.05
Model F R-Square N in Model (% of Sample)	14.4 .17 978 (97%)	<.0001

Changes in Religious Coping

Changes in religious coping over time were examined in men readmitted to the hospital during the 21-month study period. There was virtually no change in "mean" religious coping (RCI score) for the sample as a whole (Table 9.3). For individual patients, however, large changes were observed (−25 to +28) (Figure 9.2). Twenty-five percent of the sample increased by five points or more, 25% decreased by 5 points or more, and 50% changed between +5 and −5 points. Younger men as a group tended to increase in their religious coping over time more than did older men (75% vs. 50% with positive changes); again, however, the overall mean change was small. Little mean change over time was also seen for health variables such as functional status, cognitive status, and depressive symptoms; again, however, changes were marked in individual cases. Functional status showed a slight overall decline from baseline to follow up; understandably, the latter trend was particularly notable in men age 65 or over. Note also that one-third of the sample had progressive cancer.

Using a regression model (residualized change analysis), predictors of religious coping on follow up were examined (Table 9.4). A positive beta (b) coefficient indicates that a variable predicts increasing religious coping over time, whereas a negative coefficient indicates decreasing religious coping over time. The strongest positive predictor of readmission religious coping score was baseline religious coping (Time1 RCI). In other words, if patients were strong religious copers at baseline, they were more likely to use religion for this same purpose on readmission several months later; likewise, those who did not use religion at baseline, were unlikely (on the whole) to use it at follow up. However, as time interval between baseline admission and follow up increased, the likelihood of patients' using religion to cope also increased. Social support and changing physical and mental function also had an impact on religious coping. Men with high baseline social support were more likely to use religious coping at follow up, even after baseline religious coping was accounted for. As functional status improved, there was a nonsignificant trend for patients to decrease their use of religious coping.

Finally, and perhaps most interesting, is that as *cognitive* status improved, religious coping increased; conversely, as cognitive function declined, religious coping also decreased. This finding further supports the significance of the positive relationship between cognitive functioning and religious coping at baseline for the overall sample. It suggests that as cognitive impairment increases, patients become less able to use religion as a coping behavior.

TABLE 9.3. Changes in religious coping and other health variables over time (6 months average)

Variable	Baseline mean (SD)	Followup mean (SD)	Change mean (SD)	Change (range)
		OVERALL (n = 92)		
Religious Coping Index (0-30)	14.9 (8.7)	15.7 (8.8)	+0.7 (8.9)	(−25 to +28)
Spontaneous Relig Coping (0-100%)	26.7%	29.3%	+1.6%	NA
Self-Rated Relig Coping (0-100)	65.4 (30.0)	68.6 (30.0)	+3.4 (25.9)	(−75 to +90)
Observer-Rated Relig Coping (0-10)	5.7 (3.0)	6.0 (3.1)	+0.4 (2.6)	(−8 to +8)
Functional Status (ADLs) (0-17)	14.4 (3.6)	12.6 (5.0)	−1.8 (4.2)	(−15 to +13)
Cognitive Status (MMSE) (0-30)	26.8 (2.7)	26.2 (2.5)	−0.6 (2.8)	(−8 to +12)
Depression (GDS + BCDRS) (0-42)	11.5 (7.6)	12.5 (7.5)	+1.0 (6.3)	(−17 to +22)
		MEN UNDER AGE 40 (n = 12)		
Religious Coping Index	14.8 (8.6)	17.3 (10.2)	+2.5 (7.0)	(−15 to +14)
Spontaneous Religious Coping	16.7%	33.3%	+16.7%	NA
Self-Related Religious Coping	71.7 (29.2)	72.5 (33.3)	+0.8 (26.9)	(−75 to +30)

172

	Baseline	Follow-up	Change	Range
Observer-Rated Religious Coping	5.9 (3.1)	6.7 (3.7)	+0.8 (2.9)	(–7 to +4)
Functional Status	16.3 (1.2)	15.7 (1.8)	–0.7 (2.2)	(–5 to +4)
Cognitive Status	29.0 (1.4)	28.2 (1.6)	–0.9 (2.1)	(–3 to +4)
Depression	15.4 (8.3)	15.4 (10.8)	0 (–)	(–13 to +14)
MEN AGE 65 OR OVER (n = 180)				
Religious Coping Index	14.9 (8.7)	15.6 (8.7)	+0.6 (9.0)	(–25 to +28)
Spontaneous Religious Coping	27.4%	29.1%	+0.6%	NA
Self-Rated Religious Coping	65.0 (3.0)	68.4 (3.0)	+3.5 (25.9)	(–70 to +90)
Observer-Rated Religious Coping	5.7 (3.0)	6.0 (3.1)	+0.4 (2.6)	(–8 to +8)
Functional Status	14.3 (3.7)	12.4 (5.0)	–1.9 (4.3)	(–15 to +13)
Cognitive Status	26.7 (2.7)	26.0 (2.5)	–0.6 (2.9)	(–8 to +12)
Depression	11.2 (7.5)	12.3 (7.3)	+1.1 (6.3)	(–17 to +22)

*Includes patients upon whom religious coping data available at both baseline and followup

FIGURE 9.2. Change in religious coping over time for individual patients.

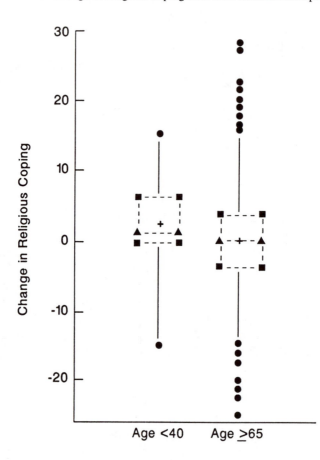

Discussion

These results from the DVAMHS indicate a high prevalence for religious coping among both younger and older hospitalized men. One out of five men spontaneously reported that religion was the most important factor that enabled them to cope with their situation. This was especially true for men age 70 or over, of whom nearly a quarter (24%) gave a religious response to the open-ended coping question (i.e., "what enables you to cope?"). When asked directly

TABLE 9.4. Predictors of change in religious coping

Variable	b (SE)	p value
Baseline Religious Coping	+.45 (.07)	<.0001
Baseline Social Support	+.62 (.32)	<.06
Time to Readmission	+.25 (.13)	.05
Improving Cognition (Time2 MMSE minus Time1 MMSE)	+.48 (.22)	.02
Improving Physical Function (Time 2 ADL minus Time1 ADL)	−.14 (.15)	ns
Model F	12.3	<.0001
R-Square	.27	
N in Model	174	

A positive value for "b" indicates a predictor of increased religious coping.

Age, psychiatric history, medical diagnoses, baseline cognitive function (Time 1 MMSE) depression status (Time1), functional status (Time 1 ADL), and change in depression status (Time2-Time1) were unrelated to Time2 religious coping (RCI) after controlling for Time 1 religious coping.

to what extent religious belief or behavior was helpful, over half of respondents (young and old) marked a 7.5 or higher on a visual analogue scale ranging from 0 to 10. Regardless of how religious coping was measured, however, older men were more likely to use it than younger men. These findings are consistent with an earlier report by our group on 100 community-dwelling elders from the Duke Longitudinal Study, where about a third of men and almost two-thirds of women mentioned religion as a coping behavior when questioned in open-ended interviews (Koenig, George, and Siegler 1988b). Given these sex differences, future studies of hospitalized elders including women are likely to yield even higher rates of religious coping than were reported for this all male sample.

Conservative protestants (mostly Baptists) were overrepresented in our sample compared with the country as a whole; this fact may have affected religious coping rates. Nevertheless, other studies have also documented high rates of religious coping among elders in different locations both in and outside the United States–Los Angeles (Nelson 1977), Kansas City (Conway 1985), Rhode Island (Manfredi and Pickett 1987), Athens, Georgia (Rosen 1982), New Orleans (Swanson and Harter 1971), Springfield, Illinois (Koenig, Moberg, and Kvale 1988a), Chicago (Pressman et al. 1990), New Haven, Connecticut (Idler 1987; Idler and Kasl 1991), Washington, DC (O'Brien 1982), and Scotland (Reid et al. 1978). National surveys of older adults have likewise indicated a high prevalence of religious coping in this population (Princeton Religion Research Center 1982; Americana Healthcare Corporation 1980-1981).

Professionals working with hospitalized elders should be aware of the function and value of religious behaviors in this setting. The strongest predictors of physicians' belief in the appropriateness of addressing religious concerns of older patients during severe illness was the physician's understanding of the importance of religion in their patients' lives (Koenig, Beearon, and Dayringer 1989). Ensuring easy access to pastoral counseling, providing the opportunity for religious ritual if desired, and allowing patients to voice concerns or conflicts in this area are interventions by health care providers which may enhance the coping of religious patients.

Details About Religious Coping

Younger men were more likely than elders to find religion helpful only recently (within the last five years). This may relate to the more recent onset of health problems in young patients. On the other hand, the decade of the 20s or 30s may be a time of growing interest in religion as young adults face the responsibilities of child-rearing or seek a source of meaning in life (*Newsweek* 1990). It is of interest that religious coping was strongest among patients who had used religion to cope for an intermediate period (10 to 25 years), rather than those reporting either recent or lifelong use. Men who had just recently turned to religion may not have had sufficient time to integrate it effectively as a coping behavior. After repeated use, religious coping may increase in its capacity for stress reduction. On the other hand, some men reporting religion's usefulness "all my life" gave this response in a haphazard way, when in actuality religion had not been used to cope with any specific problem. Those reporting religion helpful for 10 to 25 years often referred to a specific incident in the past where religion had been helpful.

Over one-third of the sample (36%) indicated an experience in their lives that significantly changed their feelings about religion. Most of these experiences strengthened religious faith and, in fact, were "conversions." These religious experiences were typically recalled and described in great detail and with great fervor, even by those with considerable cognitive impairment. Both younger and older men were more likely to have these experiences after the age of 21 (73% and 78%, respectively). The age range for such experiences was wide, with some elders reporting the change occurred as early as age 5 and others as late as age 82. In fact, more than four of every ten men over age 65 reported marked changes in their feelings about religion after they had turned age 50. Thus, it appears that older age is not a deterrent to having life-changing religious experience. Chapter 19 will address this issue in greater depth.

The impact of having a life-changing religious experience, regardless of age, was reflected in the current level of religious coping. Men who reported such changes scored significantly higher on religious coping than did those who had not. Thus, having a religious experience appears to have had a notable impact on current coping behavior. Among patients with such an experience, those who had it in mid-life were stronger religious copers than those who reported the change before the age of 21. This suggests that having a religious experience during the adult years is more likely to have an enduring effect on coping behavior than if such experiences occur in childhood or adolescence (see Chapter 7).

What effect does growing older have on the salience of religion and the likelihood of its use as a coping behavior? As noted earlier, the question of whether people become more religious as they age has been hotly debated. Some argue that older people are more religious because they have always been more so (period effect); others contend that persons are more likely to turn to religion as they grow older (developmental phenomenon). Most of these discussions, however, are based on speculation and opinion rather than on hard, objective fact. The DVAMHS has provided some facts. The majority of patients in our sample, especially the elderly, reported that religion had increased in importance as they had grown older (especially among strong religious copers). Only a small percentage said that it had decreased in importance (5%). When asked why religion's importance had increased with age, some reported that physical illness, declining health, and a realization of approaching death were important factors; the majority, however, gave a wide variety of other reasons. Whatever the grounds, those who reported an increase in religion's importance were significantly less likely to be depressed, indicating better adjustment and more effective coping. These self-report data, then, suggest that religion increases in importance with age. Increasing knowledge of and experience with the world (through exposure to different people, ideas, and problems) that occurs with aging and living may enhance the meaning and value of religion.

A mass turning to religion in response to sickness and even in the face of imminent death, however, was not observed. When religious copers were asked how religion helped them to cope, many noted that religious behaviors such as prayer or Bible reading had helped them many times in the past. In fact, only a few men who had not previously found religion helpful reported that they suddenly begin relying on these behaviors at the time of their current illness. Many men used coping behaviors other than religion to deal with their health problems, such as staying busy, keeping their minds occupied, or getting involved in social activities with friends or family. Hence, the stress of physical illness and hospitalization for the majority of patients resulted in a mobilization of previously learned coping behaviors, rather than religious behaviors in particular.

For younger men, in comparison, this was a time of more active change in feelings about religion. They were more likely to report religion to be helpful only within the past five years (31% vs. 6% for older men). Men under 40 years old also showed the largest mean increase in religious coping over time during the follow up period. These observations are consistent with national data on age of religious change collected by the Gallup organization, which indicated the age when religious faith changed most was between ages 25 and 35 years (Princeton Religion Research Center 1987a). Thus, the establishment of religious coping behaviors in young and mid-adulthood may be an important factor determining whether religion will be used to cope with stresses encountered later in life. Nevertheless, as we have seen, changes in feelings about religion frequently do occur in later life and coping behaviors at that time often reflect such changes.

What effect does parental religiosity have on the use of religion to cope during times of ill health and acute hospitalization? Not surprisingly, patients were more likely to do so if religion had been important to both parents, and were least likely to do so if religion had been important to neither parent. When looking at younger and older patients separately, however, an interesting pattern arose. For younger men, the religious orientation of their mother was more important; for older men, religiosity of the father was more influential. Why was this so? Perhaps during the time period when older men were raised (1915-1935), men in society took a greater leadership role in children's religious training than they do today. Over the past 50 to 75 years, changes in society may have resulted in women taking on greater leadership in this regard. The fact that women are more religiously oriented than men has been demonstrated repeatedly in recent times (Princeton Religion Research Center 1976; 1982; 1985; 1987b). Clearly, more systematic research is needed on the impact that childhood exposure to and training in religion has on current coping behaviors.

A PROFILE OF THE RELIGIOUS COPER

Our cross-sectional data provide a profile for the male religious coper. He is more likely to be elderly, Black, married, living alone (especially if younger), more disabled or severely ill (especially if lacking adequate social support), and more likely to have a history of psychiatric problems. Despite this, however, he is also less likely to be depressed, cognitively impaired, an alcohol user, or to report low social support. I will discuss each of these characteristics now.

Race was a significant determinant of religious coping. Again, national surveys of community-dwelling adults by the Gallup organization indicate a high prevalence of religious behaviors in Blacks compared with Whites. Religious coping studies have likewise reported these behaviors to be particularly common in the Black elderly (Swanson and Harter 1971; Rosen 1982; Conway 1985). Cultural influences and socioeconomic factors may partly explain this pattern. Religion has always been more common among persons under the greatest stress in society–the lower classes, the poor, and members of minority groups (women, Blacks, the elderly). Greater religiosity among Blacks, then, is not surprising. In America, the church is a powerful social and cultural force in this racial group today (Taylor and Chatters 1988; Taylor 1986).

Health factors also impacted on the likelihood and strength of religious coping. Men who were physically disabled or experiencing severe medical illness were more likely to use religion to cope. As physical health declines, control over one's life also decreases. Not only must sick and disabled persons depend on others for their self-care needs, they are also more likely to be unemployed and have medical bills that deplete family resources. The distress this entails arouses a sense of helplessness and loss of control. It may be easier for such persons to give up control over their lives (which they are losing control of anyway) and depend more on God for their emotional needs. In some circumstances, religion may be the only realistic hope that such persons have. Blatt (1985) has reviewed the powerful accomplishments by disabled people of strong religious faith who had only modest technical tools at their disposal.

Besides poorer health, religious copers had other characteristics suggesting exposure to increased social and emotional stresses. Men who scored higher on religious coping were more likely to be living alone and were more likely to have a past history of psychiatric problems. Religion, then, appeared to be especially valuable as a coping resource for those who were elderly, sick, living alone, or had a history of psychological problems–a group at high risk for emotional problems. Despite this, however, religious copers were more likely to be married, to report high social support, to be less depressed, less cognitively impaired, and less likely to use alcohol.

Judeo-Christian teachings strongly emphasize the importance of family, strongly denounce divorce or separation, and provide guidelines for the relationship between husband and wife which may

facilitate healthy marital functioning. Likewise, strong social relationships outside the home are encouraged by religious teachings
and may consequently enhance the individual's social support network (even if living alone). Furthermore, religious organizations
provide a ready source of age-matched peers who have a common
interest and common history (Tobin, Ellor, and Anderson-Ray
1986). Indeed, religious coping mentioned by patients often involved support from church members or pastors. Numerous studies
have now documented the extraordinary amount of informal support which older adults receive from other church members (Taylor
and Chatters 1986; Koenig, Moberg, and Kvale 1988a). One study
of geriatric clinic outpatients found that half of 106 consecutively
evaluated patients reported that 80 to 100 percent of their closest
friends came from their church congregation (Koenig, Moberg, and
Kvale 1988a).

The inverse relationships between religious coping and depression, cognitive status, and alcohol use (documented in the cross-
sectional phase of our study), are important findings that will be
discussed at length in later chapters. Although it is difficult to
determine the direction of causation from cross-sectional data, this
constellation of findings suggests that those who use religion to
cope–despite their often dismal circumstances–appear to be aging
quite successfully. However, the associations here may also indicate
an adverse effect of these conditions (depression, cognitive impairment, alcohol use) on the capacity to use religion as a coping behavior. Clearly, the issues are complex and require further analysis.

CHANGES OVER TIME

Longitudinal data may help us to better understand the dynamics
of religious change (or lack it) over time. Using a statistical method
called residualized change analysis, we examined the ability of
baseline sociodemographic and health factors to predict changes in
religious coping from one hospital admission to another. A distinct
pattern emerged.

In general, persons who had found religion helpful at their initial
evaluation were more likely to find it helpful on subsequent admission; alternatively, those who did not find religion helpful during

the initial visit were unlikely to find it helpful on future visits. This finding, at least on the surface, reflects a general pattern of stability in religious coping over the short run (six months). Support for the "stability hypothesis" also comes from a 6-year longitudinal study of change in church attendance after retirement. Glamser (1988) found little net change in religious activity for the sample as a whole. On detailed analysis, however, he found that those who attended church frequently during young and middle adulthood showed further increases in attendance after retirement, whereas those who attended church infrequently during their earlier years showed even greater declines after retirement (perhaps as normative pressures on attendance relaxed). The correlation between belief and attendance also strengthened after retirement. Glamser's findings, then, suggest a stability for religious interest over time (and perhaps some divergence).

The stability hypothesis, however, can be challenged. In the DVAMHS, religious coping on initial evaluation (Time1) accounted for less than a quarter of the variance in religious coping on readmission (Time2), indicating that other unknown factors were important and influential in this regard. Similarly, while we found little *mean* change in religious coping for the sample as a whole, wide changes did occur in individual cases–some men turning completely away from religion and others dramatically turning towards it (see Chapter 10). Changes in religious coping during medical illness, then, are heavily dependent on the individual's unique personality characteristics and situation. Wide generalizations about change in religious coping (such as stability or instability) should be made cautiously.

Besides baseline religious coping, other predictors of Time2 religious coping were level of social support, time to follow up, and change in cognitive status. Patients reporting a high level of social support on initial exam were more likely to report religious coping on follow up. Because social support may have been due in part to participation in religious groups, it is understandable that such involvement might reinforce religious coping behaviors over time. A greater time interval between initial and follow up evaluations was also a significant predictor of religious coping, suggesting that duration of illness may be an important factor in whether or not a person with health problems turns to religion for comfort. Although the relationship was weak and statistically nonsignificant, declining physical functioning did tend to predict increases in religious coping.

An interesting and most important discovery was that declining cognitive function was associated with a decrease in religious coping. This suggests that cognitive dysfunction may impair the ability to use religion as a coping behavior (or at least impair ability to communicate religion's usefulness). This is consistent with the cross-sectional finding of an inverse relationship between religious coping and cognitive status. These observations underscore the truth of comments made by James Davis (1989), a minister with Alzheimer's disease, who described the often disturbing effects that this illness had on his relationship with God ("I do not feel the Father's presence"). This topic will be discussed at length in Chapter 16.

OTHER STUDIES OF CHANGE

There are only a few longitudinal studies of religious coping in medical patients that have objectively measured change over time. O'Brien interviewed 126 chronic hemodialysis patients on this subject and re-interviewed half of the sample three years later (men composed half of those re-interviewed) (O'Brien 1982). Twenty-seven percent of the patients located for follow up three years later reported that their dependence on religion had significantly increased. Half of these patients noted that religion had changed from having no influence to having a strongly positive one; only 2% changed from a positive to a negative perception. Mean age of her sample was 45 years. Croog and Levine (1972) examined social and psychological factors in recovery from myocardial infarction. They interviewed 324 men (ages 30 to 60 years) two months after the event and then one year thereafter. Self-rated importance of religion increased in 22% and decreased in 16%; 9.3% reported a change in their feelings about religion, virtually all indicating an increase in strength of belief. Note that in our six-month follow up study, religious coping score either increased or decreased by five or more points in 50% of patients. These studies, then, indicate that a significant proportion of patients with health problems experience changes in faith during physical illness, the majority of which are positive.

SUMMARY

This chapter provides detailed information on religious coping in an all-male sample of hospitalized patients. These data were collected systematically in a sample of over a thousand consecutively admitted men, most of whom were over age 65. When asked to rate on a 0 to 10 scale the extent to which religion was helpful to them, 56% noted 7.5 or above and 20% reported that it was the most important factor that enable them to cope with their situation.

Identifying patients who find religion helpful in dealing with illness is important for clinicians who play a role in controlling access to resources that may facilitate such coping behaviors. Religious coping was more common among older men, Black men, those with severe medical illness, functional disability, or a history of previous psychiatric problems, and those who lived alone. Despite being at risk for emotional problems because of these latter characteristics, religious copers were actually less likely to be depressed, cognitively impaired, users of alcohol, and claimed high social support. These findings underscore the role that religion can play in facilitating successful aging.

Also presented here are data on the dynamics of religious change. One-third of patients reported experiencing a change in their feelings about religion at some time in their lives; a small but significant proportion of these experiences were related to physical health problems. Changes in faith were often associated with the cessation of chronic alcohol abuse. Experiences of religious change occurred throughout the life cycle, but most often in young adulthood and mid-life; among older men, however, over 40% experienced such changes after the age of 50. The majority of men indicated that religion had increased in importance to them as they had aged.

Predictors of religious change over time were also examined. Prior religious coping, high social support, time elapsed since last evaluation, and unimpaired cognitive status all predicted high levels of religious coping on follow up for the sample as a whole. While there was little mean change in religious coping during an average six-month follow up period, marked fluctuations were observed in individual cases. Younger men were more likely than older men to experience change in religious coping during the follow up period, and were more likely to report only recently finding religion helpful.

Many questions remain with unclear answers. It is not known whether religious behaviors in the medical setting are a response to the emotional stress induced by physical illness and hospitalization, whether they are a nonspecific general expression of religiosity, or both. How frequently do men who have never been religious turn to religion when faced with debilitating or life-threatening illness? Among those who do turn to religion for comfort, is this a recent new behavior in response to illness or is it a reflection of a lifelong pattern of coping developed earlier in life? What influence does age have on changes in religious coping during illness? Are individuals who have not used religion as a coping behavior in their earlier years less able to utilize it as a resource in later life? Do the answers to any of these questions differ for women? More longitudinal studies are needed to answer such questions. In the next chapter, we will explore the personal accounts of younger and older religious copers as they describe how religion seems to help.

REFERENCES

Americana Healthcare Corporation. (1980-81). *Aging in America.* Westport, CT: US-Research and Forecasts Survey Sampling Corporation.

American Society of Anesthesiologists. (1963). New classification of physical status. *Anesthesiology* 24:191-198.

Baldree, K.S., S.P. Murphy, and M. Powers. (1982). Stress identification and coping patterns in patients on hemodialysis. *Nursing Research* 31:107-112.

Blatt, B. (1985). Faith, science, and disability. *Journal of Learning Disabilities.* 18(2):122-123.

Conway, K. (1985). Coping with the stress of medical problems among black and white elderly. *International Journal of Aging and Human Development* 21:39-48.

Croog, S.H., and S. Levine. (1972). Religious identity and response to serious illness: A report on heart patients. *Social Sciences and Medicine* 6:17-32.

Davis, R. (1989). *My Journey into Alzheimer's Disease.* Wheaton, IL: Tyndale House.

Glamser, F.D. (1988). The impact of retirement upon religiosity. *Journal of Religion & Aging* 5(1):27-37.

Idler, E.L. (1987). Religious involvement and health of the elderly: Some hypotheses and an initial test. *Social Forces* 66:226-238.

Idler, E.L., and S.V. Kasl. (1992). Religion, disability, depression, and the timing of death. *American Journal of Sociology* 97:1052-1079.

Koenig, H.G., L.B. Bearon, and R. Dayringer. (1989). Physician perspectives on the role of religion in the physician-older patient relationship. *Journal of Family Practice* 28:441-448.

Koenig, H.G., L.K. George, and I.C. Siegler. (1988b). The use of religion and other emotion-regulating coping strategies among older adults. *The Gerontologist* 28:303-310.

Koenig, H.G., D.O. Moberg, and J.N. Kvale. (1988a). Religious and health characteristics of patients attending a geriatric assessment clinic. *Journal of the American Geriatrics Society* 36:362-374.

Koenig, H.G., H.J. Cohen, D.G. Blazer, C. Pieper, K.G. Meador, F. Shelp, V. Goli, and R. DiPasquale. (1992). Religious coping and depression in hospitalized elderly medically ill men. *American Journal of Psychiatry* 149:1693-1700.

Manfredi, C., and M. Pickett. (1987). Perceived stressful situations and coping strategies utilized by the elderly. *Journal of Community Health Nursing* 4(2):99-110.

Nelson, F.L. (1977). Religiosity and self-destructive crises in the institutionalized elderly. *Suicide and Life-threatening Behavior* 7(2):67-73.

Newsweek (1990). A time to seek. (December 17):50-56.

O'Brien, M.E. (1982). Religious faith and adjustment to long-term hemodialysis. *Journal of Religion & Health* 21:68-80.

Pressman, P., J.S. Lyons, D.B. Larson, and J.J. Strain. (1990). Religious belief, depression, and ambulation status in elderly women with broken hips. *American Journal of Psychiatry* 147:758-760.

Princeton Religion Research Center. (1976). *Religion in America.* Princeton, NJ: The Gallup Poll.

_____ (1982). *Religion in America.* Princeton, NJ: The Gallup Poll.

_____ (1985). *Religion in America.* Princeton, NJ: The Gallup Poll.

_____ (1987a). *Faith Development and Your Ministry.* Princeton, NJ: Gallup Poll, p. 21.

_____ (1987b). *Religion in America* (report no. 259). Princeton, NJ: Gallup Poll.

Reid, W.S., A.J.J. Gilmore, G.R. Andrews, and F.I. Caird. (1978). A study of religious attitudes of the elderly. *Age and Aging* 7:40-45.

Roof, W.C., and W.M. McKinney. (1987). *American Mainline Religion.* New Brunswick: Rutgers University Press, pp. 253-256.

Rosen, C.C. (1982). Ethnic differences among impoverished rural elderly in use of religion as a coping mechanism. *Journal of Rural & Community Psychology* 3:27-34.

Swanson, W.C., and C.L. Harter. (1971). How do elderly blacks cope in New Orleans? *International Journal of Aging & Human Development* 2:210-216.

Taylor, R.J. (1986). Religious participation among elderly blacks. *The Gerontologist* 26:630-635.

Taylor, R.J., and L.M. Chatters. (1988). Church members as a source of informal social support. *Review of Religious Research* 30(2):193-203.

Tobin, S.S., J. Ellor, and S.M. Anderson-Ray. (1986). *Enabling the Elderly: Religious Institutions Within the Community Service System.* Albany: State University of New York Press.

Chapter 10

Cases of Religious Coping in Action

Do not be surprised at the sight of simple people who believe without argument. God makes them love him and hate themselves. He inclines their hearts to believe. We shall never believe with a vigorous and unquestioning faith unless God touches our hearts; and we shall believe as soon as he does.

–Blaise Pascal

In this chapter, cases are presented which illustrate the meaning of religious coping to men involved in the Durham VA Mental Health Survey. I have included here direct quotes from patients as they responded both spontaneously and to direct questioning about their use of religion in coping with the stresses of illness and hospitalization. The cases presented here were systematically selected using a previously defined set of criteria.

In order to be included as a case below, participants had to score a maximum 30 points on the Religious Coping Index during their baseline evaluation. Thus, each had to meet three strict criteria: (1) the patient had to spontaneously (Sp) give a religious response when asked the open-ended question "What keeps you going or enables you to cope?", (2) he had to rate himself at "10" on a visual analogue scale when asked how much religious belief or activity had helped him to cope (where 0 indicated "very little or not at all" and 10 indicated "the most important thing that keeps me going"), and (3) interviewers had to rate the patient a "10" on a 0 to 10 scale, where 0 indicated the patient did not use religion as a coping behavior and 10 indicated heavy reliance on religion for this purpose. The latter rating was based on an overall assessment of both spontaneous and elicited religious responses during the interview; patients were asked a number of questions including how long religion had been helpful, in what way it was helpful, and, if they had any religious experiences in this regard, to describe them. Note that inter-rater reliability for this last item was very high (r = .87) and is particularly notable given that raters themselves came from widely disparate religious backgrounds.

Of the 1011 men evaluated during the DVAMHS, 8.1% (13/161) of younger men (age 20 to 40 years) and 8.1% (69/850) of older men (age 65 to 102 years) met all three criteria. The *spontaneous (Sp)* and *elicited (E)* comments made by these 82 men are presented below, verbatim whenever possible.

YOUNGER MEN

Case #1. A 36-year-old man admitted for nephrotic syndrome (kidney disease) due to juvenile-onset diabetes. (Sp) What enables you to cope? "My wife is very religious and I believe in God–whatever the Lord's will. A religious faith. Put the problem out of my mind." (E) Ever experience a distinct change in feelings about religion? "No sudden experiences, just ups and downs. Down when my mother and son died; up when I see how I've been able to survive these years. My mother and father were both religious. I always believed and depended on God; gets things off my mind. It has played such a big role."

Patient was readmitted five months later with worsening liver and kidney problems. (Sp) What enables you to cope? "I try to stay optimistic." (E) Has religion helped? "Yes–a great deal; I pray a lot. Was brought up in the church."

Patient again readmitted seven months later with severe chest pain from coronary artery disease. (Sp) What enables you to cope? "Mostly through prayer; wife and daughter help a lot." (E) Has religion helped? "Yes–very much. I grew up believing in the Lord. Trust in the Lord."

Case #2. A 36-year-old man admitted with achalasia (difficulty swallowing). (Sp) What enables you to cope? "My family and my spiritual beliefs and my work; also, a drink of alcohol [averages two per day, he says]." (E) How does religion help? "Can see other persons in a situation without religion. Pray for family–for health problems. Without God, nothing would be." (E) Ever experience a distinct change in your feelings about religion? "Yes, when I was 35 got involved with another church and liked their way."

Case #3. A 37-year-old man with a history of kidney disease and kidney transplant (from father), admitted for evaluation of sleep disorder. (Sp) What enables you to cope? "Lot of friends; try to keep my mind on something–antique cars, volunteer work for church, teaching English to Korean family. Have a mission in our church for Korean people. Read some, do some housework." (E) Does religion help? "Yes, it does. It's Christianity, not religion." (E) How does Christianity help? "I can go in any church–they are my brothers and sisters–God is there. That is one reason why I think the gun didn't go off (war experience?)–every person has a reason and purpose in life." (E) Ever experience a distinct change in your feelings about religion? "Yes, when I was 18. Found that there was Someone more powerful than me and more in control–and with more love than I ever experienced. I was in the hospital with kidney failure; I prayed and had a healing experience–and I mean healing experience [serum creatinine in 1976 began to reverse–unknown cause–I checked his chart]. I'm called 'the miracle man.'" (E) Were your parents religious? "My parents were not very religious."

Case #4. A 39-year-old man admitted with multiple myeloma (type of bone cancer) and chronic severe pain. (Sp) What enables you to cope? "My belief and faith and acceptance in the Lord Jesus Christ–and I believe in the word of God. If you give Him your whole life, He gives me joy." (E) How does religion help? "I love the Lord–that in itself." (E) Ever experience a distinct change in your feelings about religion? "Yes (age 31), I was having family problems, my health problems with multiple myeloma, and other real problems–trying to deal with them on my own–but then I gave them all to the Lord and I haven't worried about it." (E) Were your parents religious? "Only my mother; father was head of home and fulfilled his role, but only mother really did." (E) As you've grown older, has the importance of religion to you increased, decreased or stayed the same? "I learn something new every day; I leave myself open for more advanced knowledge." Saw patient nearly a year later; he remained in good spirits and continued to express a strong religious faith.

Case #5. A 38-year-old man with metastatic melanoma (severe form of skin cancer) and possibly brain metastasis; exposed to Agent Orange in Vietnam. He has a history of post-traumatic stress disorder; while in Vietnam saw many small children killed and friends die, and now has nightmares of this. (Sp) What enables you to cope? "Pray a lot." (E) Ever experience a distinct change in feelings about religion? "Yes, just in past year. Two months ago I got married and that was a religious experience–a year ago I was saved and joined the church." [Very involved in his church and beliefs; said that it had saved his life in many ways.]

Case #6. A 36-year-old man admitted for surgical treatment of complex partial seizure disorder; underwent temporal lobectomy (removal of a part of his brain) about three years ago. (Sp) What enables you to cope? "Just don't worry about it, cause I believe one day it will be gone, with the help of God and the doctor." (E) How does religion help? "Whenever I've been burdened down I pray to God–my needs are always met–maybe not right then, but in the right time. When I had brain surgery in 1985, felt God worked through the doctor to help me. If God wants me to lose my speech, I'll lose it anyway–so will go ahead with the surgery this time. When I've been financially down, God has always provided. Without God, my life would be like a ship without a sail." (E) Ever experience a distinct change in your feelings about religion? "When I was 12 years old, I went into prayer and felt God saved me–the spirit of God hit me at the altar."

Case #7. A 38-year-old man admitted for evaluation of seizure disorder. Patient was not working, on disability, divorced, had family and financial problems; he was treated for depression seven months prior to admission and recently went through a drug rehabilitation program. Also diagnosed with major depressive disorder during this admission. (Sp) What enables you to cope? "The Bible–the only, only, only. Best weapon I can use. Also, walking and praying; talking to people." (E) How does religion help? "It works–if a man believes and seeks Him with all he can." (E) Ever experience a distinct change in your feelings about religion? "Yes, last year. One night while on drugs, I prayed for two hours to help me and it started to happen; stopped drugs in the same way." (E) Were your parents religious? "Only my mother was very religious; father was a bad person."

Case #8. A 31-year-old man with cervical myelopathy (disease of spine affecting nerves in the neck). (Sp) What enables you to cope? "Enjoy time with family, family walks, go to church, Christian life." (E) Ever experience a distinct change in feelings about religion? "Yes, when I was 17 years old and getting ready to go to college, I accepted the Lord as Christ and savior." Patient was readmitted three months later with a change of diagnosis–now multiple sclerosis.

Case #9. A 37-year-old man with metastatic cancer (unknown type) admitted for fever evaluation. Patient had a history of chronic paranoid schizophrenia, but in remission. (Sp) What enables you to cope? "Put it in the hands of God–that's all I do–nothing else." (E) Ever experience a distinct change in feelings about religion? "Yes. When my mother died and I had to take responsibility of the household [last year]."

Case #10. A 39-year-old man admitted for treatment of right middle lobe pneumonia. (Sp) What enables you to cope? "I'm in Christ and Christ is in me, and that is what helps." (E) Ever experience a distinct change in your feelings about religion? "Yes, age 25. Some things I didn't understand that now I do."

Case #11. A 39-year-old man admitted for colonoscopy for routine follow up of colonic polyps. Also has end stage renal disease and an artificial kidney. Shares his experience with end-stage renal disease with school children on a regular basis. (Sp) What enables you to cope? "Strong belief in God; support from family, friends, and doctors." (E) How long has religion been helpful? "For the past 12 years–since I started dialysis and had my first transplant; before that, I had drifted away. Was brought up in a Christian home; always had a relationship with God, even in the midst of really hard times when not doing well on dialysis and had to accept mother's kidney."

Case #12. A 35-year-old man with multiple sclerosis, admitted for treatment of a flare. (Sp) What enables you to cope? "Dealing with the situation truly–Holy Scripture–lean on the Holy Word of Jehovah–not on your own word." (E) Ever experience a distinct change in your feelings about religion? "No distinct or sudden change. Gradually–come from a religious family, but didn't start reading the Bible until 1972 through 1976 [10-15 years ago] when I became a daily reader; now I'm satisfied."

Case #13. A 36-year-old man admitted with chest pain, probably coronary artery disease. (Sp) What enables you to cope? "Put myself in God's hands and I don't worry about it. Go about normal activities that I can do." (E) Ever experience a distinct change in your feelings about religion? "Yes, when I got saved (age 30). Started singing in the choir–got closer to God and grew and grew and grew."

OLDER MEN

Case #14. The patient was a 65-year-old man with a suspicious liver mass (possibly malignant) admitted for liver biopsy. (Sp) What enables you to cope? "I'm very religious–the Lord will carry me through." (E) How long has religion been helpful? "Raised in the church and very active now; have always relied on my religious beliefs. The Lord has brought me this far, and will carry me through."

The patient was readmitted one month later for treatment of the liver cancer that had been diagnosed. (Sp) What enables you to cope? "Go along and ask God to help me." (E) Does religion help? "I depend on my religious beliefs for help with illness."

Case #15. The patient was a 71-year-old man admitted to rule out lung cancer; despite a below the (R) knee amputation and (L) arm paralysis, he completely cared for himself at home. The diagnosis was confirmed during this admission and he never left the hospital;

over the next four months he rapidly deteriorated and died. (Sp) What enables you to cope? "I go back to the teachings of my parents; I go to my knees and talk to the Man up there–my consolation. Prayer." (E) How does religion help? "It has helped me. I don't know about the next man, but it has helped me." (E) Ever experienced a distinct change in your feelings about religion? "Yes. Around age 20, after the service (WW II), I thought about how I pulled through; seeing all the killing. Came back to it [religion] about 12 years ago. Taught by my parents and read the Bible–that's what brought me back 12 years ago."

Case #16. A 70-year-old man admitted for gastrointestinal bleeding. (Sp) What enables you to cope? "Believe the Lord will take care of me–no matter what comes or goes. He's the savior." (E) Ever experience a distinct change in your feelings about religion? "Yes. When I was seven or eight years old, had a vision of Jesus Christ; but it was a lie. Did it because others did. Then fell away and started drinking. When I was 50 years old, I experienced a fireball coming at me in a dream. Felt this was the Lord warning me, so I stopped drinking that day."

Case #17. A 69-year-old man with colon cancer diagnosed two to three years ago, now metastatic to liver, despite both radiation therapy and chemotherapy; has been weak and feverish for six weeks, now admitted for evaluation. (Sp) What enables you to cope? "Faith in Christ. Spiritual faith–when you know Jesus Christ you've got all the faith in the world. If I knew I was going to die tomorrow it wouldn't bother me a bit." (E) Ever experience a distinct change in your feelings about religion? "Yes, about three years ago when I found out I had cancer. Because He gave me a second chance. Reaccepted God and Jesus Christ. I said–I can't handle it, its up to you [God], and I haven't worried about it since; it's a wonderful feeling. I pray every night that I don't have a bad thought against anybody in the world."

Patient was readmitted seven months later for evaluation of increased blood sugar. (Sp) What enables you to cope? "God–that's the only thing. Without it, I don't think I could make it. With it, I don't worry. God never promised me a bed of roses, but He's taken care of my needs." (E) How long has religion been helpful? "Before three years ago I believed but found fault with everyone. When I got sick with cancer, I began to think I've only got a few years here anyway and that next life is never ending." (E) How is religion helpful? "When I think of all the things He's done for me, I'm so happy. Without Him, I'd have never made it. Three or four years ago–I'd a been ashamed to talk about Him–its a different story now." (E) Were your parents religious? "My father was quite religious, much more religious than my mother who was more concerned over money."

Admitted two months later for spinal cord compression due to spread of the cancer. (Sp) What enables you to cope? "I look to Jesus to cheer me up." (E) Has religion helped? "Yes, absolutely, positively. I got sick and it changed my outlook on life. I became more involved in church."

Case #18. A 66-year-old man admitted for bronchoscopic examination of his lungs to determine etiology of new lung mass; was diagnosed with squamous cell lung cancer one year prior. (Sp) What enables you to cope? "God. We are first to believe in Him. We have faith that He can get us out of anything. God is able to heal–we supply faith, He supplies grace." (E) How does religion help you to cope? "Whenever I trust in God; its your foundation to stand on. Doctors are very changeable; God is the only one that can heal you." (E) How long has religion helped? "Last 10 years I've been back to God." (E) Has your faith increased, decreased, or stayed the same with aging? "Increases in importance day by day; you grow into it 'babes in Christ'–we grow into it. Scripture says that the way is so clear that even a wayward man could find it–so you have no excuse."

Case #19. A 72-year-old man admitted with a common bile duct obstruction, rule out ascending cholangitis (infection of bile duct); had been sick and uncomfortable for several weeks. (Sp) What enables you to cope? "I leave it in His hands–nothing other than that and home life." (E) How does religion help? "When you have these problems–you'll come up feeling better and have better solutions if you ask Him." (E) Ever experience a distinct change in feelings about religion? "No sudden changes. I'm not a Christian fanatic." (E) Has your faith increased, decreased, or stayed same with aging? "Increased in importance, because we're getting closer to death."

Case #20. A 65-year-old man admitted to rule out temporal arteritis. (Sp) What enables you to cope? "Keep it in the Lord's hands. I depend on Him for everything. He is the greatest physician."

Case #21. A 65-year-old man admitted for evaluation of seizures. (Sp) What enables you to cope? "Look on the bright side. Psalm 23 has helped me."

Case #22. A 78-year-old man admitted for obstructive renal failure. Alcoholic. (Sp) What enables you to cope? "Go ahead and pray and keep getting up, and look forwards–not backwards. Nothing but prayer and thank God for letting me live." (E) Does religion really help? "Without Him you're lost." (E) How long has religion helped? "Since I was 15 or 16 years old; I wouldn't trade anything for it." (E) How does religion help? "Just makes you feel happy and good and kind to people. It will keep you out of trouble if you listen. Never been to jail in my life."

Case #23. A 72-year-old man admitted for cardiac catheterization for evaluation of aortic stenosis. (Sp) What enables you to cope? "Going to church and attending services; praying for other people–can always find someone worse than you; family going to church with me." (E) How does religion help? "If you've got religion, you feel it. And He will answer prayer if you're a born again Christian. He made us and He can bring us back. We're made in his image. I couldn't make it without it."

Case #24. An 83-year-old man admitted for cardiac catheterization for aortic stenosis. Has both a wife and a son with Alzheimer's disease. (Sp) What enables you to cope? "Through prayer and faith; or get out and do something." (E) Ever experience a distinct change in your feelings about religion? "Lord called me to my work as a minister in my college days. Didn't miss a Sunday school (except for illness) in 83 years."

Case #25. A 71-year-old man with recent stroke (right hemisphere), blind, bedridden, incontinent of stool and urine, admitted for treatment of chronic diabetes that has resulted in blindness (retinopathy), neuropathy, and kidney damage. (Sp) What enables you to cope? "I sing a lot. A reward that my church offers me (Mormon). The things that they teach me that has happened and is going to happen." (E) How does religion help? "I learned where we came from, why we came, and where we're going. And that every person will be resurrected." (E) Ever experience a distinct change in your feelings about religion? "Yes, age 26. Had a talk with the Lord and asked him to spare me from having to kill anyone (during WW II) and He did. Missionaries came to my door and I accepted it. My church is the most important thing on the topside of this earth. It's been my life ever since I first heard it." [Neither of his parents were religious.]

Case #26. A 78-year-old man recently diagnosed with lung cancer, admitted for evaluation and treatment. (Sp) What enables you to cope? "Prayer–turn it over to God and that's it." (E) How long has religion been helpful? "Stopped drinking through help from the 'Higher Power' ten years ago."

Case #27. A 68-year-old man with a stroke and nearly blind, admitted for treatment of an infected right foot. (Sp) What enables you to cope? "Take it to the Lord." (E) Ever experience a distinct change in feelings about religion? "Yes, 45 years ago. I got saved and trusted in the Lord."

Case #28. A 70-year-old man admitted for evaluation and treatment of upper gastrointestinal bleeding. Also diagnosed with major depressive disorder this admission. (Sp) What enables you to cope? "The good Lord–I believe it 100%." [First person evaluated in the DVAMHS.]

Case #29. A 65-year-old man admitted for cardiac catheterization for evaluation of heart disease. (Sp) What enables you to cope? "Get my Bible and read it. I talk with the Lord and thank Him for all He has done." (E) Ever experience a distinct change in feelings about religion? "Yes, age 25. I said take the taste of liquor and gambling from my life, and He saved me. I never did those things again. Have to be willing to let the Lord help you."

Case #30. A 65-year-old man who had recently experienced a heart attack, and was being admitted for cardiac catheterization. (Sp) What enables you to cope? "God's word." (E) Ever experience a distinct change in your feelings about religion? "Yes, I became a Christian nine years ago on November 13th at 2:30 in the morning. Read God's word."

Case #31. A 72-year-old man admitted for renal biopsy because of problems with blood pressure. (Sp) What enables you to cope? "Turned it over to the Lord completely–and have had complete peace." (E) Ever experience a distinct change in your feelings about religion? "Yes, age 35. Sing in choir–gave my life to the Lord; undergoing a divorce with first wife. Recently, I've realized that I am 71 or 72 and that I don't have much time left to go, so I've been trying to live a more Christian life–live more for the Lord each day. Everytime in the past the Lord has rescued me; I just kick myself that I don't trust more in Him now."

He was readmitted eight months later with pneumonia. Now he says (Sp) What enables you to cope? "My wife helps me." (E) Does religion help? "Definitely. Has become more important to me in the past five years. (E) Ever experience a distinct change in your feelings about religion? "Yes, around age 68. I have reevaluated my life these past few years and religion has become more important to me. Feel it should be 100% but let's say 90%."

Case #32. A 67-year-old man with severe chronic obstructive lung disease, admitted for upper gastrointestinal bleeding. Two years ago his wife died. Lost his home soon after that and was kicked out of his apartment five months after that. (Sp) What enables you to cope? "Start something; if I can't do it–I start something else; switch around. Nothing but pray." (E) Does religion help? "Does–I know it does. If it wasn't for my talk with Jesus, I couldn't make it otherwise." (E) Ever experience a distinct change in your feelings about religion? "Yes, just in the past five years. Gradually over time–still going on now. I was very selfish; He showed me the people I was stepping on and my selfishness shortly after my wife passed away."

Case #33. A 69-year-old man with heart disease. (Sp) What enables you to cope? "Turn to God–He directs my life." (E) Does religion help? "Yes–could not handle my problems without God–He will direct my doctors." [Very involved with his church and rebuilt most of it after a fire.]

Case #34. A 67-year-old man admitted with congestive heart failure. (Sp) What enables you to cope? "Read the Bible." (E) Ever experience a distinct change in your feelings about religion? "About age 62. Married my second wife in 1982–was Methodist before that. My wife is Assemblies of God and I joined her church. It has been a wonderful experience."

Case #35. A 73-year-old man admitted for evaluation of chest pain, coronary artery disease, mitral valve disease, and right hip and back pain. Cares for a sick wife at home, but is unable to drive a car. Was diagnosed with major depressive disorder this admission. (Sp) What enables you to cope? "Pray a bit about it–helps out a whole lot. He's the only source we can depend on. Living a Christian life sure helps." (E) How does religion help? "Getting on my knees and praying about it brings a calmness. I read the Bible–greatest book ever written; helps to understand about Jesus and things." (E) Ever experience a distinct change in your feelings about religion? "Yes, when I joined the church (age 35). I had something to look forward to. I've felt a lot more at ease and can take things more in stride."

Case #36. A 66-year-old man admitted for evaluation of sleep apnea (periodic cessation of breathing during sleep). (Sp) What enables you to cope? "The Holy Bible." (E) Ever experience a distinct change in your feelings about religion? "About 15-16 years ago. Things got rough–troubles with the business and having five children. Became depressed, had to take antidepressants–but they didn't work. Got more active with the help of my brother; experienced an urge to preach."

Case #37. A 70-year-old man admitted for cardiac catheterization for evaluation of coronary artery disease; history of four myocardial infarctions and chronic obstructive lung disease. (Sp) What enables you to cope? "Keep self occupied; that's the key–keep mind occupied–on the go all the time. I'm a Christian and go to church regularly. So many friends in church–I just call them and they come and help." (E) Does religion help? "You better believe it." (E) How does religion help? "By knowing God, praying about it, it helps you to cope."

Case #38. A 72-year-old man with pancreatic cancer admitted for obstructive jaundice (cancer invasion and blockage of bile duct). (Sp) What enables you to cope? "Get on my knees and pray to the Lord and read my Bible–it's the only way I can get relief. Psalms 23 and 121–read these psalms. And the doctor." (E) How does religion help? "If you take your problems to the Lord, He will solve them. Call friend, pastor, and two or three get together and pray. Pray and give it to the Lord. Then go about your business (gets relief). If I can't sleep, I read the Bible, say a prayer–then I can go to sleep." (E) Ever experience a distinct change in your feelings about religion? "Yes, around age 62. Tired of working, cheating, drinking–I'm going to put it down and live for the Lord. Before 10 or 12 years ago, I drank heavy and sold liquor; I was in jail and shot twice." [Very active as a volunteer for the VA and in his church.]

Case #39. A 73-year-old man admitted for treatment of osteomyelitis. (Sp) What enables you to cope? "Turn it over to the Lord." (E) How long have you used religion in coping? "All my life, but especially since growing older–it has been important; went to church as a child, but been at times further away."

Case #40. A 67-year-old man with unstable angina (chest pain from heart). (Sp) What enables you to cope? "I'm a Christian, do church work, try to help neighbors out; anytime I have time, I try to help." (E) Ever experience a distinct change in your feelings about religion? "Yes, got saved about 10 years ago. It was a positive experience–felt like I'd been forgiven of sins; started to love people and work in the church."

He was readmitted to the hospital 10 months later following a heart attack; once again he spontaneously emphasized the importance of religion. (Sp) What enables you to cope? "Got my friends and church."

Case #41. A 67-year-old man admitted with severe hypertension. Lived alone, no family. (Sp) What enables you to cope? "Prayer changes things." (E) Ever experience a distinct change in your feelings about religion? "No, always a strong believer; I'm a musician–play the guitar in church." [Mentioned religion frequently during interview.]

Case #42. A 70-year-old man with cancer blocking off the blood vessels returning blood back to his heart (superior vena cava syndrome), admitted for radiation therapy. (Sp) What enables you to cope? "Reading the Bible." (E) Does religion help? "That's the way I live–if you don't know how to treat people you don't know how to live. Religion is like a blueprint–if you ain't got a plan you don't know how it's going to turn out. I've had so many blessings, can't count them." (E) How does religion help? "Guideline of what you need. I put myself in God's hands–to help the doctor to understand what to do to help me. Several days ago, I prayed God to take the pain away–He did–completely." (E) Ever experience a distinct change in your feelings about religion? "Yes, age 15. Both parents religious, but father more than mother; every morning had prayer together." (E) As you've grown older, has the importance of religion increased, decreased, or remained the same? "Increased. It grows gradually–as a tree grows and blossoms."

Case #43. A 73-year-old man with a lung mass (probably cancer); awaiting results of lung biopsy. (Sp) What enables you to cope? "Going to church; getting out and talking with people; not sitting in the house or watching TV." (E) How does religion help? "That's the only way I know. I just open the Bible–no specific verse or page–and a warm feeling comes over me." (E) Ever experience a distinct change in your feelings about religion? "Yes, since I met my wife in 1944–she was very religious [wife died eight years ago]. I have a brother-in-law (a Baptist minister), and talking with him has helped me understand the Bible; my mother and father-in-law were also very religious. And there are things that have happened to me: Back in July (three months ago) was worried and depressed in the hospital; opened the Gideon Bible and read where it fell open–and depression and worry cleared away. I go and pray about something–it sort of settles me down."

(E) Were your parents religious? "My mother was very religious, my father was a drinker."

Case #44. A 67-year-old man admitted for cardiac catheterization for evaluation of coronary artery disease. (Sp) What enables you to cope? "I usually pray and read the Bible."

Case #45. A 69-year-old man admitted for treatment of lymphoma (cancer of lymph glands). (Sp) What enables you to cope? "My Christian background and faith are my main support." (E) Ever have a distinct change in feelings about religion? "No distinct changes in feelings about religion; has been important for past 50 years."

Case #46. A 65-year-old man admitted for chest pain with a diagnosis of unstable angina. (Sp) What enables you to cope? "I keep my mind occupied in spiritual church work or talking with someone about Christ." (E) Ever experience a distinct change in your feelings about religion? "Yes, when I was 48 years old; I started to go to church; the second time I went, I got in the spirit."

Case #47. A 75-year-old man with leukemia admitted for fever evaluation. (Sp) What enables you to cope? "My belief in Jesus Christ–my trust in Him–He's kept every promise He's ever made to me. If I were dead tomorrow morning, it wouldn't bother me one bit. What's also helped has been my wife's love and faithfulness to me; when I cannot depend on anyone else, she's a real pillar to lean on." (E) Has religion been of help? "Very, very much. Through the years, He has always answered my prayers–this has built up my faith." (E) How has religion helped you to cope? "It's the foundation I stand on–in a nutshell, that's it." (E) Ever experienced a distinct change in your feelings about religion? "Yes, around age 40 when I accepted the Lord. Raising my children–I could not bring up my children in the way they should go unless I got myself right. I had just had TB and came out of that. Had read about Christ–but never really knew Him and was never a friend of His. Then I really turned my life over to Him–and it made a really big change in my life. I could never make it without Him." (E) Were your parents religious? "Both parents were religious, but my mother more so than my dad; dad drank a lot but all in all I think he trusted in the Lord pretty close.''

Case #48. A 69-year-old man admitted for evaluation and treatment of possible pneumonia. (Sp) What enables you to cope? "Take life one day at a time. I've been a believer in God–that helps with any problem.'' Religion had been helpful to him all his life.

Case #49. A 66-year-old man admitted for treatment and evaluation of coronary artery disease. (Sp) What enables you to cope? "Belief in God and knowledge that He will take care of me.'' (E) Ever experience a distinct change in feelings about religion? "Yes, 26 years ago I received salvation; after reading the Bible I felt I needed the Lord. It has made a wonderful difference in my life.''

Case #50. A 65-year-old man admitted because of a recent stroke. (Sp) What enables you to cope? "Believe that I'm going to get better–the Father will help me get better if I believe.'' (E) How long have you used religion to cope? "All my life. My father was a minister; I have wanted to walk in his footsteps.'' [Visits rest homes, teaches Bible lessons, preaches and sings for people.]

Case #51. A 65-year-old man with peritonitis (infection of intestinal coverings) and renal failure. (Sp) What enables you to cope? "Look up instead of down–the best I can. Think about the Lord–to give me strength and courage to get through the day– that's the only thing that keeps me going; helps me not to worry about the kidney problem; takes a load off.'' (E) How does religion help? "It's a guide–if you follow it, it will lead you in the right direction.''

Case #52. A 88-year-old man admitted for evaluation of transient ischemic attacks (mini-strokes). (Sp) What enables you to cope? "Pray–only thing that keeps me here.'' (E) Ever experience a distinct change in your feelings about religion? "Yes, when I was 15 years old I had a sudden change in my feelings about religion.''

Case #53. A 67-year-old man admitted for a flare of chronic obstructive lung disease. (Sp) What enables you to cope? "Praying, I guess; enjoy visits from friends also.''

Case #54. A 66-year-old man admitted for chest pain and evaluation for coronary artery disease. (Sp) What enables you to cope?
"Live one day at a time–let tomorrow be for itself. God didn't
promise no tomorrow; depend on God every day for strength to go
on; put it in His hands–He will take care of me." (E) Ever experience a distinct change in feelings about religion? "Yes, when I was
38. Had been on alcohol–finding no peace. Got disturbed with
family problems. I was cleaning a gun one night and it went off and
penetrated my left chest. Told God I would serve him if I ever
survived; I did and have."

Case #55. A 70-year-old man admitted for colonoscopy because
of abdominal pain. (Sp) What enables you to cope? "I have a
strong constitution, and the Lord Jesus Christ." (E) Ever experience a distinct change in your feelings about religion? "Yes, had a
sudden change at age 15. Both my parents were strong believers.
When I was small (age seven), felt the Lord wanted me to be a
preacher; my major interests now are going to church and singing
in the choir."

Case #56. A 68-year-old man with a history of colon cancer
seven years ago, admitted for colonoscopy. Wife died two years
ago, remarried soon afterwards, but recently separated and struggling with this. (Sp) What enables you to cope? "Deal with the
Bible and believe in God. I read the Bible and quote scriptures. I
lean on God and believe in His promises; pray to God when burden
gets heavy to relieve it." (E) Ever experience a distinct change in
your feelings about religion? "Yes about five years ago. Things that
I was trying to do–I couldn't do; then I started praying and leaning
on Jesus Christ, and things got better. I've believe in Jesus Christ
totally for the past five years."

Case #57. A 67-year-old man admitted with congestive heart
failure. (Sp) What enables you to cope? "I ask God to help me in
every way; without Him we are lost." (E) Has religion helped?
"Yes. I thank God for what he has given me. Nobody can't be no
better to you than the good Lord. Get on your knees and ask God for
help." (E) How long have you used religion to cope? "All my life."
(E) Ever experience a distinct change in feelings about religion?

"No." [Cannot read or write; tries never to worry about his problems "cause the Lord will help."]

Case #58. A 69-year-old man admitted for evaluation and treatment of seizure disorder. (Sp) What enables you to cope? "Pray– that's all I know." (E) Ever experienced a distinct change in feelings about religion? "No. Always felt that way–joined the church at age 11." [Mentioned prayer and relying on God throughout interview.]

Case #59. A 69-year-old man admitted soon after a myocardial infarction (heart attack). (Sp) What enables you to cope? "Turn it over to my Lord."

Case #60. A 74-year-old man admitted for cardiac catheterization for evaluation of coronary artery disease. (Sp) What enables you to cope? "Involvement in religion–I've found a lot of strength in that. Getting involved in social activities, being with people, being around people." (E) How does religion help? "Through studying and learning about the life of humanity from a spiritual standpoint I've found in the Bible, Bible school, and Bible studies." (E) Ever experience a distinct change in feelings about religion? "No. I've been involved in religion since early childhood; it has gradually increased in importance, because I have a great desire in learning."

Case #61. A 66-year-old man admitted for treatment of cellulitis (skin and soft tissue infection); a widower and lives alone. (Sp) What enables you to cope? "I read the Bible–an answer to everything." (E) Ever experience a distinct change in feelings about religion? "Yes, in 1960 I asked Christ to save me." [Mentioned his religious beliefs quite often during interview.]

Case #62. A 67-year-old man with systemic lupus erythematosis and chronic severe pain, admitted for a pleural effusion (water around his lungs). (Sp) What enables you to cope? "Pray a lot." (E) How long helpful? "All my life."
Had many recurrent admissions after this, but usually too sick to participate in interview; however, 17 months after initial interview,

his condition permitted interview completion: (Sp) What enables you to cope? "Let the TV on, especially church programs." (E) Does religion help? "Yes. I would not be around without religion; it helps me all the time."

Case #63. A 65-year-old man admitted for cardiac catheterization; has four-vessel severe coronary artery disease. (Sp) What enables you to cope? "I depend on the Man upstairs." (E) Ever experience a distinct change in your feelings about religion? "Yes. I got saved five years ago and it brought me closer to God and the church." [Patient is a Lumbee Indian and is active in Indian affairs.]

Case #64. A 71-year-old man with transitional cell cancer of the bladder and renal cell cancer of the kidney, admitted with fever and chills probably secondary to pyelonephritis and sepsis (blood infection). He cares for a mentally ill wife at home. (Sp) What enables you to cope? "I trust in the Lord. It's the only help I've got helping me along. I feel like I am going to overcome this tumor. I don't look at the dark side of nothing." (E) Does religion help? "That's the only thing I've got to linger on–is trust in the Lord. I'm a strong believer. If I die, I don't have to worry. I like telling people that." (E) How does religion help? "Something that without religion and you get killed–you lost. If you a born again Christian living for Jesus, you don't have anything to worry about–you've got a home." (E) Ever experience a distinct change in your feelings about religion? "Yes, when I was 33 years old. Before I married, I turned my life to the Lord. I had lived a rough life before then; I drank and blew my money." (E) Were your parents religious? "My mother died when I was young; father was not religious. I lived with aunts until age 10 or 12; one of my aunts was very religious and talked with me a lot."

Case #65. A 67-year-old man admitted for cardiac catheterization for severe coronary artery disease. (Sp) What enables you to cope? "Go to church three or more times per week." (E) Does religion help? "Yes. What can you do without Him? I take life a day at a time" [prays often.]

Patient was readmitted five months later: (Sp) What enables you to cope? "Watch TV." (E) Does religion help? "Yes. God, that is the only one to go to for help."

Case #66. A 65-year-old man admitted for cardiac catheterization for coronary artery disease. (Sp) What enables you to cope? "First of all, I am a Christian and that affects my whole life. I also try to stay busy and active."

Case #67. A 75-year-old man with a history of colon cancer admitted with lower gastrointestinal bleeding and possible recurrence (he was the fourteenth of 16 children). (Sp) What enables you to cope? "I give it to Jesus. I couldn't do it through my natural sense. Jesus died for us–for our healing." (E) Ever experience a distinct change in your feelings about religion? "Yes, 34 years ago. I believe now that God–Jesus Christ–has healed my colon cancer. The Devil works his evil in the world–but Jesus has overcome. I put my faith in God." [No cancer was found during evaluation.]

Patient was readmitted 18 months later with metastatic colon cancer now involving his lungs, liver, and blocking off his kidneys, in addition to pneumonia: (Sp) What enables you to cope? "Pray!!" (delirium prevented further evaluation). [Underwent chemotherapy in a last effort. He then underwent a quite remarkable recovery and lived another five months. He remained in the hospital during these last five months; his faith remained strong and a source of comfort to him to the end.]

Case #68. A 65-year-old man with metastatic cancer in his liver, admitted with a fever, nausea and vomiting, dehydration, and pain. (Sp) What enables you to cope? "The spirit of the Lord." (E) How does religion help? "I can't make it without Jesus; He and I are all and all. When I was a sinner, didn't know that to do. When I became a Christian, I went to preach. I don't have confidence in doctors, but I have faith in Jesus–He is the healer." (E) Ever experience a distinct change in feelings about religion? "Yes. When I was 12 years old–sought Christ to live positive."

Case #69. A 74-year-old man admitted for colonoscopy. (Sp) What enables you to cope? "First, I read scriptures; second, the things I have no control over, I give to God; and third, I try to live with everybody, treat them right, do for them–and if they're my enemy, I overlook it." (E) Do your religious beliefs help? "Yes. Being a Christian, you should live as near to Christ as you can–because it will take your vile and evil thoughts away." (E) Ever experience a distinct change in your feelings about religion? "Yes. When I was 42 years old, had a vision of what it was like to live a Christian life: worship God in a temple–can't do it alone, but with your brothers and sisters; charity was the first step–helping others. Since then, I haven't missed a Sunday from 1955 through 1987. My motto is to keep on pushing ahead–no matter how long it takes–and you'll overcome it."

Patient was readmitted six months later with uncontrolled diabetes. (Sp) What enables you to cope? "Moving forward–keep mind on something positive all the time. God is the main one–consult Him all the time." (E) Ever experience a distinct change in feelings about religion? "In 1955, that when I really started knowing what God could do for me. Prayed during a nervous breakdown to get me through–didn't quit work, didn't start drinking. Had a vision–I was hanging on a limb and there was no way to get back; for six months, I prayed day and night. Really connected with God and whole life started moving with God."

Case #70. A 65-year-old man admitted with metastatic cancer of unknown type. (Sp) What enables you to cope? "Trust the good Lord. Pray every day that He will guide me in the direction he wants me to go." (E) Ever experience a distinct change in feelings about religion? "Yes, when I was 54 years old I had a sudden change in feelings about religion both positive and negative. I was diagnosed with lung cancer at that time. At first, got no response from God to prayer–as if Jesus had forgot about me. Then the Lord stopped the cancer from growing. No recurrence until five months ago."

Case #71. A 68-year-old man admitted for evaluation of a lung nodule (rule out cancer). (Sp) What enables you to cope? "I think about my Lord Jesus and what He's done for me." (E) Ever experience a distinct change in your feelings about religion? "Yes. I got saved, I walked into Emanuel Holiness Church and the power of God hit me and I passed out, and that's when I got saved."

Case #72. A 67-year-old man admitted for exercise tolerance test for evaluation of chest pain from coronary artery disease. (Sp) What enables you to cope? "A merry heart doeth good like a medicine. Jesus is my mainstay." (E) Ever experience a distinct change in your feelings about religion? "Yes, in 1944 on a boat in the Pacific when I was saved. Change and growth are constant."

Case #73. A 67-year-old man with coronary artery disease admitted for angioplasty. (Sp) What enables you to cope? "I trust in the Lord–as long as you do that, you'll get along with everything in this world." (E) How does religion help? "Helps to cope with life better. If you trust in the Lord, He'll just about look after you in anything that comes." (E) Ever experience a distinct change in your feelings about religion? "Yes, in the last six or seven years. Got to reading the Bible and really understand; so changed from Southern Baptist to Independent Baptist." [Neither of his parents were religious.]

Case #74. An 81-year-old man admitted for evaluation of left arm weakness and possible stroke. Severely disabled. (Sp) What enables you to cope? "Through faith in God, I reckon (nothing else)." (E) How does religion help? "If you are honest and sincere with Him, He's with you all the time. He's guiding you." (E) Ever experience a distinct change in your feelings about religion? "Yes (age 21), began teaching a men's Bible class; made me study more and become more familiar with the Bible."

Case #75. A 65-year-old man admitted for cardiac catheterization; told one hour before this evaluation that he had heart disease and needed surgery. (Sp) What enables you to cope? "First, I'm a born again Christian; I turn over all my problems to the Lord and I don't worry about it. Second, my family is 100% supportive." (E) How does religion help? "Talk problems with the Lord, pray about it, and I have the feelings through the Holy Spirit that relieves me of the problem. Have a very close family–prayer on the phone even." (E) Ever experience a distinct change in feelings about religion? "Yes, when I was 50 years old, was born again."

Case #76. A 72-year-old man admitted for evaluation of sleep apnea. (Sp) What enables you to cope? "Faith in the Lord Jesus Christ." (E) How long have you used religion to cope? "Thirty-two years."

Case #77. A 75-year-old man admitted to rule out tuberculosis. (Sp) What enables you to cope? "Put my trust in God; He controls all things." (E) Does religion help you to cope? "Yes! I'm a full believer in Jesus Christ." (E) Ever experience a distinct change in feelings about religion? "No. Been that way all my life. I'm a minister–same church for 15 years."

Case #78. A 68-year-old man admitted with lymphoma (cancer of lymph glands). (Sp) What enables you to cope? "I study the Word and pray. God has done it all for me." (E) Ever experience a distinct change in your feelings about religion? "Yes at age 31. I was one of the most wicked men you have ever met. The Lord spoke to me and I began to go to church and was saved. I have been a preacher for many years." [Died three months later.]

Case #79. A 68-year-old man admitted for transient ischemic attacks (mini-strokes). (Sp) What enables you to cope? "Say a prayer." (E) Ever experienced a distinct change in religious feelings? "No distinct changes; been that way all my life. Am a trustee and steward for a missionary society, and I'm active in church."

Case #80. A 67-year-old man admitted for evaluation of a lung mass (possible cancer). (Sp) What enables you to cope? "Talk with the Lord." (E) Does religion help you to cope? "Yes, very much." (E) Ever experience a distinct change in your feelings about religion? "Yes (age 35), became more interested because of my children." [Referred to religious beliefs often.]

Case #81. A 70-year-old man admitted with a history of stroke, chronic renal failure, and now congestive heart failure from cardiac valvular disease. (Sp) What enables you to cope? "Talk to the Lord about it–pray and ask Him to take it off me. And He always helps me. Don't know where we would be without Him. Don't matter whether I see tomorrow or not; I just rely on Him and try to live from one day to the next. That is the best policy." (E) How does religion help? "That's the only way that I've found that helps. As much knowledge as the Lord's given doctors, its the Lord that's more important." (E) Ever experience a distinct change in your feelings about religion? "Yes, when I got saved (age 50); when get saved and live for the Lord, it changes your life 100%."

Readmitted two months later for cardiac catheterization. (Sp) What enables you to cope? "I pray to the Lord."

Case #82. A 66-year-old man with aortic insufficiency admitted for cardiac catheterization. (Sp) What enables you to cope? "I go to church every Sunday. I'm a deacon and involved in Bible study and prayer service. I have something at church almost every night." (E) How does religion help? "When I pray–I leave the burden be-hind–so I have no fear." (E) Ever experience a distinct change in your feelings about religion? "Yes. I had been raised in the church and always had religious beliefs, but started drinking after the ser-vice. When I quit drinking 10 years ago, I came back to the church. God has been good to me."

DISTINGUISHING CHARACTERISTICS

The sociodemographic, religious, physical and mental health characteristics that distinguish these 82 men from their peers in the general sample, not surprisingly, reflect those of religious copers already discussed in Chapter 9. I will highlight the differences here focusing on younger and older men separately (see Table 10.1). Further details about these religious copers, including their survival and health care utilization compared with nonreligious copers, may be obtained from another source (Koenig, Meador, and Westlund 1992).

Younger Men

The 13 young religious copers tended to be older than their peers in the general sample. In fact, only one of them was under 35. Over three-quarters were Black (compared with half in the overall sample). Religious copers were more likely to be married, to have higher social support, and to have more education. Although they were somewhat more likely to be involved in unskilled labor or to be unemployed, their yearly incomes were actually higher than younger men in the general sample. Physical health characteristics also differed. Religious copers had more severe physical illness and disability ratings on the whole, and they were more likely to have a diagnosis of cancer (23% vs. 9%); thus, they were both more severely ill and had more serious illness.

Mental health differences are notable given the differences in physical health; these findings are presented in more detail in Chapter 11. Regardless of whether measured by observer-rated or self-rated scales, depressive symptoms were less common among the 13 younger men than in the general sample (despite the former's more severe physical illness). Likewise, major depressive disorder was also less common in this group (9% vs. 22%). Finally, only one of the 13 men used alcohol, compared with almost half of the overall sample.

The religious characteristics of this group were similarly distinctive. These men were primarily from conservative protestant or fundamentalist denominations (92%). Nearly all had experienced a distinct change in their feelings about religion at some time in their lives. Likewise, all (100%) claimed that religion had increased in importance as they had grown older (compared with only 54% of the overall sample).

Older Men

Men age 65 or over differed in numerous ways both from younger cases and from the general sample of older men. As with younger men, they differed from the overall sample in being Black (but not to the degree seen in younger cases), and were also somewhat more likely to report skilled occupations and to be currently employed (the opposite from that seen among younger cases). There was virtually no differences in age, living situation, education, income, or social support between older cases and the general population. Unlike younger patients, there were virtually no health

TABLE 10. 1. Comparison of characteristics of overall DVAMHS sample with those of Religious Copers

	UNDER AGE 40		AGE 65 or OVER	
	DVAMHS (n = 161)	Religious (n = 13)	DVAMHS (n = 850)	Religious (n = 69)
		Column % / Mean		
Sociodemographic				
Age	34 y	37 y	70 y	70 y
Race (non-white)	52%	77%	28%	39%
Married	47%	77%	70%	77%
Live Alone	14%	15%	19%	19%
Unskilled Occup Status	40%	54%	39%	33%
Currently Employed	42%	31%	4%	10%
Education	13 y	14 y	9 y	9 y
Income ($/y)	$9966	$10,700	$8587	$8653
Social Support Index	11	11	11	11
Physical Health				
Medical Diagnoses				
Malignancy	9%	23%	22%	22%
Gastrointestinal	14%	15%	15%	12%
Neurological	30%	39%	14%	15%
Respiratory	8%	8%	10%	7%
Renal	9%	8%	5%	4%
Cardiovascular	17%	8%	25%	35%
Other Disorders	31%	0%	8%	6%
Functional Status (ADLs)	16	15	14	15
Severe Med III (ASA>2)	19%	39%	53%	47%
Mini Mental State Exam	28	28	26	27
Mental Health				
Observer-Rated				
Hamilton Rating Scale	9.9	6.4	8.0	7.1
Montgomery-Asberg Scale	10.8	6.5	10.2	8.9

	UNDER AGE 40		AGE 65 or OVER	
	DVAMHS (n = 161)	Religious (n = 13)	DVAMHS (n = 850)	Religious (n = 69)
		Column % / Mean		
Self-Rated				
Geriatric Depression Scale	8.4	6.2	7.2	5.1
Carroll Depression Scale	3.6	2.8	3.6	3.0
Major Depression (by DIS)	22%	9%	13%	7%
Hx of Psychiatric Problems	42%	46%	26%	26%
Family Psychiatric Problems	22%	23%	9%	12%
Alcohol Use	47%	8%	18%	4%
Religious Characteristics				
Religious Denominations (ECA)[1]				
Liberal Protestants (7%)	3%	0%	8%	4%
Moderate Protestants (17%)	9%	8%	13%	6%
Conservative Prot (55%)	22%	15%	41%	33%
Black Protestants (26%)	40%	53%	22%	26%
Fundamental/Evangel (5%)	8%	23%	5%	19%
Protestant (unspec) (6%)	1%	0	3%	6%
Catholics (2%)	4%	0	3%	1%
Jews (<1%)	0%	0	0%	0%
Miscellaneous (3%)	4%	0	3%	4%
No Preference (5%)	11%	0	2%	0%
How Long Religious Coping				
Less than 5 years	31%	23%	6%	7%
5 to 50 years	34%	62%	46%	57%
All my life	35%	15%	48%	36%
Change Relig Feelings	54%	92%	33%	73%
Age at Change	26 y	28 y	43 y	40 y
Both Parents Religious	31%	33%	40%	52%
Religion Incr with Aging	54%	100%	61%	96%

1. ECA Piedmont Epidemiologic Catchment Area Survey (men age 55 or over in Central NC)

differences, either in terms of diagnosis or severity of illness. As with younger men, differences in mental health were present. Cases were less likely to be depressed (whether measured by self-rated or observer-rated scales) and were less likely to have a major depressive disorder (7% vs. 13%). Alcohol use was also quite low (4% vs. 18%) compared with the general sample.

The distribution of denominations in our overall sample closely paralleled that reported in a random sample of men age 55 or over in the surrounding community as determined by the 1981-82 Epidemiologic Catchment Area (ECA) Surveys. Religious characteristics differed between older cases and the overall sample just as they had in younger men. Differences in religious denomination between cases and sample, however, were less pronounced than observed in younger men. Cases were again more likely to report a distinct change in feelings about religion at some time in their lives (73% vs. 33%) and were more likely to note that religion had increased in importance with aging (96% vs. 61%). Of interest from a developmental perspective, older cases were more likely than the general sample to note that both of their parents had been religious.

SUMMARY

Reported here are verbatim accounts of men systematically selected from a consecutive series of hospitalized veterans. They were not haphazardly selected to emphasize a point. Their accounts were not modified to fit a "theory" or other preconceived notions about what investigators thought religious coping should be like. The proportion of younger and older patients who fulfilled the criteria for a strong religious coper was surprisingly the same (8%). The impact of religious beliefs and behaviors on the lives of these patients, whether young or old, is evident from their own words. These reports by themselves, without consideration of epidemiological or statistical proofs, support an important role for religion in helping men with severe and often terminal illness to better cope with their situations. It is also clear that religious coping to these men involved traditional Judeo-Christian beliefs and practices.

Let us now turn to the next chapter where we will examine the association between religious coping and depression in the overall sample, controlling for other factors that might influence this relationship.

REFERENCE

Koenig, H.G., K.G. Meador, R. Westlund, S. Ford. (1992). Health care utilization and survival of religious and non-religious copers hospitalized with medical illness. *Journal of Religious Gerontology*, (in submission).

Chapter 11

Religious Coping and Depression

This is the day the Lord has made;
let us rejoice and be glad in it.

–Psalm 118:24

As discussed in Chapters 9 and 10, religious beliefs and practices are commonly used by younger and older patients alike to manage the emotional stress conferred by physical illness and hospitalization. Religious coping is also prevalent among nursing home patients (Chapter 16), medical outpatients (Koenig, Moberg, and Kvale 1988a), and the community-dwelling elderly (Koenig, George, and Siegler 1988b). The purpose of religious behaviors, and whether they are conducive or inimical to mental health, have been avidly debated by health professionals (Bergin 1991).

Freud (1927) himself believed that religion served a coping function. Indeed, he argued that the origins of religion lie in "man's need to make his helplessness tolerable . . . and from the necessity of defending oneself from the crushingly superior forces of nature" (pp. 18, 21). As we saw in Chapter 2, Freud also did his best to convince mental health professionals of his day that religion was equivalent to neurosis, and that the suppression or renunciation of instinctual impulses by religious activities was neither completely effective nor final. The religious person was portrayed as sitting on a time bomb of repressed feelings and emotions that threatened release (Freud 1907). Nevertheless, as I have already noted, Freud's experience primarily involved religion in patients with mental illness. He had relatively little contact with general medical patients, especially those who were elderly and facing multiple social, economic, and functional losses.

A COMPLEX RELATIONSHIP

The relationship between religion and emotional disorder is a complex one. Some factors may conceal or disguise an inverse association between the two, while others may exaggerate it.

Masking Factors

Individuals who for constitutional reasons are content and mentally healthy, those who have few external stressors, and/or those who possess abundant social, economic, and health resources, may have little motivation to seek consolation in religion. Conversely, persons suffering from emotional distress, particularly those lacking other resources, may be more inclined to look to religion for comfort. Stress is a powerful motivator in this regard. Take the response of the American public to the 1991 war with Iraq, when pleas for prayer sprang up all over the United States. My point is that during a stressful period, religion may be sought after in a last-ditch effort to cope with problems not resolvable by other means.

Suppose now that religion, while bringing considerable relief and consolation, did not entirely rid the person of discomfort. This person would likely report greater distress than a more fortunate colleague with few problems (and little need for religion). Thus, it is easy to see how epidemiological studies–particularly cross-sectional ones–involving populations composed of a mixture of contented nonreligious individuals and troubled religious ones, might demonstrate a positive association between psychic distress and religion. From a clinical standpoint, the same thing may occur. If clinicians only come into contact with persons under stress from emotional or physical problems and find religion quite common in these patients, they might falsely conclude that religion was etiologically related to the emotional distress, rather than being a resource sought after in hope of relief. Because of such "contamination," the empirical demonstration of religion's positive effects on mental health is difficult.

Socioeconomic and racial factors further complicate this relationship. Minority groups (Blacks), women, and those from lower socioeconomic levels have always been the more religious element of society. The well-educated, affluent members of the upper classes, on the other hand, have tended to be less religiously inclined. Mental illness, drug and alcohol abuse, depression, and neurosis are also much more common among persons from minority groups and lower socioeconomic classes. Again, without taking such factors into account, one might mistakenly conclude that religion and mental illness were somehow related.

Amplifying Factors

On the other hand, rather than disguise an inverse relationship, intrapsychic dynamics may actually exaggerate it–especially in the case of depression. During such states, elders may lose interest in religion (just as they lose interest in other things in their lives). Indeed, "loss of interest" is a cardinal symptom of severe depression. Devoutly religious patients have told me that when they became depressed, their motivation to pray or read religious scriptures dropped off considerably; indeed, depression can result in a paralysis of the will. These persons describe a sense of feeling distant from God, as though they have been deserted by him. Anger towards God may underlie this feeling. Take Job, for instance. In a state of classical depression, he eloquently testifies to feelings of desertion by God and anger over God's failure to respond in his time of need. Thus, there are numerous forces which may affect the relationship between religious coping and depressive illness, either disguising or magnifying an inverse association.

RELIGION AND DEPRESSION IN THE MEDICALLY ILL

In designing a study to test the relationship between religious coping and depression, an investigator would like to find a large sample of persons with common social, cultural, educational, and economic backgrounds, and exposure to similar stress levels (preferably high). It would also help if there were a high prevalence of religious coping behaviors and a high prevalence of depressive illness, thus making any association between the two easier to detect. Patients hospitalized at a VA medical center with acute medical illness fulfill these criteria nicely.

Hospitalization itself is a stressful experience for most people. It interrupts work schedules and other routines, drains finances, separates families, removes people from their usual caregiving roles, and often forces them into dependency. Medical illness is also associated with limited mobility, physical discomfort, and distortions in body image. Thus, when new illness becomes evident or chronic illness worsens, coping resources are seriously tested.

THE DURHAM VA MENTAL HEALTH SURVEY

Hospitalized Veterans

In previous chapters, we have examined the prevalence of depression and of religious coping among hospitalized men participating in the DVAMHS. Here we explore the association between these two variables, controlling for socioeconomic and health factors that might conceal or magnify a relationship. Although details of the study are presented in Chapters 8 and 9, I will summarize them briefly here.

Between September 1, 1987 and January 1, 1989, 1011 men consecutively admitted to the Durham VA Medical Center were screened for depression. The final sample represented 92% of eligible participants, and included 161 men under age 40 and 850 men age 65 or over. All patients received the self-rated Geriatric Depression Scale (GDS) and Brief Carroll Rating Scale (BCRS); those scoring 14 or higher were evaluated on site by a staff psychiatrist using a DSM-III-R checklist to confirm or rule out depression. In addition, all men under age 40 or over age 70 were evaluated with a structured psychiatric interview (Diagnostic Interview Schedule–DIS) to assess patients for depressive disorder. The observer-rated Hamilton Depression Rating Scale (HRS) was used to evaluate the severity of depression.

Thus, depressive illness was determined using three different methodologies: (1) self-rated depressive symptoms (GDS and BCRS) were assessed for the entire sample, (2) observer-rated symptoms (HRS) were assessed for men under 40 and those over 70, and (3) depressive disorder was determined (a) by the DIS in men under age 40 and over age 70 and (b) by on site psychiatric exam in men aged 65 to 69 who scored 14 or higher on the GDS. Depression status was determined blind to knowledge about religious coping.

In the longitudinal phase, patients readmitted to the hospital during the 16-month study period and 5 months thereafter (September 1987 to June 1989) were approached by the social worker who readministered the self-rated depression scales (GDS and BCRS) and again inquired about religious coping. In both cross-sectional and longitudinal phases, religious coping was measured using the three-item Religious Coping Index (RCI) described in Chapter 9.

Statistical Analysis. Age-adjusted odds ratios (OR) and 95% confidence intervals (CI) were determined using the Cochran-Mantel-Haenszel method. An odds ratio of 2.0 indicates that a condition is twice as likely to occur in a particular group compared with a reference group; an odds ratio of 0.5 indicates the condition is only 50% as likely. For assessing the relationship between religious coping and depressive symptoms (self-rated and observer-rated), linear regression models were used (backward inclusion method). For testing the relationship between religious coping and major depressive disorder, logistic regression was used. Clinically plausible interactions between variables in the final models were examined and included in the model if significant (alpha < .05). Plots for figures are SAS generated using the macro RCSPLINE developed by Frank Harrell, Division of Clinical Biostatistics, Duke University Medical Center. Spline regression was used here to plot a smooth curve that might allow for changes in the relationship with depression along the entire range of the religious coping index (Smith 1979). Residualized change analysis was used to examine religious coping and other baseline variables as potential predictors of followup depression scores (after controlling for baseline depression score). A more detailed report of the methods and findings in elderly patients can be found elsewhere (Koenig et al. 1992). Here I report the results of analyses for the combined sample of younger and older patients.

Findings

Depression and Religious Denomination

Religious affiliations, described in Chapter 9, were categorized into 10 major groups as suggested by Roof and McKinney (1987). Observer-rated depressive symptoms (measured by the Hamilton Depression Scale) were less common among men affiliated with "moderate" Protestant denominations (Methodists, Lutherans, Disciples of Christ, Reformed, and so forth). This relationship persisted after controlling for 16 sociodemographic and health variables in the regression model (Table 11.1).

Major depressive disorder was only one-tenth as common among moderate Protestants as in men with other affiliations (age-adjusted odds ratio = 0.1, CI 0.0-0.5, p < .01). On the other hand, major depression was almost two-and-a-half times more common among men with no religious affiliation (odds ratio 2.4, CI 1.0-5.9), a difference that reached statistical significance in men age 65 or over. These relationships between religious denomination and major depression, however, did not persist once other covariates were controlled for.

Other mental health indicators also varied by denomination. A past history of psychiatric problems was more prevalent among Conservative White Protestants (Baptists, Church of Christ, Nazarenes, Seventh-Day Adventists, and so forth) (OR = 1.6, CI 1.2-2.1, p < .05), but less common among Black Protestants (Black Baptists, Black Methodists, and so forth) (OR = 0.7, CI 0.5-1.0, p < .05). A family history of psychiatric problems was more common among members of Pentecostal, Holiness, Assembly of God, and other Fundamentalist or Evangelical groups (OR = 3.1, CI 1.6-6.0); this difference did reach statistical significance in older men.

Depressive Symptoms and Religious Coping

RCI scores, along with the 10 religious affiliation groupings, were included in two regression models—one model examining correlates of self-rated depressive symptoms (GDS, first column, Table 11.1) and the other model examining correlates of observer-rated depressive symptoms (HRS, second column, Table 11.1). Thus, the relationship between these religious variables and depressive symptoms was examined, independent of the confounding effects of the 16 other sociodemographic and health variables measured in the DVAMHS. There was no significant relationship between depressive symptoms and any religious affiliation with the exception of Moderate Protestants as mentioned earlier.

More important, however, we found that religious coping score (RCI) was significantly and independently related to both lower

TABLE 11.1. Relationship between religious coping and depressive symptoms

Religious Variable	Self-Rated (GDS) b(SE)	Observer-Rated (HRS) b(SE)
Religious Coping	−.08 (.02)***	−.11 (.03)**
Moderate Protestant Affiliation	not significant	−2.04 (.84)*
Model F	30.7***	19.1***
R-square	.31	.31
N in model	971 (96%)	437 (87%)

* p ≤ .05, **p ≤ .0005, *** p ≤ .0001

GDS Geriatric Depression Scale (all patients < age 40 or > age 65)
HRS Hamilton Depression Scale (patients < age 40 or > age 70)

Not related to either GDS or HRS scores were education, marital status, retirement status, occupational status, living situation, or medical diagnoses. Related to either GDS or HRS and controlled for in the model were age, income, race, social support, functional status, respiratory disorder, cognitive status (MMSE), past psychiatric history, family psychiatric history, alcohol use, and five age interactions (with social support, family psych hx, past psych hx, alcohol use, and functional status).

See Koenig et al 1992a for elderly men only (results similar)

self-rated depressive symptoms (p < .0001) and lower observer-rated depressive symptoms (p = .0005). There were no significant interactions between RCI score and age or functional status. Thus, when all other factors were taken into consideration, religious coping was significantly and independently associated with fewer depressive symptoms, regardless of whether these symptoms were self-reported or observer-rated. Furthermore, this was true regardless of age or functional status. [Note, however, that when younger men were excluded from the analysis, the inverse relationship between religious coping and depressive symptoms was strongest among older patients with poorer functional status (Koenig et al. 1992)].

Major Depression and Religious Coping

Next a logistic regression model was used to examine the relationship between major depressive disorder and religious coping (Table 11.2). Of the 16 sociodemographic and health variables, only four were related to major depression: age, functional status, social support, and past psychiatric history. After controlling for these four variables, we found that the RCI score was once again significantly and independently related to major depression (p = .017). There was no interaction between RCI score and other variables in the model, including age or functional status. Overall, a 20% increase on the RCI score (approximately six points) was associated with a 19% decrease in the likelihood of major depressive disorder.

TABLE 11.2. Association between religious coping and major depressive disorder, controlling for other correlates in a logistic regression model.

Variable	beta	Std Err	OR	95% CI	P
Past Psychiatric Hx	+1.07	.27	2.92	1.70-5.00	<.001
Functional Status (3 unit or 18% change)	−.09	.03	0.76	0.64-0.91	<.01
Social Support (2 unit or 20% change)	−.38	.08	0.47	0.34-0.64	<.0001
Age (10 yr change)	−.02	.01	0.82	0.71-0.98	<.05
Age X Functional Status (interaction)	−1.50	.47	—	—	<.05
Religious Coping (RCI) (6 unit or 20% change)	−.04	.02	0.81	0.68-0.96	<.02

Model LR chi-square 80.2, p<.0001
C = 0.79, Somer D = .057
n = 500, events (major depression) = 89

OR Odds Ratio
CI Confidence Interval

Figures 11.1-11.5 display computer-generated graphs illustrating this relationship in the sample stratified by age, race, psychiatric history, social support, and degree of functional disability. Thus, regardless of demographic, social, or health characteristics, the risk of having major depression decreased in a near linear fashion with increased religious coping.

Changes in Religious Coping and Depression Over Time

Rather than being a result of religion's therapeutic or protective effects, perhaps the inverse relationship between religious coping and depression is due to a diminished interest in religion as an adverse effect of depression. To resolve this issue, we examined the relationship between *change in depressive symptoms* and *change in religious coping* during the longitudinal portion of the study. Mean changes in religious coping score (RCI) and depressive symptoms over an average 6 month time interval were small (0.7 vs. 1.3 points, respectively). We found *no relationship* between change in depressive symptoms and change in religious coping during that time (Pearson correlation = .02, p > .80). Thus, there were both increases and decreases in religious coping among patients experiencing increased depression, with no predictable pattern of change. Based on this finding, then, we concluded that the inverse relationship between religious coping and depression discovered in the cross-sectional portion of the study could not be explained by a decrease in religious coping with increased depression. A more likely explanation is that religious coping either relieved depression or prevented it from occurring. This conclusion received further support from an analysis of baseline predictors of change in depressive symptoms over time.

Religious Coping as a Predictor of Depression

Predictors of change in depressive symptoms over time were examined using data from the longitudinal portion of the study. Baseline sociodemographic and health characteristics of readmitted patients were included in a regression model to determine which of these factors might predict an increase in depressive symptoms

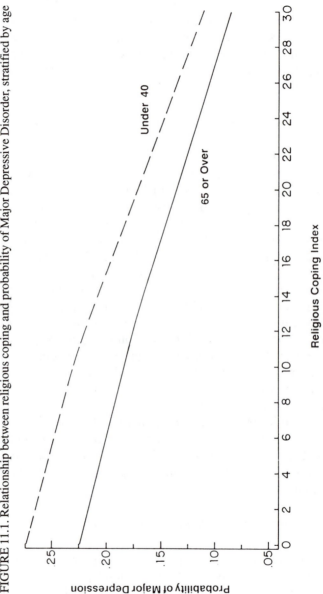

FIGURE 11.1. Relationship between religious coping and probability of Major Depressive Disorder, stratified by age

228

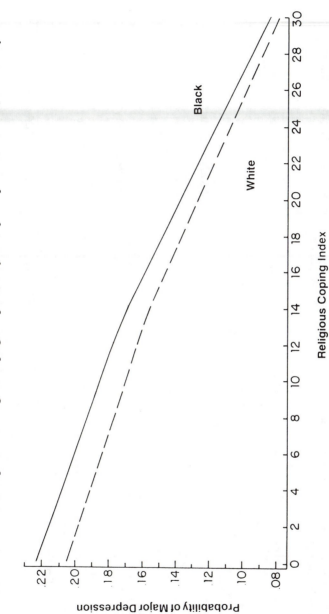

FIGURE 11.2. Relationship between religious coping and probability of Major Depressive Disorder, stratified by race

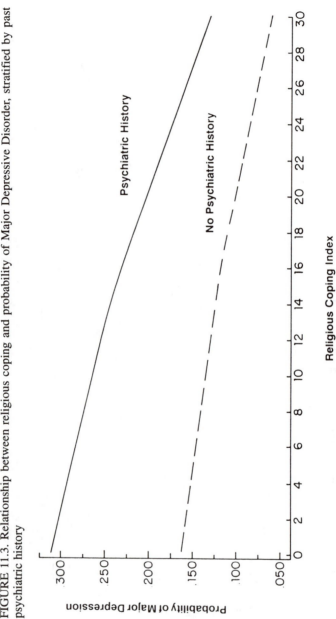

FIGURE 11.3. Relationship between religious coping and probability of Major Depressive Disorder, stratified by past psychiatric history

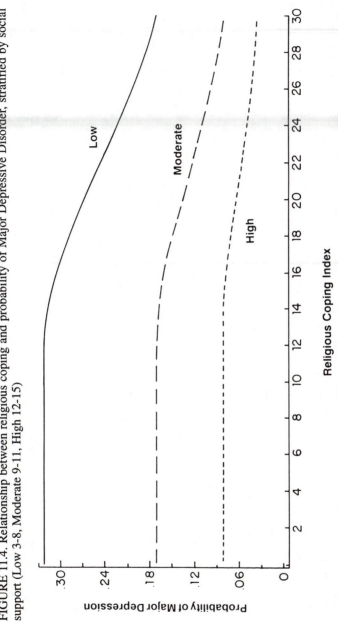

FIGURE 11.4. Relationship between religious coping and probability of Major Depressive Disorder, stratified by social support (Low 3-8, Moderate 9-11, High 12-15)

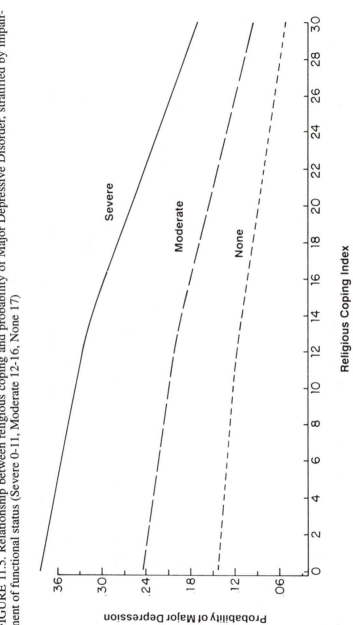

FIGURE 11.5. Relationship between religious coping and probability of Major Depressive Disorder, stratified by impairment of functional status (Severe 0-11, Moderate 12-16, None 17)

between hospitalizations. Baseline depression score was initially entered into the model, with other sociodemographic and health characteristics added successively thereafter; baseline religious coping was added in the final step (hierarchical regression or residualized change analysis) (Table 11.3).

Variables predicting high depressive symptoms on readmission were (1) a high baseline depression score, (2) a diagnosis of cancer, and (3) a diagnosis of kidney disease. Age was unrelated to follow up depression score, but was included in the model because of its importance. Baseline functional status, cognitive status, past psychiatric history, other medical diagnoses, number of hospital read-

TABLE 11.3. Baseline sociodemographic and health predictors of increasing depressive symptoms over time (residualised change analysis).

Variable	b (SE)	p value
Baseline depression score	+0.68 (0.05)	<.001
Diagnosis of cancer	+1.90 (0.86)	<.05
Diagnosis of renal disease	+5.30 (1.47)	<.001
Age	+0.05 (0.04)	ns
Religious coping (RCI)	−0.12 (0.05)	< .01

Model F = 40.5, p = .0001
R-square = .50
n = 210 in model

RCI Religious Coping Index

Not significantly related to outcome depression score were baseline functional status, cognitive status, past psychiatric history, diagnosis of respiratory disorder, level of social support, or number of readmissions. Because of its importance, age was included in the model above despite its non-significant contribution to outcome; no interactions with age were significant (p<.05).

See Koenig et al 1992 for elderly men only (results similar)

missions, and level of social support, had no ability whatsoever to predict follow up depression score. Among all baseline sociodemographic and health characteristics, the RCI score was the *only inverse predictor* of increasing depression (p = .007). No interactions between variables in the final model were significant, including age. Thus, a high level of religious coping at baseline was the only characteristic that either increased the chances of recovery from depression or protected against its development or worsening over time.

Discussion

These findings, coming from a large sample of consecutively admitted medical patients, indicate that men who use religious behaviors to cope are both less likely to be depressed during their initial hospital stay and are less likely to become depressed during future hospitalizations. Since the great majority of our sample were elderly (84%), this conclusion has special relevance for professionals in the fields of geriatrics and gerontology. Depressive disorder has an enormous impact on the lives of elders with health problems (Chapter 8). Not only does depression destroy satisfaction, joy, and meaning in life, it also interferes with the person's ability to comply with medical treatments (Rodin et al. 1981; Stoudemire and Thompson 1983; Stam and Strain 1985), increases the costs of inpatient care (Koenig, Shelp, Goli, Cohen, and Blazer 1989a), and shortens life expectancy of many institutionalized elders (Koenig, Shelp, Goli, Cohen, and Blazer 1989a; Rovner et al. 1991). Religious coping behaviors, then, by protecting against or relieving depression, may have a positive impact on each of these health outcomes.

As noted earlier, the effects of religious beliefs and behaviors on mental health have not always been clear. Some early geriatricians reported that such behaviors were a sign of trouble for the physician from an insecure individual (Covalt 1960). Albert Ellis, a giant in modern psychology and partly responsible for the development of cognitive psychotherapy, noted that "devout, orthodox, or dogmatic religion (or what might be called religiosity) is significantly correlated with emotional disturbance" (Ellis 1980, p. 637). Freud's views, as we saw in Chapter 2, were along these same lines. These and many other mental health professionals defend their position by pointing out that religion is frequently part of the thought content and delusions of mentally ill persons.

Generalizing findings from individuals with psychiatric illness to those without mental disorder or to those with medical illness, however, is unwise. Participants in the DVAMHS represented a population of mentally intact individuals who were attempting to cope with very difficult and real problems in physical health, family and social function, and finances. Far from being positively related to emotional disturbance, religious behaviors were protective against it. Recall that one-fifth of the sample reported that religious belief or activity was the most important factor that enabled them to cope, and over half claimed that this had helped to a large extent.

I recognize that the high prevalence of religious coping in this population was partly due to the location of the study in the south-eastern United States (where religion is deeply ingrained into the society and culture of the people). Nevertheless, the inverse relationship between religious coping and depression suggests an explanation different from geographical, social, or cultural ones. Religious coping is prevalent in this population because it *does* enable more effective adjustment to the severe and often uncontrollable stresses that accompany physical illness and disability. In other words, men use it because *it works*.

OTHER RECENT STUDIES

If these were isolated findings, not reported anywhere else in the literature, then perhaps they might be due to some special aspect of our sample, study design, or analysis. However, this is not the case. A brief review of recent literature finds similar reports emanating from different research groups working in a variety of locations throughout the United States (although few have concentrated exclusively on men).

Studies in Medical Inpatients

Working in the Washington, D.C. area, O'Brien found that 74% of chronic hemodialysis patients reported religious or ethical beliefs to be associated with adjustment to their disease. Those reporting a positive relationship between their beliefs and adjustment also had the highest degree of interactional behavior, the best compliance with therapy, and the least amount of alienation from others (O'Brien 1980; 1982). In a Los Angeles study, Nelson (1977) examined the adaptation of chronically ill elderly hospitalized men at a VA medical center. He found that intensity of religious belief and devotional activities varied inversely with indirect life-threatening behaviors such as refusing medications, pulling out IVs, and other self-injurious acts.

More recently, Pressman and colleagues (1990) examined religious belief, depressive symptoms, and ambulation status among 30 elderly women recovering from hip fractures in a Chicago hospital. Religious belief was measured using a 3-item Index of Religiousness composed of attendance at religious services, self-rated religiousness, and religion as a source of strength and comfort. Depressive symptoms (measured by the GDS) were inversely correlated with religiousness at discharge from the hospital ($r = -.61$, $p < .01$), a relationship that persisted after controlling for severity of illness. Among the three religious items, only God as a source of strength and comfort was related to depressive symptoms both on admission ($r = -.39$) and at discharge ($r = -.52$). Functional recovery (measured by meters walked at discharge) was also significantly related to religiousness ($r = +.45$, $p < .05$), a relationship which again remained significant after controlling for illness severity. In a Portland, Oregon study, Decker and Schulz (1985) also reported increased well-being among elders with spinal cord-injury who were more religious. These studies indicate an important role for religion in both relieving depression and facilitating functional recovery among more disabled patients (also see Idler and Kasl 1992, discussed below).

Community Studies

Several recent community studies have likewise reported an inverse relationship between religiousness and depression in older subjects. Morse and Wisocki (1987) studied a group of 156 elders recruited from 15 senior seniors in western Massachusetts. Lower levels of depression as measured by the SCL-90 and Mood Adjective Checklist were found in those elders with high scores on a religion index. Controlling for number of chronic illnesses did not alter results. The religion index included church membership, frequency of attendance, extent to which religious beliefs were a comfort in life, and extent to which religious beliefs gave meaning to life.

Nelson (1990) examined the association between religious orientation, depression, and self-esteem among 68 elderly participants of a day care program in Austin, Texas. Religious orientation (intrinsic vs. extrinsic) was measured by a modified version of the Allport and Ross (1967) Religious Orientation Scale, depression by the GDS, and self esteem by the Rosenberg Self-Esteem Scale. Fifty percent were Blacks and 78% were women. There was a significant inverse correlation between intrinsic religiosity and both depression ($r = -.23$, $p < .05$) and poor self-esteem ($r = -.38$). There was also a nonsignificant trend for church attendance to be inversely related to both depression ($r = -.08$) and poor self-esteem ($r = -.17$).

In a study of 131 elderly residents of a unit apartment facility in southern Florida, Johnson and Mullins (1989) compared the effects of involvement in various types of family and friendship relationships on *loneliness*, a psychological construct related to unhappiness and depression. After controlling for other factors, they found that a greater involvement in the social aspects of religion was significantly more likely to be related to absence of loneliness than was involvement in either family or friendship relationships. A similar trend noted for private religiousness did not reach statistical significance.

Idler and Kasl (1992) examined the prospective relationship between religious involvement and several aspects of health status, including risk of disability, depression, and mortality, over a three-year period. Their sample consisted of 2812 noninstitutionalized elders enrolled in the Yale Health and Aging project (New Haven, CT). A significant proportion of the sample was disabled and ill (between 1982 and 1989 over 1000 deaths occurred). Thirty-eight percent considered themselves "deeply religious," and 41% attended church at least weekly (a remarkable proportion given their health). This sample is unique in having high proportions of Catholics (53%) and Jews (14%), compared with other studies that have included primarily Protestants. Their results indicated significant protective effects for public religiousness (attendance at services and number of other congregation members known) against disability. Private religiousness (self-assessed religiosity and strength or comfort from religion) was especially protective against depression (CES-D) in recently disabled men. Furthermore, religious group membership for both Christians and Jews protected them against mortality in the month before their respective religious holidays.

In a fascinating study of 302 individuals age 85 or over living in and around Fort Worth, Texas, Hogstel and Kashka (1989) asked subjects (in an open-ended question) what they believed were the factors which contributed most to their long life. The three most common responses (in order) were (1) activity ("hard work, exercise, keeping active physically and mentally"), (2) a strong belief in God and Christian living, and (3) a positive attitude towards self and others. These studies stress the near universal impact of Judeo-Christian beliefs and practices on the mental health of elders in this country.

Mixed-Aged Samples

Research in mixed-aged adults report similar trends. Ellison and colleagues (1989) examined the relationship between religious commitment and life satisfaction in a national sample of Americans of all ages. They reported a small but persistent positive relationship (both statistically and clinically significant) between life satisfaction and strength of religious affiliation, frequency of church attendance, and devotional intensity. Brown and colleagues (1990) examined religiosity and psychological distress in 451 urban Black Americans in Washington, D.C. Religiosity was measured using a 10-item scale. As expected, religiosity was higher among older Blacks. Depressive symptoms, measured using the CES-D, were inversely related to religiosity among both males ($r = -.15$, $p = .01$) and females ($r = -.20$, $p = .01$). Furthermore, higher religiousness tended to buffer against the stress of personal injury in Black males. Williams and colleagues from Yale have recently examined the relationship between religion, psychological distress, health, and stressful life events among community-dwelling adults (older Blacks in particular) utilizing both cross-sectional and longitudinal data from national samples. They found that religious involvement was strongly linked with health and well-being, and buffered against the adverse effects of life events and health problems on psychological health (Williams et al. 1991; Williams, LaVeist, and Jackson 1992).

In conclusion, regardless of sample composition or geographical location, inside or outside of the Bible Belt, religious activities and cognitions appear to consistently buffer against depression in non-psychiatric populations.

EXPLANATIONS FOR THE RELATIONSHIP

As noted in the beginning of this chapter, one explanation for the inverse relationship between depression and religious coping is that religious faith weakens as depression deepens. In other words, as people become more depressed, they are less able to experience God's presence or helpfulness. Our followup data, however, do not support this explanation as a major reason for the cross-sectional findings in the DVAMHS. When religious feelings changed in response to the stress of medical illness, they either increased, decreased, or stayed the same. The direction of change, or lack thereof, was dependent on many factors, including strength of religious belief prior to illness, influence by family members, and level of depression. Several investigators have reported an increase (not decrease) in religiosity as a response to health problems (O'Brien 1982; Croog and Levine 1972).

In the present study, then, there was no consistent relationship between changes in depression and changes in religious coping. Depressions in the medical setting, however, tend to be milder than those in psychiatric settings and are usually reactive to situational factors (Koenig et al. 1991). It is possible that patients in psychiatric settings who suffer from severe depression on the basis of biological and/or genetic factors, do experience a lessening of their religious faith, although I know of no studies that have addressed this issue.

Moos and Tsu (1977) in a review of the seven most common behaviors used to cope with physical illness, provide a more plausible explanation for the inverse relationship between religiousness and depression:

> When life's happenings seem capricious and uncontrollable, as with sudden onset of serious illness, it is often easier to manage if one can find a general purpose or pattern of meaning in the course of events . . . Belief in a divine purpose or in the general beneficence of a divine spirit may serve as consolation or as encouragement to do one's best to deal with the difficulties one encounters. (p. 14)

Loss of hope is one of the most important factors associated with both depression and suicide. Religion offers a source of hope to many disabled elders that health professionals simply cannot provide.

The ability of religious cognitions and rituals to buffer against the stress of medical illness, may to some extent depend on strength of adherence to and integration of beliefs into daily life. In other words, the helpfulness of religious coping may depend on the extent to which a person's faith has been integrated with their motivations, goals, personal and interpersonal activities. Denominational affiliation has relatively little impact on this (as we observed). When faith in religion is stronger than faith in one's possessions, occupation, personal abilities, performance or productivity, declines or losses in these other areas of life may be better tolerated and less threatening to self. When self-worth and self-esteem are based upon religious identification (created in the image of God, loved by God, of importance to God), feelings about the self are less vulnerable to changes brought on by aging. In Fowler's terms, when one's "ultimate concern" is focused on God, other losses that might threaten identity and adjustment will be more easily transcended.

Because depression in later life may have a significant social component (Murphy 1982), religion may also help prevent or relieve depression by bolstering the social network of the elder (Tobin, Ellor, and Anderson-Ray 1986). In the DVAMHS, religious coping for some men involved church participation, other religious group activities, and support from a pastor or other members of their congregation. These supports are particularly important for persons with chronic medical illness, given their need for instrumental supports to maintain their independence. This was evident from our finding that in a field of 16 other sociodemographic and health factors, impaired social support was the strongest cross-sectional correlate of major depression (Koenig et al. 1991).

GENERALIZABILITY

In measuring religious coping with the RCI, we made a special point of defining the term "religious" as involving either personal belief and/or communal activity. Because of the sensitive nature of the subject and wide variety of beliefs likely to be encountered, we allowed each participant to interpret the meaning of religion for himself. Following the patients' leadings, the interviewers attempted to clarify what this interpretation was and determine the degree to which that concept of religion was used to cope. Nevertheless, it is clear from the responses documented in Chapter 10, that religion for the overwhelming majority of participants meant orthodox Christianity. Indeed, over 95% of men were affiliated with traditional Judeo-Christian denominations. Despite coming from widely different religious orientations themselves (secular humanist and conservative Christian), the investigators were able to achieve excellent agreement when using the RCI because of the almost uniform nature of patients' beliefs (inter-rater reliability coefficient 0.81). For this reason, the result of our study can be generalized only to religion based in the Judeo-Christian tradition.

Mental Health and Other World Religions

To what extent might the relationship between religious coping and mental health documented here for Judeo-Christian based religion be applicable to other world religions? Because of the difference in "content" between different world religions, it is not possible to directly generalize our findings to other traditions. As I have noted elsewhere (Chapter 7), it is the *content* of the Judeo-Christian faith that links this religion with mental health.

From an epidemiological perspective, the relationship between aging, mental health, and involvement in other religious faiths is largely unknown. Some reports on the distribution of psychiatric disorders in non-Western countries have included religious affiliation among covariables; however, such broad categorizations (Moslem, Hindu, Protestant, Catholic, Jewish, and so forth) provide data of only limited usefulness (Bazzoui 1970; Mezzich and Raab 1980; Fernando 1975; Verghese et al. 1989; Nandi et al. 1979). I could find only one study in rural India that allowed determination of rates of psychiatric disorder by religious background among the elderly (Nandi et al. 1979). Psychiatric disorders in general were most common among those age 60 or over, particularly women; Muslims had higher rates of psychiatric disorder than Hindus, although this was probably secondary to the minority status of Muslims in that country.

Other studies involve participants of all ages. In a report on affective disorders in Iraq, Bazzoui (1970) compared the religious backgrounds of depressives and manics, finding similar distributions of Moslem, Christians, and Jews among persons with these disorders as in the general population. A study comparing Jewish and Protestant depressives with nondepressed controls, found lower religiosity (measured by synagogue attendance and other Jewish practices) among depressed compared with nondepressed Jews (Fernando 1975). Another study compared depressive symptoms in Peru with those in the United States (both predominantly Christian countries), and found a similar prevalence of guilt (Mezzich and Raab 1980); they concluded that because guilt is a less frequent symptom in India and certain African countries, Christianity heightened a sense of guilt among Western depressives (a highly questionable conclusion based upon the data they present). Finally, a study of schizophrenics in India found that increased religious activity portended better overall prognosis (Verghese et al. 1989); religious activity, however, was not specified although Hindu practices were likely.

The World Health Organization is currently planning an international study to examine the role of religion in successful aging of older adults; the study should provide important data on this poorly researched topic. The examination of mental health and religion in the Eastern traditions is an exciting area for investigation, but will be challenging for a number of reasons, including cross-cultural differences in definitions of both mental health and religious behavior. Older adults in America, when questioned about their religious beliefs and ideas, are typically quite vocal; elders in other cultures, however, may be less willing and perhaps less able to express themselves on this deeply personal subject (at least in terms necessary for epidemiological research).

SUMMARY

Religious coping was found to be inversely related to depressive symptoms and major depressive disorder. This was true whether depression was measured by self-report or by investigator-ratings. We could not explain this finding by an adverse effect of depression on religious coping. Religious coping was also the only significant inverse predictor of increasing depressive symptoms over time. These results support the hypothesis that religion either protects against or helps to relieve depressive symptoms in medical inpatients. This report is not an isolated finding; in fact, it is supported by published accounts from a wide variety of other investigators working with different populations around the country.

Given both the apparent effectiveness and widespread use of religious coping behaviors by many elders with physical illness, clinicians may choose to support, encourage, and in all cases respect patients' religious beliefs and behaviors—especially in those with depression who express strong religious interests. For patients with only minor depressive reactions, pastoral counseling may be sufficient to relieve their symptoms. For those with more serious depressive disorders who require specialized mental health services, professionals may choose to supplement (not replace) traditional treatments with behavioral and cognitive strategies sympathetic to the patient's religious beliefs. Norms and guidelines for integrating religion with cognitive and behavioral approaches have been discussed elsewhere (Probst 1987; Miller and Martin 1988; Koenig, Bearon, and Dayringer 1989b) and will be addressed further in Chapter 15.

REFERENCES

Allport, G.W., and J.M. Ross. (1967). Personal religious orientation and prejudice. *Journal of Personality & Social Psychology* 5:432-443.

Bazzoui, W. (1970). Affective disorders in Iraq. *British Journal of Psychiatry* 117:195-203.

Bergin, A.E. (1991). Values and religious issues in psychotherapy and mental health. *American Psychologist* 46:394-403.

Brown, D.R., S.C. Ndubuishi, and L.E. Gary. (1990). Religiosity and psychological distress among blacks. *Journal of Religion and Health* 29:55-68.

Covalt, N.K. (1960). The meaning of religion to older people. *Geriatrics* 15:658-64.

Croog, S.H., and S. Levine. (1972). Religious identity and response to serious illness: A report on heart patients. *Social Sciences and Medicine* 6:17-32.

Decker, S.D., and R. Schulz. (1985). Correlates of life satisfaction and depression in middle-aged and elderly spinal cord-injured persons. *The American Journal of Occupational Therapy* 39:740-745.

Ellis, A. (1980). Psychotherapy and atheistic values: A response to A.E. Bergin's 'Psychotherapy and Religious Values.' *Journal of Consulting & Clinical Psychology* 48:642-645.

Ellison, C.G., D.A. Gay, and T.A. Glass. (1989). Does religious commitment contribute to individual life satisfaction? *Social Forces* 68:100-123.

Fernando, S.J.M. (1975). A cross-cultural study of some familial and social factors in depressive illness. *British Journal of Psychiatry*, 127:46-53.

Freud, S. (1907). Obsessive acts and religious practices. In *Sigmund Freud. Collected Papers, vol. 2*, edited by J. Strachey. New York: Basic Books, 1959, p. 34.

Freud, S. (1927). Future of an illusion. In *The Standard Edition of the Complete Psychological Works of Sigmund Freud, vol. 21*, edited by J. Strachey. London: The Hogarth Press, 1962, pp. 18,21,44.

Hogstel, M.O., and M. Kashka. (1989). Staying healthy after 85. *Geriatric Nursing* (January/February):16-18.

Idler, E.L., and S.V. Kasl. (1992). Religion, disability, depression, and the timing of death. *American Journal of Sociology* 97:1052-1079.

Johnson, D.P., and L.C. Mullins. (1989). Religiosity and loneliness among the elderly. *Journal of Applied Gerontology* 8:110-131.

Koenig, H.G., L.B. Bearon, and R. Dayringer. (1989b). Physician perspectives on the role of religion in the physician-older patient relationship. *Journal of Family Practice* 28:441-448.

Koenig, H.G., L.K. George, and I. Siegler. (1988b). The use of religion and other emotion-regulating coping strategies among older adults. *The Gerontologist* 28:303-310.

Koenig, H.G., D.O. Moberg, and J.N. Kvale. (1988a). Religious and health characteristics of patients attending a geriatric assessment clinic. *Journal of the American Geriatrics Society* 36:362-374.

Koenig, H.G., F. Shelp, V. Goli, H.J. Cohen, and D.G. Blazer. (1989a). Survival and healthcare utilization in elderly medical inpatients with major depression. *Journal of the American Geriatrics Society* 37:599-606.

Koenig, H.G., K.G. Meador, F. Shelp, V. Goli, H.J. Cohen, and D.G. Blazer. (1991). Major depressive disorder in hospitalized medically ill patients: An examination of young and elderly patients. *Journal of the American Geriatrics Society* 39:881-890.

Koenig, H.G., H.J. Cohen, D.G. Blazer, C. Pieper, K.G. Meador, F. Shelp, V. Goli, and R. DiPasquale. (1992). Religious coping and depression in hospitalized elderly medically ill men. *American Journal of Psychiatry* 149:1693-1700.

Mezzich, J.E., and E. Raab. (1980). Depressive symptomatology across the Americas. *Archives of General Psychiatry* 37:818-823.

Miller, W.R., and J.E. Martin. (1988). *Behavior Therapy and Religion: Integrating Spiritual and Behavioral Approaches to Change.* Newbury Park, CA: Sage Publishers.

Moos, R.H., and V.D. Tsu. (1977). The crisis of physical illness: An overview. In *Coping with Physical Illness*, edited by R.H. Moos and V.D. Tsu. New York: Plenum Press, p. 14.

Morse, C.K., and P.A. Wisocki. (1987). Importance of religiosity to elderly adjustment. *Journal of Religion & Aging* 4(1):15-28.

Murphy, E. (1982). Social origins of depression in old age. *British Journal of Psychiatry* 141:135-142.

Nandi, D.N., G. Banerjee, G.C. Boral, H. Ganguli, S. Ajmany, A. Ghosh, and S. Sarkar. (1979). Socio-economic status and prevalence of mental disorders in certain rural communities in India. *Acta Psychiatrica Scandinavia* 59:276-294.

Nelson, F.L. (1977). Religiosity and self-destructive crises in the institutionalized elderly. *Suicide and Life-threatening Behavior* 7(2):67-73.

Nelson, P.B. (1990). Religious orientation of the elderly. *Journal of Gerontological Nursing* 16(2):29-35.

O'Brien, M.E. (1980). Effective social environment and hemodialysis adaptation–a panel analysis. *Journal of Health and Social Behavior* 21:360-370.

O'Brien, M.E. (1982). Religious faith and adjustment to long-term hemodialysis. *Journal of Religion & Health* 21:68-80.

Pressman, P., J.S. Lyons, D.B. Larson, and J.J. Strain. (1990). Religious belief, depression, and ambulation status in elderly women with broken hips. *American Journal of Psychiatry* 147:758-760.

Probst, L.R. (1987). *Psychotherapy in a Religious Framework: Spirituality in the Emotional Healing Process.* NY: Human Sciences Press.

Rodin, G.M., J. Chmara, J. Ennis, S. Fenton, H. Locking, and K. Steinhouse. (1981). Stopping life-sustaining medical treatment: Psychiatric considerations in the termination of renal dialysis. *Canadian Journal of Psychiatry* 26:540-544.

Roof, W.C., and W.M. McKinney. (1987). *American Mainline Religion.* New Brunswick: Rutgers University Press, pp. 253-256.

Rovner, B.W., P.S. German, L.J. Brant, R. Clark, L. Burton, and M.F. Folstein.

(1991). Depression and mortality in nursing homes. *Journal of the American Medical Association* 265:993-996.

Smith, P.L. (1979). Splines as a useful and convenient statistical tool. *American Statistician* 33:57-62.

Stam, M., and J.J. Strain. (1985). Refusal of treatment: The role of psychiatric consultation. *Mt. Sinai Journal of Medicine* 52:4-9.

Stoudemire, A., and T.L. Thompson. (1983). Medication noncompliance: Systematic approaches to evaluation and intervention. *General Hospital Psychiatry* 5:233-239.

Tobin, S.S., J. Ellor, and S.M. Anderson-Ray. (1986). *Enabling the Elderly: Religious Institutions Within the Community Service System.* Albany: State University of New York Press.

Verghese, A., J.K. John, S. Rajkumar, J. Richard, B.B. Sethi, and J.K. Trivedi. (1989). Factors associated with the course and outcome of schizophrenia in India. *British Journal of Psychiatry* 154:499-503.

Williams, D.R., T.A. LaVeist, and J.S. Jackson. (1992). Religious involvement and health of the African American elderly. *Journal of Gerontology* (in press).

Williams, D.R., D. Larson, R. Buckler, R. Heckmann, and C. Pyle. (1991). Religion and psychological distress in a community sample. *Social Science and Medicine* 32:1257-1262.

Chapter 12

Religion and Anxiety

The fruit of the spirit is love, joy, peace . . .

–Galatians 5:22

Case. An older man was seeing a colleague of mine for treatment of a phobia. Mr. Gillis (fictitious name) was terrified of *crossing streets*. This condition had been quite disabling, since he lived in a large-sized city with many thoroughfares. The phobia had a rather sudden onset. Mr. Gillis had been an alcoholic for many years. One day two years earlier, while crossing the street in an inebriated condition, he was hit by a car. He suffered serious injuries, including a closed-head injury that left him with a brain contusion that impaired his mental capacities.

Since then, Mr. Gillis had been rather simple-minded, and was therefore not a good candidate for insight-oriented or cognitive psychotherapy. His therapist wanted to avoid benzodiazepines (minor tranquilizers) because of the prior history of alcohol abuse. A treatment plan was agreed upon using behavioral therapy that involved relaxation, desensitization, and exposure.

Prior to his first treatment, however, the man became involved in a Bible study group at the prompting of a friend. Mr. Gillis had never been particularly religious prior to this time. The members of the group prayed for him and wrote scriptures on a piece of paper for him to read while attempting to cross the street. On the first day, a member of the Bible study group crossed the street with him. The following day, he attempted to cross a major street alone with only his list of Bible verses. Repeating the verses over and over again in his mind, he successfully crossed the street alone for the first time since the accident.

Recent studies indicate a high prevalence of anxiety disorders in persons age 65 or over (5.5%), ranking them among the most common mental disturbances in later life (Regier et al. 1988; Blazer, Hughes, and Fowler 1989). Anxiety disorders (and one-year prevalence rates) in older adults include phobia (simple, social, agoraphobia) (4.8%), panic disorder (0.1%), obsessive-compulsive disorder (0.8%), generalized anxiety disorder (2.2%), and post-traumatic stress disorder (< 1%) (Eaton, Dryman, and Weissman 1991; Blazer et al. 1991). Anxiety disorders are more common in women than in men, and more common in Blacks than in Whites and Hispanics (Eaton, Dryman, and Weissman 1991). Anxiety is particularly common among older adults with psychosocial problems and/or medical illness (Derogatis et al. 1983).

WHAT IS ANXIETY?

Anxiety is basically the same emotion as fear; they are, however, distinguishable. According to Kaplan and Sadock (1988),

> Anxiety is a diffuse, highly unpleasant, often vague feeling of apprehension, accompanied by one or more bodily sensations–for example, an empty feeling in the pit of the stomach, tightness in the chest, pounding heart, perspiration, [dizziness, difficulty breathing, diarrhea], headache, or sudden urge to void. Restlessness and desire to move around are also common. . . . Fear, a similar alerting signal, is differentiated from anxiety as follows: Fear is in response to a threat that is known, external, definite, or nonconflictual in origin; anxiety is in response to a threat that is unknown, internal, vague, or conflictual in origin. (p. 310)

Thus, fear is an emotional response to a known, direct threat, whereas anxiety is a response to factors which are less easily specified and may even be unconscious. Anxiety is not always negative, and may serve an important function in motivating persons to change.

Anxiety and Depression

There is a heavy overlap between depression and anxiety in older adults (Blazer, Hughes, and Fowler 1989; Blazer et al. 1991). Nevertheless, they are distinct psychological disorders with quite different symptom profiles. With depression, particularly the more severe variety, persons may lose all motivation, desire, and energy to participate in activities or to improve their selves or situations. Rather than acting as a motivating force (as anxiety typically does), severe depression often disables the person.

Unlike anxiety, then, there is no optimum level of depression that enhances function. Depression is associated with fatigue, discouragement, hopelessness, and a desire to give up–mood states that interfere with motivation towards self-care and growth. Mild to moderate levels of anxiety, on the other hand, enhance efforts toward self-improvement and psychological/spiritual growth. Most therapists agree that a certain level of anxiety is necessary in psychotherapy to keep patients motivated to change. Because change and growth involve a lot of hard work, they usually require some type of stimulus to keep the person focused at their task. Anxiety, if not overwhelming, provides this stimulus. As indicated earlier, then, all anxiety is not dysfunctional; in fact, a certain amount of it may be necessary for optimal character development.

On the other hand, anxiety may also be excessive, noxious and without purpose. There are at least two situations in which this occurs: (1) when change within the individual or their environment is not possible, and (2) when anxiety is exaggerated out of proportion to the situation as a result of hereditary or biological influences. This leads us to a consideration of causes for anxiety.

ETIOLOGY OF ANXIETY

There are many causes for anxiety in later life. These often revolve around the threat of possible loss–including loss of financial security, loss of social position, loss of health and independence, loss of family and friends, and loss of life (death anxiety). The most common cause for anxiety that appears for the first time in old age, however, is medical illness. Thus, any elderly adult with a recent onset of anxiety symptoms requires a complete medical evaluation to rule out biological causes such as hyperthyroidism, toxic drug effect (theophylline), excessive caffeine ingestion, hypoglycemia, and so forth. Psychiatric disorders can also cause anxiety. Such conditions include major depression, schizophrenia, delusional disorders, and organic mental disorders.

Aside from medical, psychiatric, or genetic influences, anxiety may also result from external events (interpersonal and environmental), internal events (intrapsychic), or a combination of the two. Whether or not a person feels anxious in response to an external event, depends on how he or she perceives and interprets the event. Both perception and interpretation depend on a person's general view of the world and the underlying assumptions or cognitive schema associated with it. One might predict, then, that older adults with a religious worldview might experience anxiety to events differently from those with a predominantly secular perspective.

ARE RELIGION AND ANXIETY RELATED?

Freud (1927) believed that religion was a product of man's imagination to cope with anxieties aroused by his or her helplessness in the face of powerful and unpredictable natural forces:

> I have tried to show that religious ideas have arisen from the same need as have all the other achievements of civilization: from the necessity of defending oneself against the crushingly superior force of nature. (p. 21)

As we saw in Chapter 2, Freud viewed religion as a primitive way of dealing with such fears that would never be as effective as the rational intellect in containing anxiety. He predicted that intellectual operations and rational thought would eventually replace religion as the solution to man's fears.

The Judeo-Christian scriptures also have much to say about the causes and cures of fear and anxiety. Two basic messages are conveyed: (1) a need to fear God and (2) a promise of relief of fear for those who do. The word "fear" or one of its derivatives is mentioned 514 times in the Old and New Testaments, about 40% of the time admonishing believers to fear God and 40% of the time comforting them to "fear not" when calamities strike (Strong 1901). Thus, fear and its relief appear to play important roles in this religious tradition.

The Great Debate

In the past century, mental health professionals and theologians have contested over whether religion increases or decreases anxiety (Gorsuch 1988).

While this topic has been addressed elsewhere in detail (Koenig et al. 1993), I will summarize here. As noted above, Freud (1927), and more recently Ellis (1980), have maintained that religion is closely related to neurosis, causes unhealthy repression of natural drives, increases intrapsychic conflict, and results in a rigid and inflexible character style. Others–most notably Bergin, Menninger, Bandura, and Rogers–have emphasized the generally positive influences of religion on mental health, while acknowledging the potentially harmful effects of certain religious behaviors when performed in excess (Bergin 1985;1991).

Indeed, about half of all studies objectively examining this question have found an *inverse* relationship between religiousness and anxiety (Tanset 1976; Entner 1977; Sturgeon and Hamley 1979; Leming 1979-1980; Minear and Brush 1980-81; Baker and Gorsuch 1982; Richardson, Berman, and Piwowarski 1983; Finney and Malony 1985; Bergin, Masters, and Richards 1987; Kraft, Litwin, and Barber 1987; Koenig 1988; Thorson and Powell 1990). Other reports have indicated *no relationship* (Kurlycheck 1976; O'Rourke 1977; Downey 1984; Frenz and Carey 1989; Thorson and Powell 1989) or a *positive* one (Rokeach and Kemp 1960; Wilson and Miller 1968; Dittes 1969; Argyle and Beit-Hallahmi 1975; Blotcky, Cohen, Conatser, and Klopovich 1985; Francis, Pearson, and Stubbs 1985).

Those demonstrating a positive relationship between religiousness and anxiety have typically been conducted in teenagers or college psychology students–a group readily surveyed because of their ease of recruitment. The "immaturity" of young adults in terms of religious faith may understandably contribute to certain excesses of and instabilities in religious devotion–particularly during this time characterized by emotional upheaval and identity struggles. One might anticipate, however, that as persons age, mature, learn from experiences in life, and interact within the religious community, they would be more likely to experience the "fruit" of a religious life in terms of "love, joy, peace, patience, kindness, goodness, faithfulness, self-control" (Galatians 5:22).

On the other hand, if religion was a true source of neurosis, then conflicts aroused by it in early life might fixate or deepen as years passed. Neurotic conflicts might be more likely to break to the surface in late life when the stresses of health, financial and social losses reach their peak. Therefore, an ideal sample for the study of the relationship between religion and anxiety would consist of older adults. Another reason for studying this relationship in older persons is that religion and anxiety are both common in late life, thus making any association (positive or negative) more evident.

The studies which have included middle-age or older adults, however, have mostly focused on death anxiety (Jeffers, Nichols, and Eisdorfer 1961; Swenson 1961; Williams and Cole 1968; Kurlycheck 1976; Wittkowski and Baumgartner 1977; O'Rourke 1977; Leming 1979-80; Feifel and Nagy 1981; Richardson, Berman, and Piwowarski 1983; Downey 1984; Koenig 1988; Thorson and Powell 1989). About two-thirds of these report an inverse relationship between religiosity and fear of death, and the remainder found no relationship (Kurlycheck 1976; O'Rourke 1977; Thorson and Powell 1989). Interestingly, there were no reports indicating greater anxiety among the religious elderly.

A number of reports have suggested that *certainty* of belief, rather than *content* (religious or nonreligious), determines level of anxiety. In these studies, persons who were ambivalent about their beliefs or pursued a moderate or "middle of the road" commitment, were found to be more anxious than either devout believers or devout nonbelievers or the nonreligious (Hinton 1967; Alexander and Adlerstein 1959; Leming 1979-80; Smith, Nehemkis, and Charter 1983-84; Donahue 1985).

Relationship Hypotheses

Up until recently, three major hypotheses have been forwarded to explain the relationship between anxiety and religion. They are based on a combination of professional opinion and systematic research. The first hypothesis holds that religion leads to an increase in anxiety by promoting unhealthy repression of natural drives and instincts which produces intrapsychic conflict. Anxiety is further increased by the frustrating dynamics of guilt, ultimate helplessness, and lack of personal control. Religious communities are caricaturized as exerting control over their members by inducing anxiety related to the final judgement, God's anger and retribution, and eternal tortures for those who do not comply. Natural drives (anger, selfishness, sexual needs) are thus repressed and increasing anxiety is experienced as those drives threaten to be expressed. These arguments have their origin in the writings of Freud and others.

The second hypothesis refutes the first. Rather than inducing anxiety, it is claimed that devout religiousness actually protects the individual from it. Proponents of this view point out that many passages in scripture are devoted to comforting the anxious and alleviating fear. They argue that religion decreases anxiety by providing a worldview that centers on the existence of an all powerful and merciful God who is in control, cares about the welfare of each individual person, and responds to their pleas. Belief in an afterlife further diminishes anxiety by eliminating the notion of death as a final end and by conveying a sense of hope and delayed gratification to those suffering from physical or emotional sickness in the present world.

A third hypothesis contends that both of the above arguments are true to a certain extent. It tries to reconcile these conflicting views by claiming that religion first arouses anxiety and then relieves it. This hypothesis became known as *Homan's thesis* in the early 1960s after a debate on the topic by a prominent group of anthropologists and sociologists (Homan 1965). Homan contended that religion first aroused a sense of anxiety by pointing out certain realities about life which most persons repress out of awareness, such as the fact of mortality. According to this theory, religion's solution to death is seen as both comforting and anxiety provoking; comforting in dispelling the notion of death of the self, anxiety provoking in highlighting the consequences of judgement. Thus, while providing a solution to existential anxiety, it arouses a new fear–that of retribution for sin. Proponents argue, however, there is also a solution to this fear. The repentant sinner can relieve his or her guilty fear by confessing their sins and promising not to repeat them again. Religious rituals (sacrificing animals or performing acts of penance) have long existed that serve the function of facilitating this process of absolution and providing a sense of forgiveness. Professor at Cambridge University and Christian apologist, C.S. Lewis (1943), defends this view:

> All I am doing is to ask people to face the facts–to understand the questions which Christianity claims to answer. And they are very terrifying facts. I wish it was possible to say something more agreeable. But I must say what I think true. Of course, I quite agree that the Christian religion in the long run, is a thing of unspeakable comfort. But it does not begin in comfort; it begins in the dismay I have been describing, and it is no use at all trying to go on to that comfort without first going through that dismay. (p. 39)

In summary, the third hypothesis sees religion as arousing and then relieving both man's existential and religious fears. It is related to the notion that strength of belief has more to do with anxiety than content of belief (Hinton 1967; Smith, Nehemkis, and Charter 1983-84; Donahue 1985). Persons who have no existential concerns (i.e., have effectively repressed anticipations about death) and no worries about divine retribution, will feel little anxiety and therefore experience no need for the comfort that religion has to offer. Those who are devoutly religious will likewise experience little anxiety since both their existential and religious fears would be eliminated. Leming (1979-80) attempted to test Homan's thesis in a sample of 372 adults (mean age 46). He found an inverted U-shaped curve relating level of anxiety to increasing religious belief, and interpreted this as supporting the theory's truth–that religion did indeed serve the function of "afflicting the comforted and comforting the afflicted." Only about 10 to 15 percent of other studies, however, support this view.

According to these three hypotheses, then, religion may (1) increase anxiety, (2) relieve anxiety, or (3) do both. Is there any evidence from studies of older adults that supports one or the other of these hypothesized effects of religion? Apart from death anxiety, few investigators have examined the more general relationship between religion and anxiety symptoms or disorders in later life. In fact, a review of the literature revealed only one study which examined religion and anxiety *disorder* in adults. Levendusky and Belfer (1988) found that agoraphobics were more likely than simple or nonphobics to report Catholicism as their religion of upbringing; religious background, however, was the only religious variable examined.

Two other studies are of particular interest because they examine the effects of a religious intervention on anxiety symptoms. In 1982, Morris explored the effects of a religious pilgrimage to Lourdes on the mental health of 28 chronically ill middle-aged and older adults. Comparing before and after scores on state and trait anxiety measures, she found a significant drop in both types of anxiety following the pilgrimage. This effect was sustained for at least 12 months after returning home. More recently, Finney and Newton (1985) evaluated the effects of contemplative prayer as an adjunct to psychotherapy in treating nine subjects ranging in age from 21 to 58 years. In a time-series, quasi-experimental design, each subject served as his or her own control. Following the intervention, subjects reported better adaptation and lower anxiety levels.

Prior to the Duke Epidemiologic Catchment Area (ECA) study, however, there had been no research on the relationship between religion and anxiety in a general community sample of older adults. Duke was one of five sites selected by the National Institute of Mental Health (NIMH) in the early 1980s to participate in the ECA program–a survey of psychiatric symptoms and disorders in America which has since become the country's primary data base for such information. One year following the initial survey, participants were recontacted for a second interview (Wave II) that essentially repeated the same questions as in the first interview; however, included in Wave II were five questions on religiousness. The Duke site was the only ECA location that addressed religious beliefs and behaviors, in addition to denominational affiliation. Thus, the Wave II survey collected data on the religious characteristics of subjects in addition to detailed information on both recent (past 6 months) and life-rates for anxiety symptoms and disorders.

THE DUKE ECA STUDY

During this survey, data were collected on 1299 community-dwelling adults age 60 or over who were living in central North Carolina. Because the North Carolina site was chosen by the NIMH to examine rural-urban differences in rate of psychiatric disorder, the sample was composed of a mixture of older adults from the city and country. Subjects were randomly sampled in the following manner. A five-county area surrounding Duke Hospital was stratified into segments which represented racial, rural-urban, and economic characteristics of residents living in the five counties. Segments were then randomly selected, and all housing units in each segment were examined. Once a household was selected, it was rostered for all eligible participants. To ensure that a random selection of respondents was obtained, the Kish method was used to select one participant from each household. Table 12.1 gives the sociodemographic and health characteristics of the sample.

Anxiety was operationalized in two ways: (1) responses to individual questions were summed to form an *anxiety symptom* index, and (2) groups of anxiety symptoms were collected together to form clinical syndromes called *anxiety disorders*. Both recent (past six months) and life-time prevalence rates for the latter were determined using the Diagnostic Interview Schedule (DIS) (Robins, Helzer, and Croughan 1981). Anxiety disorders included simple phobia (fear of spiders, for instance), social phobia (fear of speaking in public or of participating in social settings), obsessive-compulsive disorder, panic disorder, agoraphobia (fear of open spaces), post-traumatic stress disorder, and generalized anxiety disorder. A series of questions was asked to determine whether respondents met the diagnostic criteria for each of these disorders. The anxiety symptom index was then created by summing all of the positive responses to questions asked when assessing for the different anxiety disorders

TABLE 12.1. Characteristics of the sample (n = 1299)

	%	(n)
Sociodemographic		
Age > 75 y	24.6	(306)
Sex (Male)	36.0	(467)
Race (Black)	35.3	(456)
Education (8th grade or less)	46.3	(602)
Socioeconomic Status (low)	50.0	(649)
Residence (urban)	42.7	(555)
Living Situation (alone)	38.3	(498)
Social Support (low)	48.4	(590)
Mental Health		
Anxiety Disorders (excludes simple phobia)		
Six-month prevalence	8.8	(110)
Lifetime prevalence	14.7	(186)
Negative Live Events (at least one recent)	32.4	(420)
Parental Home (unstable)	16.3	(207)
Hx Alcohol Abuse/Dependence	7.6	(99)
Physical Health		
Self-Rated Health Status (fair or poor)	38.1	(490)
Activities of Daily Living (impaired)	48.4	(628)
No. Chronic Illnesses (2 or more)	31.6	(410)
Religious		
Church Attendance (1/wk or more)	52.6	(681)
Prayer/Bible Study (sev times/wk or more)	55.9	(718)
Religious TV/Radio (sev times/wk or more)	31.5	(406)
Importance of Religion (very important)	87.9	(1138)
Religious Denominations		
Pentacostals	4.1	(53)
Conservative Protestants	61.5	(799)
Mainline Protestants	29.8	(387)
Catholics	1.2	(15)
Others	1.4	(18)
None	2.1	(27)
"Born Again" Status (yes)	69.3	(884)

Table from Koenig et al 1992. Used with permission.

(except for generalized anxiety disorder and post-traumatic stress disorder); the resulting symptom index ranged from 0 to 28 and was used as a measure of overall anxiety.

In addition to religious denomination, five items explored religious behaviors and experiences: church attendance (six categories), private religious activities (prayer and Bible reading) (six categories), religious TV viewing (six categories), importance of religion (three categories), and "born again" status (two categories). A wide variety of other information was also collected. Physical health was measured by assessing functional status (activities of daily living) and number of chronic medical illnesses. Social support was assessed using the Duke Social Support Scale (Landerman et al. 1989).

Statistical Analysis. Pearson correlations and the likelihood-ratio chi-square statistics were used to examine uncontrolled relationships. Hierarchical regression was used to control for the possible confounding effects of other sociodemographic and health variables on the religion-anxiety symptom relationship (interval-level data). The Cochran-Mantel-Haenszel method was used to control analyses involving religious variables and anxiety disorders (categorical data). A more detailed account of the methods, analysis, and results may be found elsewhere (Koenig et al. 1993).

Findings

Anxiety Symptoms

Recently reported anxiety symptoms (past 6 months) were inversely related to church attendance ($r = -.08$, $p < .01$); this association was especially strong in women, Whites, city-dwellers, the unmarried, those with moderate to high social support, and those with no history of alcohol abuse. On the other hand, recent anxiety symptoms were more common among religious TV viewers ($r = +.09$, $p < .001$); this relationship was particularly strong among the young elderly (ages 60 to 75 years), Whites, those from rural areas, those who were married, those with moderate to high social support, those from unstable homes, and those without a history of alcohol abuse. Frequency of prayer or Bible study and importance of religion were unrelated to anxiety symptoms, and subgroup analyses did not reveal significant trends in the data. Participants referring to themselves as being "born again" experienced significantly higher levels of anxiety symptoms (p = .01), as did elders from Pentecostal and conservative Protestant denominations [both recent (p < .05) and life-time symptoms (p < .01)]. Persons claiming membership in no religious denomination experienced the lowest level of anxiety.

In order to assess the possible confounding effects of other sociodemographic and health variables on the relationships, we examined the correlations between these variables and religious characteristics of respondents (Table 12.2). Frequent church attenders were significantly more likely to be younger, have higher social support, fewer chronic illnesses, and better physical function (ability to perform activities of daily living). Elders who frequently viewed religious TV, prayed or read the Bible, considered religion very important, or claimed Pentecostal or conservative Protestant affiliations, on the other hand, were *much more likely* to be Black, have low socioeconomic status, have more chronic illnesses, and experience more functional disabilities. More important, these latter characteristics were also found to be strongly associated with high levels of anxiety.

We then statistically controlled for the effects of sociodemographic and health factors on the religion-anxiety relationships reported above using hierarchical regression (Table 12.3). Interestingly, the negative association between anxiety and church attendance, and the positive association between anxiety and religious TV viewing, both *disappeared*. Fewer chronic illnesses and better functional status among church attenders accounted for the inverse association with anxiety (given the strong association between anxiety and health); thus, frequent church attendance was acting as a proxy for physical health status, and by itself was unrelated to anxiety level. In a similar fashion, the positive association between anxiety symptoms, Pentecostal or conservative Protestant religious affiliation, born-again status, and religious TV viewing, all lost their significance when demographic factors and socioeconomic status were taken into account.

We then tested Homan's thesis by comparing anxiety symptoms in participants with high, moderate, and low levels of religious

TABLE 12.2. Correlations between religious variables, sociodemographic, and health factors

	Religious Variables				
	Church Att	Prayer/ Bible	Religious TV	Impor- tance	"Born Again"
Sociodemo					
Age	−.07*	+.12**	+.05	+.07*	+.03
Sex (Female)	+.09**	+.24**	+.10**	+.19**	+.10**
Race (Black)	+.05	+.02	+.30**	+.14**	+.12**
SES (socioec)	+.02	−.06	−.38**	−.24**	−.29**
Resid (urban)	+.00	−.06	−.11**	−.09**	−.15**
Social Support	+.17**	+.06	+.04	+.12**	+.14**
Mental Health					
Parent Unstab	−.03	−.01	−.02	−.01	−.03
Neg Life Event	−.06	+.08*	+.07*	+.03	+.06
Alcohol Ab/Dp	−.09**	−.10**	+.02	−.05	−.03
Physical Health					
Chr Hlth Prbs	−.10**	+.08*	+.11**	+.10**	+.06
Impaired Func	−.29**	+.08*	+.13**	+.07*	+.05

* p < .01   ** p < .001   (Pearson correlations, uncontrolled)
Table from Koenig et al 1993. Used with permission.

activity/importance. Anxiety symptoms were lowest among those with high church attendance and highest among those with low attendance; they were equally as common among elders with moderate and high levels of prayer or Bible reading, and slightly lower among those with low levels of prayer or Bible reading. Frequency of anxiety symptoms differed little between moderate and frequent religious TV viewers and was lowest among those who were infrequently involved in such activity. Anxiety was highest among those reporting religion to be very important, and lowest in those finding religion only moderately important or not important at all; none of these differences were significant. Finally, we summed the scores on all four religious variables to obtain a "religiosity index;" this index ranged from 4 to 24. We then divided the index up into quartiles, labeling individuals falling in the top quartile as "highly religious" (20-24), the middle two quartiles as "moderately religious" (16-19), and the lowest quartile as "low or non-religious" (4-15). There was virtually no difference in anxiety symptoms between these three groups. Considering these findings, then, there is little evidence to support Homan's thesis.

Anxiety Disorders

A similar pattern of relationships was found when we examined religious characteristics and anxiety *disorders* (recent and life-time) (Table 12.4). In the uncontrolled analyses, elders who frequently prayed or read the Bible were more likely to be diagnosed with anxiety disorders ($p < .05$). Anxiety disorders were also significantly more common among elders from Pentecostal and conservative Protestant denominations. This was especially true for anxiety disorders such as agoraphobia and simple phobia. Nevertheless, when sex, health, life events, and socioeconomic status were taken into account, the associations between religious characteristics and anxiety disorder once again disappeared. Stratifying these analyses by sociodemographic and health factors did not alter the results.

As with anxiety symptoms, we found no evidence to support Homan's thesis when examining the distribution of anxiety disorders by religious characteristics. There was no suggestion of higher rates of anxiety disorder among those who scored in the moderate range of any religious variable. Unadjusted rates of anxiety disorder were the following for each level of religious activity/importance: church attendance (high 7.9%, medium 9.6%, low 10.1%); frequency of prayer/Bible reading (high 10.4%, medium 5.5%, low 8.0%); frequency of religious TV viewing (high 8.1%, medium

TABLE 12.3. Associations between religious variables and anxiety symptoms, controlling for sociodemographic and health factors

	Stage 1 b (SE)	Stage 2 b (SE)	Stage 3 b (SE)	Stage 4 b (SE)	Stage 5 b (SE)
Relig Vars					
Church Att	−.11 (.04)**	−.12 (.04)***	−.11 (.04)**	−.07 (.04)*	−.03 (.04)
Relig TV/Radio	+.13 (.04)***	+.11 (.04)**	+.06 (.04)	+.06 (.04)	+.05 (.04)
Prayer/Bible	+.02 (.04)	−.03 (.03)	−.03 (.03)	−.02 (.03)	−.04 (.03)
Import Relig	+.27 (.15)	+.08 (.15)	−.05 (.15)	+.06 (.15)	+.05 (.15)
"Born Again"	+.33 (.14)*	+.23 (.13)	+.08 (.13)	+.14 (.13)	+.16 (.13)
<u>Denominations</u>					
Pentacostal	+1.22 (.52)*	+.86 (.49)	+.71 (.49)	+.29 (.53)	+.02 (.51)
Conserv Prot	+.77 (.43)*	+.52 (.41)	+.48 (.40)	+.52 (.44)	+.46 (.43)
Mainline Prot	+.39 (.44)	+.24 (.41)	+.41 (.41)	+.41 (.45)	+.32 (.43)
Catholics	+.11 (.71)	−.01 (.66)	+.16 (.65)	+.19 (.66)	+.17 (.63)
Other	+.67 (.67)	+.37 (.67)	+.56 (.68)	+.49 (.70)	+.14 (.68)
Model R-sq	.01	.04	.06	.07	.14
N in model	1295	1262	1261	1160	1148

Stage 1 contains only the religious variable in the model

Stage 2 adds demographic and early life variables (age, sex, race, parental home) to the Stage 1 model

Stage 3 adds socioeconomic variables (SES, residence location) to the Stage 2 model

Stage 4 adds social variables (social support, marital status) to the Stage 3 model

Stage 5 adds mental and physical health variables (negative life events, hx alcohol abuse, number of chronic illnesses) to the Stage 4 model

In creating dummy variables for denominations, "none" category is missing

* $p < .05$, ** $p < .01$, *** $p < .001$

Table adapted from Koenig et al 1992. Used with permission.

TABLE 12.4. Six-month and lifetime rates of anxiety disorders by religious variables

	Church Att		Pray/Bible		Relig TV		Importance	
	Low %	High %	Low %	High %	Low %	High %	Low %	High %
All Disorders								
6-month(n = 110)	9.8	7.9	6.9	10.4	9.0	8.1	6.6	9.1
Lifetime (n = 186)	15.2	14.0	12.5	16.4	14.7	13.9	10.3	15.1
Generalized Anxiety Disorder (GAD)								
6-mo (n = 31)	2.6	2.2	2.1	2.7	2.8	1.5	1.9	2.5
Lifetime (n = 89)	6.4	7.4	5.8	7.8	7.2	6.2	5.1	7.1
Agoraphobia								
6-mo (n = 59)	5.1	4.2	3.8	5.4	4.1	5.5	2.0	5.0
Lifetime (n = 81)	7.0	5.6	5.3	7.1	6.0	6.7	3.8	6.6
Obsessive-Compulsive Disorder (OCD)								
6-mo (n = 15)	1.0	1.3	1.1	1.3	1.2	1.0	1.2	1.1
Lifetime (n = 17)	1.1	1.5	1.2	1.4	1.4	1.2	1.3	1.3
Social Phobia								
6-mo (n = 23)	2.5	1.2	2.2	1.6	2.1	1.1	2.0	1.8
Lifetime (n = 36)	3.4	2.2	3.2	2.5	3.2	1.7	2.6	2.8
Phobia (Simple)								
6-mo (n = 110)	8.8	8.5	8.1	8.7	7.9	10.1	7.1	8.9
Life (n = 154)	12.2	11.6	11.5	12.0	11.4	13.1	10.2	12.3

	Mainline Protestants %	Conservative Protestants %	Pentacostals %	Not BA %	BA %
All Disorders					
6-mo	6.5	9.4	16.0*	8.2	9.1
Lifetime	10.8	16.5	18.0*	13.0	15.1
GAD					
6-mo	1.3	3.0	3.9	3.1	2.2
Lifetime	5.4	7.9	7.8	6.1	7.1
Agoraphobia					
6-mo	2.9	5.0	11.8*	3.4	5.3
Lifetime	4.4	6.8	11.3	5.6	6.7
OCD					
6-mo	1.6	0.8	3.8	0.8	1.2
Lifetime	1.8	0.9	3.8	1.0	1.4
Social Phobia					
6-mo	1.6	1.2	3.9	1.3	2.1
Lifetime	2.1	3.1	3.8	1.5	3.3
Phobia (Simple)					
6-mo	6.3	9.2	17.7*	7.3	9.3
Lifetime	9.8	12.5	21.6	10.2	12.9

* p < .01 (uncontrolled)
No significant differences when controlled for sociodemographic and health variables
Table adapted from Koenig et al 1992. Used with permission.

9.3%, low 8.5%); and importance of religion (high 9.1%, medium 7.9%, low 0.0%).

Discussion

Let us now examine each of the three hypotheses (discussed earlier) in light of the findings from the Duke ECA Study. The first hypothesis suggested that religion might be a cause for anxiety by promoting unhealthy repression of natural instincts, by proscribing doctrines that lead to a rigid and inflexible coping style, and/or by arousing unnecessary guilt or other unpleasant emotions over sins, devils, hell, or the like. Although we did initially find higher anxiety among frequent religious TV viewers, those who often prayed or read the Bible, and members of Pentecostal or conservative Protestant denominations, these associations completely disappeared when we controlled for socioeconomic and health factors.

Rather than indicating that religious elders were more likely to be anxious, it simply meant that religious elders were more likely to have social, economic, and health characteristics which placed them in a high risk group for anxiety. Indeed, it would be difficult to argue that religious behaviors or beliefs caused chronic health problems, low socioeconomic status, stressful life events, or affected gender. A more likely explanation is that these sociodemographic and health problems had something to do with why these elders were more religious (to be addressed further below). Our findings, then do not provide support for claims that being devoutly religious increases anxiety.

The second hypothesis suggested that religion protected elders from experiencing anxiety and/or helped to relieve it (as we found in the DVAMHS for depression). At first, it looked as though frequent church attendance might be inversely related with anxiety level; however, we later found out that this was due to the confounding effects of physical health and functional status rather than the buffering or ameliorating effect on anxiety by church attendance per se. Our findings, then, also provide little support for the second hypothesis. Nevertheless, the interpretation of these results are limited by the cross-sectional nature of our data. We do not know, for instance, whether those who were more actively engaged in personal religious activities (prayer or Bible reading) had not recently increased these activities in response to chronic illness, negative life events, or other stressors. Thus, if religion did in fact shield, moderate, or suppress anxiety symptoms, then these effects might have been buried by the complex dynamics of changing religious activity in response to increasing anxiety.

Finally, we found little support for the third hypothesis which held that persons with either low religiousness or very high religiousness would be free of anxiety. Elders demonstrating moderate levels of religious activity or importance did not experience any more or any less anxiety than did their nonreligious or highly religious peers. Again, however, the proof or disproof of Homan's thesis probably requires longitudinal data, given the complex dynamics which are purported to take place over time (religion first arousing anxiety and then relieving it).

AN ALTERNATIVE EXPLANATION

None of the above three hypotheses adequately explains our data. This led us to a *fourth hypothesis*. This new theory holds that elders who are anxious as a result of declining health, unstable socioeconomic conditions, dwindling social support, or because of temperamental factors, turn to religion for comfort. Religious cognition or activity, then, while helping to relieve anxiety, does not do away with it entirely; otherwise, the motivation to continue religious behaviors would lessen. Hence, environmental factors (unrelenting poverty, chronic illness) or genetic factors (heavy loading for anxiety disorders in the family) may serve to arouse and maintain anxiety on a more continuous basis, which then drives elders to religious activities which help to keep the anxiety under control. Despite being under control, however, symptoms might still cause considerable discomfort.

On the other hand, the elder who is more constitutionally relaxed, has few environmental stressors, and/or has abundant social, economic, and health resources, might have very little to motivate him or her towards religious activities. Note the following passage in Deuteronomy (8:12-14):

> Otherwise, when you eat and are satisfied, when you build fine houses and settle down, and when your herds and flocks grow

large and your silver and gold increase and all you have is
multiplied, then your heart will become proud and you will
forget the Lord your God who brought you out of Egypt, out of
the land of slavery.

A fascinating experiment by Osarchuk and Tatz (1973) examined
the effects of increased anxiety on religiousness. Manipulating the
level of death anxiety in their subjects by experimental procedures,
they demonstrated that when death fear was intensified, there was a
concomitant increase in religious beliefs. The idea that anxiety or
environmental stressors increase religious behaviors, which then
relieve the anxiety, is also known as a "suppressor" (Krause and
Van Tran 1989) or "deprivation compensation" effect (Taylor
1986). Religious scriptures, in fact, advocate just this: "Is any one
of you in trouble? He should pray" (James 5:13).

Recall also from Chapter 9 that religious coping was highest
among those men with the most severe health problems. Other
investigators have likewise documented increased religiosity in persons coping with serious illness or approaching death (Reed 1987).
Recall even Freud believed that religion originated as a response to
fears and anxieties aroused by the dangerous and unpredictable
world in which man lived. For the aging adult with chronic health,
social, and economic problems, the world can become a pretty
hostile place.

According to this fourth hypothesis, then, there will exist among
the religious elderly a group of anxious individuals who because of
internal or external stressors have turned to religion for comfort.
Among the nonreligious, in turn, there will be secure and fortunate
individuals who have no reason to be anxious (or to seek solace in
religion). This mixture of unfortunate, highly anxious, religious
persons and fortunate, relaxed, nonreligious ones, then, would negate or mask whatever overall positive effects religion did have on
preventing or relieving anxiety. If this is true, it is likely that a
cross-sectional study would find no association between religiousness and anxiety (or might even find a positive one).

The results from our study support this reasoning. With the exception of frequent church attenders, religious elders were more
likely to have experienced recent negative life events, more likely to

have been older, chronically ill or disabled, members of minority groups such as Blacks or women, and socioeconomically deprived. Given both a higher stress level and more limited range of coping options, many of these elders may have turned to religion as a source of comfort. We cannot prove this, however, from our cross-sectional data.

RELIGION AND NEUROSIS

Based on the research described here, there is no evidence to suggest that religion is neurosis-producing. However, this is not to say that all religions or all aspects of every religion are health inducing. Indeed, some may truly induce or exacerbate neurosis. On the other hand, probably more common and more relevant here, is that even a healthy religion may attract neurotic persons to it, who then use that religion in the service of their neurosis. I will now briefly discuss several possible links between religion and neurosis.

Neurotic Religion

Great care must be taken when defining what is and what is not neurotic religious belief or practice. It is all too easy to describe any religious practice or view that differs from one's own as neurotic. Nevertheless, the task of such a description must be undertaken, regardless of the dangers involved. Seward Hiltner (1943, p. 25) addresses this topic in a reasonable and balanced fashion. In the category of "unhealthy religion," Hiltner includes (1) religion that replaces devotion to God with devotion to state, and (2) religion that emphasizes only one aspect of God's nature to the exclusion of others. I will add some others.

Religion that encourages ultimate allegiance to and dependence on a single leader, who does not him or herself have anyone to be accountable to and does not follow an established tradition, may lead to psychological domination, fanaticism, or isolation, and thus interfere with intrapsychic and interpersonal growth. In this category are religions which seek to elevate one group of persons as superior to or of greater value than another. Another type of religion that breeds neurosis is one that is so legalistic and inflexible in its tradition that it disregards the needs of individual members by a rigid proscription to group standards; such a policy can stunt religious maturation and lead to mindless adherence to rules and regulations.

Religion that leads to a marked imbalance in the emphasis placed on one of the three natures of man (body, mind, or spirit) to the exclusion of the others, can interfere with stable growth and development; perhaps an exception to this rule is in carefully selected cases of martyrdom where there is clearly a higher cause at stake. Finally, the religion that focuses entirely on the self with narcissistic gratification as its goal can promote self-absorption and hinder the growth of interpersonal relationships. In sum, any religion that does not allow for and encourage appropriate care for one's physical well-being, social and psychological needs, and enhance continued maturation in all these areas, has the potential to impact negatively on its members' mental health.

Neurotic Use of Religion

Even religion that is socially and psychologically sound and healthy may be used in the wrong way for selfish purposes that serve neurotic needs. Wise (1942) noted that the true development of religious symbols is guided more by conscious than by unconscious forces; however, they might easily degenerate to simple expressions of unconscious elements. If this were to occur, religious symbols could be used primarily for concealment and regression, rather than for synthesis and growth. Hiltner (1943) noted that as early as Cyprian's time, church leaders were careful to counsel ascetics and those seeking martyrdom to ensure that a need for self-punishment or some other conscious or unconscious psychological aberration, rather than a true spiritual intention, was not motivating these activities.

Religion may be used in a defensive attempt to resolve intrapsychic conflict or may be incorporated into an ongoing neurotic process. For instance, religious prohibitions may be utilized to repress certain drives that need to be dealt with at a more conscious level. Religion may serve as a bearer of unconscious wishes derived from the oral, dependent phase of infancy or from later developmental stages. For example, a person with a fear of independence may quickly involve him or herself with God (or other church members) in excessively dependent relationships that he or she may then use to relieve their self of responsibilities and experiences that might promote independence and growth. Similarly, an individual with a fear of depending on others may use a relationship with God to supplant other relationships; in this way, he or she avoids the anxiety that close and intimate social contacts arouse. In each of these examples, religion is *used* to serve neurotic needs.

Another example of religion becoming involved in intrapsychic conflict is the obsessive-compulsive individual who rigidly adheres to a schedule of ritual and prayer, which then more or less controls their severe anxiety or guilt over obsessive sexual thoughts. Such devout activity may, in fact, bring its practitioner praise as a strong and disciplined congregant. Freud composed a short paper on this subject entitled *Obsessive Acts and Religious Practices* (1907), in which is found the following comment:

> The protestations of the pious that they know they are miserable sinners in their hearts correspond to the sense of guilt of the obsessional neurotic; while the pious observances (prayers, invocations, etc.) with which they begin every act of the day, and especially every unusual undertaking, seem to have the significance of defensive and protective measures. (p. 31)

Freud unfortunately mistook this neurotic use of religion for the purpose of religion itself. In the Duke ECA study, we did not find a significant increase in rate of obsessive-compulsive disorder among those who prayed frequently, read the Bible, or attended church often (Table 12.4). Nevertheless, mild personality traits or temperamental dispositions may affect motivation and behavior in the absence of a clinically significant disorder. Any person for whom religion has become a compulsion, rather than a way of meaningfully relating to God, may have an underlying psychological conflict that is motivating their behavior.

Religion may also be used as a vehicle for aggressive impulses, as anger and condemnation is directed towards those who have other beliefs (or no beliefs). Destructive impulses may be justified in terms of righteously doing God's will. These individuals may point to the need for harsh punishment for any breach of rule or regulation, and yet completely ignore the overarching principles of mercy and forgiveness. Religion can also be used by the narcissist to build up his or her own self-esteem, at the expense of those whose religious beliefs differ. For instance, a person may claim that only those in his or her particular religious group are "Christian." Anyone professing doctrine that even slightly differs from their own group is criticized as being in error and thus condemnable. This provides great assurance that he or she is in the "right" group, is special in some sense, and thus worthy of esteem.

Similarly, some persons may be motivated toward religion in public ministry in order to draw the attention of others to themselves to gratify their narcissistic or control needs (Enroth 1992). Some television evangelists may fit into this category, although I believe that the majority of these individuals are motivated by healthier concerns. Persons who are intrinsically motivated towards religion, in fact, have a very low level of narcissism. Watson et al. (1990) demonstrated that individuals scoring high on intrinsic religiosity scored lowest on pathological narcissism. Intrinsically motivated persons have much of their self-esteem needs met through their relationship with God, and are thus not impelled to gratify such needs in pathological ways.

Religious elders with dementia, delusional disorders, or late-onset psychosis may present with bizarre religious ideas or delusions. Because of pathological brain processes, they may project hateful or aggressive impulses onto others or experience overwhelming guilt over imaginary shameful acts (blaspheming the Holy Spirit). Religion is often involved in psychotic processes even among those with no prior religious leanings. The tendency for psychotic persons to caricature religious behavior or belief has been called "pietism" (Group for the Advancement of Psychiatry, 1968). W.H. Auden (1964) draws a distinction between pietism and true religion in the following passage:

> The inflated egoism of the manic depressive is always con-
> spicuous whether in his elated phase, he thinks that, unlike
> other folks, he is God, or, in his depressed phase, he thinks that

unlike other folks, he has committed a sin against the Holy Ghost. The genuine mystics, on the other hand, always interpret their ecstasy as a gratuitous blessing from God which they have done nothing to deserve and their dark night of the soul not as evidence of their extraordinary wickedness, but as a period of trial and purgation. (p. 33)

Thus, while religion can in certain cases be neurotic or can foster neurotic tendencies, more often it is healthy religion that is used by neurotically or psychotically disturbed individuals who–often seeking relief from their pain–end up using religion to express or perpetuate their illness.

RELIGION AND RELIEF OF ANXIETY

Although we were unable to demonstrate a protective or therapeutic effect for religion on anxiety, several mechanisms exist by which it could do so–especially in later life. First, religion provides the elder with a social group of persons of similar age, philosophy about life, and present circumstances, who can provide emotional support and reassurance. Many persons in the religious community may be undergoing similar difficulties; those who have been successful in overcoming their fears may be able to help others do the same. A common strategy might be used to overcome a problem that many church members face, for instance, starting up a church-sponsored Alzheimer's support group, bereavement group, or even social phobia group (to help teach social skills and prevent isolation). Perhaps even more important than the social aspects of religion, however, is the cognitive framework it provides to overcome fear. Both New and Old Testament scriptures are full of encouraging words and promises of safety and care for those who believe (Deuteronomy 5:29, 6:13, 32:9-12; Job 28:28; Isaiah 26:3, 43:2-3; Psalm 91:1-7, 118:5-6; Matthew 6:31-34; 2 Corinthians 4:16-18; Philippians 4:6; 2 Timothy 1:7; 1 Peter 5:7). Exemplary, in this respect, is Psalm 91 which graphically demonstrates God's protection and love for his people. These passages suggest that relief from fear comes when people possess a cognitive awareness that God is on their side (fighting for them), is nearby (standing with them), and will not leave (remaining by them) until the problem has been resolved.

The case at the beginning of this chapter illustrates several points. Reviewing it now may refresh the reader's memory. First, this case demonstrates the impact that scripture, based on divine authority, can have on the mental state of a person operating within this cognitive framework. Second, it emphasizes the complementary relationship between secular cognitive-behavioral therapies and religious interventions. Third, it shows how group social support and reinforcement can facilitate cognitive and behavioral changes. While the above case deals with a discrete anxiety disorder (phobic neurosis), it is likely that such principles also apply to the treatment of more generalized forms of anxiety.

SUMMARY

We examined the relationship between religion and anxiety in a random sample of community-dwelling older adults. Three hypotheses were initially invoked to explain this relationship. There was no evidence to support the theory that religion causes an increase in anxiety among devout adherents (Hypothesis #1). There was also, however, no evidence that religion either protected elders from anxiety or relieved it (Hypothesis #2). Likewise, the moderately religious did not experience greater anxiety than either the strongly religious or the nonreligious, thus providing little support for Homan's thesis that religion first arouses anxiety and then relieves it (Hypothesis #3).

Religious elders tended to be members of minority groups (Blacks and women), have low socioeconomic status, recent negative life events, numerous chronic illnesses, and impaired ability to perform activities of daily living, factors which themselves were strongly correlated with anxiety. This led us to a fourth hypothesis which suggested that the therapeutic effects of religion were masked by the fact that elders who were stressed frequently turned to religion for comfort when other resources were lacking; likewise, we hypothesized that persons more prone to anxiety because of temperament, personality, or intrapsychic conflicts might also be drawn to religion and thus interfere with the detection of religion's beneficial effects (when cross-sectional data alone are examined). We also saw that not all types of religion are associated with mental health and that some may stunt spiritual and psychological matura- tion. Alternatively, "healthy" religion may become involved in neurotic or psychotic processes, as the mentally ill person uses religion to serve his or her neurosis.

The word "fear" as used in scripture to describe an attitude towards God (according to Webster's New Collegiate Dictionary) does not connotate terror; rather, fear is defined in terms of having profound reverence and awe (in a sense of worship). When religious scriptures admonish believers to "fear God," the intention is not to induce fear that immobilizes but to arouse a sense of reverence and awe for God which might motivate change in behav- ior and stimulate personal growth. Thomas à Kempis, writing in the 15th century, put it this way: "Thou oughtest to have a good hope for obtaining victory; but thou must not be secure, lest though grow either negligent or proud" (Bechtel 1980, p. 82). Also note the passage from Deuteronomy (6:13): "Oh, that their hearts would be inclined to fear me and keep all my commands always, so that it might go well with them and their children forever." According to religious scriptures, then, the only fear that religion induces is that which motivates humans to maximize their full potential–in other words, to spur them on towards successfully aging.

In Section IV we will examine some of the practical applications of theory and research to clinical practice.

REFERENCES

Alexander, I., and A. Adlerstein. (1959). Death and Religion. In *The Meaning of Death*, edited by H. Feifel. New York: McGraw-Hill.

Auden, W.H. (1964). Introduction. In *The Protestant Mystics*, edited by A. Free- mantle. Toronto: Mentor Books.

Argyle, M., and B. Beit-Hallahmi. (1975). *The Social Psychology of Religion*. London: Routledge & Kegan Paul.

Baker, M., and R. Gorsuch. (1982). Trait anxiety and extrinsic-intrinsic religious- ness. *Journal for the Scientific Study of Religion* 21:119-122.

Bechtel, P.M. (1980). Translation of *The Imitation of Christ* by Thomas à Kempis. Chicago: Moody Press.

Bergin, A.E. (1985). Proposed values for guiding and evaluating counseling and psychotherapy. *Counseling and Values* 29:99-116.

_____ (1991). Values and religious issues in psychotherapy and mental health. *American Psychologist* 46:394-403.

Bergin, A.E., K.S. Masters, and P.S. Richards. (1987). Religiousness and mental health reconsidered: A study of an intrinsically religious sample. *Journal of Counseling & Psychology* 34:197-204.

Blazer, D.G., D.C. Hughes, and N. Fowler. (1989). Anxiety as an outcome symptom of depression in elderly and middle-aged adults. *International Journal of Geriatric Psychiatry* 4:273-278.

Blazer, D.G., D. Hughes, L.K. George, M. Swartz, and R. Boyer. (1991). Generalized anxiety disorder. In *Psychiatric Disorders in America: The Epidemiologic Catchment Area Study*, edited by L.N. Robins and D.A. Regier. NY: Free Press, pp. 180-203.

Blotcky, A.D., D.G. Cohen, C. Conatser, and P. Klopovich. (1985). Psychosocial characteristics of adolescents who refuse cancer treatment. *Journal of Consulting & Clinical Psychology* 53:729-731.

Derogatis, L.R., G.R. Morrow, J. Fetting, D. Penman, S. Piasetsky, A.M. Schmale, M. Henrichs, and C.L.M. Carnicke. (1983). The prevalence of psychiatric disorders among cancer patients. *Journal of the American Medical Association* 249:751-757.

Dittes, J. (1969). Psychology of religion. In *Handbook of Social Psychology* (vol. 5), edited by G. Lindzey and E. Aronson. London: Addison-Wesley Publishing Co.

Donahue, M.J. (1985). Intrinsic and extrinsic religiousness: Review and Meta-analysis. *Journal of Personality and Social Psychology* 48:400-419.

Downey, A.M. (1984). Relationship of religiosity to death anxiety of middle-aged males. *Psychological Reports* 54:811-822.

Eaton, W.W., A.M. Dryman, and M.M. Weissman. (1991). Panic and phobia. In *Psychiatric Disorders in America: The Epidemiologic Catchment Area Study*, edited by L.N. Robins and D.A. Regier. New York: Free Press, pp. 155-179.

Ellis, A. (1980). Psychotherapy and atheistic values: A response to A. E. Bergin's 'psychotherapy and religious values.' *Journal of Consulting and Clinical Psychology*, 48:642-645.

Enroth, R. (1992). *Churches that Abuse*. Grand Rapids, MI: Zondervan Publishing House.

Entner, P. (1977). Religious orientation and mental health. Dissertation Abstracts International 38 (4-B):1949.

Feifel, H., and V.T. Nagy. (1981). Another look at fear of death. *Journal of Consulting and Clinical Psychology* 49:278-286.

Finney, J.R., and H.N. Malony. (1985). An empirical study of contemplative prayer as an adjunct to psychotherapy. *Journal of Psychology and Theology* 13(4):284-290.

Finney, J.R., and M.H. Newton. (1985). An empirical study of contemplative prayer as an adjunct to psychotherapy. *Journal of Psychology & Theology* 13:284-290.

Francis, L.J., P.R. Pearson, and M.T. Stubbs. (1985). Personality and religion among children in a residential special school. *British Journal of Mental Subnormality* 31(60, pt. 1):41-45.

Frenz, A.W., and M.P. Carey. (1989). Relationship between religiousness and trait anxiety: Fact or artifact. *Psychological Reports* 65:827-834.

Freud, S. (1907). Obsessive acts and religious practices. In *Sigmund Freud: Collected Papers*, vol. 5, edited by J. Strachey. NY: Basic Books, 1959.

―――― (1927). The future of an illusion. In *Standard Edition*, edited by J. Strachey. 21, 3-56. London: Hogarth Press, 1962.

Gorsuch, R.L. (1988). Psychology of religion. *Annual Review of Psychology* 39:201-221.

Group for the Advancement of Psychiatry (GAP) (1968). *The psychic function of religion in mental illness and health.* American Psychiatric Association Committee on Psychiatry and Religion, GAP report No. 67, pp. 653-707.

Hiltner, S. (1943). *Religion and Health*. NY: Macmillan Company, pp. 22-31.

Hinton, J. (1967). *Dying*. Baltimore: Penguin.

Homan, G.C. (1965). Anxiety and ritual: The theories of Malinowski and Radcliffe-Brown. In *Reader in Comparative Religion: An Anthropological Approach*, edited by W.A. Lessa and E.Z. Vogt. NY: Harper & Row, pp. 83-88.

Jeffers, F.C., C.R. Nichols, and C. Eisdorfer. (1961). Attitudes of older persons towards death: A preliminary study. *Journal of Gerontology* 16:53-56.

Kaplan, H.I., and B.J. Sadock. (1988). *Synopsis of Psychiatry*, 5th Ed. Baltimore: Williams & Wilkins.

Koenig, H.G. (1988). Religion and death anxiety in later life. *Hospice Journal* 4(1):3-24.

Koenig, H.G., L.K. George, D.G. Blazer, and J. Pritchett. (1993). The relationship between religion and anxiety in a sample of community-dwelling older adults. *Journal of Geriatric Psychiatry*, 26(1):65-93.

Kraft, W.A., W.J. Litwin, and S.E. Barber. (1987). Religious orientation and assertiveness: Relationship to death anxiety. *Journal of Social Psychology* 127:93-95.

Krause, N., and T. Van Tran. (1989). Stress and religious involvement among older blacks. *Journal of Gerontology* 44:s4-s13.

Kurlycheck, R.T. (1976). Level of the belief in afterlife and four categories of fear of death in a sample of 60+ year olds. *Psychological Reports* 38:228-230.

Landerman, R., L.K. George, R.T. Campbell et al. (1989) Alternative models of the stress buffering hypothesis. *American Journal of Community Psychology* 17:625-642.

Leming, M.R. (1979-80). Religion and death: A test of Homans' thesis. *Omega Journal of Death & Dying* 10:347-364.

Levendusky, P.G., and P.L. Belfer. (1988). Agoraphobia and reported religion of upbringing. *Phobia Practice and Research Journal* 1(2):121-128.

Lewis, C.S. (1943). *Mere Christianity*. NY: Macmillan Publishing Company.

Minear, J.D., and L.R. Brush. (1980-81). The correlations of attitudes toward suicide with death anxiety, religiosity, and personal closeness to suicide. *Omega Journal of Death & Dying* 11:317-324.

Morris, P.A. (1982). The effect of pilgrimage on anxiety, depression and religious attitude. *Psychological Medicine* 12:291-294.

O'Rourke, W.D. (1977). The relationship between religiousness, purpose-in-life, and fear of death (nursing home patients). Dissertation Abstracts International 37(11-A):7046-47.

Osarchuk, M., and S. Tatz. (1973). Effect of induced fear of death on belief in afterlife. *Journal of Personality & Social Psychology* 27:256-60.

Reed, P.G. (1987). Spirituality and well-being in terminally ill hospitalized adults. *Research in Nursing & Health* 10:335-344.

Regier, D.A., J.H. Boyd, J.D. Burke, D.S. Rae, J.K. Myers, M. Kramer, L.N. Robins, L.K. George, M. Karno, and B. Locke. (1988). One-month prevalence of mental disorders in the United States. *Archives of General Psychiatry* 45:977-986.

Richardson, V., S. Berman, and M. Piwowarski. (1983). Projective assessment of the relationships between the salience of death, religion, and age among adults in America. *Journal of General Psychology* 109:149-156.

Robins, L., J.E. Helzer, and J. Croughan. (1981). National Institute of Mental Health Diagnostic Interview Schedule: History, characteristics, validity. *Archives of General Psychiatry* 38:381-389.

Rokeach, M., and C. Kemp. (1960). Open and closed systems in relation to anxiety and childhood experience. In *The Open and Closed Mind*, edited by M. Rokeach. NY: Basic Books.

Smith, D.K., A.M. Nehemkis, and R.A. Charter. (1983-84). Fear of death, death attitudes and religious conviction in the terminally ill. *International Journal of Psychiatry in Medicine* 13:221-232.

Strong, J. (1901). *Exhaustive Concordance of the Bible*. McLean, Virginia: Macdonald Publishing Company, pp. 341-343.

Sturgeon, R.S., and R.W. Hamley. (1979). Religiosity and anxiety. *Journal of Social Psychology* 108:137-138.

Swenson, W.M. (1961). Attitudes toward death in an aged population. *Journal of Gerontology* 16:49-52.

Tanset, M. (1976). Religious commitment and anxiety level as function of ego strength. Dissertation Abstracts International 37 (3B):1452.

Taylor, R.J. (1986). Religious participation among elderly blacks. *The Gerontologist* 26:630-636.

Thorson, J.A., and F.C. Powell. (1989). Death anxiety and religion in an older male sample. *Psychological Reports* 64 (3, Pt. 1):985-986.

——— (1990). Meanings of death and intrinsic religiosity. *Journal of Clinical Psychology* 46:379-391.

Watson, P.J., R.J. Morris, R.W. Hood, and M.D. Biderman. (1990). Religious orientation types and narcissism. *Journal of Psychology and Christianity* 9(1):40-46.

Williams, R.L., and S. Cole. (1968). Religiosity, generalized anxiety, and apprehension concerning death. *Journal of Social Psychology* 78:111-117.

Wilson, W., and H.L. Miller. (1968). Fear, anxiety, and religiousness. *Journal for the Scientific Study of Religion* 7:111.

Wise, C.A. (1942). *Religion in Illness and in Health*. NY: Harper & Brothers.

Wittkowski, J., and I. Baumgartner. (1977). Religiosity and attitude toward death and dying in elderly persons. *Zeitschrift fur Gerontologie* 10(1):61-68.

PART IV:
CLINICAL APPLICATIONS

Chapter 13

Spiritual Needs of Physically Ill Elders

The Lord will sustain him upon his sickbed;
In his illness, Thou dost restore him to health.

–Psalm 41:3

Spiritual needs are conscious or unconscious strivings that arise from the influence of the human spirit on the biopsychosocial natures. They are a consequence of an inherent human impulse to relate to God, and also reflect God's influence on and desire to relate to humanity. Spiritual needs stem from a recognition that human life is finite and that there is a higher purpose to which people are called ("He has also set eternity in the hearts of men"– Ecclesiastes 3:11). According to D.O. Moberg (1974), spiritual needs are interwoven with all the other needs and cut across every dimension of human life. They are closely related to psychological needs, and at times may be indistinguishable from them. What separates spiritual needs into a separate category, however, is that these needs are often best met (although not always only met) through religious channels.

All persons have spiritual needs, whether they recognize them as such or not. Surveys of medically ill persons of mixed ages indicate that about 50% report spiritual needs (Martin, Burrows, and Pamilio 1983). Although little formal research has been done, recognition of spiritual needs by physically ill elders is at least as great as that by younger adults–given the existential issues which arise in later life and the greater religious-orientation at that time (at least for the current cohort of elders). As noted in Chapter 9, we found that almost 25% of older hospitalized veterans volunteered spontaneously (without prompting) that religion was the most important factor that enabled them to cope with illness; the rate was higher than in younger men (19%) (Koenig et al. 1992).

The spiritual needs of medically ill elders are similar to those of healthy older persons; however, the stress of physical illness, often chronic and irreversible, and the need to confront the reality of death, force certain spiritual concerns into awareness. Let us now examine 14 such needs below. Knowledge of spiritual needs is important both for clergy ministering to the religious needs of elders and for health professionals treating physical and psychological needs which are often affected by spiritual concerns.

FOURTEEN SPIRITUAL NEEDS

1. A Need for Meaning, Purpose, and Hope

In the face of disabling and sometimes life-threatening illness, there is a need to cultivate and strengthen a philosophy about life that gives it meaning. Viktor Frankl, a Viennese psychiatrist and survivor of a German concentration camp, noted that the search for meaning is the primary motivator in life (Frankl 1959). According to Erikson (1950), the successful resolution of the final psychosocial task of achieving integrity over despair depends heavily on the elder's assurance of life's order and meaning. This is especially true at times of physical illness, disability, and pain, when these issues press for attention. Suffering without purpose or meaning quickly becomes unbearable.

Much of the suffering from illness involves a psychological reaction to the discomfort which has meaning far beyond the physical sensations themselves. In a patient with cancer, pain may arouse fear of eventual mortality; in the elder with severe arthritis, immobility may signify a need for increasing dependence on others; in the person with early Alzheimer's disease, forgetting a name or misplacing an item may bring to mind all sorts of frightening images. Once everything has been done which can be done–by both physician and patient–the elder must find some purpose, meaning, or possible good in their illness to make it bearable. It is challenging, however, to recognize anything positive or meaningful in physical sickness and suffering that is chronic and irreversible. In such situations, the reality from a secular perspective is that life is indeed terrible, senseless, and should not be tolerated (see Chapter 22 on assisted suicide).

The religious view, however, allows for another response. The religious person may pray for a miraculous healing or for inner strength to bear up under the suffering, believing that God is by their side, desires to help, and can help (Deuteronomy 31: 6; Psalm 34:18; Isaiah 41:10,13; Hebrews 13:6). Scriptures reassure the religious elder that a good or positive outcome is possible in every situation and thus assists them in maintaining hope (Proverbs 3:5,6; Jeremiah 29:11; Romans 8:28). The person may come to accept his or her suffering in a purifying or redemptive sense, as Jesus accepted his suffering on the cross (Matthew 26:39).

The idea of rightly bearing one's suffering for an eternal purpose and good may provide great emotional comfort in the face of unalterable circumstances. The decision to carry one's burden of suffering as a sacrificial offering to God may convert even meaningless pain into an act of worship that has eternal value (1 Corinthians 15:58; Colossians 1:24).

2. A Need to Transcend Circumstances

As noted above, sometimes situations occur that are truly difficult. A person may be diagnosed with an untreatable illness associated with increasing disability, pain, and eventual death. A previously independent elder with impaired vision, uncorrectable hearing loss, arthritis, and osteoporosis, falls and breaks a hip. A frail elderly woman is caring for a husband of 60 years with advancing dementia who recently no longer recognizes his wife and repeatedly demands that she leave his house. Such persons need to be able to transcend their circumstances, or be willing to face a rough and turbulent road ahead. Religion offers a way to do this: "So we fix our eyes not on what is seen, but on what is unseen. For what is seen is temporary, but what is unseen is eternal. . . . We live by faith, not by sight" (2 Corinthians 4:18, 5:7).

3. A Need for Support in Dealing with Loss

Medical illness is often associated with losses in other spheres of life–loss of independence, loss of job and social position, loss of family roles, loss of finances, and loss of spouse or other persons in the community support network (particularly when hospitalization occurs). These losses can convey feelings of rejection, inner emptiness, boredom, loneliness and fear. This is a time when persons need validation, understanding, empathy, comfort, love, hope, and assurance of worth–out of these come the emotional strength to fight off depression and keep alive the will to live. As we saw in Chapter 11, religious cognitions and activities provide the strength to endure through such stressful times. The meeting of psychological needs, then, is an important spiritual task.

4. A Need for Continuity

Robert Atchley (1989) is credited with a relatively new theory of aging called "continuity theory." According to this view, aging persons attempt to preserve both internal and external structures in their lives. In other words, elders are motivated both toward internal psychological continuity and external continuity in their social environment. According to Atchley, motivation toward continuity arises from four needs: (1) preservation of self-esteem, (2) preservation of ego-integrity, (3) maintenance of social interaction, and (4) preservation of cognitive function.

Medical illness often disrupts the continuity of lives, particularly when associated with hospitalization. Elders are removed from their homes and familiar surroundings, forced to follow the routines of the hospital, and often have little to say about what is happening to them. For many elders, religion provides a source of both internal and external continuity (Psalm 71:9,18). Scriptures depict God as showing "no variation or shadow due to change" (James 1:17[1]) and promising that he will be "with you always, to the very end of the age" (Matthew 28:20). Even more explicitly in Isaiah is the message that God will stand by his people as they grow older: "Even to your old age, I shall be the same, And even to your graying years I shall bear you!" (Isaiah 46:4[2]). In a world that is constantly changing, older persons–whether they are sick or healthy–need something in their lives that maintains continuity from childhood, through

---

1. Revised Standard Version
2. New American Standard Version

young and middle adulthood, and into the later years. Religion serves this purpose for many. The Bible is the same Bible that was read to them by their parents or grandparents; it is the same Bible that they may have read to their children and perhaps grandchildren. Hymns and prayers remain much the same, and often arouse the same deep emotions. Thus, religion serves to maintain both internal and external continuity for elders, arousing feelings of devotion and cultivating a sense of belonging and being a part of something which is timeless and greater than themselves.

5. A Need for Validation and Support of Religious Behaviors

Elders may rely heavily on prayer, scripture reading, saying a rosary, or other religious behaviors to cope with the stress that illness conveys. They need people in their environment to recognize, support, validate, and encourage such behaviors (if the elder finds them useful), not ignore, ridicule or devalue them. When a health professional supports and validates the use of religion as an important and powerful coping mechanism, he or she may enhance religion's effectiveness and capacity for reducing stress.

6. A Need to Engage in Religious Behaviors

Elders need the opportunity to participate in activities such as prayer, scripture reading, and worship (private and communal). They need the time to pray and, sometimes, a person to pray with. They need time to visit with their clergy-person or other church members. They need access to positive and inspiring religious literature appropriate to their faith tradition, and may need it read to them. Elders need a place to worship or have access to alternative means of participation (TV or radio). Some may need to receive the Sacraments of their tradition without interruption from the routines of hospitalization. In the hospital setting, the urgency to diagnose and treat medical illness often takes precedence over these religious needs; nevertheless, taking the time to nurture the elder's spirit is essential for a rapid and complete recovery.

7. A Need for Personal Dignity and Sense of Worthiness

Experiencing physical changes induced by illness, being dependent on others, undergoing repeated hospitalizations, enduring unpleasant diagnostic and therapeutic procedures–all can have a major adverse effect on self-image and self-esteem. The person may quickly experience feelings of being a burden, being useless, and without worth.

In order to combat these assaults on self-esteem, scriptures provide a basis for personal dignity that is independent of health status or ability to produce. Every human being is created in the image of God (Genesis 1:26-27). Man is instructed to fill the earth and be its master (Genesis 6:3; Psalm 8:4-8). This includes mastering the circumstances of physical illness. Other scriptures indicate that we are "sons," "children," "heirs" of God (Romans 8:14-17; Galatians 4:6) and that our bodies are "temples of the Holy Spirit" (1 Corinthians 3:17, 2 Corinthians 6:16). This gives humans true value and worth above all else in creation:

> What is man that you are mindful of him,
> the son of man that you care for him?
> You made him a little lower than the heavenly beings,
> and crowned him with glory and honor.
>
> You made him ruler over the works of your hands;
> You put everything under his feet . . . (Psalm 8:4-6)

8. A Need for Unconditional Love

Persons need to feel that they are loved and loveable. Most persons obtain this sense very early in life from the unconditional, inbred love of a mother for her baby. To know that one is accepted, valued, and cared for, regardless of performance or productivity, is essential for mental health. Otherwise, persons spend much of their lives trying to manipulate others into providing them with the esteem they lack. Unconditional love forms the true basis for self-esteem and is the type of love that is emphasized in the Judeo-Christian religion; indeed, this is the type of love that characterizes God's love for His people.

This love is different from human love which normally occurs between adults. Human love is based primarily on a barter system: "You do this for me and I'll do this for you–but if you stop doing for me, I'll stop doing for you." This form of love is relatively unstable, for we all fail to perform up to anothers' expectations at some time or another. In later life, disease or illness may prohibit a person from keeping up their part of the bargain, thus increasing vulnerability to loss of external sources of love. When persons only see their self-worth in relation to what others think of them, they become susceptible to wide swings in emotional well-being. Knowing that he or she is loved unconditionally by God provides the frail elder with a stable of self-worth that is intrinsic and not dependent on fluctuations in their physical or social environment.

9. A Need to Express Anger and Doubt

When physical illness strikes, there is a natural tendency to question God and ask why? Feelings of anger toward and alienation from God are typical at this time, and may be followed by guilt and shame over feeling this way. An entire book in the Old Testament is devoted to the subject (Job), indicating its importance and universal relevance. Elders, however, may not volunteer such feelings without prompting.

I recently had a patient on my inpatient psychiatry service who was experiencing severe anxiety and fear over death issues. He was indeed very sick and dying, but had no peace whatsoever. In going over his past life, he talked about his experiences during World War II around the time of Pearl Harbor. He was in charge of removing Japanese civilians from the States, placing them in boats, taking the boats out into the Pacific Ocean, and directing their course toward Japan; however, there were never enough supplies to allow to survive the entire trip. These memories deeply disturbed him, and he expressed to me how angry he was at God for allowing such a terrible situation. After expressing this anger and then asking for forgiveness, his anxiety improved notably and he became better able to focus on his present circumstances and what he could do to improve them.

Gentle inquiry with an emphasis on the normality and acceptability of such feelings gives the elder permission to discuss them openly. If not expressed and worked through in a setting of tolerance and understanding, such feelings can seriously hinder emotional health and impair the person's relationship with God at a time when it is needed more than ever.

10. A Need to Feel that God Is on Their Side

Physical illness may cause psychological regression to a more dependent state of neediness. After questioning and anger has passed (and sometimes even before), many elders need to know and feel that God is with them, on their side, sympathizing with and fighting for them. This feeling of closeness can be obtained through prayer (talking to God as if God were there), reading inspiring scriptures (those promising protection and comfort from God), participating in community (or private) worship services, or relating on a one-on-one basis with a chaplain, pastor, or member of their congregation.

11. A Need to Love and Serve Others

This need stems from a belief in God's unconditional love for people. Having experienced such love in a relationship with God, elders become motivated to share this gift with others. Such sharing, then, recharges their energy and increases the love available to give. If elders are not allowed to help or serve others, well-being will suffer. Physical illness frequently impairs mobility, preventing elders from visiting others and involving themselves in the church community. However, if hearing is adequate, the telephone can be used to reach out to others. Speaker-phones may enable the homebound to participate in their regular Sunday School class and maintain contact with their friends from the class. Focusing on and ministering to the needs of those who are equally or more unfortunate than oneself often distracts a person from their own problems and facilitates appreciation of capacities that he or she does have. Even when in the hospital, elders can serve others in small but significant ways–showing kindness or appreciation to nursing staff, reassuring and encouraging their own family members, listening to problems of other patients, even cooperating the best they can with doctors, nurses, and therapists. Such actions help to restore the energy that physical illness drains: "A generous man will prosper;

he who refreshes others will himself be refreshed" (Proverbs 11:25). Referring to this point, Ralph Waldo Emerson (1883) wrote the following:

> If you love and serve men, you cannot by any hiding or strata-gem, escape the remuneration. Secret retributions are always restoring the level, when disturbed, of the Divine justice. It is impossible to tilt the beam. All the tyrants and proprietors and monopolists of the world in vain set their shoulders to heave the bar. Settles forevermore the ponderous equator to its line, and man and mote and star and sun must range with it, or be pulverized by the recoil. (p. 186)

I recently had an older woman, Mrs. Allen (fictitious name), as a patient on my psychiatry service. She had just received four electro-convulsive therapy treatments for a severe psychotic depression. We asked her to explain the procedure to another patient to reassure that patient of the safety and helpfulness of this therapy. After doing this, Mrs. Allen repeatedly told nurses how good the interaction with the other patient had made her feel–how useful. Elderly pa-tients, whether medically or psychiatrically ill, need an opportunity to help others–and in doing so, help themselves.

12. A Need to Be Thankful

If there is one key to mental and spiritual health, it is this one. There are no fewer than 154 verses in the Old and New Testaments (American Standard Version) which concern the need to be thank-ful. When faced with changes in health and other losses, it is easy and natural to focus on the negative. This, however, invariably saps energy and emotional strength. Elders with chronic or acute health problems need to search for the good things in their lives and express thanks to God for them.

There is a story about a man with an attitude of thankfulness who was walking down the street one day when he was accosted by a robber who knocked him unconscious and stole his wallet and jewelry. This man, rather than bemoaning his situation, gave four reasons why he was thankful. First, he was thankful because he was not killed or maimed. Second, he was thankful that none of his family were involved or hurt. Third, he was thankful that he didn't have much for the robber to steal. Fourth, he was thankful that he was the person robbed and not the person doing the robbing. In every situation, then, there is something to be thankful for.

There are at least two barriers to thankfulness. First, people *forget* about previous difficult situations in their lives, about the progress they have made since then, and about the good things in their lives now that weren't there before. Scripture emphasizes not forgetting to be thankful:

> Praise the Lord, O my soul,
> and forget not all his benefits–
> who forgives all your sins
> and heals all your diseases,
> who redeems your life from the pit
> and crowns you with love and compassion,
> who satisfies your desires with good things
> *So that* your youth is renewed like the eagle's.
> (Psalm 103:2-5)

This psalm suggests that remembering and being thankful actually renews one's youth and health; conversely, failing to do so may contribute to feeling old and sick.

A second barrier to thankfulness is inappropriate *comparison*, in particular, comparing oneself with others more fortunate ("upward comparisons"). An elderly disabled person sees others his or her age who are fully functional, independent, and healthy, and then compares him or herself to them. This focuses the person's attention on their deficits not their abilities, and is thus inimical to feelings of thankfulness and well-being. All situations exist on a spectrum. No matter what condition an elder finds him or herself in, there are always other persons in better or worse circumstances. Comparing oneself to those in more desperate straits ("downward" comparisons), on the other hand, arouses feelings of thankfulness and contentedness, not envy.

Finally, thankfulness is an attitude acquired through practice; in other words, it is learned. The Apostle Paul says it this way: ". . . I have *learned* to be content whatever the circumstances" (Philippians 4:11).

13. A Need to Forgive and Be Forgiven

As part of the process of "getting things in order," elders with medical illness facing an uncertain future may have a need to forgive persons in their past. Old grudges and resentments need to be released. Estranged family members and friends, whether still living or dead, need to be forgiven. Likewise, some elders have anger towards God for allowing them to get sick, for not healing them, or for seemingly deserting them in their time of need (as with Mr. Gillis); God, too, must be forgiven.

Just as elders need to forgive, they also need to *be* forgiven. Guilt may be carried for years over mistakes in the past: things said to family members that caused hurts or separations, errors in raising children, addictions to alcohol or drugs, failures in business, and so forth. The elder needs to receive forgiveness in these areas in order to put the past behind. Forgiving others and receiving forgiveness for themselves releases pent-up energy that may then be utilized for the healing of physical illness and channeled into participation in rehabilitation that may lead to a quicker recovery. The Judeo-Christian religion provides a cognitive framework and rituals that allow for the giving and receiving of forgiveness.

14. A Need to Prepare for Death and Dying

Elders may need to be reassured that all experience will not end at death and that a new and better life awaits them on the other side. Some may need assurance that retribution for past mistakes and errors is not in store. The dying elder may feel the need to make decisions at this time. He or she may need to ask for forgiveness. He or she may need to dedicate or rededicate their life to God. Preparation for death and dying has traditionally been the task of the minister, priest, or rabbi. Physicians and nurses are ill-prepared to guide elders over this threshold, although sometimes this task does fall to them when no one else is available. Traditionally, however, the clergyperson has acted as the representative of God to counsel and comfort the elder and his/her family during the dying process. Throughout the centuries, religious rituals have been used to ease the anxiety and fear associated with dying. The sacrament of extreme unction from the Roman Catholic tradition (or the "last anointing") is a primary example, as the person confesses and is cleansed of all past wrongs (imagined or real). This provides the elder with reassurance that he or she is fully prepared for the next life–whatever it may bring.

Not only must elders get ready for death, they must also plan how to spend the rest of the life that is remaining (Feder 1965). The person who has just been diagnosed with cancer will need to restructure their life to utilize the remaining time as fully as possible. Some persons may be overwhelmed or paralyzed by the prospects of their diagnosis, and thus be unable to accomplish important tasks. Addressing spiritual needs at this time may help to free elders to live as fully as possible in the time remaining and help them to prioritize those things they wish to accomplish.

SUMMARY

Acute or chronic physical illness often arouses fears and insecurities, forcing the elder to confront existential issues that previously could be avoided or denied. The disruption of routine caused by illness and hospitalization can upset that internal sense of continuity needed to maintain emotional equilibrium. The elder's sense of self-esteem may be assaulted by their changing physical condition, increasing dependency, loss of control, and sometimes humiliating diagnostic or therapeutic procedures. The need for unconditional love and a feeling of closeness to God may intensify at this time. Elders need to express their anger and disappointment, forgive and be forgiven, and be thankful. They need to be able to continue to love and give to others, in spite of sometimes limiting circumstances. Physically ill elders need an opportunity to nurture their relationship with God through prayer, scripture, and worship. They need not only preparation for death, but also for the life they have remaining. Clearly, spiritual needs are intimately related to both the physical and psychological health of the person and cannot be ignored by nurses, physicians, or other health professionals.

REFERENCES

Atchley, R.C. (1989). A continuity theory of normal aging. *Gerontologist* 29: 183-190.

Emerson, R.W. (1883). *Lectures and Biographical Sketches*. Boston: Houghton, Mifflin.

Erikson, E.H. (1950). *Childhood and Society*. NY: WW Norton Co.

Feder, S.L. (1965). Attitudes of patients with advanced malignancy. In *Group for the Advancement of Psychiatry, Death and Dying: Attitudes of Patient and Doctor*, symposium no. 11, p. 622.

Frankl, V. (1959). *Man's Search for Meaning*. NY: Simon & Schuster.

Koenig, H.G., H.J. Cohen, D.G. Blazer, C. Pieper, K.G. Meador, F. Shelp, V. Goli, and R. DiPasquale. (1992). Religious coping and depression in medically ill elderly hospitalized men. *American Journal of Psychiatry*, 149:1693-1700.

Martin, C., C. Burrows, and P. Pomilio. (1983). Spiritual needs of patients study. In *Spiritual Care: The Nurses Role*, edited by S. Fish and J.A. Shelly. Downer's Grove, IL: Inter-Varsity Press, pp. 160-176.

Moberg, D.O. (1974). Spiritual well-being in late life. In *Later Life: Communities and Environmental Policy*, edited by J.F. Gubrium. Springfield, IL: Charles C. Thomas, pp. 256-276.

Chapter 14

Meeting Psychological
and Spiritual Needs

A wise old owl sat on an oak.
The more he saw the less he spoke;
The less he spoke the more he heard.
Why can't we be like that wise old bird?

–Edward Hersey Richards

CRISIS IN MENTAL HEALTH CARE

There are many joys and deep rewards involved in caring for the psychological needs of older adults, who in my experience are generally more appreciative and more cooperative than younger adults. Elders often have much wisdom that a long and sometimes difficult life has earned them, and they are eager to share this knowledge with others. Nevertheless, few health professionals or clergy choose geriatrics as their primary specialty. Several reasons account for this. The reimbursement system under Medicare is making it financially unfeasible for psychiatrists in this field. Likewise, congregations with a preponderance of elderly members are labeled as "dying" and find it difficult to secure high quality clergy leadership. This is unfortunate, given the increasing mental health and spiritual needs of older persons today and those projected in the future.

In 1992, Medicare's allowable charges for a comprehensive initial assessment of a mentally ill elderly person was $94, of which Medicare paid 80% and the patient paid 20%. During the first five years of practice after completing residency, the physician does not receive the full reimbursable rate from Medicare; he or she receives 60% to 80%, depending on how long he or she has been in practice. Thus, for performing a comprehensive assessment that typically takes 1 1/2 to two hours of time, the new psychiatrist receives about $56 from Medicare. After paying for office personnel, building space, and malpractice insurance out of these fees, the physician may end up actually losing money. Indeed, to see a non-Medicare patient for such a visit would bring in a typical fee of about $180 (and save the time and hassle of dealing with Medicare forms). Thus, Medicare reimbursement today is simply not sufficient to motivate young professionals to pursue a career in geriatric psychiatry.

Not only is geriatric mental health care poorly reimbursed, but the work involved with older patients is frequently difficult and time consuming. Mental health problems are typically complex and involve dysfunction in multiple areas (economic, social, and physical). Thus, time is needed not only to talk with the patient, but also to consult with family members, social agencies, and medical physicians, not to mention the need to fill out reams of Medicare forms and hassle with government agencies over payment.

Why go through all of this trouble, when one can see younger, less complicated patients for higher fees with less bother? As a consequence, fewer and fewer talented professionals are choosing geriatric mental health care as their field of expertise. With a four trillion dollar federal debt, a 320 billion dollar per year federal deficit, and plans to reduce Medicare spending by 65 billion over the next 5 years, it is unlikely that federal resources will be diverted to this area in the near future. Thus, in all likelihood the deficit of specialists in mental health problems of the aged will become greater and greater as time passes. Poor reimbursement schedules have already resulted in psychiatrists limiting routine office visits to 15 minutes, during which they primarily manage the elders' medication and monitor for side-effects; consequently, there is little time left over to provide verbal support or psychotherapy. Thus, elders are being trained to expect that all their emotional problems are physical and can be treated with medication. Those who simply need reassurance, encouragement, support, practical advice and counseling, are left out in the cold or inappropriately treated with medications.

In the meantime, mental illness and psychosocial problems are on the rise. As discussed in Chapter 21, suicide rates in the elderly are moving upward. Between 1980 and 1986, the rate of suicide in Americans age 65 or over jumped by over 20% (by 42% in older Black males) (Meehan, Saltzman, and Sattin 1991). Nearly epidemic rates of depression and drug and alcohol abuse have been reported in the post-World War II baby-boom generation which is now in middle-age (Klerman and Weissman 1989). The middle of this generation will reach age 65 in about 25 years; at that time nearly one-third of all Americans will be over age 55. Who is going to care for the mental health needs of this population? What seems clear to me is that neither funds nor mental health professionals will be enough to go around. While family physicians and internists will be forced to take up much of the slack, they too will be overwhelmed with the needs of elders who will make up one-half to two-thirds of all medical patients (American Geriatrics Society 1991). America's secular health care system will soon be under heavy pressure to find alternative sources of mental care for older adults with adjustment and coping problems.

COMMUNITY CLERGY

A significant proportion of mental health care services in this country are provided by the clergy. Even though the use of clergy is less common today among younger persons socialized to secular psychology, most pastoral counselors' practices are completely filled with younger persons and consequently rarely see the elderly. Family physicians and parish clergy provide the bulk of care to the elderly in our society whether trained for this or not. Table 14.1 illustrates the sources of mental health care sought by Americans during the latter half of this century. In 1957, Congress sponsored a landmark survey of American mental health care entitled *Action for Mental Health*. The survey indicated that 14% of people (all ages) sought help for mental problems; only 32% of these sought help from mental health professionals, while 43% sought help from clergy. Twenty years later, in 1977, a repeat survey found that more

TABLE 14.1. Sources of mental health in the United States (all ages)

Year	Type of Sample/ Reference	Seeking Help	Source of Help			
			Mental Health	Clergy	Doctor	Other
1957	Community (national) Kulka et al 1979	14%	32%	43%	30%	21%
1977	Community (national) Kulka et al 1979	26%	49%	39%	21%	11%
1982	Urban (NIMH-ECA) Larson et al 1988	18%[1]	83%[2]	34%	–	–

Rows for source of help total > 100% because some respondents mentioned more than one source

1. Unlike the total figures for the community studies, does not include mental health visits to general physicians or other sources; the latter makes up an additional 15 to 20%

2. Included in these ECA figures are 17% of respondents who saw both clergy and mental health professionals

persons sought help for mental health problems (26%), with 55% visiting mental health professionals and 39% seeing clergy (Kulka, Veroff, and Douban 1979).

In 1980-82, the National Institute of Mental Health (NIMH) sponsored the Epidemiologic Catchment Area (ECA) surveys in five U.S. metropolitan areas (New Haven, Baltimore, Durham, St. Louis, and Los Angeles), to examine the prevalence of mental disorder and patterns of mental health service use. This study found a lower proportion of persons seeking assistance from clergy than previous studies had indicated; however, the urban nature of their sample probably disallows comparisons with earlier studies involving national samples which contained much greater numbers of rural participants (who are more likely to be religious). Furthermore, none of these studies focused specifically on the elderly.

One finding from the ECA study, however, was that a higher

proportion of patients seen by clergy were elderly than seen by mental health professionals (9.9% vs. 5.8%, respectively) (Larson et al. 1988). Even more interesting was that the types and severity of mental disorders did not differ between those seeing clergy and those seeing mental health professionals. Although it would appear that most persons go to clergy for problems in living and questions of meaning, those with more serious mental disorders often find themselves in their minister's office. Given that most psychiatrists would prefer to work with younger persons and that older persons, at least in the current generation, are often more comfortable with religious professionals, the clergy will continue to serve an increasingly important role in the delivery of mental health care to this population. It also underscores the need for clergy to obtain proper education on the mental health problems of elders and the treatments (social, psychological, and biological) available for management. Unfortunately, clergy receive about as much training in counseling and human relations as do physicians. At many masters of divinity programs (a 3 to 4 year professional degree for ordination) students take one course in pastoral care and counseling, and may use an elective for another. Clergy need to know about biological treatments for mental disorders just as physicians need to know about the spiritual aspects of elder care (and both need knowledge about social gerontology and psychology). This knowledge will help clergy and physicians distinguish conditions which they can treat themselves from those which require referral (Koenig 1993a).

Unfortunately, many clergy have a work-load similar to that of physicians; where will they get the time to minister to the mental and spiritual needs of elders? Clearly, they cannot do it all themselves. Interestingly, the answer to this dilemma is provided by Jethro, Moses' father-in-law, in the Book of Exodus (18:18-23). Moses faced a situation of being over-burdened by the needs of the people. Jethro suggested that he choose able, honest, and truthful men and women from among the Israelites, and then train them to minister to the needs of the people. This is precisely what clergy must do. First, they must focus their sermons from the pulpit on the topic of helping one's neighbor (Matthew 25:31-46); the purpose of this is to inspire and motivate congregants to become involved.

Then they must train these volunteers on counseling techniques and on what types of mental illness they can and cannot handle.

This can also be effectively accomplished by the creation of "home cell groups." Here, a leadership position is given to persons in the congregation who are assigned five families (or approximately ten adults) who then meet on a weekly basis for fellowship, prayer, and support. In this way, the clergy can transfer the burden of ministry back onto the people and free themselves to do other things. Nevertheless, the responsibility of training such home group leaders remains on the clergy who themselves must be competent in counseling and in recognizing mental problems that need referral.

CHAPLAINS: WHO ARE THEY AND WHY ARE THEY NEEDED?

While community clergy are frequently called on to minister to members of their own congregation when hospitalized, most of the work-load of meeting the mental and spiritual needs of physically ill elders–particularly those in public hospitals, nursing homes, VA hospitals, and state psychiatric facilities–falls on chaplains. Chaplains are paid employees of such facilities where they represent a stable clerical presence, available to patients of all denominations, at all times of the day and night. Elders who are not regular members of any particular congregation or whose pastors, priests, or rabbis do not routinely make hospital or nursing home visits, are totally dependent on chaplains for meeting their spiritual (and often emotional) needs.

As Chapter 8 indicated, between 40% and 50% of older adults hospitalized with medical illness suffer from symptoms of depression, anxiety, or despair. Who is to provide the psychological support necessary to help these individuals cope with their often realistic concerns about health, independence, meaning in life, and issues surrounding death? Who is to provide for the spiritual needs of this population, given that less than 29% of physicians can identify in themselves the skills needed to address the spiritual dimension (Fichter 1981)? Due to dramatic improvements in medical care, persons with chronic illness are surviving past the age of 65; because of recurrent flares of their illness, repeated hospitalization or nursing home placement is common, making older persons the predominant occupants of hospital beds in America. The need for mental health services for this segment of the older population threatens to overwhelm available resources (even more so than in the community). Chaplain services, however, are frequently unappreciated and underutilized.

Modern hospital chaplaincy has been around since 1914 when it was founded by Dr. Richard Cabot, a physician at Massachusetts General Hospital. The clergy, however, were involved in hospital work long before that. As Chapter 1 indicated, monks, priests, and religious personnel were instrumental in *starting* the first hospitals and frequently cared for the sick themselves. Given the wide use of religion by medically ill elders to cope (Chapter 9), the demonstrated stress-buffering capacity of religious cognitions and behaviors (Chapter 11), the high prevalence of spiritual needs (Chapter 13), and the greater acceptability and affordability of clergy (compared with mental health specialists), chaplains should play an instrumental role in providing emotional and spiritual support to this population.

THE RESEARCH IMPERATIVE

Unfortunately, the value and importance of chaplains is not well appreciated by many administrators, who, under an enormous pressure to contain hospital costs and limit "unnecessary" expenditures, are seeing this particular service as expendable. As of October 31, 1991, chaplains in Georgia state psychiatric hospitals and prisons received their final paycheck. Because the state budget had fallen 415 million dollars short, legislators decided that one way to make up this deficit was to eliminate all clinical chaplain positions in state operated facilities (Bailey 1991; Association of Mental Health Clergy 1991; Carter 1991; White 1991). Now, chaplains are no longer on the payroll as employees of these facilities; instead, the needs of patients are served by "volunteer community clergy" or "contract chaplains" (the latter without fringe benefits such as health insurance, retirement program or liability protection). Similar events are happening in the state of Michigan (personal communication, Thomas Harries, PhD). Thus, chaplains will need to provide proof (through traditional scientific research) that they do indeed provide a necessary service to hospitalized patients; otherwise, their jobs are likely to be in very real danger.

Studies are now beginning to examine the impact of chaplain services on health outcomes and service utilization. Demonstrated benefits include shorter hospital stays (Florell 1973), decreased demands on nursing time, increased patient satisfaction with care (Parkum 1985), and other financial savings (McSherry 1987; Gartner et al. 1990). These studies, however, are few and far between. The general rule is that most chaplain programs are clinically oriented and not very motivated (or trained) to collect outcome data on the effectiveness of their methods. According to Elizabeth McSherry (1987),

> the chaplaincy health care discipline lags very far behind the clinical sciences of somatic medicine and psychiatry-psychology in (1) basic science and (2) clinical intervention literature, in (3) patient diagnostics using objective instruments, in (4) numbers of subspecialties, (5) amount of professional school curriculum dedicated to clinical science instruction, and (6) number of courses developed to teach other health professionals. This lack of professionalism in clinical science standards by the caregivers for the spiritual dimension results in inferior quality of care in the spiritual dimension for hospitalized patients. (p. 4)

Five years later, despite this warning, clinical research in pastoral care remains underdeveloped relative to other health professions. Nevertheless, corrective efforts are being attempted (Hover et al. 1991).

HEALTH PROFESSIONALS' ATTITUDES TOWARD CHAPLAINS

Although chaplains have failed to provide objective evidence of their contributions through systematic research, negative attitudes of medical and psychiatric professionals toward chaplains–reflected by their underutilization and perhaps undervaluation–are also partly to blame. A number of reasons exist why chaplain services are frequently passed over by health professionals as a possible resource. Most important of these, and perhaps most remedial, is the medical and psychiatric community's general lack of awareness of hospitalized patients' spiritual needs and of the complex interaction between religion and mental health in this setting. This may stem from a simple lack of knowledge, or it may go deeper than that.

Perspectives and personal biases of health care providers concerning religion have been shown to differ from those of their patients. In a recent study at Duke Hospital in Durham, North Carolina, we examined religious background, belief, behavior, and coping style of nurses and doctors, comparing them with those of hospitalized patients and their families (Koenig et al. 1991). Religious affiliations of physicians, nurses, and patients differed widely. Almost 50% of patients and families came from conservative or fundamentalist religious backgrounds, compared with only 3% of physicians and 34% of nurses. Likewise, 9% of physicians described themselves as agnostic, atheist, or with no religious affiliation, compared with 0% of patients and families. Approximately 60% of patients attended church one or more times per week, compared with only 35% of physicians. Finally, 44% of patients noted that religion was the most important factor that enabled them to cope with stresses in their life, compared with only 9% of physicians and 26% of nurses. Psychiatrists were among the least religiously oriented of all medical specialists. These findings reflect religious trends among health professionals noted for the past 75 years (Leuba 1916, 1934; APA Task Force Report 1975; Ragan, Malony, and Beit-Hallahmi 1980).

Thus, either because of their own biases against religion and/or lack of knowledge concerning the role of religion in the lives of older patients (Koenig et al. 1989), physicians–particularly psychiatrists–may tend to undervalue the contributions that chaplains can make. Physicians and other hospital personnel not attuned to the spiritual needs of patients are less likely to detect such needs and make appropriate chaplain referrals. In our study at Duke Hospital, 55% of 130 physicians had never worked with a chaplain; 72% of psychiatrists had never done so. Almost 50% of physicians had made no referral to clergy in the past six months (compared with

14% of nurses); again, psychiatrists made the fewest referrals among all specialists.

Exposure to and experience with chaplains tend to break down barriers to communication, clear up misconceptions, and pave the way for future referrals. We examined some of the fears that physicians had about chaplains seeing their patients (Hover et al. 1991). Table 14.2 compares two groups of physicians in this regard: (1) a group who had never worked with chaplains before and (2) a group that had. The results were enlightening. Physicians who had not interacted with chaplains before were likely to have many fears that were perhaps unjustified. Unless medical professionals are convinced of the important contributions that chaplains can make, they are unlikely to work with them and may consequently harbor unrealistic notions about the harm that chaplain interventions may cause. Thus, it is important that physicians and other medical per-

TABLE 14.2. Physician concerns about chaplains

Concerns About Chaplain	Never Worked with Chaplains (n = 71)	Have Worked with Chaplains (n = 59)
Too pushy	48%	2%
Too preachy	52%	0%
Would not listen	30%	0%
Not talk enough about God	11%	4%
Conflict with patient's beliefs	48%	0%
Not from same denomination	20%	4%
Interfere with medical care	17%	2%
Wear patient out	13%	0%
Make patient feel guilty	33%	0%

sonnel be adequately informed of the beneficial services chaplains render and the needs they serve. On the other hand, chaplains have the task of demonstrating that their services are needed and that they have an impact which benefits patient care (from a medical, psychological, spiritual, and/or economic perspective).

THE SPECIAL ROLE OF THE CHAPLAIN

While meeting the psychological and social needs of patients is one of the tasks that chaplains may provide, it cannot be their only concern. Psychiatrists, psychologists, and social workers exist for this purpose. Whatever chaplains do with patients, their focus needs to remain on that area of ministry which sets them apart from other service providers. Only chaplains are specifically trained to provide spiritual support and consolation to patients. While training in psychotherapy has been a major part of many clinical pastoral education programs since 1960, it is not this expertise that makes chaplains who they are. Rather, it is their religious training, their sensitivities in detecting spiritual needs, and their ability and skills in meeting those needs that makes chaplains special. As we saw in Chapter 13, there is a heavy overlap between spiritual and psychological needs; they are not, however, synonymous. Providing emotional or psychological support to patients and their families should always be given a high priority; nevertheless, it must remain of secondary importance for chaplains. If it were primary, there would be no need for chaplains; indeed, money would best be spent on social workers or psychologists who are experts in these matters and are fully trained to provide such services.

I recognize, however, that the situation is often not simple. As we saw in Chapter 13, spiritual and psychological needs are frequently difficult to separate. Likewise, chaplains are often called on to minister to nonreligious patients or those from nontraditional religious orientations. In these cases, chaplains need to focus on "higher values" (meaning and purpose, death and life, joy and suffering) not necessarily associated with a religious context or language; chaplains have expertise over other health professionals in these areas.

ATTITUDES TOWARD AGING

In approaching older patients, chaplains must reexamine their own views on aging, physical and emotional illness, and theology itself. With regard to aging, there are two prevalent views. One paints an overly optimistic picture that portrays old age in terms of the "joy of aging," "old is beautiful," or "a time of golden opportunity." Some writers have challenged this view as simply unrealistic. While later life does bring with it many opportunities and joys for some elders, it does not appear to do so for many others (Koenig 1993b). Stephen Sapp articulately defends this perspective to the Christian community, suggesting a different viewpoint that is more authentic and useful in stimulating personal growth (Sapp 1987).

Sapp refers to this approach as the "Theology of the Cross." The basic premise is that, like it or not, old age is often associated with much suffering. This is especially true for elders with chronic health problems, declining function, pain from diseases such as arthritis or cancer, or progressive memory loss and personality disintegration from Alzheimer's disease or multiple strokes. What is the purpose of such suffering? Is their any possible meaning or religious value to pain and suffering? These questions are particularly important because suffering is always more easily tolerated if it has some type of meaning or purpose attached to it.

For the Judeo-Christian elder, individual suffering can have purpose or at least can be transformed into having a purpose. As I have noted before, scriptures indicate that being willing to "carry one's cross" is an important aspect of the Christian life. John 16:33 states "If anyone would come after me, let him deny himself and take up his cross daily and follow me." H. Kung in his book, *On Being a Christian* (1976), notes that "Discipleship is always–sometimes in a hidden way, sometimes openly–a discipleship of suffering, a following of the cross" (p. 580). How can value be derived from chronic, irreversible illness, loss of control and independence, or death of loved ones? Sapp gives two ways in which aging may allow Christian growth and maturity: first, through an acknowledgement of dependence and, second, through a reckoning with the true basis for personal value.

Dependence and Loss of Control

First, aging and illness force one to acknowledge dependence on God's grace and accept human limitations. In this country, where independence and self-sufficiency are so highly valued, the greatest fears about growing old center around losing independence and becoming a burden. Thus, there is a struggle to maintain personal control to the end and, at whatever cost, to avoid dependency. One lesson that aging and health problems drive home is that humans are not independent, self-sufficient, and able to make it entirely on their own.

Persons report that depending on God and releasing control of a situation to him seems to help them to cope (Chapter 10). This makes sense, since much of the psychological distress associated with chronic illness and forced dependency is the individual's intense struggle to maintain control in situations where loss of control is inevitable. Freed of the need to maintain control, the person who gives up control to God may be able to relax a little and take advantage of whatever pleasures are available to him or her–knowing that their future is safe (Romans 8:28). This is not an impractical, trite, or pious notion. For reasons that are not entirely clear, it happens to work (Chapter 11).

This principle also works for the suffering associated with caring for dependent elders. If caretakers can see their job as a God-given task that is a necessary part of the Judeo-Christian life and a practical application of Judeo-Christian principles (relying on God to give them the strength to perform the job well), then they might be able to more easily cope with their predicament. Perhaps the ideal situation is when both caregiver and dependent elder are willing to compromise and suffer–"suffering of each for Christ's sake" (Sapp 1987). With this comes a shift in emphasis from that on the individual to that on the community–from self to other, from independence to interdependence, from self-fulfillment to sacrifice. Indeed, this is the heart of the Judeo-Christian message.

Like all things in life, however, either extreme–excessive dependence and reluctance to do for oneself or exaggerated independence and refusal to rely on others–can result in problems. A prime example is the older adult who refuses to seek proper medical or psychiatric attention because of dependence on God to heal them or otherwise solve their problem. Another example is the disabled elder who refuses to move from their home into a nursing home, despite dangers to their safety, for fear of having to depend on others. Finally, there is the adult child who takes on heavy caregiving responsibilities without acknowledging their physical or psychological limitations (see Chapter 19). For both older patient and caregiver, then, achieving a balance in issues of dependency, control, and level of personal responsibility can help maximize adaptation and help bring about spiritual growth.

Basis for Self-Worth

Second, aging and illness can cause a person to confront the true basis for self-worth. In childhood and adulthood, the lesson that parents, teachers, and bosses drove home is that one's value depends on what one does, produces, accomplishes. Old age and disability force the individual to find some other basis for value besides productivity. Sapp notes the following:

> Reflecting the Biblical teachings of the creation of all human beings in the image of God and of Christ's death for the sake of all, Christian theology affirms strongly that one's value does not rest in what one does or has but merely in the fact that one is. The true impact of this truth, however–as well as the significant function that the losses of aging can play in bringing one to realize it–cannot be gained unless a realistic view of aging is presented and not just empty platitudes and words of encouragement. (p. 11)

Thus, rather than deny the realities of aging or try to escape the suffering, pain and loss that sometimes come with it, chaplains might best accept and acknowledge the importance, value, and meaning of the Cross as central to the Christian life and as offering an opportunity for growth and maturation. This approach makes particular sense in cases where illness is chronic and suffering irreversible.

INTERVENTIONS WITH THE CHRONICALLY DISABLED AND THE TERMINALLY ILL

What can chaplains and other health professionals do to meet the physical, psychological and spiritual needs of elders with severe disability, irreversible chronic or terminal illness? Ned Cassem (1988) notes eight essential features of *whole person care* for such patients.

1. Competence

Patients need to have confidence in the skills of their physician, nursing staff, and chaplain. Although a caring attitude and warm bedside manner are important, they cannot take the place of careful clinical assessment and management of the underlying medical, psychological, or spiritual illness. For example, Cassem notes that "no matter how charming the physician, nurse, or intravenous technician may be . . . the approach of the person who is most skillful at venipuncture brings the greatest relief to an anxious patient." The same applies to mental health professionals who perform psychotherapy, prescribe medicine, or administer electroconvulsive therapy, or to chaplains who assess the spiritual needs of older patients and pray at the bedside to meet those needs.

Religion may be a factor in motivating health professionals to develop and improve their technical skills, as a matter of achieving excellence and providing a witness. It may also provide a balance in perspective, helping health professionals not to rely too heavily upon their own skills and enabling them to recognize limits. A religious perspective may help to reduce the frustration and discouragement that often come when the healer discovers that their technical expertise and medical wisdom are insufficient to reverse many of the problems that face chronically ill, disabled older adults.

For the chaplain or clergyperson, acquiring good training in their ministry can help them achieve clinical competence. Competence involves taking a complete and thorough religious history in a cautious, sensitive, and respectful fashion, getting to know the patient as a unique individual on a unique spiritual path. Before this is done, any intervention such as praying or giving of spiritual advice is likely to be less effective.

2. Concern

Among all personal qualities of the health professional that patients admire, the ability to have compassion ranks number one. This involves being able to communicate that he or she truly understands and is moved by the patient's predicament. To do so, one must become emotionally involved. There is no other way. The word "compassion" comes from the two Latin words "passio" (to suffer) and "con" (with). Thus, to have compassion means literally *to suffer with the patient*, or in other words, to take on some of the patient's burden to make it lighter for them to carry. Many professionals will shy away from doing this, because of the price it extracts.

Religious faith, in my opinion, enables one to have more compassion than one would have otherwise. Without such faith, it is simply difficult to see any realistic reason for hope in many of these circumstances. If the professional can see no purpose in or possibility of a good result from suffering, progressive disability, or approaching death–particularly when it cannot be altered–then this feeling of helplessness arouses intolerable anxiety and discomfort (just as it does in the patient). Most professionals are not willing to experience emotional distress of this magnitude for much time, and thus tend to withdraw. Viewing a case from a religious perspective gives a sense of hope and final justice. By giving meaning and purpose to suffering, this perspective can help avoid the experience of senseless pain for both the patient and the provider.

3. Comfort

Providing comfort for the elder with incurable chronic illness and/or severe disability often involves as much, if not more, activity than trying to cure or treat. Many details need to be attended to. For the chronically ill patient with severe arthritis, this includes relief of physical pain through appropriate use of analgesics; for the elder suffering from severe anxiety and/or depression, this means appropriate and timely use of tranquilizers and antidepressants; for the terminally ill, this means careful attention to mouth care, skin care, and bowel problems, maintenance of a clean and bright environment, and rigorous management of pain or other distressing symptoms through the appropriate use of narcotics. Inquiry into the small needs and wants of such patients can make their remaining days of life more pleasant. The hospice movement has made enormous strides in maximizing the comfort of the dying by enabling patients to remain in the familiar environment of their homes for as long as possible.

The hospital chaplain or the patient's own minister can bring great comfort by relieving spiritual concerns and taking care of "unfinished business." Likewise, providing access to worship services, religious TV programs, and scriptural readings or tapes, can keep hope alive, and thus enhance the meaning and quality of remaining life for many older patients. Being terminally ill does not negate the possibility of successful aging, for in a sense, we are all in that predicament.

4. Communication

What do you say to a severely disabled elder, one who is suffering with an untreatable chronic illness, or facing death in the near future? Cassem notes that practically every empirical study that has ever been done has come up with the same result: it really doesn't matter what you say. What matters is if you *listen*. This seems to be one of those universal truths that has few exceptions. Giving a person the opportunity to talk about whatever they wish to share, in an accepting and validating atmosphere, can provide immense relief to those experiencing emotional pain.

Many therapists and pastoral counselors underestimate the power of "just listening." Perhaps this seems too simple to be of any value to patients. As simple as listening appears to be, it is actually quite a complex and fatiguing endeavor. It takes a great deal of effort to listen. Self-restraint is needed to avoid commenting on, reacting to, or otherwise providing input into the ideas, thoughts, or ruminations of another as they talk. In such a situation, the therapist's thoughts can easily wander and it may be difficult to sustain attention. This takes a great deal of concentrated effort and psychological energy, more effort than friends or family are often able or willing to give–especially over a long period of time. Thus, in order to get someone to "just listen," patients typically have to pay them as in the case of hiring a therapist. While professional psychotherapists often proceed using techniques based on elaborate theoretical schemas, it may be that listening is the key therapeutic element–that works *in spite of* the theory (see Chapter 3).

Listening can be improved by training. "Reflective" listening is a technique whereby the therapist takes what the patient says and paraphrases it to demonstrate that he or she has been listening and really understands what the patient means. This prevents boredom and distraction in the therapist because it demands active involvement through careful attention and synthesis, allows the patient to correct any misunderstandings, and keeps the focus on what the patient is saying and away from the temptation to make value judgements or offer advice. The result is that the patient feels understood and accepted, which achieves a major goal of supportive therapy, strengthens the therapeutic alliance, and builds trust between patient and therapist.

Listening allows for several things to happen when working with older adults: reminiscence, validation and affirmation, confession, abreaction, catharsis, and personality reorganization. Reminiscence involves the patient talking about important events or experiences in his/her past. This is actually a natural and important psychological process during which the older person reviews, organizes, and evaluates their successes and failures in life in an attempt to establish a sense of integrity (Erikson's final life task). Such reminiscence, when conducted in the presence of a chaplain or religiously oriented therapist, often includes religious issues that involve conflict and require resolution.[1]

Listening gives value and importance to the elder's life story, and enhances the integration and acceptance of past experiences, i.e., provides validation and affirmation. Validation facilitates the construction of a meaningful continuity between past and present.

---

1. While reminiscence is a natural, healthy process, it can like any psychological process become derailed. Reminiscence can be destructive to mental health if it involves brooding or obsessing on past negatives and prevents the elder from moving on. As discussed in Chapter 6, dwelling in the past can be used defensively to avoid taking responsibility and making needed changes in the here and now. Again, Judeo-Christian teachings emphasize both a dealing with the past through confession and forgiveness, and then a changing of behavior in the present to reflect the new attitude.

Affirmation comes through understanding and uncritical acceptance of decisions and paths taken during a lifetime, and gives a sense that experiences thus learned had meaning, purpose, and connection to one's overall life story. Recall Frankl's notion that the quest for meaning and purpose is the primary motivation in life. In earlier years, individuals obtained meaning through their jobs, families, or possessions (productivity); in later life, as productivity declines, there comes a struggle to find new sources of meaning or to retrieve old sources from the past. Listening facilitates this process.

Listening also allows for confession. A long life invariably involves many mistakes, failures, regrets, and hurts. These past experiences cause conflict and unhappiness if they are dwelled upon, particularly when seen as unchangeable and irreversible. Such events can imprison the elder in the past, negatively impacting on self-image and sense of integrity. Confession involves the disclosure in a penitent manner of past wrongs that have caused continued feelings of shame or guilt. Telling another person about such events somehow gets them into the open and helps the person release them.

The chaplain, who acting as God's representative, may be of particular help in facilitating the process of forgiveness and release. Because God is not limited by time, wounds and hurts from the past can be forgiven and released. Using the technique of guided imagery, the chaplain can take the elder back into his or her past to either give forgiveness to or receive forgiveness from important individuals who are no longer living or are otherwise inaccessible. With a sense of forgiveness, there often comes abreaction or catharsis–an emancipation of pent-up emotions associated with the original events–resulting in psychological (and spiritual) healing. As the elder reviews past events, recognizes their meaning, confesses and releases them, there comes a personality reorganization.

Cassem notes that listening is often not enough to maximize communication. Few people are willing to reveal their uttermost struggles to a stranger. One must also get to know the patient and show interest in them as a unique person. Inquiring about family, prior work, and hobbies, may reveal common interests and unique traits about the individual. Having a common religious faith can facilitate a rapid development of trust. As we have seen in earlier chapters, religion is a central motivating force for many elders and provides a basis for hope. Supporting and encouraging the patient's own religious beliefs are appropriate interventions that chaplains, nurses, and physicians can do to help maintain morale and facilitate bonding (Koenig et al. 1989). This is not a time, however, to try to convert a person to the counselor's own religious views. While there is nothing wrong with sharing experiences, imposing one's beliefs or arguing with the patient does more harm than good, serves to block communication, and demonstrates a fundamental lack of respect.

5. Visits from Children

There is little question that visits from children, grandchildren, or great-grandchildren usually have a beneficial effect on the mood of a sick elder. Whether or not this is advised in the acute hospital setting, however, should be determined by the feelings of the elder and the feelings of the child. If the child wants to visit and the elder is willing, then these visits should by all means be encouraged. Likewise, if the patient and all involved family members approve, the child may participate in prayer for healing, emotional strength, or family closeness.

6. Family Cohesion

Family members often experience as much, if not more, suffering than their sick or dying relative. The family needs support and encouragement, and needs to be listened to. Again, in order to effectively support the family, time must be set aside to get to know family members, understand their situations, and hear their struggles. Sometimes health professionals need to assist the older patient to understand the stresses on family members, and may need to encourage him or her to try to be supportive of them. Provision of such support on the patient's part not only improves communication, but often gives him or her a sense of worth and value that enhances self-esteem. Encouraging joint family and patient participation in prayer, religious services, or receiving of Sacraments can link family members together in a way that death cannot break.

7. Cheerfulness

A gentle and appropriate sense of humor can go a long way toward relieving tension and diffusing uncomfortable situations. "A cheerful heart is good medicine, but a crushed spirit dries up the bones" (Proverbs 17:22). Sick elders can often read the faces of their caretakers. A sad or somber expression on the face of medical, nursing or chaplaincy staff can communicate to the patient that he or she is truly hopelessly ill. On the other hand, when the patient is despondent or in pain, undue cheerfulness or insensitive joking conveys a lack of understanding that is likely to increase suffering and isolation. Again, it is best to follow the patient's lead–be ready to "Rejoice with those who rejoice" and "mourn with those who mourn" (Romans 12:15).

8. Consistency and Perseverance

Regular visits from health care providers and chaplains are indisputable proof of concern and caring. Cassem emphasizes that it is not the amount of time that is spent, but the quality of the time that is important. Sitting down for a moment at the bedside, placing a hand on the patient's shoulder, and focusing all one's attention on what the person is saying, can make a five-minute visit seem much longer. Thus, brief, well-timed visits can mean much more to the patient than infrequent, extended stays.

Many elders who are suffering emotionally, may become bitter and irritable; this can cause them to react quite negatively towards health professionals and visitors. Despite a tremendous need for closeness, such persons may withdraw into themselves and alienate those around them. Persistence and consistency, however, will often win these patients' trust and allow them to unburden some of their troubles. Again, having a strong religious faith helps one to persist even when a show of appreciation from the patient is lacking.

APPROACHING PATIENTS ON MATTERS OF RELIGION

The topic of religion is best approached in a respectful, sensitive, and cautious manner. This is true regardless of whether a chaplain, physician, nurse, or other health professional is involved. The spiritual journey of every person through life is highly individualized and must be examined gently and with the utmost respect. The need for religious freedom was incorporated by the founders of our nation in the First Amendment to the U.S. Constitution ("Congress shall make no law respecting an establishment of religion or prohibiting the free exercise thereof"). Their is seldom, then, justification for either a chaplain or other health professional initiating religious interventions (prayer, Bible reading, etc.) as a matter of routine, before completing a full assessment of that patient's spiritual needs. Failure to do so treats all persons the same and gives no credence to the individual's unique religious quest.

The first step in broaching the subject of religion, then, is assessment. To start, a general question may be asked, such as "What enables you to cope? Where do you get the strength to go on, despite your condition and circumstances?" The patient should be allowed to elaborate on this and be prompted to give examples of several coping resources. Next, if no reference to religion is made, a more direct question about religion might be asked, such as "Some people have found religion helpful in this regard, others have not. What has been your experience?" This usually opens up the subject for discussion. Now the primary task of the professional is to listen. Later, questions may be asked to help clarify exactly what the patient means by "religion;" in other words, does this involve faith in themselves, faith in God or Jesus Christ, a higher Power, meditation, attending church, temple or mosque, support from church members, or performance of religious rituals? Especially important is inquiry into *how* religion is helpful. Does it give the person emotional strength, peace of mind and relief of worry, a greater sense of control, hope for healing, or relief from loneliness? Finally, any previous strong experiences with religion, either good or bad, should be explored. The patient may be encouraged to describe these experiences in detail. This can help them recall times when religion had been helpful and may thus facilitate its usefulness in the present situation.

If the elder has not found religion helpful in the past, a gentle question may be asked concerning any experience that may have turned them off to religion. A quarrel with a pastor, hypocritical behavior of religious persons on TV or in church, or a sense that God has deserted them or let them down may be recalled. Listening in an understanding manner, avoiding any argument or defense of religion, is perhaps the best approach in this situation. One must be particularly cautious in questioning nonreligious elders about religion, for this may reawaken painful memories and give rise to hostility and offense. The latter, however, does not happen nearly as often as one might fear. Most of the time, simply giving the elder a chance to discuss their feelings–both good and bad–in an atmosphere of openness and acceptance is greatly appreciated. This may enable the person to put into perspective and integrate their experiences in this area. Elders with mental health problems are often stuck in obsessing over past mistakes and lost opportunities as they review their life. By emphasizing Christianity's central message of mercy, forgiveness, and making a new start, the professional can help the elder get unstuck and enable them to construct a new or different story beginning in the here and now.

Prayer, in my opinion, can be utilized by physicians to facilitate healing in the same way it is used by chaplains or clergypersons. Unless specifically asked to do so by the patient, however, prayer should not be engaged in until a full assessment has been made of the patient's religious perspective and experiences as outlined above. Even then, it is best if the patient is encouraged to say the prayer him or herself, since it is the patient who knows best what their needs are. If the patient prefers the professional to pray instead, a short prayer emphasizing God's interest, love, mercy, and power is best.

SPECIAL TOOLS OF THE RELIGIOUS PROFESSIONAL

In working with the sick elderly, there are tools available to the religious professional that are unavailable to those using purely secular techniques. These tools include the use of ultimate forgiveness, scripture, prayer, worship, and sacraments. According to traditional Judeo-Christian teachings, complete and absolute forgiveness is possible for those who believe and are truly repentant. Scriptures provide promises of God's protection and care both in this life and the next life. Prayer can be a powerful tool to relieve anxiety, fear, provide hope, and even clarify problems. Worship enables the patient to express thankfulness, reverence, and praise towards God, actions which stimulate positive emotions.

Finally, the sacraments provide powerful symbols and rituals which may be used to assist with resolution of psychic conflict. As described in Chapter 18, the celebration of the Eucharist can facilitate the process of mourning (Wilson 1984). The sacraments of confession and extreme unction (last rites) are likewise powerful rituals for dealing with unresolved guilt and fears.

SUMMARY

The need for mental health services by community-dwelling and hospitalized elders is increasing rapidly as the United States population over 65 expands due to demographic factors and improving medical care. A deficiency of mental health professionals attuned to the emotional and psychosocial problems of older persons is developing and is likely to worsen in the future. Community clergy and hospital chaplains may be increasingly called on to minister to the spiritual and mental health needs of older persons. This is particularly true in the acute hospital setting, where these needs are so pervasive.

Because of economic pressures, however, many hospitals are seeking to cut unnecessary expenditures. Unless chaplains are able to objectively demonstrate that their contributions improve health care and meet patient needs, their jobs will become increasingly vulnerable to administrators' efforts at cost containment. Chaplains must also educate physicians and other health professionals about the spiritual and psychological needs of patients and about their expertise in meeting those needs. Chaplains and community clergy, in turn, must learn about the special needs of elders with chronic or acute health problems and how to best meet those needs.

Finally, there are certain principles of whole-person care that can help professionals to meet the mental and spiritual needs of older patients with severe illness. Emphasis should be placed on competence, compassion, comfort, listening, communication, cheerfulness, persistence and perseverance, and attention to family support and cohesion. A religious view may facilitate the implementation of each of these aspects of care. A gentle, competent, and respectful approach to assessing and meeting spiritual needs is always warranted.

REFERENCES

American Geriatrics Society. (1991). *Geriatrics Review Syllabus: A Core Curriculum in Geriatric Medicine*. New York, NY: American Geriatrics Society.

American Psychiatric Association Task Force Report 10. (1975). *Psychiatrists' Viewpoints on Religion and Their Services to Religious Institutions and the Ministry*. Washington, DC: APA.

Association of Mental Health Clergy. (1991). Here we are again! Crisis in Georgia. *AMHC Newsletter*, vol. III, no. 10 (September):1.

Bailey, J. (1991). Legislature approves budget cuts: Cuts also endanger Central State chaplaincy program. *The Union-Recorder* (Milledgeville, Georgia), vol. 173 (no. 174., August 29):1.

Carter, H.B. (1991). Save prison, mental hospital chaplains. *The Atlanta Constitution* (September 12), A14.

Cassem, N. (1988). The person confronting death. In *The New Harvard Guide to Psychiatry*, edited by A.M. Nicholi. Cambridge, MA: Harvard University Press.

Fichter, J.H. (1981). *Empirical Studies on the Spiritual Dimension of Modern Health Deliverers*. Waltham, MA: Crossroads.

Florell, J.L. (1973). Crisis intervention in orthopedic surgery–empirical evidence of the effectiveness of chaplain working with surgery patients. *Bulletin of the American Protestant Hospital Association* 37:29.

Gartner, J., J.S. Lyons, D.B. Larson, J. Serkland, and M. Peyrot. (1990). Supply and demand for chaplaincy services in a post-DRG environment. *Journal of Pastoral Care* (in press).

Harries, T. (1991). Conversation at Veterans Administration Hospital in Durham, North Carolina.

Hover, M., J.L. Travis, H.G. Koenig, and L.B. Bearon. (1992). Pastoral research in a hospital setting: A case study. *Journal of Pastoral Care* 46:283-290.

Klerman, G.L., and M.M. Weissman. (1989). Increasing rates of depression. *Journal of the American Medical Association* 261: 2229-2235.

Koenig, H.G. (1993b) Religion and hope in the disabled elder. In *Religious Factors in Aging and Health*, edited by J. Levin. Newbury Park, CA: Sage Publications (in press).

_____ (1993a). Trends in geriatric psychiatry of relevance to pastoral counselors. *Journal of Religion and Health* 32:131-151.

Koenig, H.G., L. Bearon, P. Dayringer (1989). Physician perspectives on the role of religion in the physician-older patient relationship. *Journal of Family Practice* 28:441-448.

Koenig, H.G., M. Hover, L.B. Bearon, and J.L. Travis. (1991). Religious perspectives of doctors, nurses, patients and families: Some interesting differences. *Journal of Pastoral Care* 45(3):254-267.

Kulka, R.A., J. Veroff, and E. Douban. (1979). Social class and the use of professional help for personal problems: 1957 and 1976. *Journal of Health and Social Behavior* 20:2-17.

Kung, H. (1976). *On Being a Christian*, (tr. E. Quinn). Garden City: Doubleday.

Larson, D.B., A.A. Hohmann, K.G. Kessler, K.G. Meador, J.H. Boyd, and E. McSherry. (1988). The couch and the cloth: The need for linkage. *Hospital and Community Psychiatry* 39:1064-1069.

Leuba, J.H. (1916). *The belief in God and immortality.* Boston: Sherman, French.
_____ (1934). Religious beliefs of American scientists. *Harper's* 169 (August):291-300.

McSherry, E. (1987). The need and appropriateness of measurement and research in chaplaincy: Its criticalness for patient care and chaplain department survival post-1987. *Journal of Health Care Chaplaincy* 1:3-41.

Meehan, P.J., L.E. Saltzman, and R.W. Sattin. (1991). Suicides among older United States residents: Epidemiologic characteristics and trends. *American Journal of Public Health* 81:1198-1200.

Parkum, K.H. (1985). The impact of chaplaincy services in selected hospitals in the eastern United States. *Journal of Pastoral Care* 39:262.

Ragan, C., H.N. Malony, and B. Beit-Hallahmi. (1980). Psychologists and religion: Professional factors and personal belief. *Review of Religious Research* 21 (Spring):208-217.

Sapp, S. (1987). An alternative Christian view of aging. Consider aging from the perspective of the Cross. *Journal of Religion and Aging* 4(1):1-13.

White, G. (1991). Prison ministry, Department of Human Resources chaplains face budget ax. *The Atlanta Constitution* (August 24):E6.

Wilson, W.P. (1984). *The Grace to Grow.* Waco, TX: Word Books.

Chapter 15

Use of Religion in Psychotherapy

Lord, make me an instrument of thy peace.
Where there is hatred, let me sow love;
Where there is injury, pardon;
Where there is despair, hope;
Where there is darkness, light;
Where there is sadness, joy.

—Francis of Assisi

In this chapter, I will review the major psychotherapies in vogue today, examine their utility for older adults, and demonstrate how the religious approach is consistent with and complementary to many of these secular methods. I will also examine issues of transference and countertransference that affect the therapeutic alliance between religious therapists and religious patients. First, let us review some general aspects of psychotherapy with older adults.

There is surprising agreement between mental health professionals on the best psychotherapeutic approach with elderly patients. Brief, time-limited treatments that focus on the here and now are advocated (Gallagher and Thompson 1982, 1983; Lazarus, Sadavoy, and Langsley 1988; Thompson, Gallagher, and Breckenridge 1987; Kirshner 1988). Most psychological problems in older adults stem from situational difficulties in their present life, rather than from intrapsychic conflict, transference distortions, or genetic factors (as in younger adults). Thus, the goals and techniques of therapy in the elderly must often be modified. In younger adults, there is often an attempt to encourage independence and discourage denial. For older persons, dependence and denial may serve useful functions–particularly in situations of irreversible chronic, disabling physical illness or in other circumstances characterized by loss of control.

The therapeutic alliance between patient and therapist, while important in younger patients, is especially consequential for therapy with elders. The stone-faced, uninvolved, unreactive therapist is unlikely to be successful with older adults; instead, an active, empathetic, self-revealing stance is more effective. These considerations influence the choice of psychotherapy optimally effective in treating elders, and also affect possibilities for integration with the religious approach. Structured psychotherapies in common use today include psychoanalytic, existential, interpersonal, supportive, and cognitive-behavioral therapies.

PSYCHODYNAMIC PSYCHOTHERAPY

A major goal of classical psychodynamic psychotherapy (psychoanalysis) is a restructuring of personality, and involves repeating, remembering, and working through. This is often accomplished by daily to weekly sessions with an analyst and may extend for several years. The characteristics of patients amenable to analysis include relatively good ego function, capacity for insight, psychological mindedness, motivation, time, and adequate finances. Because of these requirements, psychoanalysis is available to only about 5% or less of all persons seeking psychiatric help. The cost of long-term psychoanalytic treatment ($15,000/yr in 1990) has made it impractical for the treatment of most geriatric mental disorders, given that third-party payers (Medicare in particular) are not willing to reimburse psychotherapy at this rate, and given that the median family income in the U.S. is about $24,000 per year.

Not only is the cost of such therapy prohibitive, but there is also little evidence that analysis is particularly effective in the elderly. Even Freud (1905) questioned its value in older patients, claiming that individuals over the age of 55 are unanalyzable; in later publications, he reiterated this view referring to the inelasticity of the mental processes in old age and the ineducability of older persons; the mind after age 40 or 50 was seen as too cluttered to change. A textbook widely used today in psychiatry residency training programs is Dewald's *Psychotherapy: A Dynamic Approach* (1971). A chapter entitled "Indications and Evaluation for Therapy" differentiates the characteristics of patients suited for insight-oriented (psychodynamic) versus supportive therapy.

> . . . the young adult is best suited for insight-directed therapy. Patterns of response and reaction in the young adult tend to be more flexible, and less stereotyped or rigid than in the older person, and the young adult will usually find it easier to learn new modes of reaction and adaptation than will the elderly person whose capacity to experiment and try new things will often be impaired. Insight-directed psychotherapy is frequently a long-term procedure so that the younger person who has successfully completed such a therapeutic undertaking will have a longer time to make use of the changes that have resulted within himself, and the total effect of the treatment is likely to be greater since benefits accrued in his treatment may be passed on to his children in terms of reduction of emotional disturbance in the family. . . . Furthermore, the elderly person by virtue of the insight gained through his therapy, may come to recognize important neurotic forces in such things as his patterns of choice of work, of a marital partner, or of other relationships and activities in life, and then become significantly depressed since it may now be too late in life to change. (pp. 125-126)

The application of insight-oriented therapy, then, is discouraged by Dewald, who implies that elders are best treated with supportive techniques. He indicates that this is particularly true when psychological problems are reactive to real situational difficulties.

> Neurotic symptom formations which appear as a part of a reaction to significant external stress or change in the individual's life situation are often indications more for a supportive than insight-directed therapeutic approach. Often when the response to the external stress has been dealt with at supportive levels, the neurotic regression and symptom formation proves to be transitory and reversible, and further treatment

may be unnecessary. . . . In other words, in any situation of major change in his life, an individual may have transient neurotic symptom formation, but it may not be necessary to explore the deeper unconscious conflicts in a long-term therapeutic venture. It may instead be sufficient to deal with the situation at the level of immediate support and symptom relief. . . . At the other extreme are those patients whose symptoms have been in existence at an essentially constant level or degree for many years or for large parts of the person's life. The more that the neurotic adaptation and symptom formation have been firmly entrenched and "calcified" and the more that the patient and family have adjusted to the disability, the more difficult will it be for the patient to change, and hence the poorer the prognosis for insight-directed treatment. (pp. 127, 128)

Psychoanalytic and other rational-based therapies (Freud or Ellis) work best in healthy young adults who have control over their external circumstances and have conflicts primarily of intrapsychic origin. They are relatively less effective when reality is truly difficult, as is the case for many elders disabled with chronic illnesses such as arthritis, loss of vision and/or hearing, advanced cancer, diabetes, chronic respiratory or cardiac disease. Elders beset with chronic, irreversible health problems and other real problems in the environment over which they have little ability to control or modify, must be able to *transcend*, not focus on, these problems.

Insight-oriented therapies, then, are relatively less helpful in treating emotional disorders in later life (as well as long-term neurotic adaptations that have become "entrenched and calcified") than are other approaches (Gallagher and Thompson 1983; Sadavoy and Robinson 1989). This is not to say, however, that psychodynamic techniques have no place in the treatment of older adults. Elders can benefit from these methods and do possess potential for personality change if motivated to do so (Abraham 1919; Kaufman 1963; Abraham 1965; Kahana 1979), and this approach has been used successfully in treating elders with long-held, seemingly intractable symptoms (Myers 1984).

Religion and Psychoanalytic Therapy

As noted above, psychoanalytic psychotherapy and other psychodynamic therapies seek to accomplish a significant structural change in the patient's personality that will help that person relate to self and others in a more effective and satisfactory manner. According to Dewald (1971), this includes

> . . . a modification of super-ego functions, with a decrease in primitive or authoritarian moral precepts, and an increase in conscious personal decisions by the patient regarding his own moral value system. (p. 283)

On the surface, this goal seems directed at uprooting religious influences. In actuality, however, the therapeutic goals of mature religion and psychoanalysis are similar, though couched in quite different language. Judeo-Christian and psychoanalytic approaches parallel each other in a number of ways which provide possibilities for integration. This was noted over 20 years ago by the *American Psychiatric Association's Committee on Religion and Psychiatry* in a 1968 GAP report:

> The combination of belief and mood stimulates a regressive process that is important to many of the psychological effects of religion. In reactivating the magical thinking of childhood, it is a potentially enriching experience, inasmuch as it may bring to awareness some of the workings of the mind that have been until then repressed or denied. Psychoanalytic therapy shares this process with religious experience: it too induces a state of regression with the intention of facilitating growth. . . . Ritual not only stimulates regression, but controls and guides it by stipulating its form, depth, duration, and intensity. (pp. 703-704)

The goals of psychoanalysis, then, may be viewed as consistent with those of religion. Both seek to free the person from primitive or neurotic influences, including the neurotic use of religion (see Chapter 12). Recall from Chapter 7 that intrinsic religiosity reflects a mature-love relationship with God based upon a conscious and free decision to do so. Primitive, immature forms of religious faith, on the other hand, frequently involve an unconscious manipulation of religious teachings and symbols to disguise or compensate for personal inadequacies; a goal of spiritual maturation is to uncover these motivations and replace them with healthy, stable, and conscious ones.

Compared with the religious approach (employed for many centuries), the use of psychoanalytic techniques to treat neuroses is a relatively recent therapeutic strategy. Paul Wachtell (1977) notes the following in *Psychoanalysis and Behavior Therapy*:

> The role of the priest was perhaps one of the few that matched that of the doctor in engendering trust and raising the expectation of a wise and understanding response to the divulgence of shameful and guilty thoughts. Most of the crucial data from which psychoanalytic theory was constructed were probably reported in the confessional box long before they were reported on the couch. Certainly there is little that Freud found in the Id that would have shocked Augustine, and Freud's shattering of the myth of childhood innocence would no doubt have seemed to the Christian saint a rather dated rerun. (p. 14)

Religious scriptures recognize and address the problem of intrapsychic conflict. A number of passages refer to "the battle within" (Romans 7:14-25; Galatians 5:17; James 4:1-3) using a tone that sounds a lot like psychodynamic descriptions of conflict between the id drives and the superego. Although the solutions to such conflict proposed by religion (James 4:7-10) differ quite markedly from those suggested by psychoanalytic theory, they at least agree on the problem. Other psychodynamic issues addressed by religious scriptures include the need to confront problems and work them out (Matthew 18:15; Luke 12:58) and warnings against countertransference when counseling others (Luke 6:41). Just as psychoanalysis emphasizes abreaction and emotional understanding as important outcomes of therapy, so too does religion seek to free persons of unhealthy mental states brought on by bitterness and resentment. It does so by encouraging repentance, penance, and receipt or giving of forgiveness, which like dynamic therapy often lead to emotional release and understanding.

Religious scriptures also encourage mature intrapsychic defense mechanisms such as altruism (being concerned about others and their welfare), asceticism (self-discipline and self-denial for a higher cause), sublimation (expression of sexual or aggressive drives in constructive and socially acceptable ways), and suppression (consciously deciding to deny or postpone drive gratification to more appropriate circumstances); on the other hand, religious teachings discourage infantile or neurotic defenses such as acting out (destructive behavioral manifestations of intrapsychic conflict) or projection (projecting one's own negative feelings onto others). This does not repudiate the fact that *neurotic* uses of religion can involve immature defenses such as controlling, displacement, dissociation, repression, or undoing; however, these defenses do not characterize mature religious faith (Chapter 7).

Religion, like psychoanalysis, seeks to mold and restructure character in cases where long-term destructive attitudes or behaviors have become habitual. In Judeo-Christianity, the concept of sin involves a conscious and willful decision not to follow religious or ethical guidelines for interacting with others, self, and God. These guidelines are internalized as part of the conscience or superego and are linked with an emotional enforcer called guilt. When functioning properly, guilt acts as a psychological warning system to help the individual avoid self-destructive or other-destructive behavior, and in cases where such behavior has occurred, it motivates actions to reverse or minimize the damage done (by repentance and making amends). Religion provides a framework by which guilt can be relieved and further destructive behaviors avoided. Through confession, persons consciously admit the error of their ways and profess a determination to compensate for damage done and avoid future repetition, thus initiating character change.

Religious guidelines for human behavior may also be preventative in a primary sense. By promoting positive interpersonal behaviors and discouraging discord within the family, religion may help block the development of intrapsychic conflict at its source in early childhood. Scriptures emphasize the importance of the nuclear family, promote healthy marital relationships, and stress the value of children and their early training. This enhances the chances that early development will proceed unhindered, in an intact and stable environment.

Thus, increasing conscious awareness of one's motivations, preventing and resolving internal conflict, and stimulating character change for those with disordered personalities are major goals of both religion and psychoanalysis. Each system, while utilizing different methods, seeks the same outcomes. As discussed in Chapter 4, psychoanalytic and religious approaches to mental health problems each have unique strengths which complement each other. The religious framework is more acceptable and understandable to many older persons who might otherwise reject explanations based on classical psychoanalytic theory. The elder's view of God, on the other hand, may be heavily influenced by negative influences from early childhood which psychoanalytic strategies could help to uncover and free the person of, resulting in a greater capacity for spiritual growth and maturation.

The work of Oskar Pfister in blending psychoanalysis with religion is a prime example of this. Pfister was a contemporary of Freud's who found psychoanalysis immensely helpful toward increasing his effectiveness as a Protestant minister (Meng and Freud 1963). Thus, the integration of religious and analytic methods in the treatment of older adults may enhance and extend the capacity for successful aging beyond that accomplished by either method alone. A more contemporary author and pastoral counselor, David Seamands, in his book *Healing of Memories* (1985) describes a method of exploring traumatic memories of negative childhood experiences buried deep in the unconscious which interfere with present day functioning; he does a fine job of incorporating Judeo-Christian teachings into a psychoanalytic-like approach that uses imagery and prayer to achieve insight and healing.

EXISTENTIAL PSYCHOTHERAPY

Existential psychotherapy is a dynamic therapy based on existentialism, an approach which borders on psychology, religion, and philosophy. This perspective comes largely from the teachings of Soren Kierkegaard, Martin Heidegger, Jean Paul Sartre, and Martin

Buber. Existentialism departs from other theories that explain behavior in terms of outward observation of human responses to stimuli; furthermore, it avoids the nature vs. nurture arguments. Instead, existentialism focuses on man's awareness of his or her being and non-being, especially with regard to feelings aroused over the anticipation of death.

According to Lester Havens (1974), existential therapy involves *being* with the patient, *staying* with the patient, and *leaving behind*. The existential therapist tries to place him or herself where the patient is, relying heavily on empathy to do so. Empathy involves "the power of projecting one's personality into, and so fully understanding the object of contemplation" (Oxford Universal Dictionary). Every attempt is made to avoid preconceptions about the patient and to suspend judgement during the course of therapy. The therapist keeps looking and listening in an effort to come into contact with the patient's deepest thoughts, feelings, and motivations. The objective is to help patients discover who they are–to assist in their search for being. As persons age, the search for meaning and identity intensifies; losses accumulate and challenge previous bases for self-concept (work, parenthood, social position, physical prowess). Thus, many existential issues arise with aging and, if not adequately dealt with, can give rise to existential anxiety or despair.

Existential psychotherapy addresses questions of meaning and being, using a philosophical approach that closely parallels religion. The Judeo-Christian religious tradition has provided–and continues to provide–sensible answers to questions of meaning and being that are easily understood by and acceptable to persons of all ages, intellectual capacities, educational levels, and cultural backgrounds. Empathy, understanding, and compassion are cornerstones of both existential therapy and religion (Isaiah 53:3-5; 54:10; Joel 2:13; Mark 1:41, 3:5, 6:34, 8:2; Luke 6:36, 7:13; Hebrews 2:17-18). Just as existential therapists seek to avoid preconceptions and judgements, scriptures also advocate suspending judgement of others, reserving this task for God alone (Genesis 18:25; Psalm 19:9; Acts 10:42; 1 Corinthians 5:13; 2 Corinthians 5:10; Hebrews 12:23). Because of these similarities, existential and religious views are easily integrated.

INTERPERSONAL PSYCHOTHERAPY

Another form of dynamic therapy, interpersonal psychotherapy focuses on problems in relating to other persons in the social environment (family and friends). The underlying premise is that man is predominantly a social animal and almost all of his or her behavior is motivated by relationship needs. The interpersonal method attempts to identify social distortions acquired during early childhood from interactions with powerful others. Neuroses are believed to originate from impaired relations with parents and caretakers; difficulties in current relationships are seen as learned patterns that have persisted from childhood.

As noted earlier, research has shown that older age does not prevent persons from relearning and establishing new patterns of interpersonal relating (Labouvie-Vief and Gonda 1976; Willis 1985). Inflexibility is less a function of age than of prior personality style. Persons who are rigid and close-minded as young adults are likely to have difficulty changing as they get older; in the same way, however, those who were open and flexible in youth typically remain so in old age. Thus, while elders may take longer to learn, those without significant cognitive impairment can often do so as well as younger persons. In fact, because of their maturity and life experiences, older adults have a broader perspective on many issues and thus may learn quicker than would be expected, particularly when instruction is presented in a cognitive framework that is familiar to them. Even institutionalized elders can learn new interpersonal skills that may enhance their relationships (Berger and Rose 1977).

The increasing emphasis by psychodynamic therapists on interpersonal relationships (Guntrip 1971; Wachtell 1977) has provided new possibilities for the integration of religious and secular approaches. Interpersonal psychotherapy focuses on the relationship between the patient and other persons in their life both past and present–including the therapist. It explores how people use and influence others to meet their own needs.

Likewise, the Judeo-Christian tradition deals almost exclusively with relationships. Man's relationship with man is given an importance in both the Old and New Testaments that is second only to his or her relationship with God. Scriptures repeatedly emphasize that while the relationship with God is always primary, this is not intended to compensate for or replace relationships with humans (1 John 4:20-21). Much of the content of the Judeo-Christian scriptures deals with laws governing social interaction. Individual well-being and psychological stability are strongly linked with concern for others, unselfishness, and service to others, especially those within one's own family. These teachings aim to increase community and family stability, and ensure that infants and children obtain the secure and consistent human interaction necessary for optimal growth and development.

As persons age, they tend to lose important family members and friends through death. Because some individuals never experienced deep and fulfilling relationships as children, much of their lives are spent longing for such relationships. In later life, such longings may intensify. The religious approach addresses these needs directly. First of all, it discourages a neurotic dependence on others to fulfill one's deepest needs and encourages a relationship with God to provide this *primary satisfaction*. Scriptures indicate that God can make up for deficiencies in past or present relationships; he can be a father to the fatherless, a spouse to the widowed, a friend to the friendless (Psalm 68:5; Isaiah 63:16; Matthew 23:9; 2 Corinthians 6:18; Ephesians 3:18-19; 1 John 3:1-2). Having a source of unconditional love is what many people need to feel whole, complete, and capable of reaching out to others. Relationships with others, then, take on an entirely new meaning. Instead of being desperately driven to seek relations for personal fulfillment, the individual becomes free to love and serve others because of his or her free choice–rather than out of compulsion.

Just as with psychoanalytic therapy, using a religious perspective in interpersonal therapy may have certain advantages in the elderly. Trying to change an elder's habitual way of relating to others, while possible, is not an easy task–particularly when the therapist is using concepts foreign to the worldview of the older adult. The Judeo-Christian perspective, on the other hand, involves time-tested principles of interpersonal relating based on a cognitive framework familiar and acceptable to many older adults, especially those who are less psychologically oriented.

SUPPORTIVE PSYCHOTHERAPY

Supportive therapy involves the strengthening of defenses and coping behaviors, rather than their breakdown and reconstruction (as in psychoanalysis). Dewald (1971) describes the function and technique of supportive therapy:

> One of the therapist's tasks in supportive treatment is to survey the various defenses available to the patient and determine which of these can most effectively be introduced, strengthened, encouraged or reinforced. . . . He tries to help the patient more effectively use *pre-existing defenses which for him are familiar, rather than introduce new ones the patient is not able to use himself* [my italics]. But when new defenses are to be introduced by the therapist, they are chosen to be compatible with the patient's overall ego structure and already existent major defenses . . . the strategy is based on a dynamic assessment of the patient's pre-morbid defensive patterns, and interventions are designed to best make use of these patterns in furthering the patient's ego controls and re-establishing a more comfortable and stable level of equilibrium. . . . Neurotic symptom formations which appear as part of a reaction to significant external stress or change in the individual's life situation are often indications more for a supportive than an insight-oriented approach. (pp. 105, 127)

Supportive therapy, then, is especially appropriate for elders suffering acute emotional distress over real problems associated with aging (Weinberg 1975). As we have seen, such problems include a loss of physical health or cognitive functioning because of illness, a loss of social status or occupational role because of retirement, a loss of family or friends through death, and a loss of economic security through increasing expenses and decreasing income.

Supportive techniques may be especially useful for treating older adults with *situational depressions*. In his book *Depression, Stress, and Adaptations in the Elderly* (1986), Fry states the following:

> Although psychotherapy has been practiced with the elderly to a limited degree, evidence suggests that the supportive mode is

the single most innovative and effective approach to the treatment of depressed elderly. The time-honored, face-to-face interaction mode of therapy with the elderly not only has the weight of tradition but provides the maximum flexibility and adaptability to those needs of the elderly person that are age and stage specific. The supportive interpersonal relation that the mental health practitioner establishes is designed to bring about modification of feelings, cognitions, attitudes, and behavior that have proven troublesome or problematic to the elderly. (pp. 275-276)

The religious approach to psychotherapy includes a strong element of support. While large portions of scripture deal with God's laws and commandments, justice, judgment, and punishment for sin, the central message is that of God's mercy, love and concern for human welfare. The majority of scripture is, in fact, supportive and encouraging in providing role models and promises that inspire hope. Not only does scripture emphasize the love and care of God for each individual person, but also commands that people care and show concern for each other in a supportive community. Many passages refer to people struggling with emotional states such as depression, anxiety, or fear (Numbers 11:10-15; 1 Samuel 1:5-18; 16:14; 1 Kings 19:4-10; Job 3:20-26; 7:4-5; 16:1-22; Psalm 6:2-6; 13:1-6; 31:9-13; 34:18; 88:1-18, 102:1-11; Jeremiah 20:7-18; Isaiah 38:13-16; Jonah 4:1-10). In response, numerous passages offer encouragement and support to those so afflicted (Deuteronomy 32:9-12; Psalm 34:18, 118:5-6; 147:3; Matthew 6:31-33; Romans 8:28, 15:13; Philippians 4:11; 1 Peter 5:7). Referral to such passages by the therapist when working with religious elders may help strengthen, inspire, and reinforce healthy defenses in a way that the older patient can readily understand and accept.

While supportive therapy often involves simple encouragement, listening, and empathy–methods with little structure–its effectiveness may be enhanced by including a psychodynamic perspective which takes into account the life-long personality characteristics of the patient (Hine 1963; Werman 1984). Elders with conflicts in their ability to trust or affiliate with others ("trust-fear conflict") will often react with increased anxiety, fear, and anger when the therapist approaches too closely with kindness, empathy, and under-standing. In such cases, the way to relieve anxiety is to back off and respect the patient's need for distance in the relationship. Likewise, the elder with a fear of submitting to or being dependent on others ("submission or dependence-fear conflict") will also react with anxiety or hostility to supportive techniques that threaten to take control away from him or her (despite the best intentions of the therapist). Thus, every person has a unique history and psychologi-cal makeup that must be considered and taken into account when offering supportive therapy. While techniques involving kindness, encouragement, listening, and empathy are essential components of any type of support, these must be tailored to the long-standing personality traits of the patient.

When distress is acute and severe, regardless of etiology, persons typically lack the motivation or cognitive capacity necessary for psychodynamic and cognitive-behavioral interventions. Treatments at this time should be directed at immediately relieving the psycho-logical distress and helping the individual to adjust to their new environment by providing support in the amount and form that he or she needs. There comes a time after the acute distress has dimin-ished, however, when support must be gradually withdrawn in order to facilitate psychological (and probably spiritual) growth. To con-tinue to foster dependence on others for guidance and support, par-ticularly in patients who already have an "independence-fear con-flict," may lead to an unwitting collusion between therapist and patient to maintain neurosis. In this case, support does not foster the growth needed for either psychological or spiritual change, but rather encourages the person to remain as they are–thus preventing their exposure to situations and consequences needed for reeducation and relearning (Hine 1963; Hine et al. 1972; Wachtell 1977). Religion, while emphasizing a need to support those in distress, makes clear demands on behavior once that distress is relieved; in fact, much of the support that religion offers is conditional on behavior.[1]

---

1. As I understand it, this does not mean that God's love is conditional. Even though God still loves a person (and sometimes because of that love), one may have to suffer the painful consequences of a behavior in order to induce changes that will ultimately be beneficial.

As in Chapter 4, this discussion stresses how religious and secular approaches complement and extend the gains achieved by either method used alone. Because of the importance of *identification with the therapist* in supportive therapy (Dewald 1971, p. 306), it may be difficult for the religious elder to identify with someone who is not sympathetic to, understanding of, and/or accepting of their religious views. Thus, mental health professionals may enhance their ability to support elders in times of crisis by utilizing religious beliefs and rituals; likewise, ministers and religious counselors may heighten the effectiveness of supportive interventions by taking into account psychodynamic principles.

COGNITIVE-BEHAVIORAL PSYCHOTHERAPY

Therapies derived from learning theory (cognitive and behavioral techniques), as well as insight-directed therapies (psychoanalysis and other psychodynamic techniques) involve a process of *reeducating* the patient–in other words, changing the way he or she thinks, feels, and behaves. This type of therapy is quite different from supportive therapy, where benefits to the patient are more immediate (in terms of relief of distress). Relearning is a hard process that requires motivation and cognitive flexibility; it may even temporarily increase the person's discomfort (in hope of a long-term better adjustment). Reeducative therapies, then, are more useful in patients with milder distress who are motivated to change, rather than those who are overwhelmed with discomfort and unable to muster the strength to make changes in their lives (persons better helped by support and/or medication).

Cognitive-behavioral therapy (CBT) involves structured interventions to help alter the dysfunctional cognitions and maladaptive behaviors which are believed to fuel many emotional disorders. Old patterns of thinking and behaving that involve pessimism, overreaction, exaggeration and catastrophizing are identified, challenged, and replaced by new healthy patterns of thinking. The first goal of CBT is belief assessment. The therapist seeks to identify the patient's beliefs about the world and the role he or she plays in it. Attempts are then made to help the patient correct their dysfunctional beliefs and cognitive errors. Selective abstraction of the negative aspects of situations, while ignoring the positive features, is characteristic of the cognitive distortions typifying many of the emotional disorders in later life–especially depression.

Aaron Beck (1963;1976) is given credit for developing the technique of CBT used in treating depression. He described a "cognitive triad" in depressed patients: (1) a negative view of self, (2) a negative interpretation of experiences, and (3) a negative expectation of the future. The goal of therapy, then, became to change negative thought patterns and underlying assumptions in the hope that depressive symptoms would diminish as the person began to think more rationally and positively. This method has been used to treat not only patients with depressive illness, but also those with panic attacks, obsessive-compulsive disorders, paranoid disorders, and somatoform disorders. A number of studies have now demonstrated the efficacy of cognitive-behavioral therapy in treating mild to moderate depression and anxiety in older adults (Gallagher and Thompson 1982; 1983; Gottlieb and Beck 1987; Thompson, Gallagher, and Breckenridge 1987; Beutler et al. 1987).

Many of the basic principles of cognitive therapy are contained in Judeo-Christian teachings. Consider the following passages: Matthew 15:18-20 (thought life makes persons unclean, not the food they eat), Mark 7:15-20 (same idea–thought life pollutes), Romans 12:2 (renewing of your minds), and especially Philippians 4:8 ("Finally, brothers, whatever is true, whatever is noble, whatever is right, whatever is pure, whatever is lovely, whatever is admirable–if anything is excellent or praiseworthy–think about such things"). Scriptures emphasize the positive outcomes that are possible in every situation ("And we know that in all things God works for the good of those who love him"–Romans 8:28), and thus encourage positive rather than negative thinking.

Behavioral Therapy

CBT involves not only changing the way people think, but also the way they act. This is the "behavioral" part of CBT. One might say that behavioral therapy operates on the religious notion that "faith without works is dead." Based on learning theory, behavioral therapy relies heavily upon classical (Pavlov) and operant (Skinner) conditioning techniques to either reinforce behaviors that are desired or extinguish those which are disliked. Behavioral therapy may also involve the repeated exposure to a feared stimulus or situation in order to lessen the anxiety associated with it. An example of the latter is "graded exposure," where the person is exposed to the feared stimulus little by little until he or she no longer experiences any fear. Another is the technique of "systemic desensitization" developed by Joseph Wolpe (1973) for the treatment of various anxiety disorders. Systematic desensitization involves relaxation training (tensing and relaxing of muscles, along with focused breathing), visualization of the anxiety-provoking stimulus, and desensitization of the stimulus by associating it with a deeply relaxed state. This method has been used most successfully in the treatment of phobias, obsessions, compulsions, and sexual disorders.

Besides graded exposure and systematic desensitization, other behavioral techniques include flooding, participant modeling, assertiveness and social skills training, aversion therapy, and positive reinforcement. Behavioral therapies focus on changing behavior and interactions that occur in the real world in the here and now, and are less concerned with the origins of these behaviors in the distant past. The basic premise is that no matter when or why a behavior started, its persistence depends on feedback from experiences with situations or people in the present environment. While older patients may require more therapy sessions than younger patients, behavioral therapy has been shown to be quite effective in this age group (Cautella and Mansfield 1977). Operant conditioning (Hussian 1981), token economies (Mishara 1978), and other structured behavioral programs (Gallagher and Thompson 1981) have also been successful in changing behavior of older adults.

Judeo-Christian scriptures heavily emphasize behavior. The Old Testament describes in great detail the blessings that follow good behavior and obedience to the laws (Leviticus 26:3-13) (positive reinforcement), whereas it promises disastrous consequences for those who disobey or otherwise conduct themselves inappropriately (Leviticus 26:14-39) (aversive conditioning). Rituals involving the sacrifice of animals or household goods were instituted in order to appease God and help ward off the consequences of negative behavior. The New Testament, while more cognitively oriented than the Old Testament because of an emphasis on faith, still underscores the importance of actions and behavior (James 2:24). While Jesus's death on the cross represents to Christians the final sacrifice for man's sins, each person is expected to confess their individual sins, seek forgiveness, and change their behaviors to avert negative spiritual/emotional consequences.

Role Models

Another common strategy in both religion and behavioral therapy is that of modeling. "Modeling" involves the patient's learning to act in a certain way or perform a task by imitating the actions of the therapist or other role model. Even mental health professionals have pointed out that religious scriptures contain men and women who might be looked on as role models and identified with (GAP 1968, pp. 705-707). Biblical figures are typically portrayed with faults and weaknesses that make them genuinely human. Arlow (1951) notes that "in every generation individuals with similar conflicts may find, through identification with the prophet, a model for the resolution of their own conflicts." Such identifications may contribute to identity formation through channeling, regrouping, or otherwise modifying behavior in highly specific ways.

Religious scriptures contain a number of examples of people who suffered, endured, and overcame their disturbed emotions (Moses, Jonah, Job, Hanah, David, Elijah, Isaiah, Jeremiah, and others). Jeremiah experienced classical symptoms of depression (Jeremiah 20), including disappointment ("O Lord, you deceived me, and I was deceived"–verse 7), rejection ("I am ridiculed all day long; everyone mocks me"–verse 7), fear and paranoia ("I hear many whispering. . . . 'Report him. Lets report him!' All my friends are waiting for me to slip . . ."–verse 10), self-condemnation ("Cursed be the day I was born! May the day my mother bore me not be blessed!"–verse 14), hopelessness ("Why did I ever come out of the womb to see trouble and sorrow and to end my days in shame"–verse 18).

Jeremiah coped with his depression using a mixture of cognitive and behavioral techniques. First, he restructured his cognitions by self-talk; then he became behaviorally engaged in activity that would get his energy going again. He reminded himself that God was with him ("The Lord is with me like a mighty warrior"–Jeremiah 20:11) and then began offering praise to God ("Sing to the Lord! Give praise to the Lord! He rescues the life of the needy from the hands of the wicked"–Jeremiah 20:13). Thus, by challenging his previous assumption that he had been deserted and by refocusing his thoughts on the idea that God was close at hand and would not leave him, his perspective began to change. Next, he became behaviorally engaged in activity that would help get him going–singing and praising God. In this way, Jeremiah used religion both cognitively and behaviorally to help relieve his depression.

The New Testament includes other role models such as the Centurion (an example of unwavering faith) (Matthew 8:5-13) and Peter (an example of someone who failed but later regained his strength and accomplished much) (Luke 22:55-62; Acts 3). Likewise, Paul often used himself as an example of someone experiencing troubles and hardships, which were overcome through perseverance. The portrayal of his struggles in the following passage illustrates human qualities that are easily identified with:

> We know that the law is spiritual; but I am unspiritual, sold as a slave to sin. I do not understand what I do. For what I want to do I do not do, but what I hate I do. . . . For I have the desire to do what is good, but I cannot carry it out. For what I do is not the good I want to do; no, the evil I do not want to do–this I keep on doing. (Romans 7:14-15, 18-19)

Finally, the New Testament presents Jesus as the exact human likeness of God on earth (John 14:9; Colossians 1:15,19; 2:9), and encourages adherents of the Christian faith to imitate his life and follow in his steps to the best of their ability. For the Christian, Jesus is a role model for obedience, suffering, honesty, compassion, mercy, and care for others; he represents an ego-ideal, the ultimate model of spiritual maturity.

Besides modeling, other behavioral techniques are commonly advocated in the Bible. These include prayer and meditation, behaviors that have been associated with deep states of relaxation. Much advice is also given on how to treat and relate successfully to other people; this instruction, then, can be viewed as a form of social skills training. From these examples it is clear that the Judeo-Christian approach relies heavily on cognitions and behaviors, making integration with secular CBT a relatively easy task. L. Rebecca Propst (1987) has integrated the techniques of cognitive-behavioral therapy within the context of Christian spirituality in a book entitled *Psychotherapy in a Religious Framework.* By increasing self-awareness, altering thoughts, and changing perspective, Propst uses Biblical passages to treat depression, anxiety, and better control anger and other responses to stress. She has also demonstrated the usefulness of religious imagery in the treatment of depression (Propst 1980). *Telling Yourself the Truth* (Backus and Chapian 1980) is a self-help book written in layman's terms which takes a similar orientation using cognitive-behavioral techniques to help persons with mild depressions or adjustment difficulties. Although there are numerous secular psychotherapies in addition to the five techniques reviewed above, they are less relevant to an older population and will not be considered here.

I have pointed out the many parallels that exist between secular psychotherapies and religion with the hope of facilitating their integration when working with older adults. Now for some comments on an all-important entity, the *therapeutic alliance*, as it develops between religious therapist and religious patient in analytic therapy.

FACTORS AFFECTING THE THERAPEUTIC ALLIANCE

Therapeutic alliance is a term used for the personal relationship that develops between patient and therapist. The therapeutic alliance is sometimes contaminated by unrealistic emotional elements called "transference" and "countertransference" reactions. Transference is a psychoanalytic concept that involves the patient's reactions to and feelings for the therapist that are exaggerated and distorted. These responses are more a function of the patient's needs and conflicts than of any real characteristics of the therapist. Transference occurs when the patient reacts to the therapist as if he or she represented some significant figure in the patient's past (a parent, for instance). Countertransference, on the other hand, is the term given to the therapist's emotional reactions to the patient that are based on the therapist's own needs and conflicts, rather than on any real characteristics of the patient.

Transference and countertransference issues between religious therapists and religious patients often hinder or disrupt therapy, especially insight-oriented therapy. While having a similar belief and value system often strengthens the therapeutic alliance, unanticipated problems may arise. Older patients, by virtue of their age, may react to the therapist as to a younger child (transference); the elder patient, in turn, may easily be associated with the therapist's parents or grandparents (countertransference). In psychoanalytic therapies, the patient's transference is actually used as part of the treatment; by working through the transference, the therapist helps the patient resolve related intrapsychic conflicts at the core of their emotional problems. Countertransference, however, can significantly interfere with therapy, and therefore must be recognized and dealt with immediately by the therapist.

Moshe Spero (1981) provides a well-rounded discussion of transference-countertransference issues surrounding the treatment of religious patients. He notes that despite similarities in religious belief, there may often be idiosyncratic and conflicting differences based on differing personal needs for religion (neurotic and non-neurotic) in patient and therapist. The religious therapist may have reactions to the patient ranging from rescue fantasies to feelings of disdain stemming from projection of insecurity or guilt. On the other hand, patients may have expectations and fantasies of a magical cure. Unsatisfied needs for love or nurturance may stimulate feelings of adoration; on the other hand, neurotic fears and aggressive or paranoid feelings may be projected onto the therapist.

Because the therapist may be acquainted with the patient's minister, there may be a temptation to share information about the patient without the patient's knowledge or consent. This breach of confidence can markedly interfere with trust, however, and add to resistance encountered in treatment. Finally, the religious therapist may fall into the trap of resolving ideological problems for the patient and providing them with "correct" religious views; by doing this, the therapist may become involved in religious debates or overextend him or herself into a position that can bring attack or devaluation by the patient.

Spero gives seven ways to manage countertransference for religious therapists doing psychodynamic therapy with religious patients. While countertransference issues are most relevant for cases that involve psychoanalysis, these strategies (especially the first three) are important regardless of therapy type, whether supportive, cognitive or behavioral.

First, the therapist must develop an understanding of the neurotic and normal needs of the person for religious practice and belief. The following areas should be explored: attitudes toward the spiritual world and the present world here on earth, attitudes toward and conceptualizations about God (especially any parallels with early parental figures), the use of religious belief in coping with death and loss, issues of conscience and degree of self-centered narcissism, and moral values. Second, the therapist must be able to identify neurotic or immature forms of religious belief that reflect underlying conflict, and distinguish these from mature belief that is adaptive and free from pathological influences. Third, the therapist must be able to examine his own religious belief from the two perspectives above and recognize differences and similarities to those of the patient.

Fourth, when feelings of anxiety and anger arise in the therapist from interaction with religious patients, he or she must recognize and accept these feelings as arising from within the therapist's over-concern or identification with the patient and not allow them to interfere with the therapeutic relationship. Fifth, religious similarities between therapist and patient should not be grounds for either more appreciation or less appreciation for the patient. Distorted countertransference reactions must be distinguished from the religious commitment to "love one another" (brotherly love). By avoiding countertransference distortions based on religious similarities between patient and therapist, the therapist may be in a better position to identify contaminating factors in the therapeutic relationship that may interfere with therapy.

Sixth, there must be a recognition of the limits placed on therapeutic goals when religious commitments by patient and therapist are the same: "The therapist must be able to distinguish when the commitment to values is being used as a defense and when such values must be accepted as constraints and as representing valid goals which the patient may be helped to achieve in a non-defensive way." Seventh, the therapist must control the urge to impart his or her own religious insights into each of the patient's religious dilemmas, given that the therapist's major focus should be on how religious beliefs cause or are involved with neurotic conflict.

The last four steps are designed to help the therapist maintain a more neutral and objective stance necessary for insight-oriented therapy, where the goal is to interpret defenses and resolve inner conflict. This stance may be less appropriate for supportive therapy where personal and empathic involvement by the therapist is more important. A similar religious orientation may have a strong impact on the quality and depth of the therapeutic alliance and the degree of trust between therapist and patient. In supportive and interpersonal therapies, a strong alliance may be of particular usefulness in furthering the aims of therapy. In order to use the therapeutic relationship most effectively for the healing of psychological wounds and the enhancement of growth, the therapist must "know him or herself" in terms of his or her own psychological vulnerabilities and religious biases, and not allow these countertransference issues to impede therapy.

When reference is made by the patient to issues of religious doctrine, belief, or practice, the therapist's first task is to explore in an objective and non-judgmental manner how the patient understands the issue. The personal view of the therapist on a religious issue–if requested by the patient–should be withheld until a thorough knowledge is acquired about what the issue means to the patient. Once this information is obtained, I believe it is appropriate to share with the patient how the therapist views the issue. This should be presented as simply an opinion, with the admission that the therapist is likewise proceeding along the path of growing religious maturity and does not possess absolute spiritual truth.

For example, a patient of mine in supportive therapy once asked me how I understood a passage from the Bible. Since I believed I had an understanding of the passage, my first urge was to expound on this knowledge. Restraining myself, however, I asked the patient what the passage meant to him. The patient's response provided me with considerable insight on his view of himself and of God, that enabled me to later tailor my response (in the form of an opinion) to better meet his needs.

Many experts would disagree strongly with the therapist's giving personal opinions on religious doctrine or belief. Often, however, the patient who is depressed or demoralized will selectively pick out biblical passages with a judgmental or condemning tone completely out of context, or they will interpret a passage in an overly harsh and guilt-provoking manner. Once the therapist explores the patient's understanding and how it relates to his or her psychopathology, then the therapist may offer a corrective interpretation if the patient requests and if the therapist is sufficiently knowledgeable to do so. It is always best to focus interpretations on God's love, compassion, and forgiveness, rather than on judgment or retribution for sin, given the high prevalence of low self-esteem, feelings of worthlessness, guilt, and lack of self-efficacy in patients suffering from anxiety or depressive disorders.

SUMMARY

As indicated in Chapter 4, the similarities and consistencies between religious and secular psychological approaches allow for easy integration of these techniques. This is particularly true for supportive, cognitive-behavioral, and interpersonal psychotherapies, which are especially useful for treating emotional disorders in older adults. Combined approaches, then, should further enhance the efficacy and acceptability of psychotherapy in this age group. The use of religion in psychotherapy, however, is not without problems. Transference and countertransference reactions between patient and therapist–based on religious beliefs or values–may adversely affect the therapeutic alliance unless understood and anticipated.

REFERENCES

Abraham, K. (1919). The applicability of psychoanalytic treatment to patients at an advanced age. In *Selected Papers on Psychoanalysis*, edited by D. Bryan and A. Strachey. NY: Basic Books, 1959.

_____ (1965). The applicability of psychoanalytic treatment of patients at an advanced age. In *Selected Papers of Karl Abraham*, edited by D. Bryan and A. Strachey. London: Hogarth Press, pp. 312-317.

Arlow, J.A. (1951). The consecration of the prophets. *Psychoanalytic Quarterly* 20(3):374-397.

Backus, W., and M. Chapian. (1980). *Telling Yourself the Truth*. Minneapolis, MN: Bethany Fellowship.

Beck, A.T. (1963). Thinking and depression. *Archives of General Psychiatry* 9:324-333.

_____ (1976). *Cognitive Therapy and Emotional Disorders*. NY: International Universities Press.

Berger, R.M., and S.D. Rose. (1977). Interpersonal skill training with institutionalized elderly patients. *Journal of Gerontology* 32:346-353.

Beutler, L.E., F. Scogin, P. Kirkish, D. Schrethen, A. Corbishley, D. Hamblin, K. Meredith, R. Potter, C.R. Bamford, and A.J. Levenson. (1987). Group cognitive therapy and alprazolam in treatment of depression in older adults. *Journal of Consulting Clinical Psychology*, 55:550-556.

Cautella, J.R., and L.A. Mansfield. (1977). Behavioral approach to geriatrics. In *Geropsychology: A Model of Training and Clinical Service*, edited by W.D. Gentry. Cambridge, MA: Balinger Press, pp. 21-42.

Dewald, P.A. (1971). *Psychotherapy: A Dynamic Approach*. NY: Basic Books.

Freud, S. (1905). On psychotherapy. In *The Standard Edition of the Complete Psychological Works of Sigmund Freud* (vol. 7), edited by J. Strachey. London: Hogarth Press, 1957. pp. 257-268.

Fry, P.S. (1986). *Depression, Stress, and Adaptations in the Elderly: Psychological Assessment and Intervention*. Rockville, MD: Aspen Publishers.

Gallagher, D., and L.W. Thompson. (1981). *Depression in the Elderly: A Behavioral Treatment Manual*. Los Angeles, CA: University of Southern California Press.

_____ (1982). Differential effectiveness of psychotherapies for the treatment of major depressive disorder in older adult patients. *Psychotherapy: Theory, Research and Practice* 19:42-49.

_____ (1983). Effectiveness of psychotherapy for both endogenous and nonendogenous depression in older adult outpatients. *Journal of Gerontology* 38:707-712.

GAP. (1968). The psychic function of religion in mental illness and health. Group for the Advancement of Psychiatry (prepared by the American Psychiatric Association Committee on Psychiatry and Religion), GAP Report #67, pp. 653-707.

Gottlieb, G., and A.T. Beck. (1987). Cognitive therapy and pharmacotherapy in geriatric depressants: a pilot random clinical trial. Paper presented at 140th Annual Meeting of American Psychiatric Association, Chicago.

Guntrip, H. (1971). *Psychoanalytic Theory, Therapy, and the Self*. NY: Basic Books.

Havens, L. (1974). The existential use of the self. *American Journal of Psychiatry* 131:1-10.

Hine, F.R. (1963). Improvement of emotional support through differential diagnosis of inner conflict. *Psychosomatics* 4:191-198.

Hine, F.R., E. Pfeiffer, G.L. Maddox, P.L. Hein, and R.O. Friedel. (1972). *Behavioral Science: A Selective View.* Boston: Little, Brown, & Co.

Hussian, R.A. (1981). *Geriatric Psychology: A Behavioral Perspective.* NY: Van Nostrand Reinhold Co.

Kahana, R.J. (1979). Strategies of dynamic psychotherapy with the wide range of older individuals. *Journal of Geriatric Psychiatry* 12:71-100.

Kaufman, S.R. (1963). *The Ageless Self: Sources of Meaning in Late Life.* Madison, WI: University of Wisconsin Press.

Kirshner, L.A. (1988). A model of time-limited treatment for the older patient. *Journal of Geriatric Psychiatry* 21:155-168.

Labouvie-Vief, G., and J.N. Gonda. (1976). Cognitive strategy training and intellectual performance in the elderly. *Journal of Gerontology* 31:327.

Lazarus, L.W., J. Sadavoy, and P.R. Langsley. (1988). Individual psychotherapy. In *Comprehensive Review of Geriatric Psychiatry,* edited by J. Sadavoy, L.W. Lazarus, L.F. Jarvik. Washington, DC: American Psychiatric Association Press, pp. 487-512.

Meng, H., and E.L. Freud. (1963). *Psychoanalysis and Faith: The Letters of Oskar Pfister.* London: The Hogarth Press.

Mishara, B.L. (1978). Geriatric patients who improve in token economy and general milieu treatment programs: A multivariate analysis. *Journal of Consulting and Clinical Psychology* 46:1340-1348.

Myers, W.A. (1984). *Dynamic Therapy of the Older Patient.* NY: Jason Aronson.

Propst, L.R. (1980). The comparative efficacy of religious and non-religious imagery for the treatment of mild depression in religious individuals. *Cognitive Therapy and Research* 4:167-178.

_____ (1987). *Psychotherapy in a Religious Framework: Spirituality in the Emotional Healing Process.* NY: Human Sciences Press.

Sadavoy, J., and A. Robinson. (1989). Psychotherapy and the cognitively impaired elderly. In *Psychiatric Consequences of Brain Disease in the Elderly,* edited by D. Conn, A. Grek, and J. Sadavoy. NY: Plenum Press, pp. 101-135.

Seamands, D.A. (1985). *Healing of Memories.* Wheaton, IL: SP Publications (Victor Books).

Spero, M.H. (1981). Countertransference in religious therapists of religious patients. *American Journal of Psychotherapy* 35:565-575.

Thompson, L.W., D. Gallagher, and J.S. Breckenridge. (1987). Comparative effectiveness of psychotherapies for depressed elders. *Journal of Consulting and Clinical Psychology* 55:385-390.

Wachtell, P. (1977). *Psychoanalysis and Behavioral Therapy: Toward an Integration.* NY: Basic Books.

Weinberg, J. (1975). Geriatric psychiatry. In *Comprehensive Textbook of Psychia-*

try, 2nd ed., edited by A.M. Freeman, H.L. Kaplan and B.J. Sadock. (vol. 2). Baltimore, MD: Williams & Wilkins, pp. 2405-2420.

Werman, D. (1984). *The Practice of Supportive Psychotherapy*. NY: Brunner-Mazel.

Willis, S.L. (1985). Towards an educational psychology of the older adult learner: Intellectual and cognitive bases. In *Handbook of the Psychology of Aging*, edited by J.E. Birren and K.W. Schaie. NY: Van Nostrand Reinhold, pp. 818-847.

Wolpe, J. (1973). *The Practice of Behavior Therapy*, 2nd edition. NY: Pergamon Press.

PART V:
SPECIAL CONCERNS IN LATER LIFE

Chapter 16

The Nursing Home
and Alzheimer's Disease

The community, moreover, may need its aged and dependent,
its sick and its dying, and the virtues which they sometimes
evince–the virtues of humility, courage, and patience–just as
much as the community needs the virtues of justice and love
manifest in the agents of care.

–William F. May

THE NURSING HOME

While only about 5% of persons age 65 or over reside in a
nursing home, nearly 20% of those over age 80 do so, and the
lifetime risk of spending at least some time in a nursing home is
40%. At the age of 75, 20% of adults need help from another person
for basic needs; at age 80, 40% need such assistance. The annual
cost of nursing home care in this country is currently 50 billion
dollars and rising. Because of the fast pace of society, the changes
in family structure and composition, the aging of our population,
and the medical advances allowing persons to live longer with
chronic illness, nursing home enrollments are on the rise. By the
year 2030, the number of nursing home patients is expected to
triple. Thus, a considerable proportion of Americans, if they live
long enough, can expect to spend time in an institutional setting.

When timely, the admission of an older adult to a nursing home
can improve physical care, increase feelings of independence, relieve a sense of being a burden on family, and result in supportive,
fulfilling relationships with aged peers and staff. Relationships with

family members may improve and the time spent together can become more enjoyable, due to greater freedom and well-being of all
parties concerned. On the other hand, admission to a nursing home
may also indicate family withdrawal and abandonment. Many "first
generation" elderly have expectations based in their culture of origin, while their adult children have become Americanized and may
not share in their elders' expectations. In such cases, nursing home
placement is often accompanied by intense feelings of anger, disappointment, and loneliness.

For an older person, the mere fact of leaving their home represents an enormous loss. The home is the most perfect expression of
the self, containing treasures and memories collected over a lifetime
of living, playing, loving, and grieving. Loss of the home has a
direct impact on a person's sense of self. If this wasn't enough, the
transition to a nursing home generally occurs at a time when physical health is poor and ability to care for self is limited–factors that
negatively impact on self-esteem. This, combined with a loss of
control over one's environment, loss of one's home, and confine-
ment with others who are disabled and helpless, produces a threat to
the integrity of the self that is second to few other negative life
events.

Studies of the physical and psychological impact of nursing
home placement appear to confirm these speculations. Jerome
Frank (1974) discovered an increased death rate of aged persons
shortly after admission to state mental hospitals; in many cases no
clear cause of death could be found at autopsy. Many such patients
may have suffered from a severe form of reactive depression, where
the person loses interest in their environment, regresses, stops eating, and takes a progressive downward course both physically and
mentally. George Engel (1968) called this type of psychological
state the "giving up-given up" complex. Such persons seem to have
lost the will to live. Once this attitude becomes firmly entrenched,
Engel found that death often ensued.

Because of the high prevalence of functional impairment in this
population (over 90% needing assistance in bathing, dressing,
transferring, toileting, and so forth), elders in nursing homes are
heavily dependent on others for meeting even their most basic daily
needs. Poor staffing in such facilities commonly results in a high

patient to staff ratio; consequently, services must be provided in a highly organized fashion that allows little room for individual variation or patient preference. When elders are admitted to a nursing home, they often lose control over their lives. Eating, bathing, getting up in the morning, going to bed at night, are all arranged by others. This loss of autonomy and assault on personal dignity are highly distressing for many individuals, particularly those who possess the cognitive awareness to appreciate their tragic circumstances. Loss of control and loss of individuality, then, are major factors that trigger and maintain emotional problems in this setting.

While only 20% of nursing home patients have a primary psychiatric diagnosis, 70% have psychiatric problems contributing to their condition (Borson et al. 1987) and 40% may experience some form of depression (Morley 1988; Parmelee, Katz, and Lawton 1989; Rovner 1991). Such depressions markedly diminish the subjective quality of life and adversely affect survival rates (Rovner et al. 1991; Parmelee, Katz, and Lawton 1992). These depressions are frequently associated with severe physical disability and/or recent nursing home admission. Studies have shown that over 90% of nursing home patients who require a specific psychiatric intervention do not receive such care (Burns et al. 1988; Burns 1991). Only about 1 percent of nursing home patients are appropriately evaluated by psychiatrists, and only 5 percent see any type of mental health provider at all (Burns 1991). What else can be done to enhance quality of life and increase the likelihood of successful aging for such persons?

Enhancing Quality of Life

One way to improve this situation is to focus on maximizing patient autonomy as a vital component of nursing and medical care plans. Nursing staff needs to understand and appreciate the role that autonomy and control play in the elder's overall mental and physical health. Providing choices for the patient is as important for viability of the human spirit as the daily insulin injection is to a diabetic or the digitalis pill is to a heart failure patient. Unfortunately, issues of autonomy and individual choice are seldom treated with the same reverence as medications or other treatments.

Autonomy can be enhanced by small, minor alterations in everyday care. Examples include allowing nondemented patients to decide when and where they wish to take their daily bath, how long they wish to sit up in a chair, what television program they would like to watch, where and with whom they would like to eat their meals, and when to get up in the morning or go to bed at night. In some settings where staffing shortage is a serious problem, these options are simply impractical. Nevertheless, efforts in this direction are sure to have large payoffs in terms of enhancing quality of life for institutionalized elders. Volunteers from local churches who wish to live out their Christian faith could help alleviate some of the pressure from staffing shortages by pitching in for brief periods each day.

Harvard psychiatrist Ned Cassem notes that the physician [or clergyperson] can play a major role in influencing nursing staff's attitudes toward patients by educating them about aspects of each patient's life that makes him or her special (without compromising patient confidentiality, of course). For instance, an elderly patient may have been a teacher at the local high school, a registered nurse, or a librarian; he or she may have traveled extensively throughout the world, fought in a World War, helped build or design a well-known building, and so forth. These details give the patient distinction and uniqueness as a person. Such information may also help staff understand and tolerate behaviors by the patient related to their former lifestyles (desire for privacy, independence, or need for social interaction).

In some cases, however, interventions to increase autonomy and allow choices are insufficient to stave off emotional problems. When a clinical depression settles in, interventions of a different nature may be required to reverse feelings of hopelessness and despair. While biological treatments for depression are invaluable in such situations, counseling and psychotherapy are also essential for changing attitudes that foster the development and maintenance of depressive illness. In such cases it is vital that someone communicates to the elder that there are things that he or she can still do to help themselves and to *give of themselves* to help others (Frank 1974).

Role of Religion

Religion can facilitate a change of attitude and outlook both in patients and caretakers. First, religion provides a worldview in which suffering has a place and meaning. Second, it affords the hope of compensation in the next life for difficulties endured during this one. Third, through a personal faith, the elder can experience God's love for them and come to comprehend their eternal value and priceless worth. Fourth, a religious faith can motivate elders to reach out to others–thus giving them a sense of purpose and participation in God's overall plan (as well as enhanced well-being as Neal Krause (1992) has so eloquently shown). Finally, religion can motivate other people (family, staff, friends, other patients) to provide the elder with a sense of being important and cared for.

While there has been little empirical research on this topic, what information is available confirms the valuable function of religion in this setting. The only study that I am aware of is that of Nelson (1989), who surveyed a sample of 26 institutionalized elders in Austin, Texas. She found a significant inverse relationship between involvement in religious activity and depressive symptoms measured by the Geriatric Depression Scale. Social support was also a significant inverse correlate of depression; clergypersons, however, made up a disappointingly small percent (5%) of patients' support network. As noted earlier, the heavy responsibilities of community clergy frequently prevent them from personally ministering to nursing home patients on a regular basis; however, they need to realize the important role they play in motivating lay ministers and in establishing a lay visitation program to these homes.

Epidemiological research suggests that religious cognitions and behaviors play an important role in facilitating adjustment to the nursing home. The evidence for this lies in the frequency of these activities and in patients' testimonials of their effectiveness.

Prevalence of Religious Beliefs and Behaviors

Again, the number of published reports on the prevalence of religious cognitions and behaviors in the nursing home are few and far between. Among the many logistical barriers to such studies is the fact that many nursing home residents are cognitively impaired and are thus unable to cooperate and/or give informed consent to participate in such surveys. Pan (1950) reported that of 597 women from Protestant church homes (many homes in those days were church sponsored), 67% regularly listened to church services over the radio and 84% attended church at least once a week. Scott (1955) found that of 78 nursing home patients in Austin, Texas (most from proprietary homes), 33% read the Bible at least once a week and 20% attended church at least once a month. In Nelson's (1989) more recent study of nursing home patients in Austin, Texas, she reported that 69% regularly participated in religious activity and 19% occasionally participated.

Finally, we have recently completed a small prevalence study in High Shoals, Georgia, which I will report here. Magda D. and Joseph R. Bennett, administrators at the Family Enrichment Center (FEC) in High Shoals, Georgia, conducted a comprehensive assessment of residents' religious cognitions and behaviors in December of 1988. All 101 elderly residents at this nonprofit, private, skilled nursing facility were eligible for the survey. Although not directly associated with any religious institution, this facility has indirect ties to the Disciples of Christ. The study was approved by the Human Investigations and Ethics Committee of the Family Life Center; participating elders were required to give their permission to be included in the research study. Elders were excluded if their mental status was severely impaired (delirium/dementia) (n = 30), if they were unable to speak (aphasic) (n = 25), had severe hearing impairment (n = 4), if they were unavailable because of recent discharge or rehabilitation (n = 4), or if they refused (n = 10). Thus, of those available and capable of being interviewed (n = 38), 74% (n = 28) of patients completed the questionnaire.

The Springfield Religiosity Schedule (SRS) (Koenig, Kvale, and Ferrel 1988a) was administered by two staff members who made efforts to remain impartial during the process; questions were asked in a monotone voice without encouraging one response over another. The SRS measures religious beliefs, behaviors, and attitudes. This instrument includes portions of several other religious scales including the Hoge Intrinsic Religiosity scale (Hoge 1972), the Spiritual Well-Being scale (Palouzian and Ellison 1982), and questions from an instrument developed by Glock and Stark (1965); in addition, there are a number of questions concerning organizational and nonorganizational religious behaviors, support from church members, and desire for prayer with their medical physician. The SRS has been validated in older and younger religious professionals from a wide variety of Christian faiths (Koenig, Kvale, and Ferrel 1988a).

Because the SRS has been administered to elderly outpatients attending a geriatric medicine clinic (Koenig, Moberg, and Kvale 1988b) and to community-dwelling elders participating in senior centers in Iowa, Missouri, and Illinois (Koenig, Smiley, and Gonzales 1988c), we have data for comparison with the current sample. Table 16.1 summarizes and compares the responses to the SRS in these three elderly populations.

The nursing home sample was older (mean age 84), had a greater percentage of women (83%), more Protestants (93%), and was more financially secure than either the geriatric outpatient or the senior center samples. Religious belief, while prevalent in both groups, tended to be higher among nursing home patients than medical outpatients. Personal devotional activities, such as private prayer and Bible reading, were especially common among nursing home patients. The salience of religion and its perceived role in coping was similar between the groups; over 80% found religious cognitions and activities–especially prayer–very helpful. As far as religious attitudes were concerned, nursing home patients demonstrated a higher level of intrinsic religiosity than either of the other two groups, with over 90% of the former claiming that faith was involved in every aspect of their lives, that they experienced the presence of God, and that they sought God's guidance whenever making an important decision.

These findings suggest that religion plays an important role in the lives of nursing home patients–at least those residing in the deep South. The reader should recognize the limitations of the current study in terms of small sample size and location in the Bible Belt region of the United States. Our nursing home sample was somewhat atypical in that participants were better off financially and perceived their health status as better than did elders in the other samples. This may not be the case in other nursing home settings.

TABLE 16.1. Religious behaviors and attitudes of elderly nursing home patients compared with those of elders from a geriatric assessment clinic and from senior centers

Characteristics	Nursing Home (n = 28)	Geriatric Clinic* (n = 106)	Senior Centers** (n = 298)
Demographic and Health			
Mean Age, y	83.8	74.4	74.3
	%	%	%
Male	16.6	27.6	27.2
Financial Status (> $1000/mo)	67.9	12.1	5.4
Subjective Health (fair or poor)	28.6	48.1	31.5
Religious Denomination			
Protestant	93.0	58.5	76.5
Catholic	7.0	31.1	22.4
Jewish	0.0	1.9	0.0
None	0.0	4.9	1.1
Religious Belief			
Belief in a personal God	96.4	90.5	—
Belief in Jesus as Divine	100.0	83.9	—
Belief in miracles (literally)	85.2	75.7	—
Belief in the Devil	88.5	75.7	—

Religious Behaviors			
Church Attendance (> once/wk)	46.5	54.4	57.9
Religious Community Activity (> 1/wk)	25.0	27.0	31.3
Private Prayer (> once/daily)	78.6	71.5	63.1
Religious TV/Radio Programs (daily)	7.4	6.8	8.8
Read Bible/Religious Lit (> once/daily)	40.7	28.0	38.0
Miscellaneous			
Recognition of Old Testament Prophets (correct on all 6 names)	25.0	33.8	—
Number of Patient's Five Closest Friends Who are Members of Same Church (4 or 5)	53.6	52.2	—
If in great emotional stress, very sick or near death, would like personal physician to pray w them (very much)	60.7	47.0 (n = 38)	53.0 (n = 34)

TABLE 16.1. (continued)

Salience of Religion & its Perceived Role in Coping	Nursing Home	Geriatric Clinic	Senior Centers
		% strong or moderate agreement	
Rely very little on religion	28.6	27.3	—
Prayer not helpful in coping with stress	14.8	19.0	—
Prayer important in my life	85.7	82.1	88.9
God not a source of strength	14.8	14.6	31.7
Do not experience God's interventions	23.0	18.7	—
Experience God's love and care	85.1	87.7	—
Relationship w God helps me not feel lonely	75.0	80.5	—
Most fulfilled when close communion w God	82.1	84.8	—
Relig faith most important influence in life	89.3	82.1	85.6

Intrinsic Religious Attitudes (Hoge 1972)

		% definitely true or tends to be true
My faith involves all my life	92.8	74.5	84.5
I experience the presence of God in my life	92.9	76.6	88.0
Refuse to let religious considerations influence my everyday affairs (extr)	44.4	41.7	55.0
Nothing is as important to me as serving God as best as I know how	88.9	81.0	85.4
My faith sometimes restricts my actions	81.5	69.3	62.6
My religious beliefs are what really lie behind my whole approach to life	88.9	79.0	78.3
I try hard to carry my religion over into all my other dealings in life	89.3	79.6	79.1
One should seek God's guidance when making every important decision	92.6	85.4	85.6
Although I believe in religion, there are many more important things in life	21.5	27.4	34.3
It doesn't matter so much what I believe as long as I lead a moral life	67.9	48.4	61.3

* Data from Koenig, Moberg, and Kvale 1988b
** Data from Koenig, Smiley, and Gonzales 1988c

Nevertheless, the rates of religious belief and activity here are not greatly different from those documented in elderly persons sampled in Missouri, Iowa, and Illinois. The slightly higher rates in nursing home patients is expected, given the higher stress typically experienced in those in institutional settings. The pattern of religious activities indicated that private devotional activities were especially prevalent in this disabled population.

In conclusion, religious beliefs and behaviors are common among nursing home patients without cognitive impairment, and appear to facilitate coping in this setting. Future studies are needed to further examine the role of religion in the nursing home, since our results reflect a rather atypical, small population of financially secure and relatively healthy elders without cognitive impairment. Given the evident importance of religion to institutionalized elders, how might counselors and religious professionals best minister to the spiritual needs of this group?

Role of the Chaplain

A clerical presence in the nursing home helps to facilitate religious expression and orchestrate the meeting of spiritual needs. Henry Simmons (1991) discusses the tasks of the chaplain in the nursing home, especially the task of helping new residents adjust to their environment. For many elders, nursing home placement initially arouses a sense of abandonment and anger that is often directed towards both family and God. The universe becomes less trustworthy and one's relationship with God is deeply affected. What can the chaplain do to help? Simmons emphasizes the role of prayer.

Pardue (1989) examined the pastoral needs of residents of three long-term care facilities. Residents agreed unanimously that the single factor most helpful in reorganizing themselves and adapting to the nursing home was *personal prayer*. Interestingly, this response contrasted to those of their pastors (also surveyed), who believed that communal worship and social activities were the most important factors. Pardue concluded that the "subjective, personal elements of the recreative process" were most important in allowing elders to reestablish their sense of self in the new environment. Communal religious activities are of secondary importance. A vital task of the chaplain, then, is to help elders develop the inner side of their devotional lives–help them to deepen their prayer lives. This will then initiate the healing process, assist in rebuilding their relationship with God, and facilitate the reconstruction of self. Equipped with the ability to pray, the resident will have a tool that can be used at any time, day or night, whenever loneliness, pain, or discomfort creeps into his or her life.

The chaplain will not find the task of teaching elders how to pray an easy one, for there are many resistances within the chaplain that seek to defeat this effort. According to Simmons,

> Because to come close to the inner life of another in such a moment of darkness puts to the test the depth of our own life of prayer, puts to the test the adequacy of our meditation on the mysteries of faith, puts to the test whether our own psyche and souls are refined by fire, puts to the test the quality of our own inner lives. What is needed by the new resident is a guide whose qualifications are rooted in a serious struggle with the same ultimate realities and some sureness of knowledge about the inner life of prayer. (p. 173)

There are four things the chaplain can do to help the elder pray. First, is to understand the importance of personal prayer in the reconstruction of a meaningful life and relationship with God (as distinct from community worship). Second, is to understand the difficulty in recreating meaning, given the powerfully negative effects of homelessness, feelings of abandonment, irreversible and progressive physical disability, and loss of control over life. Third, is to uncouple prayer from formal or communal worship. Most people have prayed personally, but this prayer has typically been supported by familiar persons and familiar places. Patients recently admitted to a nursing home experience a sense of "uprootedness" that must be dealt with up front. In order to pray in a way that will rebuild their personal and spiritual lives, the elder must give up their old ways of praying and start anew.

Finally, the chaplain must weather and tolerate the new resident's anger and frustration that may be directed at them because of their association with God. Anger is a normal and expected stage in the mourning process that all humans go through when adapting to loss.

The "why me?" question is universal. Such persons feel disap-
pointed and cheated by God. Instead of being accompanied by
feelings of warmth, peace, and consolation, prayer at this time may
be characterized by feelings of "desolation, by no sense of center,
by no sense of connectedness, by no sense of the mystery of the
presence of God" (Simmons 1991, p. 174). The chaplain must be
able to sit with patients in silence, experiencing their sense of desperation and abandonment with them; no words of consolation are
necessary or even useful. This is why the chaplain's own inner
religious life needs to be strong. Empathy of this type is emotionally
draining, and extracts a price. The effort, however, is not without
reward.

When Jesus was undergoing his deepest hour of suffering in the
Garden of Gethsemane, he asked his disciples to accompany and *sit
with him*: "remain here and keep watch with me" (Matthew 26:38).
This is the primary task of the chaplain in the nursing home. In
ministering to residents in this way, one is following the desires
expressed by Jesus in the Garden. Indeed, not long before his time
in the Garden, Jesus had just spoken to his disciples about the need
to visit the sick and attend to those in prison: "Truly I say to you, to
the extent that you did it to one of these brothers of Mine, even the
least of them, you did it to Me" (Matthew 25:40). Thus, for the
Christian chaplain (or lay visitor) sitting in silence with an elderly
nursing home patient is equivalent to "keeping watch" with Jesus.

Other Duties

Although helping patients to develop their inner spiritual lives is
the most important task of the nursing home chaplain (in my opinion), there are many other duties that must be attended to as well
(Phillips 1973). Orchestrating regular communal services and administering sacraments (the Eucharist, penance, anointing of the
sick) are among these. Once the resident has adapted to their new
environment, gathering together with others in the community to
worship and socialize will help keep personal faith alive and will
provide an opportunity to share the hope and meaning in their life
with others.

For cognitively impaired elders, singing hymns, receiving the
sacrament of communion, and exposure to other religious symbols

or rituals can arouse spiritual feelings that are unaccessible by other routes. For cognitively intact residents, the chaplain may form a Bible study group that meets weekly to encourage communication and socialization. Another task includes communicating with pastors in the community and encouraging their participation in the nursing home–particularly when a number of residents are former congregants. This communication may also facilitate the enlistment of volunteers from the local churches to visit patients, help relieve loneliness, and perhaps provide practical services to ease the workload of already overburdened nursing staff.

At times, the chaplain will also be called upon to provide personal counseling to residents who have adjustment problems. Supportive and cognitive-behavioral approaches that integrate religious and secular methods (as described in Chapter 15) are particularly helpful. The chaplain, however, needs to be able to recognize psychiatric problems that require input from mental health professionals (Koenig 1993). An adjustment disorder may deepen into a major depression, for which antidepressants (Katz et al. 1990) or electroconvulsive therapy (Koenig 1991) may be necessary. Delusional disorders involving religious themes may also be encountered, requiring major tranquilizers for their management. The chaplain must have sufficient knowledge about these conditions to make appropriate referrals when indicated. Ministering to residents' family members and arranging for family meetings may also be a task of the chaplain in some institutions. Thus, the job of the chaplain in the nursing home is a challenging one in which he or she must wear many hats.

However, a word of caution is once again in order. The nursing home chaplain is a specialist in the area of religion–not social work, psychology, or nursing home administration. Because of staff shortages characteristic of most homes, there will be pressure to have the chaplain take over some of these other duties. When this happens, the chaplain may not have sufficient time to perform the duties most directly related to his or her area of expertise. Thus, it is necessary to establish and maintain a clear boundary between the responsibilities of the chaplain and those of other staff personnel.

There is no doubt that the chaplain plays a vital role in institutional settings. Unfortunately, not all persons are cut out for such a position. The job is often associated with little glamor and much hard work to the one who accepts it. The opportunity to make a real difference in people's lives comes only infrequently, however; the occasion to do so certainly exists for the nursing home chaplain, who has the opportunity to profoundly influence the mental and spiritual well-being of elders at a particularly vulnerable time in their lives.

ALZHEIMER'S DISEASE AND OTHER DEMENTIAS

Among residents of nursing homes, 60% to 80% experience significant cognitive impairment (Teeter et al. 1976; Rovner et al. 1986; Parmelee, Katz, and Lawton 1989; Rovner 1991). At least 75% of cognitive impairment is long-standing and irreversible, with Alzheimer's disease being the primary cause in 50% to 60% of cases. Other causes of progressive mental decline in later life include multiple strokes (10-20%), chronic alcoholism (6-11%), normal pressure hydrocephalus (4-12%), and a wide range of other more rare neurological disorders (Kaufman 1990). The prevalence of Alzheimer's dementia among all persons age 65 or over living in the community is much lower (3%) than in the nursing home, although the rate of Alzheimer's disease among community-dwellers age 85 or older may reach nearly 45% (Evans et al. 1989). Since Alzheimer's disease accounts for only about 50% to 60% of all dementias, the total proportion of older adults with cognitive dysfunction that impairs self-care and overall function is quite large. The clinical course of Alzheimer's disease and related dementias is described by Kaufman (1990):

> In the early stage, patients may be conversant, sociable, and physically intact, but testing reveals impaired judgment and memory. These individuals may be confused either at night or when they are moved to new surroundings . . . . When casually seen, these impairments are liable to be misinterpreted as depression or benign senescence. The middle stage of Alzheimer's disease is marked by overt memory loss accompanied by impairment in other intellectual functions . . . language impairments. . . .The impairments in expression are followed by a

decline in comprehension of written and verbal communications. . . . In addition, patients commonly suffer depression, hallucinations, and, in 20 to 40 percent of cases, prominent paranoid ideation that sometimes reaches psychotic proportions. . . . In the late stage, physical as well as cognitive deficits become profound. Patients tend to be mute, unresponsive to verbal requests, and bedridden in a decorticate (fetal) posture. (pp. 116-117)

During the earlier stages of dementia, the person begins to experience difficulty with memory, concentration, or performing calculations. Depending on the amount of insight and their premorbid personality adjustment, the elder may struggle coming to terms with their gradually shrinking world; many may experience anxiety or depression (perhaps 50%) at this time (Reifler, Larson, and Hanley 1982). The family may likewise experience fear and confusion over what is happening to their loved one. As the disease progresses, loss of the ability to recognize close family members occurs, judgment worsens, restlessness and wandering increase, personality changes and outbursts of anger may occur, and communication skills diminish. Because patients with dementia may survive anywhere from 2 to 16 years (average 7 years), the elder and his or her family often must struggle with this disorder for a considerable period of time (Walsh, Welch, and Larson 1990).

As the disease progresses, the person becomes less aware of their dysfunctions; consequently, depression and other affective symptoms tend to diminish. The family, however, faced with an ever increasing burden of responsibilities, may now begin to experience severe emotional turmoil and/or physical exhaustion, as they witness their loved one change into a different person before their eyes. While nursing home placement is the best option for some families, others for personal or financial reasons attempt to provide this care themselves. A spouse or child, then, may take on the responsibility of providing 24-hour-a-day care at home–a job that is seldom easy. At times like this, religion may be turned to by either the patient or the family caregiver as a source of comfort.

Cognitive Impairment and Religious Coping

There are virtually no empirical studies which examine the relationship between increasing cognitive impairment and use of religious beliefs or activities to cope. In our study of hospitalized veterans, we documented an inverse relationship between cognitive impairment (measured by the Mini-Mental State Exam) and religious coping (Koenig et al. 1993). This was particularly true in men previously employed in unskilled occupations. There are two possible explanations for these findings. Religion may "protect" the person against the development of cognitive dysfunction in later life, or cognitive impairment may interfere with the capacity to use religion as a coping resource.

If the former explanation is true, then the mechanism by which religion might enhance cognitive function is unclear. The inverse relationship between religious coping and depression may have some effect in this regard, given the adverse impact of depression on cognition. The religiously involved individual may also experience more social interaction and exposure to people from different educational and occupational levels. Given the impact of educational level and occupational status on cognitive performance, one might speculate that increased social interaction in this setting leads to greater transmission of information and cognitive processing. Another possibility is that men from lower social classes, if not depending on religion to cope, may be more likely to depend on alcohol to do so. In support of this hypothesis, we found a strong inverse relationship between use of alcohol and religious coping. Thus, the adverse effects of alcohol on cognitive function may be less common among lower class persons who use religion instead of alcohol to cope.

A second, and more likely, explanation for the inverse relationship between religious coping and cognitive impairment is that as memory and concentration decline, the ability to use religion as a coping resource (especially the use of religious cognitions) diminishes. This explanation is further corroborated by results from the longitudinal portion of our study. As cognitive function declined over time, religious coping did likewise. This finding is understandable given that the ability to read the Bible, pray, listen to sermons, and process religious cognitions all decline with loss of the ability to focus one's attention and remember. Further research is needed to better understand the effects of dementing illnesses on religious faith and the capacity for a conscious relationship with God.

A Presbyterian minister, Robert Davis, has written a book entitled *My Journey into Alzheimer's Disease* (1989) that describes his own battle with Alzheimer's disease and the impact of this illness on his religious faith. Pastor of a 4000-member congregation in Miami, Florida, Davis began having memory and concentration problems at the peak of his career in the ministry. His book contains deep insights into the interaction between cognitive impairment and religious faith:

> The sunlight of Christ had always filled and thrilled my soul in those drifting moments before sleep carried me away. Now I discovered the cruelest blow of all. This personal and tender relationship that I had with the Lord was no longer there. This time of love and worship was removed. There were no longer any feelings of peace and joy. I cried out to God for it to be restored. I howled out to the Lord to come back and speak to my spirit as he had done before. (p. 47)

> By sheer faith I prayed, 'O God, I cannot see you through the darkness that fills my mind and so terrorizes me, but please see me and take care of me in my absolute confusion.' (p. 50)

> I could not read the Bible. I could not pray as I wanted because my emotions were dead and cut off. There was no feedback from God the Holy Spirit. (p. 53)

Despite these early difficulties, Davis notes that his persistent faith eventually brought him to a profound spiritual experience:

> One night in Wyoming, as I lay in a motel crying out to my Lord, my long desperate prayers were suddenly answered. As I lay there in the blackness silently shrieking out my often repeated prayer, there was suddenly a light that seemed to fill my very soul. The sweet, holy presence of Christ came to me. He spoke to my spirit and said, "Take my peace. Stop your struggling. It is all right. This is all in keeping with my will for

your life. I now release you from the burden of the heavy yoke of pastoring that I placed upon you. Relax and stop struggling in your desperate search for answers. I will hold you. Lie back in your Shepherd's arms, and take my peace." (pp. 54-55)

Nevertheless, Reverend Davis must continue to struggle. He later writes the following:

The private emotional relationship with the Lord that I enjoyed is distorted and does not comfort me now. When I pray, I often pray in silent blackness of spirit . . . . I am so changing that my old Bible study habits are disappearing. Now when I read the Bible, I often read the same short passage over and over again. (p. 110)

. . . the mind that remains assures me on the basis of God's own word that he will never leave me nor forsake me. I fear the day when my mind will lose this capacity as well. Then I must rely solely on those who love me to keep me close to the Father by their prayers, and to reassure me with songs and touch and simple words of Scripture. (p. 110)

Davis advises that Christian counselors or family members should not spiritually exhort or preach to demented persons, thinking they can force Jesus into them; this may arouse guilt and increase their feelings of alienation from God. Instead, he suggests that efforts be made to comfort and reassure such persons of God's continual presence, doing this through gently touching them, lovingly holding them, or even singing to them.

Meeting Spiritual Needs

The attitude that persons with dementia receive no benefit from spiritual care and worship must change. Demented elders have many spiritual needs; these needs, however, do vary depending on the stage of the disease process (Richards 1990; Fisher 1990). In all but the final stages, cognitively impaired elders can sing or listen to hymns and experience a wide range of emotions during a worship service. Sometimes, however, it requires ingenuity and persistence to reach these persons:

It takes patience, knowledge of the disease, a tub full of love, and acceptance of failure to minister to the demented person. There will be times when nothing a chaplain tries can reach them. Not even the spirit of God can penetrate their troubled minds. The chaplain must adjust his/her style, change his/her mind, study, develop new techniques, use all available resources, be creative, and use all their God given, as well as, acquired gifts in assisting these struggling souls in maintaining a relationship with God. (Fisher 1990, p. 3)

Chaplain Fisher goes on to describe the specific techniques that he learned during years of daily work with demented elders in a VA hospital. For readers with a special interest in this topic, I strongly urge you to obtain a copy of a short paper he has written on the subject (see References for address). His insights should be enormously helpful to those working with the cognitively impaired. Although space is limited to elaborate further here, I will briefly list some of his suggestions:

1. Know as much as possible about the patient's religious background.
2. Look like a chaplain (wear a collar–even if not from a liturgical background).
3. Visit every person unless they are asleep, calling them by their surname or title.
4. Approach patient using conversational tone, consider hearing or visual impairments.
5. Prayer with patients is vital; keep it short, simple, supportive, positive, familiar.
6. Recite familiar scripture passages with patients; start them out, keep them short.
7. Visual cues help; symbols are an important way of communicating (cross or rosary especially).
8. Provide weekly communion (or other sacrament) to those accustomed to receiving it.
9. Singing/whistling hymns; get right down in their face and prompt them.

10. Involve family members; tape record grandchildren reading scripture/hymns and play back.

Helping Caregivers to Cope

For over 10 years, the Duke Family Support Program (headed by Lisa Gwyther) has been investigating factors which maximize the coping of family caregivers of patient's with Alzheimer's disease (70% of whom are women). During that time, discussions with family members and systematic research, has uncovered four major factors which facilitate caregiver adjustment:

1. A sense of humor
2. Good friends and family
3. Old-fashioned ingenuity
4. The grace of God

Having a *sense of humor* undoubtedly helps to maintain sanity. The situations that some family members find themselves in, can be seen as either humiliating and embarrassing–or simply funny. The ability to laugh in such circumstances, without demeaning the patient or injuring their self-esteem, can be life-saving for the caregiver. Sharing such experiences with those who understand can be truly heart-warming and spirit-elevating.

Good friends and family are needed for emotional support and for companionship. No one survives long without such support when caring for a moderately or severely demented relative. This is why the Alzheimer's disease support programs have been so successful. There are times when the burden becomes overwhelming and the caregiver needs nurturance from others. The fact that elder abuse in the setting of dementia is so high should not be surprising. Frustration, rage, entrapment, and guilt are frequent emotions that caregivers experience. Sharing these feelings with others in similar circumstances can be immensely relieving. During caregiver support meetings, vital information can be learned from those who have suffered through and survived caring for a demented relative. Much of this information cannot be obtained elsewhere.

Old-fashioned ingenuity is necessary for survival. Assisting demented relatives with personal hygiene and other physical activities of daily living can be a frustrating task. Getting them to take a shower or bath, brush their teeth, take their medicine, eat, dress appropriately for the weather, travel to the doctor's office, not drive their car, and so forth, require careful thought, planning, and use of novel strategies. There are ways, however, to accomplish these tasks while preserving the patient's dignity and self-esteem. For instance, many demented elders will be more willing to go to day-care if they are told that they are acting as volunteers to help out the other patients. Telling such "white lies" is a necessary (and appropriate) trade-off for the benefits accrued to both loved-one and caregiver.

Last, but not least, is the *grace of God*. Sophisticated scientific research is not needed to conclude that both the personal and communal aspects of religion are important factors enabling many caretakers to cope. Talking with relatives of demented patients will convince even the hard core skeptic. The stress of caregiving pushes persons to their psychological limits, forcing them to mobilize all and every possible resource. Church communities can be an invaluable support in this regard, providing both companionship and respite.

Although systematic research has been scant in this area, reports from reputable investigators are beginning to appear which support the clinical observations noted above. In a study of 85 female caregivers of Alzheimer's disease patients in Richmond, Virginia, Wood and Parham (1990) found that God was perceived by Black caregivers in a very personal way as part of their support system, along with family, friends, or neighbors. Dr. Peter Rabins, renowned Alzheimer's disease researcher from Johns Hopkins University, followed over a two-year period 32 caregivers of patients with Alzheimer's disease and 30 caregivers of patients with recurrent metastatic cancer (Rabins et al. 1990). Both groups showed a decline in anxiety and negative mood over time; dementia caregivers also experienced a decline in anger. After statistically controlling for other factors, Rabins and colleagues found that self-reported strength of religious belief was a significant predictor of good adaptation.

Likewise, Keilman and Given (1990) studied caregivers of patients with another feared disease–cancer. Their sample consisted of 100 caregivers of all ages in East Lansing, Michigan. These investigators reported a significant inverse relationship between depression (measured by the CES-D) and spirituality ($-.24$, p < .001). Thus, evidence from systematic research seems to indicate an important role for religion in enabling caregivers to cope.

Tough Decisions

The decision to place a loved one in a nursing home is invariably a painful and agonizing one, both for the elder being institutionalized and the relative initiating the process. Despite sometimes tremendous efforts made by relatives to keep an elder at home, there comes a time when no other alternative exists. Many spouses, less often children, will continue to care for their loved one at home to the detriment of both themselves and their loved one (Chapter 18). Religious issues commonly surface at this time. Some spouses feel committed by their marriage vows "until death do us part," and show nothing less than heroic devotion in their efforts to avoid placement. Religious motivations may underlie these efforts in some cases. Spouse and family may feel a moral and religious obligation to provide such care based on scripture (1 Timothy 5:3-5,8,16).

Nevertheless, while Paul's letter to Timothy underscores the responsibilities of children to parents, other scriptural passages equally emphasize parents' responsibilities to their children–"Fathers, do not embitter your children, or they will become discouraged" (Colossians 3:21). As I noted above, discouragement and depression are common among caregivers. In a book entitled *When Love Gets Tough*, Douglas Manning (1990) reflects about the decision to place a parent in a nursing home. Although this book paints a somewhat rosy picture of life in the nursing home, it will help those struggling with guilt and other emotions that accompany to this tough decision.

In choosing a nursing home, family members often ask about the best facility in the area. My response is that there is no "best one." Because of the tremendous heterogeneity of needs which elders have, a home that is good for one person is not good for another. Different homes cater to different needs. The way to find out about the quality of a nursing home is to ask friends who have parents or spouses in that home; they will know the good and bad points about the facility. Another piece of advice is to always choose a home that is convenient enough to maximize the frequency of visits by family members. The greatest predictor of quality of care in nursing homes is the *frequency of visits* by family. If nursing home personnel see that family members are invested in the elder's welfare, they will often "go the extra mile" to ensure that needs are met. Thus, even after nursing home placement, family can continue to make a significant impact on the quality of their loved one's care. The worst situation is when, out of guilt, the elder is abandoned.

SUMMARY

The nursing home experience is not an easy one for many older adults. Adjustment problems often occur soon after admission and sometimes evolve into a clinical depression where hope is lost, life loses meaning, and the will to live vanishes. Religious cognitions and behaviors are prevalent in this setting and serve to help elders survive both emotionally and physically in a situation of dependency and loss of control. The chaplain or clergy person plays a major role in helping residents develop their inner spiritual lives from which they can reorganize themselves and find new meaning and purpose.

One of the most common causes of nursing home admission is cognitive impairment, often as a result of Alzheimer's disease. Religion has meaning to demented elders even in the final stages of the disease, when religious symbols, rituals, and songs continue to provide comfort. Little is known about the effects of impaired cognition on religious faith, although research efforts are now beginning to address this issue. The stress of caring for a demented relative can place an enormous psychological burden on caretakers; for them, both the personal and social components of religion are important sources of support, providing the inner strength to endure and friends with whom trials and information may be shared.

REFERENCES

Borson, S., B. Liptzin, J. Nininger, and P. Rabins. (1987). Psychiatry and the nursing home. *American Journal of Psychiatry* 144:1412-1418.

Burns, B.J. (1991). Mental health services research on the hospitalized and institutionalized CMI elderly. In *The Elderly with Chronic Mental Illness*, edited by E. Light and B.D. Lebowitz. NY: Springer Publishing Co.

Burns, B.J., D.B. Larson, I.D. Goldstrom, W.E. Johnson, C.A. Taube, N.E. Miller, and E.S. Mathis. (1988). Mental disorder among nursing home patients: Preliminary findings from the national nursing home survey pretest. *International Journal of Geriatric Psychiatry* 3:27-35.

Cassem, N. (1988). The person confronting death. In *The New Harvard Guide to Psychiatry*, edited by A.M. Nicholi. Cambridge, MA: Harvard University Press, pp. 728-758.

Davis, R. (1989). *My Journey into Alzheimer's Disease*. Wheaton, IL: Tyndale House.

Engel, G.L. (1968). A life setting conducive to illness: The giving up-given up complex. *Annals of Internal Medicine* 69:293-296.

Evans, D.A., H.H. Funkenstein, M.S. Albert, P.A. Scherr, N.R. Cook, M.J. Chown, L.E. Hebert, C.H. Hennekens, and J.O. Taylor. (1989). Prevalence of Alzheimer's disease in a community population of older persons. Higher than previously reported. *Journal of the American Medical Association* 262: 2551-2556.

Fisher, G.F. (1990). *The role of the chaplain in ministering to persons with Alzheimer's and related disorders*. Department of Veterans Affairs Medical Center, Salisbury, North Carolina 28144.

Frank, J. (1974). *Persuasion and Healing*. Baltimore: Johns Hopkins Press.

Glock, C.Y., and R. Stark. (1965). *Religion and Society in Tension*. Chicago: Rand McNally.

Hoge, D. (1972). A validated intrinsic religious motivation scale. *Journal for the Scientific Study of Religion* 11:369-376.

Katz, I.R., G.M. Simpson, S.M. Curlik, P.A. Parmelee, and C. Muhly. (1990). Pharmacologic treatment of major depression for elderly patients in residential care settings. *Journal of Clinical Psychiatry* 51(7)(suppl.):41-47.

Kaufman, D.M. (1990). *Clinical Neurology for Psychiatrists*. Philadelphia: WB Saunders Co.

Keilman, L.J., and B.A. Given. (1990). Spirituality: An untapped resource for hope and coping in family caregivers of individuals with cancer. *Oncology Nursing Forum* 17(2) (suppl.):159.

Koenig, H.G. (1991). Electroconvulsive therapy for treatment of depression in older patients. *Geriatric Consultant* 9(5):14-16.

Koenig, H.G. (1993). Trends in geriatric psychiatry of relevance to pastoral counselors. *Journal of Religion and Health* 32:131-151.

Keonig, H.G., D.G. Blazer, S.M. Ford (1993). The Mini-Mental State Exam and assessment of mild to moderate cognitive dysfunction in hospitalized medically ill patients. Unpublished manuscript. Duke University Medical Center, Durham, NC.

Koenig, H.G., J.N. Kvale, and C. Ferrel. (1988a): Religion and well-being in later life. *The Gerontologist* 28:18-28.

Koenig, H.G., D.O. Moberg, and J.N. Kvale. (1988b): Religious activities and attitudes of older adults in a geriatric assessment clinic. *Journal of the American Geriatrics Society* 36:362-374.

Koenig, H.G., M. Smiley, and J.P. Gonzales. (1988c). *Religion, Health, and Aging*. NY: Greenwood Press.

Koenig, H.G., H.J. Cohen, D.G. Blazer, C. Pieper, K.G. Meador, F. Shelp, V. Goli, and R. DiPasquale. (1992). Religious coping and depression in hospitalized elderly medically ill men. *American Journal of Psychiatry* 149:1693-1700.

Krause, N. (1992). Providing support to others and well-being in later life. *Journal of Gerontology* 47:P300-P311.

Manning, D. (1990). *When Love Gets Tough*. San Francisco: Harper Collins.

Morley, J.E. (1988). Medical problems in nursing homes. In UCLA Board Review Course Syllabus, pp. 63-68.

Nelson, P.B. (1989). Social support, self-esteem, and depression in the institutionalized elderly. *Issues in Mental Health Nursing* 10:55-68.

Palouzian, R.F., and C.W. Ellison. (1982). Loneliness, spiritual well-being, and quality of life. In *Loneliness: A Sourcebook of Current Theory, Research and Therapy*, edited by A. Peplau and D. Porlman. NY: Wiley InterScience, pp. 224-237.

Pan, J. (1950). Personal adjustments of old people: A study of old people in protestant church homes for the aged. *Sociology and Social Research* 35:3-11.

Pardue, L. (1989). *Models for Ministry: The Spiritual Needs of the Frail Elderly Living in Long-Term-Care Facility*. Ashville, NC: Mars Hill College.

Parmelee, P.A., I.R. Katz, and M.P. Lawton. (1989). Depression among institutionalized aged: Assessment and prevalence estimation. *Journal of Gerontology* 44:M22-M29.

_____ (1992). Depression and mortality among institutionalized aged. *Journal of Gerontology* 47:P3-P10.

Phillips, A.K. (1973). The chaplain's role in a nursing home. *Hospital Progress* (June):75-78.

Rabins, P.V., M.D. Fitting, J. Eastham, and J. Zabora. (1990). Emotional adaptation over time in care-givers for chronically ill elderly people. *Age and Ageing* 19:185-190.

Reifler, B.V., E. Larson, and R. Hanley. (1982). Coexistence of cognitive impairment and depression in geriatric outpatients. *American Journal of Psychiatry* 139:623-627.

Richards, M. (1990). Meeting the spiritual needs of the cognitively impaired. *Generations* (Fall):63-64.

Rovner, B.W. (1991). Much major depression in nursing homes said to be overlooked. *Clinical Psychiatry News* 19(5):12.

Rovner, B.W., S. Kafonek, L. Filipp, M.J. Lucas, and M.F. Folstein. (1986). Prevalence of mental illness in a community nursing home. *American Journal of Psychiatry* 143:1446-1451.

Rovner, B.W., P.S. German, J. Broadhead, L. Burton, M. Folstein. (1991). Depression and mortality in nursing homes. *Journal of the American Medical Association* 265:993-996.

Scott, F.G. (1955). Factors in the personal adjustment of institutionalized and non-institutionalized aged. *American Sociological Review* 20:538-546.

Simmons, H.C. (1991). "Teach us to Pray": Pastoral care of the new nursing
    home resident. *Journal of Pastoral Care* 45:169-175.
Teeter, R.B., F.K. Garetz, W.R. Miller, and W.F. Heiland. (1976). Psychiatric
    disturbance of aged patients in skilled nursing homes. *American Journal of
    Psychiatry* 133:1430-1434.
Walsh, J.S., H.G. Welch, and E.B. Larson. (1990). Survival of outpatients with
    Alzheimer-type dementia. *Annal of Internal Medicine* 113:429-434.
Wood, J.B., and I.A. Parham. (1990). Coping with perceived burden: Ethnic and
    cultural issues in Alzheimer's family caregiving. *Journal of Applied Gerontol-
    ogy* 9:325-339.

Chapter 17

Alcoholism/Sexual Dysfunction

ALCOHOLISM

> Who has woe?
> Who has sorrow?
> Who has strife?
> Who has complaints?
> Who has needless bruises?
> Who has bloodshot eyes?
> Those who linger over wine . . .
>
> *–Proverbs 23:29-30*

Many elders in later life use alcohol. Because it acts as a central nervous system depressant, alcohol helps with relaxation and socialization. Studies have shown that mild alcohol use is inversely related to depression (Warheit and Auth 1984; Koenig, Meador, Goli, Shelp, Cohen, and Blazer 1991) and may even help maintain cardiovascular integrity and lengthen life (Cornaro 1563; Yano, Rhoads, and Kagan et al. 1977). Indeed, older persons residing in nursing homes or in other institutionalized settings may derive considerable benefits from an occasional glass of wine or beer (Chien, Stotsky, and Cole 1973). With heavy use, however, alcohol has both adverse medical and social consequences. Older alcoholics are more likely than nonalcoholics to commit suicide, live alone, have marital problems, be divorced or separated, live transient lifestyles, have health problems, and experience organic mental disorder (Schuckit and Pastor 1979). Heavy alcohol use increases blood pressure, has cardiotoxic effects, impairs the functioning of the liver and other vital organs, and has adverse effects on the brain. Because of a decreased physical tolerance for alcohol with aging, some elderly alcoholics may achieve toxic serum levels with amounts of alcohol that would be considered social drinking at a younger age. Even with mild or moderate usage, however, serious interactions may occur with chronic medical illnesses and with the drugs used to treat them.

Definition

Alcoholism, and alcohol dependency are terms describing a habitual pattern of excess alcohol intake. There are four criteria necessary for the diagnosis of alcoholism: (1) tolerance to the effects of alcohol, (2) withdrawal symptoms on discontinuing or cutting back on alcohol, (3) loss of control of drinking behavior, and (4) social decline (Beresford, Blow, and Brower 1990). The presence of any one of these criteria should raise suspicion for alcohol dependence.

Tolerance indicates a need to drink more and more alcohol to achieve the desired effect. This criterion may be less valid in the elderly since tolerance actually decreases with age (Hartford and Samozajski 1982). Thus, an elderly person, despite drinking the same amount or even cutting back, may still show evidence of increasing tolerance. As tolerance develops, the likelihood of withdrawal symptoms increases if alcohol intake lessens or stops. Approximately 6-12 hours after the last drink, or after blood alcohol level starts dropping, the alcoholic may experience tachycardia (rapid heart beat), tachypnea (rapid breathing), increase in the blood pressure, mild fever, tremor, nausea, sweating, and anxiety. These withdrawal symptoms are more debilitating in the elderly who are physiologically less able to recover from the toxic insult. Increasing confusion is a prominent symptom of withdrawal in the elderly, and the latter should always be considered in the differential diagnosis of cognitive impairment of unknown etiology. One study showed that 28% of elderly persons admitted with chronic brain syndrome had alcohol abuse as their underlying diagnosis (Epstein and Simon 1967). Impaired sleep and sexual dysfunction are other symptoms associated with alcohol abuse. Loss of drinking behavior control occurs when the elder cannot stop or cut back in spite of damage done to self and/or others. Social decline is evident by loss of job, divorce, separation, estrangement from family, or loss of social position in the community.

Prevalence and Characteristics

Alcoholism affects one out of every three families in the United States. According to the National Institute on Alcohol Abuse, the rate of alcohol abuse among older persons ranges from 2 to 10% (Zimberg 1987). Among elders with medical and psychiatric problems, 15% to 25% have significant alcohol problems. About 20% of older medical inpatients will have a history of alcohol abuse. Many cases, however, go undiagnosed and only come to the attention of physicians because of health problems related to alcoholism. Self-neglect, confusion, and repeated falls are often accepted as being due to aging (Estes and Heinemann 1986). Heavy drinking usually peaks in the 40s and 50s and then declines until age 70 after which it rises again (McCourt, Williams, and Schneider 1971).

The age-related decline in alcohol abuse has been challenged for a number of reasons. First, alcohol abusers probably die off from alcohol-related accidents or physical illness, leaving fewer to survive into old age (Glynn et al. 1985). Second, health problems often prevent elders from obtaining access to alcoholic beverages. Third, elders may be more likely to deny alcohol use in self-report surveys–especially those who grew up during a time or in an area of the country where there were legal or social prohibitions against alcohol use (Mishara and Kastenbaum 1980). Fourth, most data are cross-sectional (collected at one point in time) and thus may represent cohort or period effects. "Cohort effects" indicate the impact on drinking behavior of persons being born at the same time in history and aging together; "period effects" mean the impact on drinking behavior of a particular period of history (the Great Depression, for instance). One longitudinal study has demonstrated stability in alcohol use among males during a nine-year period (Glynn et al. 1984).

Epidemiological studies indicate the existence of two types of alcoholics among the elderly (Gaitz and Baer 1971; Mishara and Kastenbaum 1980). The early-onset alcohol abuser has a long history of excessive drinking beginning in early adulthood (ages 20 to 40). They are typically well known to social service agencies as public drunks and have personality characteristics similar to those of younger drinkers. The other type is the late-onset variety (one-third of cases), in which heavy drinking begins after age 50, usually as a reaction to negative life events associated with aging (loss of spouse, adverse health events, retirement, loss of income, and so forth); this contrasts with early-onset drinkers who may have lost jobs and families as a consequence of their drinking.

Late-onset alcoholics are less likely to drink in public, more often choosing the privacy of their own homes. Encounters with the criminal/legal system are less frequent because they are less likely to drive cars or commit drug-related crimes. Late-onset drinkers often live alone, depressed and grieving from losses (Williams 1984; Jinks and Raschko 1990; Schonfled and Dupree 1990). Psychosocial and health problems are prevalent in this group. Chronic physical illness, disability, dependency, social isolation, cognitive dysfunction, and depression are widespread among late-onset drinkers. It is not surprising then that community agencies (social services and home health nurses) are frequently the first ones to detect elders with drug or alcohol abuse problems (Jinks and Raschko 1990; Krach 1990).

One study of alcohol and prescription drug abuse among 1668 clients of the Elderly Services of Spokane, Washington in 1989, discovered 161 alcohol abusers (10%) and 50 prescription drug abusers (5%) (Jinks and Raschko 1990). Ninety percent of drug abusers were women, whereas the great majority of alcohol abusers were men. Psychological evaluation of the elderly alcoholics revealed a primary diagnosis of alcohol abuse and secondary diagnosis of depression in 37%; a primary diagnosis of depression with secondary alcohol abuse in 29%; a primary diagnosis of cognitive impairment with secondary alcohol abuse in 22%; and other primary psychiatric disorders with secondary alcohol abuse in 14%. Thus, 63% of cases had a primary diagnosis of a psychiatric illness, with alcoholism occurring as a secondary diagnosis.

There are numerous other studies which implicate depression as predisposing to alcohol abuse (alcohol being used in an attempt to self-medicate) (Pottenger et al. 1978; Behar, Winokur, and Berg 1984; Daley, Moss, and Campbell 1987). Krach (1990) reported that 97% of alcohol abusers seen in their homes had a concurrent diagnosis of depression. Most studies indicate that heavy alcohol use leads to depression in the vast majority of cases (85%), and if this is so, then stopping alcohol use often alleviates depressive symptoms within one month or less.

Finlayson and colleagues (1988) at the Mayo Clinic reported on the characteristics of 216 elderly persons admitted to an inpatient setting for the treatment of alcoholism. They found that the concern of friends and family was the number one factor motivating patients to seek help. They confirmed that late-onset drinking was more likely than the early-onset variety to be associated with stressful life events such as retirement, death of a spouse, family conflict, health problems, employment stress or psychologic symptoms. Again, comorbid psychiatric illness was frequently present. Associated mental disorders were organic brain syndrome (44%), affective disorder (12%), drug abuse or dependence (14%), and other psychiatric disorders (8%). It is safe to conclude, then, that psychological stressors underlie many cases of alcohol abuse in later life. Indeed, elders may turn to alcohol as a coping strategy when other efforts fail to relieve the stress associated with problems of aging.

Treatment Programs

While it is commonly assumed that the community-based elderly have family or social agencies to care for them, this is frequently not the case. Many elders living at home may resist the services of social agencies or minimize their problems for fear that they will be removed from their homes and placed in a nursing home. In an attempt to deal with problems on their own, alcohol may be seen as a solution. Consequently, elderly alcoholics seldom seek services from mental health providers. Even if they did, there is widespread concern that available resources would not be sufficient to provide the needed services. Most public-sponsored treatment programs are inundated by younger alcoholics or drug abusers, and private programs are often unaffordable. This is unfortunate given that older alcoholics frequently respond as readily, if not more readily, than younger alcoholics (Mishara and Kastenbaum 1980; Kofoed et al. 1987).

A new treatment approach for older alcoholics has focused on "age-specific" treatment, where elders are treated separately from younger persons (Mishara and Kastenbaum 1980). In such programs efforts are directed at increasing socialization, improving attitudes and thinking patterns (cognitive restructuring), and teaching coping skills for dealing with loss. At present, however, there are only a handful of such programs in the country.

Long-Term Prognosis

Only one study has followed alcoholics for longer than two years to determine factors that predict recovery (Vaillant 1983). Four factors were found to relate to long-term prognosis:

1. Finding a substitute dependency
2. Enhancement of hope and self-esteem
3. Social rehabilitation
4. Behavioral modification

Finding a substitute dependency involves filling time (that otherwise would have been spent drinking) with healthful activities such as community work, educational activities, involvement in Alcoholics Anonymous (AA), or church. *Enhancement of hope* means conveying to the elder that they are suffering from an illness–a disease–rather than a moral or characterological weakness. Since many elders grew up in the prohibition years and often have a religious background, they may feel intense guilt over their behavior and thus condemn themselves–an action which only increases the likelihood of a relapse into drinking. *Social rehabilitation* means the institution of a caring relationship with someone who accepts the person, but not their drinking (spouse, physician, psychotherapist, AA sponsor, clergy-person). Careful limit-setting is necessary on the part of the support person in such cases. *Behavioral modification* involves providing a clearly noxious and predictable response to drinking (incarceration, expulsion from family, threat of loss of independence, use of disulfiram). Behavioral modification is the least powerful of all four prognostic features and is poorly correlated with long term sobriety.

Role of Religion

A close examination of the strategies employed by treatment programs and suggested by prognostic factors reveals that many of these are already part of normal operations in religious communities. Nearly all older persons are members of a religious congregation. Churches or synagogues encourage socialization and provide the elderly person with age-matched peers with whom supportive relationships may develop. Judeo-Christian principles place a high value on caring for others. The religious approach to the problem of alcohol abuse involves a cognitive restructuring which enhances self-esteem, provides a mechanism for obtaining forgiveness, and teaches healthy attitudes and ways of coping with loss (Nelson 1990).

Because older persons comprise a significant proportion of the membership of many American denominations (almost 30% in some cases), efforts by churches to minister to the special needs of elderly alcoholics are quite appropriate. The need for such services is expected to increase dramatically in the years ahead as the "graying of America" takes place. Drug and alcohol problems are particularly prevalent among the generation of Americans now in their 20s, 30s, and 40s who have grown up in an era of relaxed social prohibitions. Religious organizations, to which many of these persons currently (or will) belong, may need to pick up where public service agencies leave off. It remains to be seen, however, whether American churches will do so. Indeed, to not do so would represent a failure to fulfill a fundamental Judeo-Christian imperative.

If churches and synagogues fail to meet this responsibility, or if elderly alcoholics find it difficult to utilize services from this source, then persons seeking such assistance will have to turn to self-help groups such as AA. This organization relies heavily on the supportive fellowship of former alcoholics who have succeeded in achieving abstinence. AA has had enormous success in helping persons of all ages stop drinking. Prior to AA, only 10% of alcoholics quit drinking apart from a terminal illness. Of those who did quit drinking, 30% did so as a consequence of religious experience (Lamere 1953). Indeed, AA's success has been largely attributed to the spiritual dimension that is central to its twelve steps to recovery (Wilson 1968).

Religion and Alcohol Use

Religion provides the elder with an alternative strategy for coping with stress. Data from the Durham VA Mental Health Survey (DVAMHS) demonstrated a rather marked inverse relationship between religious coping and use of alcohol. Recall from Chapter 10 that only 9% of religious copers under 40 used alcohol compared with 44% of nonreligious copers; for the elderly, these figures were 5% and 21%, respectively (Koenig, Meador, Westlund, and Ford 1992). This inverse association has been reported by a number of other investigators (Blum and Associates 1970; Tennant, Detels, and Clark 1975; Parfrey 1976; Larson and Wilson 1980; Khavari and Harmon 1982) and is particularly relevant in a VA population where heavy alcohol use is associated with major medical morbidity. Among the men in the DVAMHS who reported a sudden and significant change in feelings about religion at some time in their lives, 8% linked this experience with the emergence from an addictive pattern of smoking and/or drinking.

In a classic study, Harvard psychiatrist George Vaillant followed the adjustment patterns of four hundred inner city men from ages 14 through 47. Of this group, 110 men met research criteria for alcohol abuse. Of these, 20% achieved three years or more of sobriety ("stable abstinent"), 47% achieved abstinence for at least one year ("ever abstinent"), and 33% continued to abuse alcohol on a progressive downhill course ("progressive"). Of the "stable abstinent" group, 19% noted increased religious involvement and 38% noted involvement in AA as a primary factor contributing to sobriety. In an article published in the *Archives of General Psychiatry*, Vaillant and Milofsky (1982) conclude the following:

> . . . it is important to appreciate that a major source of help in changing involuntary habits may come from increased religious involvement. Only recently have investigators like Frank (1961), Bean (1975), and Mack (1981) begun to elucidate the nature of this process. Alcoholics and victims of other incurable habits feel defeated, bad, and helpless; invariably they suffer from impaired morale. For recovery, powerful new sources of self-esteem and hope must be discovered. Equally important is the fact that religious involvement facilitates deployment of

the defense of reaction formation, wherein an individual abruptly rejects and hates what he once cherished and loved, or vice versa. Reaction formations are essential to abstinence, and they are often stabilized by surrendering commitments to one set of desires up to a 'higher power' that dictates the exact opposite. (p. 132)

Later in his seminal work on the topic, *The Natural History of Alcoholism*, Vaillant (1983) reports the following insight:

In the treatment of addiction, Karl Marx's aphorism "religion is the opiate of the masses" masks an enormously important therapeutic principle. Religion may actually provide a relief that drug [and alcohol] abuse only promises. . . . First, alcoholics and victims of other seemingly incurable habits feel defeated, bad, and helpless. They invariably suffer from impaired morale. If they are to recover, powerful new sources of self-esteem and hope must be discovered. Religion is one such source. Religion provides fresh impetus for both hope and enhanced self-care. Second, if the established alcoholic is to become stably abstinent, enormous personality changes must take place. It is not just coincidence that we associate such dramatic change with the experience of religious conversion. Third, religion, in ways that we appreciate but do not understand, provides forgiveness of sins and relief from guilt. Unlike many intractable habits that others find merely annoying, alcoholism inflicts enormous pain and injury on those around the alcoholic. As a result the alcoholic, already demoralized by his inability to stop drinking, experiences almost insurmountable guilt from the torture he has inflicted on others. In such an instance, absolution becomes an important part of the healing process. (p. 193)

Religion may then provide a powerful source of self-esteem and hope, relief from guilt, and commitment to a group or belief system that displaces the desire for alcohol. Persons who abuse alcohol frequently have underlying personality disorders. The treatment of severe personality disorders, such as borderline or antisocial types (sociopath), requires a total personality reorganization. These disor-

ders are notoriously resistant to virtually all forms of psychotherapy. A life-altering experience of the magnitude seen in religious
conversion, however, can effect such a radical change (Carothers
1970; Donnelly 1990). Following that, involvement in a religious
community willing to include, support, and nurture the person may
help to maintain such changes and stimulate further growth. In
another classic article "Sociopathy as a Human Process," published
in the *Archives of General Psychiatry*, Vaillant (1975) notes the
following about treatment of patients with this severe personality
disorder:

> Finally, one-to-one therapeutic relationships are rarely ade-
> quate to change the sociopath. A therapist even five times a
> week–is not enough to satisfy an orphan. At the start of the
> recovery process, only the church, self-help residential treat-
> ment, and addicting drugs provide relief for a sociopath's pain;
> they all work 24 hours a day. . . . Only group membership or
> caring for others, or both, can eventually provide adults with
> parenting that they never received . . . the psychopath needs to
> absorb more of other people than one person, no matter how
> loving, can ever provide. Sociopaths need to find groups to
> which they can belong with pride. (p. 183)

Thus, religious communities may contribute to the treatment of
both alcoholism and the personality disorders associated with it.

Alcoholism and Sexual Dysfunction

Because alcohol is a central nervous system depressant, it re-
laxes and often greases the wheels of social interaction. It may
stimulate sexual desire and lessen inhibitions in this area. On the
other hand, alcohol often impairs sexual performance among men.
Thus, while alcohol may be used to suppress feelings of shame or
guilt related to sexual activity, it may actually increase these negative emotions as a consequence of adverse effects on erectile function. Furthermore, an elder may attempt sex after becoming intoxicated and find that he cannot perform; this may then lead to "fear
of failure" and thus lead to psychogenic impotence. Chronic alco-

hol use may actually lead to permanent, irreversible sexual impotence by its direct toxic effects on the sexual organs, leading to peripheral neuropathy, testicular atrophy, and decreased androgens (male sexual hormones). Thus, alcoholism and sexual dysfunction are frequently related.

MALE SEXUAL DYSFUNCTION

An old couple went to a psychiatrist for help with their marital problems. The psychiatrist found out that the wife was starved for affection. He said to the husband, "Let me show you what your wife needs." And he gave the wife a big hug and kiss. "Now she needs that at least three times a week." The husband responded, "I think we could arrange that. She could come in here on Monday, Wednesday, and Friday."

–Unknown author

Despite the implication given by the above vignette, sexual activity is an important part of life for both older men and older women. The ability to perform sexually is integrally related to self-esteem issues. For those married to younger partners, such performance is often necessary to keep the relationship alive. In the absence of illness, potency can be maintained well into the 70s, 80s, and even 90s. Studies have shown that while a slowing of response is considered a normal accompaniment of aging, most men do not lose the capacity for erection and ejaculation (Kinsey, Pomeroy, and Martin 1948; Pfeiffer, Verwoerdt, and Wang 1968). The work of Masters and Johnson (Masters 1986) demonstrated that 75% of men in their 70s engage in sex at least once a month, and that 37% of those age 61-65 and 28% of men age 66 to 71 have intercourse at least weekly. The average male age 60 to 64 has coital activity approximately three times per month. The primary reason why couples stop sexual activity in later life is because of the man (Pfeiffer, Verwoerdt, and Wang 1968; Pfeiffer, Verwoerdt, and Davis 1972).

The most common cause of sexual dysfunction in older men is impotence. Forty percent of older men cease having sexual relations because of erectile dysfunction (Pfeiffer, Verwoerdt, and Davis

1972). The Kinsey Report (1948) indicated that 55% of men by age 75 were impotent or totally sexually inactive. In a more recent survey of 2801 patients attending a urology clinic, Pearlman and Kobash (1972) found that 59% of those 70 to 80 years of age and 85% of those over age 80 were sexually impotent. Similarly, one study of U.S. veterans attending a VA medicine clinic, found that 27% of those age 65 to 75 and 47% of those over age 75 were impotent (Mulligan et al. 1988). Thus, impotence poses a problem for a very large percentage of older men.

Organic factors (diabetes, prostate cancer, prostatic surgery, and so forth) frequently cause impotence in later life. In a high proportion of cases, however, psychological factors either contribute to or represent the primary etiology for this dysfunction (Finkle 1979). Psychosocial and cultural factors such as education, occupation, marital status, and religious background may have an immense impact on sexual attitudes and functions. Although systematic research on this topic is quite rare, there is some evidence that counseling and education are effective in the treatment of sexual dysfunction of psychogenic origins and can also help men better adapt to organic impotence that is irreversible (Finkle and Finkle 1975, 1977).

We have already seen in previous chapters that religion may play an important role in enabling older men with medical illness to better cope with their condition. What about coping with sexual impotence? To what extent does conservative religious background or active involvement in the religious community help adjustment in such cases? Alternatively, one might hypothesize that devout religiousness might lead to conflict in this area. Religious prohibitions might result in an unnecessary restriction of sexual expression, and if problems develop, may hinder help-seeking efforts.

In order to answer these questions, Steve Herman and I embarked on a study that examined the relationship between religious background (denominational affiliation), frequency of church attendance, and older men's ability to cope with sexual impotence (Koenig and Herman 1992). Healthy and unhealthy coping behaviors were examined. Healthy coping was viewed as seeking help early, seeking it from a variety of sources, seeing one's partner as supportive, and being relatively free of psychological distress. Compensating for erectile dysfunction by employment of a variety of sexual behaviors was also considered a healthy coping behavior.

Our sample consisted of 83 men age 55 or over seen in the urology outpatient clinic at Duke University Medical Center with a chief complaint of sexual impotence. These patients had been seen by a urologist and were now referred for psychological evaluation. All men referred between January 1989 and July 1990 were eligible for the study. Of the 182 men referred during this time, 89 (49%) were age 55 or over. All received complete psychological evaluations. Six of these men had sexual problems other than impotence and were excluded.

As part of their routine assessment, men were asked to complete a questionnaire that collected information on sociodemographics, medical history, and sexual functioning (Herman 1987). Questions about religious affiliation and frequency of church attendance were included. Sensitive and detailed information about current and past sexual functioning were inquired about (frequency of intercourse, preferred frequency by both patient and partner, frequency of masturbation, length of foreplay, type of foreplay, and so forth). Information was also gathered on how long impotence had been a problem, whether it had begun suddenly or gradually, whether the patient had problems with impotence in the past, and how their partner had reacted to the current problem. Global ratings were obtained on the quality of the sexual relationship before and after impotence developed. Psychological health was measured using the SCL-90-R (Derogatis 1977), which provides scores of overall functioning as well as scores on specific psychological traits such as somatization, obsessive-compulsive tendencies, interpersonal sensitivity, depression, anxiety, hostility, phobic anxiety, paranoid ideation, and psychoticism.

Findings

The sociodemographic and religious characteristics of men in our sample were compared with those of men age 55 or over living in the Piedmont area of North Carolina. Our sample tended to be younger, of Caucasian race, better educated, and less likely affiliated with conservative Protestant congregations; they did not differ, however, on marital status and frequency of church attendance. Forty-five percent attended church weekly or more often.

We then split our sample by frequency of church attendance. Men attending once a week or more were labeled "high attenders" and those attending once a month or less as "low attenders." We then compared sociodemographic, health, and sexual behaviors between the two groups. High church attenders were significantly more likely than low attenders to be Black (28% vs. 9%) and were less likely to use alcohol (35% vs. 73%). High church attenders also tended to be younger (61 vs. 64 years) and less educated (56% vs. 74% with college). High attenders were more likely than low attenders to see their partners as supportive of attempts to seek help for the problem (93% vs. 76%).

We then compared the help-seeking activity and sexual behaviors of high and low attenders. High attenders were more likely than low attenders to have consulted a medical specialist for their impotence; otherwise, help-seeking behaviors between the two groups were roughly equivalent. As far as sexual behaviors were concerned, several significant differences emerged between the two groups (Table 17.1). High attenders were less likely to kiss their partners on the lips, kiss their partner's breasts, engage in oral-genital sex (either partner), and were more likely to have intercourse in the traditional position of man on top (vs. sideways or woman on top). Using the SCL-90-R, psychological stability was compared between high and low attenders. There was no significant difference in psychiatric symptomatology between the two groups; however, high church attenders tended to be slightly more depressed than low attenders (63 vs. 58 depression subscale score, $.05 < p < .10$).

Next, the sample was divided into men from conservative or fundamentalist Protestant affiliations (37%) versus those from other religious denominations (primarily moderate Protestants, liberal Protestants, Protestants unspecified, and those with no religious affiliation). We compared sociodemographic, health, and sexual behaviors between the two groups. As with frequent church attenders, conservative affiliates were less likely to use alcohol and were *more likely* to have sought help from a medical specialist or to have tried hormone pills or injections. They also had a more constricted range of sexual behaviors than did nonconservative affiliates (less

TABLE 17.1. Comparison of sexual function/behaviors between frequent (once/wk or more) and infrequent church attenders

	High Attenders (n = 36)	**Low Attenders** (n = 43)
	Mean (SD) / %	Mean (SD) / %
Sexual Function		
Satisfactory sex before prob	91%	98%
Quality of sex before (0-8)	5.6 (1.7)	5.6 (1.5)
History of sexual problems	18%	17%
Onset of impotence (sudden)	16%	16%
Duration of impotence (months)	44.8 (69.0)	60.7 (55.4)
Sexual Activity		
Frequency of Sexual Intercourse (% once/wk or more)		
Current	15%	7%
Before impotent	56%	50%
Patient prefers	61%	62%
Spouse prefers	44%	50%
Masturbation (self) (> once/mo)	53%	64%
Foreplay (5 to 15 min or more)	66%	71%
Behaviors During Foreplay (rated 1–6 in frequency)		
Kissing on the lips	4.0 (1.4)	4.5 (0.8) **
Caressing breasts	4.4 (1.2)	4.6 (0.7)
Kissing breasts	3.9 (1.4)	4.5 (0.8) **
Caressing vagina with hand	4.1 (1.2)	4.4 (0.9)
Stim vagina with mouth	1.4 (0.8)	1.8 (1.0) **
Partner caressing penis	3.4 (1.7)	3.9 (1.3)
Partner stim penis with mouth	1.3 (0.8)	2.2 (1.2) ****
Intercourse with man on top	4.3 (0.9)	3.4 (1.4) ***
Intercourse with woman on top	1.9 (0.8)	2.1 (1.0)
Other positions	1.7 (0.8)	1.9 (1.1)

Table adapted from Koenig and Herman (1992); used with permission

* $.05 < p < .10$ ** $p < .05$ *** $p < .01$ **** $p < .001$

(N's may vary by up to 18%)

kissing partner's lips, caressing or kissing breasts, vaginal stimulation with hand or mouth) (Table 17.2). There were only minor differences in psychiatric symptomatology between the two groups, although conservative affiliates tended to score higher on the psychoticism and interpersonal sensitivity subscales of the SCL-90-R. Stratifying the analyses by both race and educational level did not alter these results.

Discussion

Although frequency of church attendance and conservativeness of religious affiliation did not have a marked impact on the adjustment of men to their impotence, some interesting findings did emerge. Frequent church attenders and conservative affiliates were more likely than others to have already sought help from medical specialists or tried hormone pills or injections, prior to evaluation at the Duke urology clinic. This greater likelihood of seeking help from a variety of sources is indicative of healthy coping. There was no evidence, then, that the more religiously conservative or religiously active men were any less willing than others to seek professional help for their problem. Other investigators have also found that religiously active adults are especially likely to seek help for health symptoms or participate in a health screening program (Naguib, Beiser, and Comstock 1968; Koenig, Smiley, and Gonzales 1988). This finding goes directly against the claims of some that highly religious persons are less likely to see a doctor for health problems, relying instead on Divine intervention (Goulder 1986; Coakley and McKenna 1986). Given the increasing numbers of older adults in America, the high prevalence of religious behaviors in this group, and the generally positive impact of these behaviors on seeking health care, counselors and clinicians are likely to see religious elders with sexual dysfunction in their practices and should be prepared to deal with the special problems that they experience.

Our results indicate that professional counseling may be of considerable benefit to religious elders experiencing sexual dysfunction. We found that both frequent church attenders and conservative affiliates were more restricted than other groups in their range of sexual behaviors during sexual activity. The lower prevalence of

TABLE 17.2. Sexual function/behaviors of men from conservative/fundamentalist religious affiliations compared with men from other denominations

	Conservative (n = 27)	Other Denominations (n = 46)
	Mean (SD) / %	Mean (SD) / %
Sexual Function		
Satisfactory sex before prob	96%	96%
Quality of sex before prob (0-8)	5.3 (1.5)	5.7 (1.6)
History of sexual problems	21%	19%
Onset of impotence (sudden)	13%	17%
Duration of impotence (months)	49.1 (67.1)	53.4 (45.9)
Sexual Activity		
Freq of Sexual Intercourse (once/wk or more often)		
Current	12%	9%
Before impotent	62%	44%
Patient prefers	69%	54%
Spouse prefers	56%	43%
Masturbation (self) (> once/mo)	58%	61%
Foreplay (5 to 15 min or more)	73%	67%
Behaviors During Foreplay (frequency rated 1-6)		
Kissing on the lips	3.9 (1.3)	4.6 (0.8) ***
Caressing woman's breasts	4.3 (1.2)	4.7 (0.5) *
Kissing woman's breasts	3.9 (1.3)	4.5 (0.9) **
Caressing vagina with hand	4.2 (1.1)	4.4 (1.0)
Stimulate vagina with mouth	1.4 (0.6)	1.9 (1.1) ***
Partner caressing penis	3.3 (1.7)	3.9 (1.4) *
Partner stim penis with mouth	1.6 (1.1)	2.0 (1.2)
Intercourse with man on top	3.9 (1.0)	3.7 (1.4)
Intercourse with woman on top	2.0 (0.8)	2.1 (1.1)
Other positions	1.7 (0.9)	1.8 (1.1)

Table adapted from Koenig and Herman (1992); used with permission

* $.05 < p < .10$ ** $p < .05$ *** $p < .01$ **** $p < .001$

(N's may vary by up to 22%)

behaviors such as kissing, caressing or fondling a partner's breasts or vaginal area, and oral-genital stimulations may indicate greater inhibition for religious elders in these activities. This may be to their detriment, given that such behaviors during foreplay enhance partner arousal and satisfaction in the event that impotence precludes intercourse. Thus, therapists and counselors who advise religious elders on these matters may need to encourage and give permission for a wider range of sexual behaviors.

We suspect that many elderly men with impotence simply attribute this to aging, and consequently do not seek professional help for the problem. Others may simply be too embarrassed to do so. Nevertheless, when impotence is due to psychological factors–which is frequently the case even among elders with physical health impairments–it is often readily reversible with appropriate education and behavioral techniques that can be implemented by a primary care physician, a psychologist, or a pastoral counselor.

SUMMARY

Alcoholism. While less common than at younger ages, approximately 2 to 10% of older adults abuse alcohol; this proportion is probably an underestimate, given the difficulties in diagnosing alcoholism among older adults. Excess alcohol use may have serious health consequences, in terms of both physical, emotional, and cognitive functioning. In perhaps one-third of cases, such abuse begins in later life as a reaction to physical, social, and economic stresses. There is little reason for therapeutic nihilism in such cases. With appropriate treatment, elders are as likely (if not more likely) than younger persons to respond to treatment. The inverse relationship between alcohol use and religious coping suggests that religion may represent an alternative coping strategy to alcohol. Religious doctrines, through their prohibition of excesses and promotion of respect of the body, may also prevent the development of alcoholism. Finally, religious conversion can help older alcoholics to become abstinent and then maintain it. According to George Vaillant, the addiction of alcohol needs to be replaced by something equally as powerful. Religion is often that "something." Support from the religious community is a vital component of any abstinence program for the religious elder; churches need to work with secular and self-help organizations (AA) to provide services in a nonjudgmental manner which preserve self-esteem yet set clear limits on behavior.

Sexual Impotence. We found little evidence of greater sexual dysfunction or intrapsychic distress among more religiously active or religiously conservative older men (compared with others). We also, however, found little support for the notion that religion buffers against the psychological stresses caused by sexual impotence. Nevertheless, it appears that religious elders are not reluctant to seek professional assistance for their sexual dysfunction, which is itself a healthy coping behavior. Our findings indicate that the range of sexual activities displayed by religious elders may be somewhat constricted, thus impairing their ability to adapt effectively to impotence problems when they arise. Counselors should be aware of this fact, and may need to encourage or give permission for a wider variety of sexual behaviors that may both facilitate adaptation and enhance partner satisfaction when intercourse is prevented.

REFERENCES

Bean, M. (1975). Alcoholics Anonymous. *Psychiatric Annals* 5: 5-64.

Behar, D., G. Winokur, and C.J. Berg. (1984). Depression in the abstinent alcoholic. *American Journal of Psychiatry* 141:1105-1107.

Beresford, T.P., F.C. Blow, and K.J. Brower. (1990). Alcoholism in the elderly. *Comprehensive Therapy* 16(9):38-43.

Blum, R.H. and Associates (1970). *Students and Drugs.* SF: Jossey-Bass.

Carothers, M. (1970). *Prison to Praise.* Plainfield, NJ: Logos International.

Chien, C.P., B. Stotsky, and J.O. Cole. (1973). Psychiatric treatment for nursing home patients: Drug, alcohol, and milieu. *American Journal of Psychiatry* 130:543-548.

Coakley, D.V., and G.W. McKenna. (1986). Safety of faith healing. *Lancet* i:444.

Cornaro, L. (1563). *Sure and Certain Methods of Attaining a Long and Happy Life.* Reprinted (1979). NY: Arno Press.

Daley, D., H. Moss, and F. Campbell. (1987). *Dual Disorders: Counseling Clients with Chemical Dependency and Mental Illness.* Center City, MN: Hazelden Foundation.

Derogatis, L.R. (1977). *The SCL-90-R Administration, Scoring and Procedures Manual I.* Baltimore: Clinical Psychometric Research.

Donnelly, P. (1990). A light in the darkness. Unpublished manuscript. Duke University Department of Psychiatry.

Epstein, L.J., and A. Simon. (1967). Organic brain syndrome in the elderly. *Geriatrics* 22:145-150.

Estes, N., and M. Heinemann. (1986). *Alcoholism Development, Consequences, and Interventions*. St. Louis: CV Mosby Co.

Finkle, A.L. (1979). Psychosexual problems of aging males: Urologist's viewpoint. *Urology* 13:39-44.

Finkle, P.S., and A.L. Finkle. (1975). Urologic counseling can overcome sexual male impotency. *Geriatrics* 30:119-120.

_____ (1977). How counseling may solve sexual problems of aging men. *Geriatrics* 32:84-86.

Finlayson, R.E., R.D. Hurt, L.J. Davis, and R.M. Morse. (1988). Alcoholism in elderly persons: A study of the psychiatric and psychosocial features of 216 inpatients. *Mayo Clinic Proceedings* 63:761-768.

Frank, J.D. (1961). *Persuasion and Healing: A Comparative Study of Psychotherapy*. Baltimore: Johns Hopkins University Press.

Gaitz, C.M., and P.E. Baer. (1971). Characteristics of elderly patients with alcoholism. *Archives of General Psychiatry* 24:372-378.

Glynn, R.J., G.R. Bouchard, J.S. LoCastro, and J.A. Hermos. (1984). Changes in alcohol consumption behaviors among men in the Normative Aging Study. In *Nature and Extent of Alcohol Problems Among the Elderly*, edited by G. Maddox, L.N. Robins and N. Rosenberg. NY: Springer Publishing Co., pp. 101-116.

Glynn, R.J., G.R. Bouchard, J.S. LoCastro, G.R. Bouchard, J.S. LoCastro, and N.M. Laird. (1985). Aging and generational effects on drinking behaviors in men: results from the normative aging study. *American Journal of Public Health* 75:1413-1419.

Goulder, T.J. (1986). Scientific evaluation of complementary medicine. *Lancet* i:158.

Hartford, J.T., and T. Samozajski. (1982). Alcoholism in the geriatric population. *Journal of the American Geriatrics Society* 30:18-24.

Herman, S. (1987). Initial assessment of men with sexual complaints: The male sexual dysfunction protocol. In *Applications in Behavioral Medicine and Health Psychology: A Clinician's Source Book*, edited by J.A. Blumenthal and D. McKee. Sarasota, FL: Professional Resource Exchange, pp. 115-140.

Jinks, M.J., and R.R. Raschko. (1990). A profile of alcohol and prescription drug abuse in a high-risk community-based elderly population. *DICP Annals of Pharmacotherapy* 24:971-975.

Khavari, K.A., and T.M. Harmon. (1982). The relationship between the degree of professed religious belief and use of drugs. *International Journal of Addictions* 17:847-857.

Kinsey, A.C., W.B. Pomeroy, and C.E. Martin. (1948). *Sexual Behavior in the Human Male*. Philadelphia: WB Saunders.

Koenig, H.G., and S. Herman. (1992). Religion and coping with sexual impotence in later life. *Journal of Religious Gerontology* (in press).

Koenig, H.G., K.G. Meador, R. Westlund, and S. Ford. (1992). Health care utilization and survival of religious and non-religious copers hospitalized with medical illness. *Journal of Religious Gerontology* (in submission).

Koenig, H.G., M. Smiley, and J.P. Gonzales. (1988). *Religion, Health, and Aging.* NY: Greenwood Press.

Koenig, H.G., K.G. Meador, V. Goli, F. Shelp, H.J. Cohen, and D.G. Blazer. (1991). Self-rated depressive symptoms in medical inpatients. *International Journal of Psychiatry in Medicine* 12:409-429.

Kofoed, L.L., R.L. Tolson, R.M. Atkinson, R.L. Tolson, R.M. Atkinson, R.L. Toth, and J.A. Turner. (1987). Treatment compliance of older alcoholics. *Journal of Studies in Alcoholism* 48:47-51.

Krach, P. (1990). Discovering the secret: Nursing assessment of elderly alcoholics in the home. *Journal of Gerontological Nursing* 16(11):32-37.

Lamere, F. (1953). What happens to alcoholics? *American Journal of Psychiatry* 109:673.

Larson, D.B., and W.P. Wilson. (1980). Religious life of alcoholics. *Southern Medical Journal* 73:723-727.

Mack, J. (1981). Alcoholism, A.A., and the governance of the self. In *Dynamic Approaches to the Understanding and Treatment of Alcoholism*, edited by M.H. Bean and N.E. Zinberg. NY: Free Press.

Masters, W.H. (1986). Sex and aging–expectations and reality. *Hospital Practice* (August 15): 175-198.

McCourt, W.F., A.F. Williams, and L. Schneider. (1971). Incidence of alcoholism in a state mental hospital population. *Quarterly Journal of Studies on Alcohol* 32:1085.

Mishara, B.L., and R. Kastenbaum. (1980). *Alcohol and Old Age.* NY: Grune and Stratton.

Mulligan, T., S.M. Retchin, V. Chinchilli, and C.B. Bettinger. (1988). The role of aging and chronic disease in sexual dysfunction. *Journal of the American Geriatrics Society* 36:520-524.

Naguib, S.M., P.B. Beiser, and G.W. Comstock. (1968). Response to a program of screening for cervical cancer. *Public Health Reports* 83:990-998.

Nelson, P.B. (1990). Religious orientation of the elderly: Relationship to depression and self-esteem. *Journal of Gerontological Nursing* 16 (2):29-35.

Parfrey, P.S. (1976). The effect of religious factors on intoxicant use. *Scandinavian Journal of Social Medicine* 3:135-140.

Pearlman, C.K., and L.I. Kobash. (1972). Frequency of intercourse in men. *Journal of Urology* 197:298-301.

Pfeiffer, E., A. Verwoerdt, and G.C. Davis. (1972). Sexual behavior in middle life. *American Journal of Psychiatry* 128:1262-1267.

Pfeiffer, E., A. Verwoerdt, and H.S. Wang. (1968). Sexual behavior in aged men and women. *Archives of General Psychiatry* 19:753-758.

Pottenger, M., J. McKernon, L.E. Patrie, M.M. Weissman, H.L. Ruben, and P. Newberry. (1978). The frequency and persistence of depressive symptoms in the alcohol abuser. *Journal of Nervous and Mental Disorders* 166:562-570.

Schonfled, L., and L.W. Dupree. (1990). Older problem drinkers–long-term and late-life onset abusers: What triggers their drinking? *Aging* 361:5-11.

Schuckit, M.A., and P.A. Pastor. (1979). Alcohol-related psychopathology in the aged. In *Psychopathology of Aging*, edited by O.J. Kaplan. NY: Academic Press, pp. 153-168.

Tennant, F.S., R. Detels, and V. Clark. (1975). Some childhood antecedents of drug and alcohol abuse. *American Journal of Epidemiology* 102:377-384.

Vaillant, G.E. (1975). Sociopathy as a human process. *Archives of General Psychiatry* 32:173-183.

———— (1983). Paths into abstinence. In *The Natural History of Alcoholism: Causes, Patterns, and Paths to Recovery*, edited by G.E. Vaillant. Cambridge, MA: Harvard University Press, pp. 193-194.

Vaillant, G.E., and E.S. Milofsky. (1982). Natural history of male alcoholism. *Archives of General Psychiatry* 39:127-133.

Warheit, G.J., and J.B. Auth. (1984). The mental health and social correlates of alcohol use among differing life cycle groups. In *Nature and Extent of Alcohol Problems Among the Elderly*, edited by G. Maddox, L.N. Robins and N. Rosenberg. NY: Springer Publishing Co., pp. 29-82.

Williams, M. (1984). Alcohol and the elderly: An overview. *Alcohol Health Research in the World* 8:3-9.

Wilson, B. (1968). The fellowship of alcoholics anonymous. In *Alcoholism*, edited by E. Cantanzaro. Springfield, IL: Charles C. Thomas.

Yano, K., G.G. Rhoads, and A. Kagan. (1977). Coffee, alcohol, and risk of coronary heart disease among Japanese men living in Hawaii. *New England Journal of Medicine* 197:405-409.

Zimberg, S. (1987). Alcohol abuse among the elderly. In *Handbook of Clinical Gerontology*, edited by L.L. Carstensen and B.A. Edelstein. NY: Pergamon Press, pp. 57-65.

Chapter 18

Family and Bereavement Issues

THE FAMILY

But if a widow has children or grandchildren, these should learn first of all to put their religion into practice by caring for their own family and so repaying their parents and grandparents, for this is pleasing to God.

—1 Timothy 5:4

The importance of the family in providing both physical care and emotional support to chronically ill, dependent older members cannot be overemphasized. Much has been written about the highly mobile, fragmented, self-centered American family that has "abandoned" its elders (compared with other cultures). This is simply not true. Despite the very real and difficult problems associated with providing care to ill or disabled older adults (Zarit, Todd, and Zarit 1986), 85% of all such care is provided by family members (many of whom are elderly themselves) (Brody 1986). The willingness and ability of family to provide such services are the primary factors that enable chronically ill elders to live outside of institutional settings (Lawton 1981). During times of stress, family members also provide the bulk of emotional support needed by dependent elders (Shanas 1980; Wortman and Conroy 1985). Studies have shown that disruptions in family relationships, rather than disruptions in friendships, have the greatest negative impact on elders' support networks (Crohan and Antonucci 1989).

To better understand the cognitive framework by which an older adult is operating, it is essential to examine the assumptions that guide behavior within the elder's family (Qualls 1988). Important in this regard are shared beliefs, often unspoken. For example, the husband of a patient with Alzheimer's disease might have great difficulty leaving his wife in the care of others in order to participate in a social event that might provide him with rest and needed respite from his caregiving role. His action (or failure to act) is often based on a set of beliefs such as "I am responsible for my wife's behavior," "she cannot feel safe and comfortable without my being near her," or "I cannot participate in pleasurable social activity in my wife's absence."

These beliefs may be further grounded on a shared assumption both within his family of origin and his current family that to be a good husband or wife means providing personal care for one's spouse and being there when needed. Even a brief separation, then, may arouse guilt and signify a breach of contract. While such beliefs and underlying assumptions may be helpful in maintaining family solidarity and support, if not tempered by reality, the husband or wife may become overburdened and exhausted with caregiving responsibilities to the detriment of themselves and their loved one. Studies have shown that family members who care for chronically ill or disabled relatives are at high risk for deterioration of physical health, well-being, relationships with other kin, and social activities outside the home (Cantor 1983; Poulshock and Deimling 1984; George and Gwyther 1986).

Caregivers require time off for their own rejuvenation, physical and mental health. Nevertheless, they may have difficulty doing so on their own without prompting and support by other family members and by health-care professionals. As discussed in Chapter 16, a family's belief system and the rules derived from it may have a profound impact on decisions about nursing home placement, and may arouse distressing feelings of guilt after such placements are made.

Besides decisions about where the elder is to be cared for, family belief systems also affect many other issues related to elder's physical and mental health: decisions on when or whether to seek professional help for physical or emotional symptoms, decisions on whether to comply with medical/psychiatric treatment, decisions about resuscitation in event of sudden death, decisions about continued life support, and perhaps soon, decisions about euthanasia. Thus, health-care providers and religious professionals must seek out and try to understand family beliefs that motivate health decisions. Knowledge of the underlying cognitive framework of the family system may assist professionals in making important clinical decisions and in understanding the decisions made by family members.

Impact of Religious Beliefs

Religious beliefs can and often do profoundly affect the overall family belief system. They often define what is "right," "appropriate," or "acceptable" behavior by family members. The Judeo-Christian scriptures encourage family solidarity through their emphasis on responsibilities of husbands to wives (1 Corinthians 7:11; Ephesians 5:25-33; 1 Timothy 5:8; 1 Peter 3:7), wives to husbands (Ephesians 5:33; 1 Corinthians 7:10; Titus 2:4; 1 Peter 3:1-6), parents to children (Genesis 18:19; Deuteronomy 4:9, 6:6-7; 21:18-21; 2 Corinthians 12:14; Ephesians 6:4; Galatians 4:1-2; Colossians 3:21; Hebrews 11:23), and children to parents (Exodus 20:12; Leviticus 19:3; Deuteronomy 30:2; Ephesians 6:1-3; 1 Timothy 5:4,8; Hebrews 12:9). Take the following verses, for instance:

> For God said, "Honor your father and mother" and "Anyone who curses his father or mother must be put to death." But you say that if a man says to his father or mother, "Whatever help you might otherwise have received from me is a gift devoted to God," he is not to "honor his father" with it. Thus you nullify the word of God . . .
>
> *(Matthew 15:4-6)*

> If anyone does not provide for his relatives, and especially for his immediate family, he has denied the faith and is worse than an unbeliever.
>
> *(1 Timothy 5:8)*

Such proscriptions, in general, maintain a secure setting for the raising of children, ensure the safety of weaker or less able family members (the retarded or sick), and provide care and support for family members as they age. They also indicate that, just as in our times, these types of family matters were of concern, otherwise they would not have been discussed, prohibited or proscribed, as the case may be. The duties described above are necessary for the survival of civilization as we know it. Religious principles encourage an attitude of caring for others, while dissuading inappropriate selfishness and self-centeredness.

If any one of these principles, however, is followed to an extreme–without balance, temperance, or common sense–then problems can and often do develop. It is important to keep in mind that the responsibilities of each family member must be balanced against those of other members. Children have responsibilities to parents, but parents also have responsibilities to children. Husbands have responsibilities to wives, but wives also have responsibilities to husbands. Finally, there are duties that family members also have to themselves–to maintain their own physical and emotional health. The primary goal is to achieve a healthy balance and distribution of responsibility within the family. A parent who coerces a child to care for them in their home, thus causing a disruption in that child's emotional health or ability to carry out responsibilities to their own family members, is not fulfilling his or her scriptural duties to that child. Such actions may "exasperate" (Ephesians 6:4) or "embitter" (Colossians 3:21) children, and thus go against scriptural teachings.

Another example where a lack of perspective or balance can be detrimental is the case described earlier of the devoted husband caring for his wife with Alzheimer's disease. Perhaps the husband was raised in a religious home and determined throughout his life to guide his family by religious principles. When confronted with the need to separate briefly or more permanently from his demented wife, he resolutely adheres to his wedding vows "to have and to hold until death do us part;" this resolve may be further strengthened by the biblical notion of a husband and wife "becoming one" (Genesis 2:24; Matthew 19:6; 1 Corinthians 7:10; Ephesians 5:31) and of the call upon husbands to "love your wives, just as Christ loved the church and gave himself up for her . . ." (Ephesians 5:25). These underlying religious beliefs and assumptions, when taken to an extreme, may cause distress and guilt when separation becomes necessary and essential for the mental and physical health of both partners.

Some family members give religious grounds for refusing to institutionalize or separate from a parent or a spouse, when what is really driving this behavior are their own neurotic fears (cloaked in terms of religious piety). There may be fears of independence, being alone, or losing one's role as caregiver (or martyr). Thus, intrapsychic motivations–both religious and neurotic–must be carefully explored, particularly in situations where the physical or emotional health of either the dependent elder or the family caregiver is being seriously compromised.

Religious beliefs may also influence a family's decision concerning medical or psychiatric care. There may be a family belief that to rely on "worldly" medical interventions is a sign of spiritual weakness or lack of trust in the power of God to heal. Although this is less common today in America, it may still be a factor in the failure to seek appropriate health care by elders affiliated with certain fundamentalist religious groups. More common, perhaps, is the distrust that many religious elders have of members of the mental health profession–the feeling that psychiatrists are immoral, godless, or operating on principles that are inimical to their own belief system. To have a psychiatric illness may be especially embarrassing to some elders who feel that "good Christians" shouldn't have mental health problems; this may contribute to denial and failure to seek necessary treatment. The guilt thus aroused by illness may further increase a sense of separation from God and thus adversely affect their own spiritual growth.

Another instance where family religious beliefs are influential is the decision about cardiopulmonary resuscitation (whether or not to allow "no code" orders to be written). The issue of "salvation" may come up at this time. Some family members may be reluctant to allow the death of a relative whom they believe is not saved. The death of the unsaved relative may mean to family members the damnation of their loved one and eternal separation from him or her. This belief can affect the grieving process and the ability to let go. Thus, religious beliefs within the family and the assumptions that underlie these beliefs can influence decisions surrounding death and its impact on the mental health of survivors. An exploration by the therapist of how religion affects the family's belief system and rules, then, is essential for understanding behavior and for eventually influencing it.

BEREAVEMENT

When Uriah's wife heard that her husband was dead, she mourned for him.

–2 Samuel 11:26

According to the Holmes and Rahe's (1967) Stressful Life Events Scale, death of a spouse ranks number one in magnitude of stress. Numerous studies have demonstrated an increase in physical health problems and emotional disorder in the surviving spouse during the year following bereavement.

Physical Health Problems

Maddison and Viola (1968) examined the health of 375 widows in the year following bereavement, comparing it with that of 199 married controls matched by age and other sociodemographic factors. "Health deterioration" was 3 to 16 times greater in the bereaved sample compared with controls. Clayton (1974) documented a 50% increased risk of hospitalization and 20% greater likelihood of seeing a physician in the year following bereavement (three times that for matched controls). Fenwick and Barresi (1981) collected health data from 246 low-income and disabled elderly before and after bereavement over one year; a significant change in perceived health was noted among the bereaved compared with controls.

Mortality rates are also increased. Rees and Lutkins (1967) prospectively examined death rates among 156 spouses over two years following bereavement. Mortality was highest in the first year for the bereaved (12.2% for cases vs. 1.2% for controls); figures for the second year were 18.8% and 4.2%, respectively. Parkes, Benjamin, and Fitzgerals (1969) examined the mortality rate among 4,486 widowers (all over age 55) six months after bereavement, documenting a 40% increase in mortality among the bereaved compared with controls. The impact of bereavement on health appears to affect men more than women (Glick, Weiss, and Parkes 1974); specific illnesses behind this excess mortality include influenza, tuberculosis, pneumonia, cirrhosis and alcoholism, suicides and accidents (Helsing and Szklo 1981; Helsing, Comstock, and Szklo 1982). While health changes following bereavement are less prominent in women, they are still a concern and seem to be due to increased heart disease and cancer.

Emotional Problems

In addition to physical health problems, death of a spouse can cause enormous emotional pain in the survivor. The normal grief process takes anywhere from 6 to 12 months, although this time period varies widely depending on the suddenness of the death, surrounding circumstances, and quality of the relationship. Many elders may never get over the death of their spouse. The old saying, "You never get over it, you just get used to it," has particular applicability here.

When two people fall in love, marry, raise a family, and live together for 40 to 60 years or more, their individual identities and senses of self begin to blend together, particularly when the marriage is a good one (and sometimes even more so if the marriage is filled with disharmony and conflict). To some extent, then, there is an instillation of part of each spouse into the other, with an accompanying cathexis of emotional energy. Death, then, represents a tearing away of part of the person of the surviving spouse.

The process of grieving involves a psychological deinstillation (separation) and a decathexis (removal) of emotional energy from the dead spouse, and a reconstruction of the bereaved's personal identity. These adjustments to the death of a spouse are especially difficult for the elder whose entire social world up to that point involved relating to others as part of a couple, and thus possesses few intimate one-on-one relationships outside of the marriage (absence of a confidant). Bereavement seems to be particularly hard on older men who after focusing much of their energy during life on

job or career, now have a more limited social support network
outside of the home (unlike older women).

Anticipatory and Normal Grief

Mental preparation for the death of a loved one (anticipatory
grieving) may ease family members' adjustment to the eventual loss
of a loved one. It does so by emotionally finalizing the relationship
with the dying person, allowing time for resolution of conflicts with
the person while still alive, and by allowing for financial planning
and preparation for funeral arrangements (Rando 1986). There is a
growing literature, however, that has questioned the benefits of
preparing for a loved one's death, suggesting that even such preparation often does not soften the blow of the loss once it occurs (Hill,
Thompson, and Gallagher 1988).

Because of the magnitude of this loss, elders must have an opportunity to grieve after the event has actually taken place. Grieving is
a psychological process that involves working through the pain of
loss. It is essential that elders take the time to experience the pain of
grief, and not try to avoid it by numbing themselves with sedatives
or filling their time with social or work activities. Crying and talking about the deceased with friends, family members, or interested
professionals (clergy, personal physicians, and so forth) may facilitate the grief process. Helpers must listen and validate the bereaved
elder's emotional response to their loss. The absence of grieving is a
danger signal that should alert both religious and health professionals that there is a problem. Elders with delayed grief or inhibited
grief often experience physical symptoms or have catastrophic reactions on anniversary dates or after other minor stressors.

Normal grief proceeds along more or less predictable phases.
The first phase involves shock, numbness, a sense of disbelief.
During the first few weeks, the bereaved often experiences a sense
of deep yearning and may even unconsciously search for their loved
one. The elder may have vivid dreams of their spouse as if he or she
were still alive. At times, the person may hear their loved one's
voice, footsteps in the hall, or even may see them on the street; this
is all part of normal grief and does not indicate that the person is
going crazy. The second phase of grief involves separation anxiety,
protest, and anger–anger at oneself for real or imagined failures in

their relationship with the deceased, anger against the loved one for leaving, anger at God for taking him or her. The third phase involves depression, despair, apathy, and aimlessness as the person comes to accept the fact that their loved one is really gone.

The final stage of grief involves gradual recovery and movement out of depression, as the person slowly adapts and reorganizes their life. Little by little, previously enjoyed activities once again become pleasurable and meaningful. Evidence for this happening may be a return to work, a return to social life, and/or a return to cultural activity including amusements. By four to six months, the peak intensity of grief has usually passed and reorganization has begun (Bankoff 1983; Jacobson 1986). As noted earlier, no end point has been established, although it usually occurs sometime after the first year and generally not later than two years after the death.

Pathological Grief

Pathological grief involves an arrest of the grieving process and failure to move through the normal stages towards resolution. In such cases, chronic depression and loneliness may set in and inhibit the elder from getting on with their life (Clayton, Halikas, and Maurice 1972). While symptoms of depression such as difficulty sleeping, loss of appetite, decreased energy and concentration, and ruminating thoughts about the deceased are common during normal grief, the persistence of such symptoms for months and months without apparent lessening of intensity–particularly when associated with feelings of worthlessness, low self-esteem, and suicidal thoughts–indicates a pathological process that probably requires professional intervention.

Religion and Bereavement

Studies have shown that having a strong religious belief may ease the grief process and promote quicker adaptation (Berardo 1967; Heyman and Gianturco 1973; Peterson and Briley 1977; Vachon et al. 1982). More recently, Rosik (1989) examined the relationship between religious attitudes and adaptation among 159 elderly widows and widowers involved in southern California support groups. Distress and depression were lower among both men and women with high levels of intrinsic religiosity (measured using an intrinsic-extrinsic religiosity scale) compared with those who were either indiscriminately pro-religious or extrinsically religious. These findings indicate that religious beliefs may be particularly helpful in coping with bereavement when they are intrinsically motivated (see Chapter 7). When a person derives their sense of value and purpose from religion, the loss of a spouse may represent less of a threat to self than it would if their life centered around that spouse.

Another way that religion may facilitate adjustment is by reducing the loneliness associated with the third phase of grief. Although no systematic research has examined the connection between religiosity and loneliness in the bereaved, some investigators have explored this issue among mixed-age groups and elderly populations in general (Ellison 1978; Paloutzian and Ellison 1982; Koenig, Moberg, and Kvale 1988; Johnson and Mullins 1989). In a study of 106 consecutively evaluated patients seen in a geriatric medicine outpatient clinic, over 80 percent strongly or moderately agreed with the statement "My relationship with God helps me not to feel lonely" (Koenig, Moberg, and Kvale 1988). Belief in a personal God who is concerned with and responsive to the needs of people, then, may be an important way that elders compensate for social losses in later life.

Johnson and Mullins examined the relationship between loneliness (UCLA Loneliness Scale) and two dimensions of religiosity (the social and personal) among 131 residents of a 199-unit apartment facility for the elderly in Southern Florida. They reported that the social aspects of religion were significantly related to less loneliness more consistently than involvement in either family or friendship relations. Loneliness was also inversely related to personal religiosity, although this association did not reach statistical significance once social contact variables were controlled for. Personal religiosity may have motivated elders to be more involved in the social aspects of religion, which in turn, decreased their loneliness.

It is clear that support from the religious community often enables elders to work through their grief and reinvolve themselves in group activities (Berardo 1970). Such participation may help to combat social withdrawal that can isolate bereaved elders. Involvement in a religious community may also provide an outlet for psychological energy (as it becomes available) which can then be reinvested in the lives of others who need support and understanding for their own situations. Efforts to help others, then, may build self-esteem and thus expedite reorganization of the self following bereavement.

Clinical Applications

Religious rituals and ceremonies may facilitate the work of grief, and can help in the treatment of elders who get stuck during this process. The funeral ceremony, the soliloquy by the minister or others recounting the good characteristics of the deceased, the prayers, the burial process–all are heavily invested with symbolism to help the bereaved let go and separate from their loved one. At the funeral, there is an opportunity to express emotion and experience the pain of loss while receiving comfort and support from friends and family. When grief is prolonged and the bereaved is unable to separate fully from the deceased, the therapist can use religion to help complete the processes of deinstillation and decathexis, even if many years have elapsed since the death.

Techniques include the use of scripture and prayer to reassure the bereaved of the deceased one's safety, emphasizing God's love for and protection over him or her and God's promise of eventual reunion in the after life (Talbot, date unknown). Belief in an afterlife can lessen the impact that an eternal and permanent separation would have if all life ceased at death. During the celebration of the Eucharist, the Christian elder may symbolically be reunited with their loved one as part of the "communion of saints" that occurs as they receive the communion host and drink the wine. The belief involved here is that all Christians throughout time are united in Christ's body. This experience can arouse deep emotion and facilitate abreaction.

If getting on with life is the problem (because of excessive focus on the deceased), the elder may be encouraged through prayer to commit or release their spouse to the care and protection of God. Visualization can be used to help the elder let go of their loved one. This is accomplished by using progressive relaxation (muscle tensing and releasing, controlled breathing) to first induce a state of deep relaxation and peace. Then the elder is asked to visualize themselves in a beautiful place holding hands with their loved one. God (or Jesus) is then imagined to come walking up to them with his arms open, ready to receive the deceased. The person is instructed to give their loved one a deep embrace, put their loved one's hand into the hand of God, and let him or her go. The final scene is their spouse walking away with God (who has his arm around their shoulder) until they are completely out of sight.

If the bereaved has difficulty with visualization, he or she may be instructed to write a letter to the deceased. In the letter, he or she is instructed to tell the deceased how much they are loved and missed. Included here may be regrets, apologies, or requests for forgiveness for hurts inflicted by the bereaved on the deceased during their life together. Even more important, forgiveness may be given to the deceased spouse for actions that may have hurt the bereaved person and for which the latter may harbor resentment or bitterness. Good-bye is said and the deceased is again placed in the care of God (or Jesus) for protection and safety until they are reunited again in the next life. The therapist may include the use of ritual in this process. For instance, a special worship service or Requiem mass (for the Catholic) can be held with only a few close friends or relatives, the therapist, and minister or rabbi. During the service, the bereaved elder may receive communion while holding the letter of goodbye in their hand. They may then give the letter to the priest or pastor who may offer it to God through symbolically burning it and burying the ashes.

Such a ritual can powerfully impact on the elder's ability to successfully separate from the deceased, and has in clinical practice resulted in the relief of grief-related depressions lasting 30 years or more (personal communication 1991, William P. Wilson, Duke professor emeritus in psychiatry). The religious or mental health professional will need to use their ingenuity in thinking of rituals that are acceptable to the bereaved elder and appropriate for the characteristics of the deceased and their relationship together.

SUMMARY

Family members provide the vast majority of personal physical care and emotional support to the disabled elderly in America. By its emphasis on the importance of family cohesion and its proscription of interpersonal behaviors to maintain it, religion may help to provide the stability needed to assure that older family members are cared for and not neglected. Religion provides the basis for many belief systems that operate within families, determining what behaviors are appropriate. Religious beliefs may impact on whether elders seek help for physical or psychiatric symptoms, comply with proscribed medical regimens, and/or seek relief from caregiving responsibilities when necessary (such as placement of a spouse in a nursing home or acceptance of respite from caregiving duties). To enhance the effectiveness of interventions and better understand elders' responses to them, clinicians should explore the underlying religious belief systems of families in order to determine how these may be affecting healthcare decisions.

Loss of important family members, through bereavement may be associated with increased physical health problems and even adversely affect mortality. The grief process usually follows a fairly predictable pattern. Whether one is religious or not, the initial pain is severe and at times overwhelming. Studies have shown, however, that religious beliefs and activities often help to cushion the impact of such losses and facilitate adjustment over the long-run. Besides supplying a cognitive framework for dealing with death, religion provides a community where emotional support may be obtained and where psychic energy can be reinvested as grieving comes to an end. Clinicians and religious professionals may take advantage of religious rituals, scripture, prayer, and visualization to help ease normal grieving and, if necessary, to intervene when complications develop. I have approached bereavement primarily from a Christian background; Jewish readers are referred to Dr. Grollman's work (1974) on mourning among Jews.

REFERENCES

Bankoff, E.A. (1983). Social support and adaptation to widowhood. *Journal of Marriage and the Family* 45:827-839.

Berardo, F.M. (1967). Social adaptation to widowhood among a rural-urban aged population. *Agricultural Experiment Station Bulletin*, No. 689. Washington State University.

_____ (1970). Survivorship and social isolation. The case of the aged widower. *Family Coordinator* 19:11-25.

Brody, E. (1986). *Informal support systems in the rehabilitation of the disabled elderly.* In *Aging and Rehabilitation*, edited by S.J. Brody and G.E. Ruff. NY: Springer Publishing Co.

Cantor, M.H. (1983). Strain among caregivers: A study of experience in the United States. *The Gerontologist* 23:81-93.

Clayton, P.J. (1974). Mortality and morbidity in the first year of widowhood. *Archives of General Psychiatry* 30:747.

Clayton, P.J., J.A. Halikas, and W.L. Maurice. (1972). The depression of widowhood. *British Journal of Psychiatry* 120:71.

Crohan, S.E., and T.C. Antonucci. (1989). Friends as a source of social support in old age. In *Older Adult Friendships*, edited by R.G. Adams and R. Blieszner. Newbury Park, CA: Sage, pp. 129-146.

Ellison, C.W. (1978). Loneliness: A social-developmental analysis. *Journal of Psychology and Theology* 6:3-17.

Fenwick, R., and C.M. Barresi. (1981): Health consequences of marital-status change among the elderly: A comparison of cross-sectional and longitudinal analyses. *Journal of Health and Social Behavior* 22:106.

George, L.K., and L. Gwyther. (1986). Caregiver well-being: A multidimensional examination of family caregivers of demented adults. *The Gerontologist* 26:253-259.

Glick, I., R.S. Weiss, and C.M. Parkes. (1974). *The First Year of Bereavement.* NY: Wiley Interscience.

Grollman, E.A. (1974). The Jewish way in death and mourning. In *Concerning Death: A Practical Guide for the Living*, edited by E. Grollman. Boston: Beacon Press, pp. 119-140.

Helsing, K.J., and M. Szklo. (1981): Mortality after bereavement. *American Journal of Epidemiology* 114:41.

Helsing, K.J., G.W. Comstock, and M. Szklo. (1982). Causes of death in a widowed population. *American Journal of Epidemiology* 116:524.

Heyman, D.K., and D.T. Gianturco. (1973). Long-term adaptation by the elderly to bereavement. *Journal of Gerontology* 28:359-362.

Hill, C.D., L.W. Thompson, and D. Gallagher. (1988). The role of anticipatory bereavement in older women's adjustment to widowhood. *The Gerontologist* 28:792-796.

Holmes, T.H., and R.H. Rahe. (1967). The social readjustment rating scale. *Journal of Psychosomatic Research* 11:213-218.

Jacobson, D.E. (1986). Types and timing of social support. *Journal of Health and Social Behavior* 27:250-264.

Johnson, D.P., and L.C. Mullins. (1989). Religiosity and loneliness among the elderly. *Journal of Applied Gerontology* 8:110-131.

Koenig, H.G., D.O. Moberg, and J.N. Kvale. (1988). Religious activities and attitudes of older adults in a geriatric assessment clinic. *Journal of the American Geriatrics Society* 36:362-374.

Lawton, M.P. (1981). Community supports for the aged. *Journal of Social Issues* 37:102-115.

Maddison, D., and A. Viola. (1968). The health of widows in the year following bereavement. *Journal of Psychosomatic Research* 12:297.

Paloutzian, R.F., and C.W. Ellison. (1982). Loneliness, spiritual well-being and the quality of life. In *Loneliness: A Sourcebook of Current Theory, Research and Therapy*, edited by L.E. Peplau and D. Perlman. John Wiley and Sons, Inc., pp. 224-237.

Parkes, C.M., B. Benjamin, and R.G. Fitzgerals. (1969): Broken heart: A statistical study of increased mortality among widowers. *British Medical Journal* 1:740.

Peterson, J.A., and M. Briley. (1977). *Widows and Widowhood.* NY: Association Press.

Poulshock, S.W., and G.T. Deimling. (1984). Families caring for elders in residence: Issues in the measurement of burden. *Journal of Gerontology* 39: 230-239.

Qualls, S.H. (1988). Problems in families of older adults. In *Cognitive-behavioral therapy with families*, edited by N. Epstein, S. Schlesinger, and W. Dryden. NY: Bruner-Mazel, pp. 215-253.

Rando, T.A. (1986). *Loss and anticipatory grief.* Lexington, MA: DC Heath.

Rees, W.D., and S.G. Lutkins. (1967). Mortality of bereavement. *British Medical Journal* (Oct 7):13.

Rosik, C.H. (1989). The impact or religious orientation in conjugal bereavement among older adults. *International Journal of Aging and Human Development* 28:251-260.

Shanas, E. (1980). Older people and their families: The new pioneers. *Journal of Marriage and the Family* 42:9-15.

Talbot, J.F. (date unknown). A Christian ministry to the bereaved. Dissertation Abstracts International (Ann Arbor, MI: University M-films, No 77-20,780).

Vachon, M., J. Rogers, W.A. Lyall, W.J. Lancee, A.R. Sheldon, and S.J. Freeman. (1982). Predictors and correlates of adaptation to conjugal bereavement. *American Journal of Psychiatry* 139:998-1002.

Wilson, W.P. (1991). Discussion in Dr. Wilson's home in Durham, NC.

Wortman, C.B., and T.L. Conroy. (1985). The role of social support in adaptation and recovery from physical illness. In *Social Support and Health*, edited by S. Cohen and S.L. Syme. NY: Academic Press, pp. 281-302.

Zarit, S.H., P.A. Todd, and J.M. Zarit. (1986). Subjective burden of husbands and wives as caregivers: A longitudinal study. *The Gerontologist* 26:260-266.

Chapter 19

Religious Conversion

Each man can interpret another's experience only by his own.

–Henry David Thoreau

As discussed in Chapter 9, there has been much speculation about whether people become more religious as they grow older. Most studies demonstrate that the current generation of elderly Americans are more religiously oriented than are their younger peers. How older persons got that way, however, is less clear. Although alternative explanations abound (i.e., cohort effect, period effect, selective mortality, and so forth), one possibility is that religious faith does change as one grows older. In this chapter I will discuss the topic of religious conversion, with a focus on religious change in later life.

DEFINITION

According to Max Heirich (1977), religious conversion means different things to different people:

> In some descriptions, conversion involves a dramatic turn-about–either accepting a belief system and behaviors strongly at odds with one's previous cognitive structure and actions or returning to a set of beliefs and commitments against which one has been strongly in rebellion. In other descriptions conversion involves a *qualitative* change [my italics] in experience and in level of commitment, regardless of previous mindset. (p. 654)

James Fowler (1981) likewise views religious conversion as "those sudden or *gradual* processes that lead to significant changes in the contents of faith" (p. 285). Thus, conversion may involve a change in faith that occurs either suddenly and dramatically or evolves more slowly over a period of time. In both cases, there is an increased depth of religious understanding and commitment that is recalled by the person because of the changes in behavior and attitude that follow.

From the Judeo-Christian perspective, conversion indicates a profound change in the person's world view–the view of self and the view of other people; it is a time when God (or Jesus for the Christian) becomes the focus of that person's *ultimate concern* (the *"habitual centre of his personal energy,"* according to William James). The experience is not easily forgotten. In a follow up study of one hundred or so persons years after their conversion experience, Starbuck (1899) concluded that this event resulted in:

> a changed attitude toward life which is fairly constant and permanent, although the feelings fluctuate. . . . In other words, the persons who have passed through conversion, having once taken a stand for the religious life, tend to feel themselves identified with it, no matter how much their religious enthusiasm declines. (pp. 360, 357)

Perhaps this is why the scriptures describe such religious change in terms like "new birth" and "death of the old self" (John 3:3,7; 2 Corinthians 5:17; 1 Peter 1:3,23). True conversion often produces a complete transformation of the personality, a change in interests and motivations–in essence, it produces a new person. Again, however, this transformation may occur suddenly or only gradually over a period of time. Of course, many conversion experiences are transient and do not result in any lasting change in attitude or impact on behavior.

STUDIES ON CONVERSION

Religious conversion–particularly the sudden type–has received a lot of bad press in the mental health literature. Opinions have changed little since 1924, when Freud wrote a short piece on the subject (Freud 1925). He analyzes a letter written to him by an American physician about his conversion experience. The physician's conversion took place in the morgue when he saw an older woman's corpse (who, according to Freud, represented his mother). Freud explained that the conversion resulted from the physician's intense oedipal hatred for his father. This hatred, intensified by the sight of the woman's corpse, aroused such overwhelming anxiety and conflict that he completely submitted to his father represented by Christ. This interpretation was consistent with Freud's reductionistic view of God as psychodynamically symbolizing the "exalted father."

In a seminal and widely acclaimed review of the topic, prominent psychiatrist and psychoanalyst Leon Salzman (1953) wrote that Freud's psychoanalytic explanation "went to the very core of the conversion process" (p. 181). Salzman then reviewed three cases from his own clinical experience that justified Freud's interpretation, and concluded that "it is clear that hatred, resentment, and hostile, destructive attitudes seem in each case to have been involved in the preconversion experiences" (p. 183). The suggestion is that conversion experiences are rooted in psychopathology and internal conflict. Salzman calls this type of conversion "regressive" since it occurs in the context of severe emotional stress and attempts to deal with "pressing psychological problems" (p. 181).

Although he does mention a more progressive or maturational type of conversion, Salzman spends little time on it and instead focuses on the type of conversion associated with sudden and dramatic change (the more common type, in his estimation). Other mental health professionals in the early 1900s likewise emphasized that religious conversion typically took place in the context of emotional disturbance–be it severe depression (as in Tolstoy's case), guilt and conviction of sinfulness (Bunyan in *The Pilgrim's Progress*), or during the marked identity crisis that occurs during adolescence (James 1902; Coe 1916; Pratt 1920).

In the past 75 years, there has been little change in psychiatry's view of religious conversion (Christensen 1963; Witztum, Greenberg, and Dasberg 1990), with a continuing focus on inner conflict and psychopathology. Much of this literature, however, is based on clinical experience with a small number of mentally ill patients, not individuals selected randomly from the community or those without mental disorder. It is not surprising that the religious conversion which takes place in persons with mental illness is often associated with symptoms of emotional distress and intrapsychic conflict. Indeed, mental health professionals might seldom come into contact with mentally healthy persons who have had conversion experiences.

There are also problems with studies which examine new converts to particular religious groups within the community. First is the issue of generalizability. Reports from investigations of new converts to religious cults like the Subud, Moonies, or other unconventional religious sects (Kiev and Francis 1964; Galanter 1980) are unlikely to produce findings applicable to converts to more traditional, established Judeo-Christian groups. The ideologies of cults differ so radically from the cultural norms of American society that motivations underlying conversion are unlikely to compare with those of converts to more integrated religious groups. I would challenge the argument that ideology (the content of faith) makes little difference in such research. It is the specific belief that determines attitudes and behaviors which over the long-run can have profound psychological and sometimes physical consequences (the Jones massacre in British Guiana, for instance, or David Koresh incident in Waco, Texas).

A second problem in many studies is the failure to include matched controls (nonconverts) from the general population for comparison. Heirich (1977) has underscored the importance of including such controls when testing hypotheses concerning the etiology and consequences of religious conversion. In an indepth study of 152 recently converted Catholic Pentecostals, Heirich tested the three major hypotheses forwarded by social scientists to explain religious conversion: (1) conversion as a fantasy solution to a stressful life situation, (2) conversion as a consequence of socialization experiences in childhood, and (3) conversion as a result of patterns of interpersonal influence. In this study, he compared converts' responses to those of 158 unconverted controls of similar background. When looking at the results for the convert sample alone, it appeared that life stress and emotional upheaval were unusually common among religious converts, as was a history of devout religious upbringing, thus confirming the first two hypotheses. However, when he examined the prevalence of these characteristics among unconverted controls, they were practically the same.

More important in predicting conversion status, according to Heirich, were *interpersonal influences* which caused would-be converts to take on the religious frame of reference. The consistent, reinforcing input from trusted friends, relatives, and teachers (many of whom were converts themselves) was instrumental in this regard. This study dealt primarily with college students and is thus not directly applicable to older adults. Nevertheless, it makes the point that not all conversions are solely a consequence of intrapsychic conflict, emotional disturbance, or even religious upbringing, but instead often result from interpersonal influences.

Unfortunately, there has been virtually no systematic research on the causes and consequences of religious conversion in later life. Previous reports have typically focused on young adults and college students, since this group is most frequently seen by psychiatrists, is more likely to be accessible for study (on college campuses), and is more likely to be involved in new religious movements that attract the attention of researchers. There may also be a general feeling that as persons age they become more rigid in their belief systems and are less likely to change, particularly in the area of religion. Changes in religious faith, however, may be common among older adults as they experience health changes, social losses, and struggle with issues involving control and dependency. For some, the road to integrity may require a "starting over" that religious conversion can facilitate.

The rest of this discussion will focus around the following questions. Is there a special age or time during the life cycle when religious conversion or change is especially likely to occur? How likely is it that this will occur in later life? What intrapsychic or environmental causes initiate such changes in faith? In particular, how does the emotional stress of physical illness and approaching death impact on this likelihood? Finally, what are the psychological consequences of religious conversion?

CONVERSION AND AGE

Articles in psychiatric journals that discuss the psychodynamics of religious change or conversion frequently emphasize the occurrence of such experiences in adolescence (Salzman 1953; Christensen 1963; Draper et al. 1965). Coe (1916) noted that most converts were adolescents, and made a connection between conversion and the sexual instinct. By denying and repressing sexual needs, religion was seen as providing a neurotic solution to the conflict between these desires and prohibitions by parents and authority figures. Recall from above that Freud also linked oedipal issues (sexual and aggressive strivings) to religious conversion.

How much truth is there in these psychodynamic speculations? If religious change indeed happened primarily during adolescence, then perhaps such an explanation would have merit. However, if dramatic changes in religious faith occur at other times during the life cycle as well–when sexual issues are less pressing–then there may be some grounds for doubt. Responding to assertions during his day that religious conversion was related to sexual needs during adolescence, William James (1902) gives the following opinion:

> The two main phenomena of religion, namely, melancholy and conversion, they will say, are essentially phenomena of adolescence, and therefore synchronous with the development of sexual life. To which the retort again is easy. Even were the asserted synchrony unrestrictedly true as a fact (which it is not), it is not only the sexual life, but the entire higher mental life which awakens during adolescence. One might then as well set up the thesis that the interest in mechanics, physics, chemistry, logic, philosophy, and sociology, which springs up during adolescent years along with that in poetry and religion, is also a perversion of the sexual instinct:–but that would be too absurd. Moreover, if the argument from synchrony is to decide, what is to be done with the fact that the religious age *par excellence* would seem to be old age, when the uproar of the sexual life is past? (p. 19)

Since 1902, no systematic research has established that religious change of any enduring significance takes place more commonly during adolescence than at times later in the life cycle. In fact, recent community and institutional surveys have provided information about age of conversion or religious change that indicates a different pattern than reported in the early 1900s–suggesting that either the age at conversion has changed or current sampling methods are now providing more accurate data.

The Gallup organization recently conducted a survey of adults of all ages randomly selected across the United States to determine the age when Americans' religious faith changed (Princeton Religion Research Center 1987). Only 22% of those who experienced such a change reported that it occurred before the age of 18 (see Figure 19.1). In fact, the average age was 28, well beyond adolescence.

Recall also from Chapter 9 that in the DVAMHS we asked hospitalized patients if they had ever experienced a distinct change in their feelings about religion and at what age this occurred (as a means of eliciting age at conversion). This sample consisted of consecutively admitted men in the age ranges 20 to 40 and 65 to 102 who were systematically sampled using a set of clearly defined criteria independent of religious affiliation or experience. Many more older people were included in this sample compared with the Gallup sample (73% over age 65 vs. 39% over age 50 for Gallup survey). Figure 19.2 gives the distribution of ages at which faith was reported to change among the 276 VA patients having such experiences. Only 11% indicated that significant changes took place prior to age 18. In fact, over 40% of men age 65 or over who had experienced such a change reported that it occurred after the age of 50. The lower percentage of conversion experiences reported by the Gallup sample in the later years is probably due to the fact that fewer participants were over age 65 (10% or less). Thus, as more older adults are included in such studies, the average age of religious conversion or significant religious change falls far beyond adolescence. The failure of earlier reports (Freud, Salzman, Christensen, Witztum) to include older adults and, especially, those without mental illness, probably accounts for the differences between their reports, Gallup's and our own.

Significant changes in religious faith, then, are not restricted to adolescence or the teen years; rather, such changes may occur at any time during the life cycle. If religious change is not restricted to

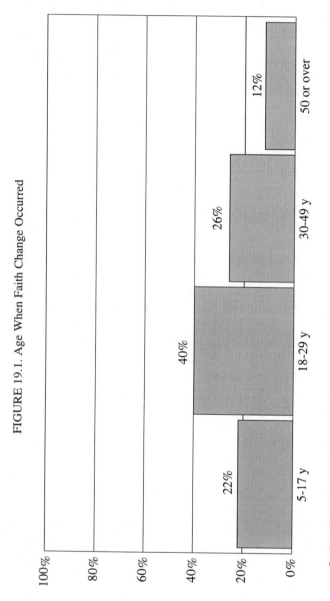

FIGURE 19.1. Age When Faith Change Occurred

Gallup Poll 1987 Report (n=708)
(39% of sample age 50 or over when surveyed)

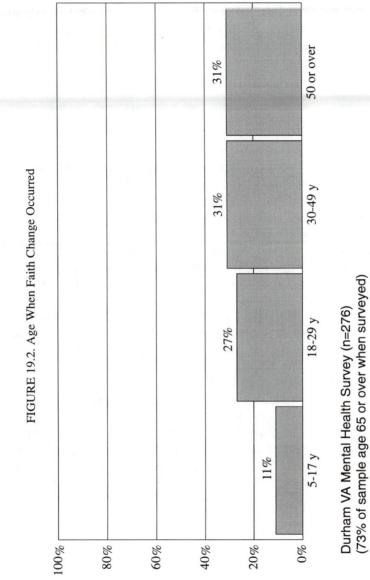

FIGURE 19.2. Age When Faith Change Occurred

Durham VA Mental Health Survey (n=276)
(73% of sample age 65 or over when surveyed)

adolescence, then the psychodynamic mechanisms used to account for conversion at this age may be inadequate to explain religious faith changes during adulthood or later life (as James pointed out). Even the validity of classical psychodynamic explanations for adolescent conversion may indeed be questioned.

CAUSES FOR CHANGE

Although there is some doubt concerning the role of psychic stress in the religious conversion of younger adults (where interpersonal influences may be more consequential) (Heirich 1977), it is likely that life crises do play a role in conversions that occur in middle adulthood or later life. The Gallup study, which included many middle-aged and some older adults, reported that those who experienced a marked change in faith were more likely to have undergone a divorce and to have felt lonely for a long period of time (Princeton Religion Research Center 1987). Subjective reports by those in our VA study also indicated that negative life events were often central to conversion experiences (see Chapter 10). Theories of religious faith development in later life (Chapters 6 and 7) indicate a need for crisis or emotional distress to catalyze changes in faith that lead to maturity. Fowler (1981) notes that transitions between faith stages often occur after a period of emotional stress or depression. In order for God to become the object of a person's ultimate concern (as occurs in true religious conversion), the possession, person, or goal that served this purpose beforehand must be displaced. This displacement often occurs through *loss* (loss of a loved one through death or divorce, loss of a career goal through failure of a business, or loss of independence and physical prowess through illness).

Mid-Life Conversions

During mid-life, there comes a time when persons realize that they are no longer young adults and that their time for achieving life goals (success in business, family, etc.) is limited. Likewise, this is a time when physical stamina and attractiveness may be lessening, children may be leaving the home, and a need to care for aging parents may arise. These changes arouse anxiety and stimulate a search for meaning and alternative sources on which to base one's identity. This quest may find its end in religion.

Some mental health experts attribute mid-life conversions to what is called "deferred obedience":

> As the individual enters middle age, he begins to lose some of his vigor. Even though he may not be conscious of it, a mild sense of depression may start to creep over him. He becomes mellower and gradually reorients himself toward his parents. The values and ideals that he had learned from them and perhaps since discarded now become attractive in his eyes. To the extent that the parents participated in the religious life of the community, he now obediently follows their example. His deferred obedience expresses in this way his need for parental appreciation of "good" behavior. (Group for the Advancement of Psychiatry 1968, p. 672)

This and earlier explanations underscore the role that age-related changes play in stimulating transformations in religious outlook.

Late-Life Conversions

As the person moves into older adulthood, events may occur which more directly threaten the individual. As noted in earlier chapters, later life can be a time of loss–loss of health, physical abilities, finances, and social supports. A goal of our studies of hospitalized veterans (DVAMHS) was to examine the nature of significant changes in religious faith and determine the circumstances involved in their occurrence. Conversions both toward religion and away from it were examined. Experiences that strengthened belief and dependence on God varied widely in nature. While some resulted from the influence of family or friends and from personal decisions to change, unrelated to an identifiable stressful event, many others came during a time of crisis–after an addiction to alcohol, a traumatic war experience, an accident, or some other stressful period.

Physical illness played a role in a number of cases, but was not as

influential in initiating change as expected. Among men who did
report a significant change in their feelings about religion at some
time in their lives, only about 15% attributed this change to physical
illness. In a minority of cases, health problems actually led to a
lessening of faith or turning away from religion.[1] In general, however, when illness was associated with changes in religious faith it
usually involved a strengthening of belief and greater dependence
on religion for support. Despite increasing disability and often life-
threatening illness, as noted in Chapter 9, we did not observe a mass
turning to religion by those who had not previously been religious.
Most elderly men continued to cope with their circumstances in the
same way that they had always coped. Those who had previously
turned to religion during crisis tended to do so when faced with
health problems at this time. In general, those who had not turned to
religion earlier in their lives did not do so when their health failed;
instead, they depended on family members or friends, the skill of
their doctors, their own personal resources, and some on alcohol.

Two older participants in the DVAMHS exemplify the dramatic
changes in faith that can occur in later life, whether initiated by
physical illness or not. Sometime in the year between their first and
final evaluations, both of these men had a profound change in their
behavior and feelings toward God. The first patient was a 65-year-
old man with unstable angina who, on initial evaluation, reported
that religion was seldom of any help to him since he had severe
hearing loss that prevented his participation in church services. At
the next evaluation (eight months later) he noted that his daughter
had begun bringing him religious books to read. Not long thereafter,
he stopped drinking and smoking, and began daily reading of the
Bible and other religious literature, depending heavily on this activity for comfort. Follow up two months later found that religion
remained a strong and important source of support for him.

The second case was an 86-year-old man with acute myeloge-
nous leukemia (cancer of the blood) who, like the first patient,

1. Experiences that had a negative effect on faith varied widely in nature. Almost
a quarter of such changes occurred during wartime; others were related to loss of
family members, conflicts at church, and bad examples set by church members or
religious leaders. Only a few (approximately 5%) were a negative reaction to
physical illness.

claimed during his first evaluation that religion had been of little or no help to him; on reevaluation one year later, however, he reported that physical illness had strengthened his belief in God and then proceeded to recount the following events. Shortly before Easter, eight months prior to his second evaluation, he underwent a profound religious experience during which he sensed God's presence at his bedside. At that time, he felt a tremendous release from the emotional distress and anxiety that he had been experiencing. It is of interest that on subsequent evaluations, he would repeatedly retell his story to examiners; he continued to do so up until his death nearly a year distant from the event. Old age, then, is clearly not a limiting factor in the capacity to experience a significant change in faith that might profoundly affect one's world view and thus enhance the quality and meaning of life.

Neither of the above conversions were church-based. Could this be a factor that distinguishes the conversions of the elderly from those who are younger? If that is true, then might it also help to explain why "everyone knows" that conversion is for the young, since the two elderly conversions noted here (and many others in Chapter 10) were private? Further research on this topic is needed.

PSYCHOLOGICAL EFFECTS OF RELIGIOUS CONVERSION

Of the 69 cases of strong religious copers identified in Chapter 10, 73% reported having a conversion-like experience at some time during their lives. It is evident that this experience had a profound effect on the way these men would deal with crisis thereafter. Compared with older men who did not rely on religion to cope, religious copers were less likely to drink alcohol or to be depressed, indicating better adjustment to current circumstances. This finding supports claims by these men that their conversion experiences had been beneficial in helping them cope with problems in life since then. Older men who showed positive changes in religious faith during follow up evaluations typically reported a lessening of psychological symptoms. Unfortunately, no study has yet systematically examined the mental health effects of conversions which take place in later life. Several studies, however, have examined the topic among younger and middle-aged subjects.

Most of the psychopathology associated with religious conversion has been documented prior to religious change rather than after (Salzman 1953; Christensen 1963; Kiev and Francis 1964; Levine and Salter 1976; Clark 1979; Ullman 1982). William James (1902) first reported on the beneficial effects of conversion, noting that religious experience often enhanced well-being and happiness:

> . . . and we must acknowledge that the more complex ways of experiencing religion are new manners of producing happiness, wonderful inner paths to supernatural kind of happiness, when the first gift of natural existence is unhappy, as it so often proves itself to be. (p. 71)

A number of empirical studies have now substantiated these claims. Stanley (1965) reported lower neuroticism scores on the Maudsley Personality Inventory among converted compared with nonconverted theology students. Wilson (1972) examined the mental health effects of religious conversion in a sample of 63 subjects, a number of whom were elderly (age range 15 to 75). Wilson reported positive cognitive and behavioral changes following the religious experience, including an increased ability to communicate with others, a decreased use of alcohol, and a decline in symptoms of depression, anxiety, confusion, and anger.

In a survey of 2500 American women responding to a magazine questionnaire, Shaver, Lenauer, and Sadd (1980) also reported that converts had greater well-being than nonconverts. Some investigators have even shown that religious change may produce changes in sexual orientation in homosexuals (Pattison and Pattison 1980) and have positive rehabilitation effects on criminals with severe personality disorder (Cromer 1981). Religious conversion has also been associated with spontaneous resolution of depression (Group for the Advancement of Psychiatry 1968; Cavenar and Spaulding 1977) and emergence from chronic alcohol addiction (Lamere 1953; Vaillant 1983). In a seminal review, Bergin (1983) concluded that conversion significantly reduced pathological symptoms and led to improved adjustment.

Of particular relevance to this discussion is a case which William

Wilson, colleague and former head of the division of biological psychiatry at Duke Medical Center, recently shared with me. It concerned a 79-year-old woman admitted to his psychiatric inpatient service at Duke Hospital sometime during the 1970s. She had a diagnosis of severe dementia of the Alzheimer's type, and was being admitted for evaluation of reversible causes and possible interventions. The patient's agitation had made life at home quite difficult for her family who cared for her. In the month prior to admission, she became so agitated that the family began to seriously consider admitting her to a local nursing home. Before doing this, however, they decided to have one final evaluation.

At some point during her hospital stay, one of the staff members talked with her about her religious beliefs (not a typical policy at Duke), after which she experienced a religious conversion. This experience was accompanied by an outpouring of positive emotions. In addition, she became decidedly more manageable for nursing staff. The patient was able to recount this experience for the next five days, but because of her severe dementia she was unable after that to recall what exactly had happened to her, although she knew that something had changed. Dr. Wilson followed her for the next five years, during which her mental condition progressively deteriorated. The positive mood and behavioral changes, however, persisted for many months beyond her memory of the incident, which enabled her care at home to proceed more smoothly.

Her story is a remarkable one; however, it is not outside the realm of possibility. Recall from Chapter 16 the religious experience of Robert Davis which occurred when he was in the early to middle stage of Alzheimer's disease. Emotional experiences are much more deeply ingrained in memory than are purely cognitive ones. I myself have cared for a patient in his 90s who had advanced cognitive impairment from multiple strokes (multi-infarct dementia) who could not recount a thing about his past medical or psychiatric history except for his religious conversion in middle age, about which he gave a remarkably detailed and prolonged account (with obvious pleasure). Thus, even moderate to severe cognitive impairment does not rule out the possibility of profound religious experience and change.

ADVERSE MENTAL HEALTH EFFECTS

Although I have not encountered older patients in whom a conversion experience had negative mental health effects, there are cases in the literature of middle-age adults whose conversion was followed by tragic consequences such as suicide (Cavenar and Spaulding 1977). Witztum and colleagues report that a high percentage of referrals to a community mental health center in Jerusalem were new converts to ultra-orthodox Judaism (13%). In these reports, however, patients had serious psychiatric illness prior to their conversion (affective disorder and schizophrenia). Because of the importance placed by religious communities on caring for the physically and mentally ill, it is not surprising that many new members have a history of mental illness. Because most mental illness tends to be chronic and recurrent, exacerbations are to be expected even in the nurturant atmosphere of the religious community. Although it has been suggested that entry into a society which advocates a "repressive religious ethic" may cause mental illness (Goshen-Gottstein 1987), there is no research to date that documents an induction of mental illness by religious conversion in previously stable individuals.

MECHANISM OF POSITIVE EFFECTS

Precisely how religious conversion produces increased well-being, spontaneous resolution of depression, freedom from an addictive pattern of alcohol abuse, decreased anxiety, decreased selfishness, greater concern for and desire to help others, and a new sense of purpose and hope, is not clear. However, several mechanisms exist by which such changes could occur.

James (1902) explained it as a coming together of the "divided self." He notes that in some people there are discordant strivings within the personality and an "incompletely unified moral and intellectual constitution" (p. 140) (inherited temperament). According to James, "Their spirit wars with their flesh, they wish for incompatibles, wayward impulses interrupt their most deliberate plans, and their lives are one long drama of repentance and of effort to repair misdemeanors and mistakes" (p. 141). Indeed, this description parallels St. Paul's account of the war within (Romans 7:23, 8:6-7) and other scriptures (James 4:1; 1 Peter 2:11). According to this explanation, religious conversion marks a unification of these drives within the person and a coming together of the divided self. Psychic energy, once needed to contain the battle within, is now released in the form of positive emotions and unopposed spiritual strivings (at least temporarily). For the older adult facing difficulties and stresses in life, there may be a part of him or her that struggles to maintain control in the face of declining health, independence, and other resources. In the process of conversion, he or she gives up this control to God and places their trust in him. This may then relieve the distress of trying to control the uncontrollable.

A second explanation for the mental health effects of conversion, particularly in middle age and later life, involves the relief of existential despair. As persons age, they may experience disappointments in life–failure to achieve that which they had hoped for in their career, marriage, or other areas of ultimate concern. Life then begins to lose its meaning and purpose, and despair creeps into their lives. Religion represents a solution to this dilemma. By placing God at the center of ultimate concern, the person may experience a return of meaning and purpose in life–this time linked with goals that are psychologically more attainable.

A third explanation is suggested by Lombillo (1973) from his examination of the conversion of Ignatius of Loyola (founder of the Jesuit Order). A Spanish nobleman of prominent rank in the military, Ignatius was injured in battle, requiring a prolonged convalescence and the cessation of his previous work, thus initiating an identity crisis and emotional upheaval. The transformation from a military identity to a religious one resolved the crisis. Using Ignatius as an example, Lombillo compares religious conversion to the process of "working through" in psychotherapy. Both involve a change in psychic structure and may be followed by resolution of intrapsychic conflict. The altered state of consciousness sometimes experienced during conversion shakes up the existing personality structure enough so that it can be replaced by a new structure, this time based on a religious worldview. This explanation, if true, may explain religious change in later life that occurs in response to threats to personal identity, such as declining health, social and occupational status. Thus, as earlier sources of self-esteem and self-worth diminish with age, religion may be sought as a more durable base for identity formation.

SUMMARY

Religious conversion involves a profound reorientation of goals and motivations in life so that God (or Jesus for the Christian) becomes the object of ultimate concern. Such religious change is not restricted to adolescence or early adulthood, but may occur at any time during the life span–including old age. The fact that 40% of elderly men experience such changes in religious faith after the age of 50 is clear evidence for the possibility of real and sometimes dramatic spiritual growth in later life. Such religious change seldom occurs in the absence of some type of psychological stress or conflict that displaces whatever existed previously as the object of ultimate concern.

While physical health problems may initiate the process of religious change, a wide variety of other experiences and changes associated with aging–acting alone or in concert with health changes–are often responsible. Influences of friends and relatives, changes in occupational and social identity, struggle with an addictive pattern of alcohol use, existential anxiety, and religious background and upbringing each play a role in different cases. Whatever the cause, true religious conversion produces a marked and enduring effect on the personality, enhances well-being and adjustment, and provides meaning, purpose, and new identity. Even conditions such as Alzheimer's disease and other dementias may not preclude the possibility of religious change and the positive psychological effects that accompany it. In some cases, especially where there is a prior history of severe psychiatric illness, some dangers may attend the profound emotional upheaval that conversion sometimes involves (Cavenar and Spaulding 1977). Such persons should be monitored carefully and provided with professional guidance to help them integrate the experience into their lives.

Finally, can religious conversion be explained entirely by psychological, sociological, or interpersonal processes? Certainly, all human experience is filtered through the psyche and is profoundly affected by the influence of others. Nevertheless, there are few other forms of human experience that have the effects that religious conversion has, particularly in terms of arousing zeal for greater morality and self-sacrifice (James 1902; Moreland 1987). Whether or not something beyond the psychological or sociological takes place, however, is beyond our discussion here. One can only wonder and marvel at the changes in personality and behavior that do take place and transform the individual in a way that months or years of psychotherapy were often unable to accomplish.

REFERENCES

Bergin, A.E. (1983). Religiosity and mental health: A critical reevaluation and meta-analysis. *Professional Psychology: Research and Practice* 14:170-184.

Cavenar, J.O., and J.G. Spaulding. (1977). Depressive disorders and religious conversions. *Journal of Nervous and Mental Disease* 165:209-12.

Christensen, C.W. (1963). Religious conversion. *Archives of General Psychiatry* 9:41-50.

Clark, J.G. (1979). Cults. *Journal of the American Medical Association* 242: 279-281.

Coe, G.A. (1916). *The Psychology of Religion.* Chicago: University of Chicago Press.

Cromer, G. (1981). Repentant delinquents. A religious approach to rehabilitation. *The Jewish Journal of Sociology* 23:113-122.

Draper, E., G.G. Meyer, Z. Parzen, and G. Samuelson. (1965). On the diagnostic value of religious ideation. *Archives of General Psychiatry* 13:202-207.

Fowler, J.W. (1981). Stages of Faith. SF: Harper and Row.

Freud, S. (1925). A religious experience. *Collected Papers* 5:243-246. London: Hogarth Press.

Galanter, M. (1980). Psychological induction into the large-group: Findings from a modern religious sect. *American Journal of Psychiatry* 137:1574-1579.

Goshen-Gottstein, E.R. (1987). Mental health implications of living in an ultra-orthodox Jewish subculture. *Israel Journal of Psychiatry* 24:145-166.

Group for the Advancement of Psychiatry. (1968). *The Psychic Function of Religion in Mental Illness and Health.* NY: Mental Health Materials Center.

Heirich, M. (1977). Change of heart: A test of some widely held theories about religious conversion. *American Journal of Sociology* 83:653-680.

James, W. (1902). *The Varieties of Religious Experience: A Study in Human Nature.* NY: Longmans, Green and Co.

Kiev, A., and J.L. Francis. (1964). Subud and mental illness: Psychiatric illness in a religious sect. *American Journal of Psychotherapy* 18:66-78.

Lamere, F. (1953). What happens to alcoholics? *American Journal of Psychiatry* 109:673.

Levine, S.V., and N.E. Salter. (1976). Youth and contemporary religious movements: Psychosocial findings. *Canadian Psychiatric Association Journal* 21:411-420.

Lombillo, J.R. (1973). The soldier saint–A psychological analysis of the conversion of Ignatius of Loyola. *Psychiatric Quarterly* 47:386-418.

Moreland, J.P. (1987). *Scaling the Secular City.* Grand Rapids, MI: Baker Book House.

Pattison, E.M., and M.L. Pattison. (1980). "Ex-gays": Religiously mediated change in homosexuals. *American Journal of Psychiatry* 137:1553-1562.

Pratt, J.B. (1920). *The Religious Consciousness.* NY: Macmillan.

Princeton Religion Research Center. (1987). *Faith Development and Your Ministry.* Princeton, NJ: The Gallup Poll.

Salzman, L. (1953). The psychology of religious and ideological conversion. *Psychiatry* 16:177-187.

Shaver, P., M. Lenauer, and S. Sadd. (1980). Religiousness, conversion, and subjective well-being: The 'healthy-minded' religion of modern women. *American Journal of Psychiatry* 137:1563-1568.

Stanley, G. (1965). Personality and attitude correlates of religious conversion. *Journal for the Scientific Study of Religion* 4:60-63.

Starbuck, E.D. (1899). *The Psychology of Religion.* NY: Charles Scribner and Sons.

Ullman, C. (1982). Cognitive and emotional antecedents of religious conversion. *Journal of Personality and Social Psychology* 43:183-192.

Vaillant, G.E. (1983). Paths into abstinence. In *The Natural History of Alcoholism: Causes, Patterns, and Paths to Recovery,* edited by G.E. Valliant. Cambridge, MA: Harvard University Press, pp. 193-194.

Wilson, W.P. (1972). Mental health benefits of religious salvation. *Journal of Diseases of the Nervous System* 36:382-386.

Witztum, E., D. Greenberg, and H. Dasberg. (1990). Mental illness and religious change. *British Journal of Medical Psychology* 63:33-41.

PART VI:
THE FINAL FRONTIER

Chapter 20

Hope for the Dying

Even though I walk
through the valley of the shadow of death,
I will fear no evil,
for you are with me;
your rod and your staff,
they comfort me.

–Psalm 23:4

Death is a subject of relevance to all. It is the one fact about the future that can be counted on for certain ("for death is the destiny of every man; the living should take this to heart"–Ecclesiastes 7:2). In all the animal kingdom, presumably only humans must deal with the foreknowledge of their own death and the array of possible experiences that may precede (or follow) that event. Many persons who acknowledge death's existence for others, deny it for themselves. In fact, the amount of psychic energy spent on denial of one's inevitable mortality is quite astounding. Freud (1915) was aware of this massive denial, for he wrote that despite the ubiquitousness and certainty of death, most people had difficulty facing this concept. In fact, he believed that it was actually impossible for a person to conceptualize his or her own death. Thus, Freud rationalized that the fear of death was not really a fear of a specific known entity, but rather a displaced anxiety–the fear of castration. Irving Yalom, in his seminal work Existential Psychotherapy (1980), sums up nicely the impact on human behavior of conscious and unconscious fear of death:

The terror of death is ubiquitous and of such magnitude that a considerable portion of one's life energy is consumed in the denial of death. Death transcendence is a major motif in human experience–from the most deeply personal internal phenomena, our defenses, our motivations, our dreams and nightmares, to the most public macro-societal structures, our monuments, theologies, ideologies, slumber cemeteries, embalmings, our stretch into space, indeed our entire way of life–our filling time, our addiction to diversions, our unfaltering belief in the myth of progress, our drive to 'get ahead,' our yearning for lasting fame. (p. 41)

As a person ages and faces threats to health, denial of death becomes increasingly difficult. With the experience of loss of health, friends, and family, the older person is forced to confront the meaning of life and death in a way that is foreign to the young and healthy. This is perhaps not possible in young adulthood, for it is easy to become engrossed in the activity of work and play. Because death is a remote and unfamiliar concept, many experience a false sense of immortality and see their future as limitless. Yet the time allotted each person is limited.

As for the days of our life, they contain seventy years,
Or if due to strength, eighty years,
Yet their pride is but labor and sorrow;
For soon it is gone and we fly away. (Psalm 90:10)

Despite tremendous advances in medicine, we have been unable to extend life much beyond King David's figure given almost 3000 years ago. Studies have now shown that healthy human cells are capable of replicating only a certain number of times before they cease and die (Hayflick phenomenon); this number seems to be genetically programmed for each animal species (Hayflick 1965). Thus, while medicine has the potential of enhancing the quality of life in the latter years by the *compression of morbidity* (Fries 1980), we may never be able to lengthen life much beyond that limit specified in the Old Testament (which in Genesis 6:3 notes a maximum human life-span of 120 years).

Knowledge of inevitable mortality, however, allows a person to set priorities and structure time accordingly. The writings of 17th-century philosopher Thomas a Kempis (1617) make the point that such knowledge should be used to make every moment of life count:

> Of what use to us is a long life, if we amend so little? Alas, a long life often adds to our sins rather than to our virtue. Would to God that we might spend a single day really well! Many recount the years since their conversion, but their lives show little sign of improvement. If it is dreadful to die, it is perhaps more dangerous to live long. Blessed is the man who keeps the hour of his death always in mind, and daily prepares himself to die. . . . When that last hour shall come, thou wilt begin to have a far different opinion of thy whole life that is past, and be exceedingly sorry thou has been so careless and remiss. Oh how wise and happy is he that now laboreth to be such a one in his life, as he wisheth to be found at the hour of his death! (pp. 73-74)

On the other hand, to be constantly aware of and concerned about one's eventual mortality would be disabling (Yalom 1980). There is again a need for balance. Conscious knowledge and consideration of one's eventual mortality, when of a moderate degree, can enhance functioning because it assists the individual in deciding what is really important in life. As people age and death approaches, priorities, goals, and even experience of time may change. Kalish and Reynolds (1981) asked persons of all ages what they would do if they had only six months remaining in their life. Younger persons mentioned traveling and accomplishing things they had not done before; older people, on the other hand, were three times more likely than younger to focus on inner behaviors and spiritual needs. In fact, elders were more likely to desire no changes at all in their lives.

Some investigators have maintained that confronting death is easier for older than younger persons. The psychoanalyst Felix Deutsch (1933), after studying a sample of dying patients, observed that the decline in vital processes was accompanied by a parallel decline in the intensity of instinctual aggressive-erotic drives. He hypothesized that the fear of dying might be reduced as the pressures of inner instinctual demands diminished. Thus, if aging is associated with a lessening of aggressive-erotic drive, then perhaps death anxiety may be diminished as well. Furthermore, the social, cognitive, and physical health losses that accompany aging, combined with the lower likelihood of reversible losses and the fear of being a burden on others, may lessen the anxiety associated with dying at a younger age.

While anxiety about death may diminish in later life, it does not extinguish. At least 50% to 75% of older adults living in the community say they experience fear or anxiety about death (Gubrium 1973; Koenig 1988). Even these figures, however, may be suspect given that many of the healthy elderly participants in community surveys may still be in a state of denial as far as death is concerned. Indeed, Carl Jung believed that the major concern and motivation in later life was the conscious or unconscious fear of death (Jung 1934). There are many things to fear about dying and death: loss of autonomy, disfigurement, letting family members down, physical discomforts (pain, shortness of breath, nausea), and facing the unknown (Cassem 1988). Fear of the unknown and of death of the self can be paralyzing. In one study, elderly veterans in a nursing home were asked what their preferences would be if they were fatally ill, in great distress, and under heavy medical expense. Almost half desired that physicians do everything possible to keep them alive (Preston and Williams 1971), indicating that almost any kind of life was worth more than no life at all.

Many other elders, on the other hand, may consciously deny such fear to protect others. Rather than drain the emotional or financial resources of the family, they may ask to be allowed to die even though they themselves may desire to live longer (Kalish 1976). Family, employer, community, government, and many older persons themselves may feel that since there is less future to invest in an older person's life, perhaps resources should be allocated elsewhere. Such attitudes encourage social and psychological disengagement. Kalish (1972) notes that the decreasing attachments to possessions, groups, friends, and family may help to diminish the loss that accompanies death, reduce anxiety, and make death more acceptable. The actual meaning of disengagement, the factors which initiate the process, and the consequences of it, however, are far from clear.

It is well known that withdrawal from activities and loved ones is also associated with feelings of hopelessness, helplessness, worthlessness, and being a burden, well known symptoms of *depression*, the most common treatable psychiatric disorder in late life (Koenig and Blazer 1990). Disengagement by elders during the process of dying may represent a response to abandonment by family, friends, and health care professionals who are threatened by the dying process which disturbs their own sense of immortality. When patients are asked what they fear most about dying, however, the most common response is abandonment by loved ones (Weissman 1972; Becker 1973; Saunders 1959). Thus, disengagement from others as death approaches does not necessarily indicate progress towards a "good death." Indeed, it may reflect a pathological process that may interfere with tasks which the dying person must accomplish in order to achieve true peace of mind in their final days.

What are the tasks of dying? Kubler-Ross (1969) talks about the unfinished business that confronts the dying person, particularly the need for reconciliations and resolution of conflict with loved ones. This is the time to let bygones be bygones; to forgive others and to receive forgiveness from them. *This is not a time to withdraw or disengage*. Rather, this is an opportunity for developing a closeness with loved ones which will leave them with a real treasure–an experience which will later comfort them in their grief and live on as a warm memory for years to come. I am not saying that it is easy for family and friends to stand near the dying person, particularly in circumstances where death is disfiguring or painful. Nevertheless, a certain amount of emotional pain will be experienced anyway in the process of mourning after the loved one's death. It is probably better to experience this pain with the dying person while they are still alive, since much of the suffering involved in grief has to do with not being able to communicate to the deceased things which had not been discussed previously. Clinical experience has shown that when a spouse or child is at their loved one's bedside at the time of death, they cope better with their loss than they do in situations where travel difficulties or heroic measures by medical staff prevented this from happening.

RELIGION, DEATH, AND DYING

> And Abraham breathed his last and died in a ripe old age, an old man and satisfied with life . . .
>
> *–Genesis 25:8, ASV*

The premise here is that religion helps the elder achieve a "good death." This does not mean that all religious elders are without fear or anxiety during the dying process or will not need to face the physical discomforts that can occur at this time. Nevertheless, the religious elder is assured in their worldview, based on scripture, that he or she will not be alone during their final hour (Matthew 28:20). The image is that God will guide them across this threshold. The religious elder has a promise that all will not end at the moment of death. There will certainly be change, but the change will be for the better. Medical science cannot make this promise.

As I have noted earlier, the existence of life after death is not a topic for science to address, for it is not in the natural realm in which scientific laws operate. The deterioration and decomposition of the physical body at death is a scientific fact that can be observed and verified by those of us still alive. However, whether there is any type of experience that occurs after death is a notion that cannot be proven or disproven by experiment or observation. Such a phenomenon is supernatural and is thus outside the natural system where science and logic are helpful. The supernatural phenomenon of life after death, then, is totally in the province of religion. To science, it is unknown and unknowable.

However, the mental health of persons holding a particular set of beliefs or a specific worldview can be observed, measured, and compared with that of others with different belief systems or no belief system at all. Thus, the important question to health professionals caring for the dying elder is not whether there is life after death, but whether a religious cognitive framework provides more comfort during the dying process and a better death than alternative worldviews. The most common competing worldview in this society is that death is the end, results in permanent separation from loved ones, total annihilation of the self, absence of all experience, and nonexistence for the rest of eternity.

Here is a scientific question. Does a religious belief system enhance the quality of life during the terminal stages of illness, allow for more meaningful and satisfying relationships with family and friends, relieve anxiety, or help the elder to better cope with the pain and suffering that often accompanies the dying process? The psychological and social ramifications of a religious perspective in later life have only begun to be explored systematically.

The Evidence

One approach to this question is to examine prevalence. In other words, how common is the religious worldview among older adults nearing death? We have shown that the overwhelming majority of older adults with health problems adhere to a religious belief system and rituals which ease the transition from life to death (Koenig, Moberg, and Kvale 1988). Over 70% of Americans age 50 or over believe in life after death (Princeton Religion Research Center 1976). In fact, the United States is second only to India in prevalence of this belief, a situation which has not changed since 1948, despite rapid advances in education, science and technology (Princeton Religion Research Center 1976). This high prevalence of belief in an afterlife testifies to the importance of its function.

Likewise, a number of scientific investigators who have looked deeply into this subject have come away with a belief themselves. Five years after her widely-acclaimed book, *Death and Dying* (1969), Elizabeth Kubler-Ross (1974) wrote: "Before I started working with dying patients, I did not believe in a life after death. I now do believe in a life after death without a shadow of a doubt" (p. 167). After reviewing Kubler-Ross's book and several others on this subject, M.G. Michaelson (1974) commented:

> Damned if I know what's going on here, but it does seem that everyone who's gone into the subject comes out believing in something crazy. Life after death, transformation, destiny, belief. . . . These are the words of hard-nosed scientists fresh from their investigations. (p. 6)

Research on the relationship between religiosity and death anxiety is not something recent. The topic has received intermittent attention for almost 100 years, since the birth of psychology and its separation from philosophy. As Thorson and Powell (1990) note, some of the earliest survey research in psychology focused on this topic (Hall 1896; Scott 1896). Theories on religion's role in existential reconciliation soon came about. According to Hall, "Thus never was the greatest *Vergrangung* [fear] that ever oppressed the human race so completely removed . . . by this most masterly of all psychotherapies" (1915, p. 561).

As noted in Chapter 12, several epidemiological studies have more recently examined the relationship between religion and death anxiety in middle-aged or older adults. About two-thirds found an inverse relationship between religiosity and fear of death (Jeffers, Nichols, and Eisdorfer 1961; Swenson 1961; Williams and Cole 1968; Wittkowski and Baumgartner 1977; Leming 1979-80; Feifel and Nagy 1981; Richardson, Berman, and Piwowarski 1983; Koenig 1988); the remaining studies found no relationship (Kurlycheck 1976; O'Rourke 1977; Downey 1984; Thorson and Powell 1989). No reports, however, indicate greater anxiety among religious elders. Several investigators have now forwarded the hypothesis that the certainty, rather than content of belief is what matters (Hinton 1967; Alexander and Adlerstein 1959; Leming 1979-80; Smith, Nehemkis, and Charter 1983-84). In other words, it is not so important whether one has a religious or non-religious view of death, but rather if the person is absolutely convinced that theirs is the correct view. Those who are less certain about their beliefs and thus follow a "middle of the road" commitment, will suffer the greatest anxiety. While this is an interesting hypothesis, we have been unable to replicate this phenomenon in our studies of anxiety and religion in general (Koenig et al. 1993) or death anxiety in particular (Koenig 1988).

Studies of survivors of life-threatening illnesses contribute further to our understanding of this subject. These survivors can report themselves from first-hand experience what types of thoughts and feelings they had. Hawley (1990) explored the personal experiences of 16 survivors of deadly cancer (eight men and eight women). She found that all but three subjects attributed their survival to nontraditional methods of healing, even though all had received traditional treatments. Instead, most attributed their healing to God or nonallopathic treatments. These patients often described the turning point in their illness as characterized by spiritual insights, spiritual callings, or prayers. Religious faith was reported to lessen fear and increase hope. Thus, when persons face death, religious cognitions become increasingly important as a source of comfort.

As I have noted in Chapter 12, the dynamics of religious change over time and in response to approaching death, may actually underestimate the strength of the inverse relationship between religiosity and death anxiety in some studies. For instance, an elder may not seek religious comfort until their anxiety about death escalates; in other words, religion may not be employed until "all else has failed." Recall Osarchuk and Tatz's (1973) report of an experiment in which they artificially increased the intensity of death fear in subjects. With an increase in death anxiety, they found a concomitant increase in intensity of beliefs in an afterlife. If, however, the effect of religion on relieving anxiety was not immediate or only partial, then the likely outcome from a cross-sectional survey exploring religiosity and death anxiety (which most studies have been) might demonstrate either no association or a positive one. Through a process of self-selection, religious persons might appear to be more anxious than the nonreligious, thus concealing any protective effects that religion may offer.

A related idea is the following. If anxiety motivates people towards religion, then persons with a hereditary or biological propensity to nervousness and insecurity might be more attracted towards religion than those with a more relaxed disposition. Freud himself claimed that religion was born from man's insecurity over the enormous and uncontrollable forces of nature (Freud 1927). Again, such a dynamic would likely result in a positive association between religion and anxiety, despite a possible therapeutic effect by religion. For example, even though doctors help treat disease, a community survey that included patients in doctors' offices would likely discover that the sickest individuals were most commonly found in these places; one could hardly conclude that seeing the doctor makes one sick! It is remarkable that despite these considerations, the majority of cross-sectional studies still report an inverse relationship between religiosity and death anxiety. Harvard psychiatrist Ned Cassem (1988), in a seminal review of the topic of death and dying, nicely summarizes the clinical and research findings when he writes: "In general, those who possess a sense of the presence of God, of being cared for or watched over, are more likely to manifest tranquility in their struggle with terminal illness" (p. 738).

Mechanism of Effect

According to Robert Kastenbaum (1985), belief in an afterlife enables the dying elder and his or her loved ones to share a common frame of reference. In addition, such a belief relieves the rehearsal anxiety of caretakers (and the patient) and minimizes the pain or social disruption of dying and death. By performing such functions, Kastenbaum notes that such a belief "helps to support the status quo, both in terms of individual psychodynamics and the interpersonal network" (p. 624). Underscoring the importance of religious cognitions, Ellison (1989) note the following:

> . . . cognitive reorientation of such experiences [turning to religion] may facilitate individual resolution of ego integrity versus despair through ego transcendence. . . . A new awareness of oneself as intimately known and valued by God might well result in the perception of enduring significance beyond one's physical self and life. (p. 10)

For the religious elder, there appears to be little to fear in death. Often, this event may even be regarded as a time for joyous reunion with a beloved husband, wife, or child, who has already passed on. For the faithful elder who has spent his or her life in the worship and service of their Creator, death may represent a time when he or she will finally meet their master and experience his love more fully and directly (2 Corinthians 5:6-8). According to the Christian religion, man was created to live in eternal fellowship with God; when sin came into the world, death accompanied it. Because of Christ, the "sting of death" has been removed, and therefore eternal life once again becomes possible and death only represents a transition point from this worldly life into spiritual life.

For religious elders who are less certain about their relationship with God, however, the anticipation of death may be a time of anxiety over the unknown future (which may involve retributions). The Judeo-Christian religion, however, has a belief system which includes mercy and forgiveness as central to its message, and provides a mechanism by which guilt can be relieved through confession. Therefore, no person need live in this fear.

In cases of exaggerated guilt over real or imagined sins, which may be viewed by the elder as unforgivable, the health professional, minister or priest should be alerted to the fact that such fixed false beliefs may involve psychiatric illness. Delusional disorders or severe depressions, often based on an organic cause such as stroke or other brain disease, can be responsible for such convictions of sinfulness and fear of eternal damnation, particularly when such convictions are at wide variance from a previous life of faith and relative equanimity. A mental disorder such as this may unnecessarily disturb the final days of life for even the most devout and faithful elder. In such cases, either psychotropic medication or even electroconvulsive treatment may be needed, along with absolution.

I am reminded of an elderly woman (Mrs. Smith, I will call her) who had been a pillar in her local church for many years, teaching Bible classes and organizing various religious outings until the age of 85. In the previous eight months, however, Mrs. Smith had become convinced that she had made a pact with the devil and was being forced to commit suicide as her part of the bargain. This elaborate delusion involved an elderly man at the nursing home who was wheelchair-bound and severely demented, whom she was extremely afraid of. She thought he was forcing her to carry out the pact. Mrs. Smith had both visual and auditory hallucinations, the latter involving voices calling her to get ready for a trip that would result in her committing suicide. She was very distraught. For months, Mrs. Smith had felt strangely distant from God, and feared that if she carried out the pact, that she would be forever separated from him. She remarked to me that she had never dreamed that her final days on earth would be like this. Despite ardent attempts to dissuade her of these fantastic beliefs, she remained unconvinced. I tried to reassure her that God was still close by, that he understood her situation, and that her many years of faithful service would not go unrewarded. While this temporarily brought her some relief, her fear returned after returning to the nursing home.

Mrs. Smith's strange ideas about her pact with the devil began soon after contracting an influenza-like illness which may have involved the coverings of her brain (encephalitis), and perhaps even precipitated a small stroke (she had high blood pressure). In addition, she had been treated for depression with a medication which had mild delirium as a side-effect. Consequently, we rearranged her antidepressant regimen and began her on a small dose of a major tranquilizer. She eventually responded completely. In this case, a combination of reassurance, support, and biological therapy directed at the underlying illness was necessary.

Scripture as a Source of Support

Just as medical professionals base their opinions and recommendations on scientific papers and reputable medical texts, so many religious persons base their observations about the world around them (and the world to come) on what they see as a credible and reliable source, religious scripture. As they approach death, many elders find consolation from reading scriptures that assure them that the current physical or emotional sufferings are only temporary, and that a new life awaits them on the other side. The following are examples of passages from the Christian Bible (Psalms, Isaiah, the Gospels, and the Epistles of Paul) and passages from the Jewish Talmud which dispel fear and convey the hope of a future for the dying elder who has lived righteously (or who has at least asked for and received forgiveness).

The Bible[1]

> For thou wilt not leave my soul to Sheol; Neither wilt thou suffer thy holy one to see coruption.

> Your dead will live; their corpses will rise.
> You who lie in the dust, awake and shout for joy,
> For your dew is as the dew of the dawn,

---

1. Unless otherwise specified, the following excerpts are from *New American Standard Bible* (1977).

And the earth will give birth to the departed spirits. (Isaiah
    26:19)

The righteous man perishes, and no man takes it to heart;
And devout men are taken away, while no one understands.
For the righteous man is taken away from evil,
He enters into peace;
They rest in their beds,
Each one who walked in his upright way. (Isaiah 57:1-2)

But regarding the resurrection of the dead, have you not read
that which was spoken to you by God, saying "I am the God
of Abraham and the God of Isaac, and the God of Jacob?" He
is not the God of the dead but of the living.
[Jesus's response to a question about life after death]
(Matthew 22:31; the same response is given in Mark 12:26-27
    and Luke 20:37-38)

If there is no resurrection of the dead, then not even Christ has
    been raised.
And if Christ has not been raised, our preaching is useless and
    so is your faith.
More than that, we are then found to be false witnesses about
    God,
for we have testified about God that he raised Christ from the
    dead.
But he did not raise him if in fact the dead are not raised.
For if the dead are not raised, then Christ has not been raised
    either.
And if Christ has not been raised, your faith is futile. . . . If
    only for this life we have hope in Christ, we are to be
    pitied more than all men. (I Corinthians 15:13-19 NIV)

In the same way, our earthly bodies which die and decay are
different from the bodies we shall have when we come back to
life again, for they will never die. The bodies we have now
embarrass us for they become sick and die; but they will be
full of glory when we come back to life again. Yes, they are
weak, dying bodies now, but when we live again they will be

full of strength. They are just human bodies at death, but when they come back to life they will be superhuman bodies. For just as there are natural, human bodies, there are also supernatural spiritual bodies. (1 Corinthians 15:42-44, Living Bible)

For this perishable must put on the imperishable, and this mortal must put on immortality. But when this perishable will have put on the imperishable, and this mortal will have put on immortality, then will come about the saying that is written, "Death is swallowed up in victory. O death, where is your victory? O death, where is your sting?" (1 Corinthians 15:53-55)

For we know that if the earthly tent which is our house is torn down, we have a building from God, a house not made with hands, eternal in the heavens. For indeed in this house we groan, longing to be clothed with our dwelling from heaven; inasmuch as we, having put it on, shall not be found naked. For indeed while we are in this tent, we groan, being burdened, because we do not want to be unclothed, but to be clothed, in order that what is mortal may be swallowed up by life. (2 Corinthians 5:1-4)

But we do not want you to be uninformed, brethren, about those who are asleep, that you may not grieve, as do the rest who have no hope. For if we believe that Jesus died and rose again, even so God will bring with Him those who have fallen asleep in Jesus. For this we say to you by the word of the Lord, that we who are alive, and remain until the coming of the Lord shall not precede those who have fallen asleep. For the Lord Himself will descend from heaven with a shout, with the voice of the archangel, and with the trumpet of God and the dead in Christ shall rise first. Then we who are alive and remain shall be caught up together with them in the clouds to meet the Lord in the air, and thus we shall always be with the Lord. Therefore comfort one another with these words. (1 Thessalonians 4:13-18)

Now the dwelling of God is with men, and he will live with them.
They will be his people, and God himself will be with them,

and be their God.

He will whip every tear from their eyes.

There will be no more death or mourning or crying or pain, for
the old order of things has passed away. (Revelation
21:3-4 NIV)

The Talmud[2]

I rise early and they rise early, I rise early to engage in the
study of Torah, and they rise early to engage in frivolous talk;
I labor and they labor, I labor and gain a reward, but they labor
without receiving a reward; I run and they run, I run toward
the life of the world to come, while they run toward the pit of
destruction. (28b, Tractate Berakhot) (p. 68)

R. Hiyya B. Va prayed thus: May it be your will, O lord our
God, to stir our hearts to full penitence, that we do not suffer
embarrassment in the presence of our ancestors in the world to
come. (Yerushalmi 4:2, 7d, Tractate Berakhot) (p. 69)

A favorite saying often repeated by Rav: [The world to come
is not like this world]. In the world to come there will be no
eating, or drinking, or procreation, or business, or jealousy or
hatred or competition, but the righteous will sit with crowns on
their heads feasting on the radiance of the divine presence.
Thus it is written: 'And they beheld God, and did eat and
drink' [Exodus 24:11, the divine presence was their food and
drink]. (17a, Tractate Berakhot) (p. 72)

A heavenly voice came forth saying: How fortunate are you,
R. Akiba, that your soul has departed with the word ehad. The
ministering angels said before the Holy One, praised be He: Is
this the Torah, and is this its reward? [He should have been]
'of those who die by Your hand, O Lord' [Psalm 17:14]. A
heavenly voice came forth saying: How fortunate are you R.
Akiba, that you are destined for the life of the world to come.
(61b, Tractate Berakhot) (p. 81)

---

2. All excerpts are from Bokser BZ (1989). *The Talmud: Selected Writings.*

Said Rava: When a person is brought before the heavenly tribunal for judgment he is asked: Did you conduct your business with integrity? Did you set aside time for the study of the Torah? Did you raise a family? Did you persist in the hope for redemption? Did you search after wisdom? Were you able to infer one truth from another? Nevertheless, if 'the fear of the Lord is his treasure' [Isaiah 33:6], all will be well, but if not, not. (30b-31b, Tractate Shabbat) (p. 87)

How can the belief in the resurrection of the dead be proven from the Torah? Because it is written: "and you shall contribute from it the Lord's offering to Aaron the priest" [Numbers 18:28]. Would Aaron live forever? He did not even enter Eretz Yisrael that offerings should be given him. But this indicates that he was to be resurrected and the children of Israel would give him offerings. Thus the resurrection of the dead is implied in the Torah. It has been taught: R. Similai said: How can we prove the resurrection of the dead from the Torah? From the verse: "And I have established my covenant with them [the patriarchs] to give them the land of Canaan" [Exodus 6:4]–it does not say to give you but to give them [the patriarchs]. This proves the resurrection of the dead from the Torah. (90b, Tractate Sanhedrin) (p. 211)

Thus, while there is the fear of judgment (Revelation 20:12), most scriptures (Christian and Jewish) promise a new and better life than would ever be possible for the chronically ill older person in their future worldly existence. So important for Christians is the existence of an afterlife that Paul bases the entire truth of Christianity on it (1 Corinthians 15:13-19). For some hurting and severely disabled persons, such a belief is the only rational basis for hope. For elders who doubt whether they have lived a "good enough" life, there is always the promise of forgiveness and mercy for those who ask. It is never too late for that (Isaiah 1:18; Luke 15:11-24; 1 John 1:9).

THE HEALTH CARE PROFESSIONAL

Because of the ubiquity of religious beliefs among older adults, and their use of these beliefs to cope with illness, disability, and death, spiritual needs will become evident to health professionals during their contact with religious elders in many settings: the acute care hospital, the outpatient clinic, the emergency room, the nursing home, the hospice. Inclusion of clergy as part of the health care team in these settings is, thus, essential. Physicians and nurses themselves, however, must be prepared to help elders meet their spiritual needs when time is short, clergy are unavailable, or the patient refuses to see the clergy. In a study of physicians' attitudes towards religious issues in older patients, we found that the majority agreed that some of these issues could and should be dealt with by physicians and not always delegated to the clergy (Koenig, Bearon, and Dayringer 1989). Some dying elders will feel closer to a physician, nurse, or social worker than to anyone else. They may be unwilling to bring up sensitive spiritual issues with others, even the clergy. In such cases, health professionals need to understand the vital importance of spiritual needs in achieving a good and peaceful death, and then be willing to listen with respect and, if necessary, support the elders in their religious struggles. The excellent book by Sharon Fish and Judith Shelly, *Spiritual Care*, has principles and clinical guidelines that are appropriate for all the helping professions (Fish and Shelly 1983).

OTHER WAYS OF COPING

One of the most common sources of strength at this time, besides religion, is family and friends. The family, particularly when in the caregiving role, needs support and encouragement itself. Without this, family members will be unable to provide the support which their dying relative needs. This is especially true when the dying process is painful and/or protracted; it often takes enormous strength on the relative's part to remain close to the patient during these times. Support groups, depending on the particular illness, are useful in helping families share their burden with others undergoing a similar plight, and help to develop new relationships that will sustain them after their loved one's death.

A variety of other ways besides religion are used by the elderly to relieve anxiety over death and thus compensate for this expected loss. Some may see themselves surviving after death by dwelling in the memory of others, some by living on through progeny, and some by living on through works and accomplishments. Others simply accept the idea of total extinction or put it out of awareness, and focus attention on the usual activities that have kept them busy throughout their life (if they are physically able). Thus, religion is not the only way that older persons deal with dying and death; however, few methods of coping are as powerful.

NEAR DEATH EXPERIENCES

Recently, there have been highly publicized reports, both in newspapers and on TV, about the pleasant experiences people have during near-death experiences. Nearly everyone today is familiar with such accounts that are surprisingly similar in nature and often involve moving through a dark tunnel with a bright light at the end; as the light is approached, profound feelings of peace and well-being are reported, and sometimes the presence of a loving supernatural Being is felt. This, however, is only one side of the near-death experience. Very little attention has been paid to negative experiences reported by others. The latter have been described in detail by Maurice Rawlings, MD, of the University of Tennessee Medical College, who for many years taught cardiopulmonary resuscitation to physicians around the world as member of the National Teaching Faculty of the American Heart Association. His work is summarized in two books, *Before Death Comes* (Rawlings 1980) and *Beyond Death's Door* (Rawlings 1987).

Dr. Rawlings notes that only about 20% of those who survive clinical death describe any experience at all of "a life beyond." About half of these persons report pleasant visions and thoughts during that time. The other half–immediately after their return to consciousness–report a horrendous, hellish terror. Within a very short time, however, they have psychologically *repressed* this experience because of its overwhelming and terrifying nature. These experiences, then, seldom get told–since most interviews with these patients by psychologists, psychiatrists, or others take place days, weeks, or even years after the event. This means that the pleasant accounts come form only about 10% of those with near-death experiences, while the other 10% with negative ordeals are seldom heard from and the remaining 80% have no immediate or deferred sensations at all. Thus, there is probably little grounds for feeling much consolation about death from the glowing reports of near-death experiences so often publicized by the media.

SUMMARY

The view of death described in this chapter maintains that there is nothing to fear in it. Rather than fear death, it would be wiser to worry about one's attitudes and behaviors in the present; for the latter is what largely determines the quality of life here on earth and—if there is life after death—perhaps the nature of that existence as well.

REFERENCES

Alexander, I., and A. Adlerstein. (1959). Death and religion. In *The Meaning of Death*, edited by H. Feifel. New York: McGraw-Hill, pp. 271-283.

Becker, E. (1973). *The Denial of Death*. New York: The Free Press.

Bokser, B.Z. (1989). *The Talmud: Selected Writings*. New York: Paulist Press.

Cassem, N.H. (1988). The person confronting death. In *The New Harvard Guide to Psychiatry*, edited by A.M. Nicholi. Cambridge, MA: Harvard University Press, pp. 728-758.

Deutsch, F. (1933). Euthanasia, a clinical study. *Psychoanalytic Quarterly* 5: 347-368.

Downey, A.M. (1984). Relationship of religiosity to death anxiety of middle-aged males. *Psychological Reports* 54:811-822.

Ellison, C.G. (1989). Religious involvement, stress, and psychological well-being. Dissertation proposal. Department of Sociology, Duke University, Durham, NC.

Feifel, H., and V.T. Nagy. (1981). Another look at fear of death. *Journal of Consulting and Clinical Psychology* 49:278-286.

Fish S., and J.A. Shelly. (1983). *Spiritual Care*. Downers Grove, Ill: Inter Varsity Press.

Freud, S. (1915). Thoughts for the times on war and death. In *S. Freud, Collected Papers, Vol. 4*. London: The Hogarth Press, 1959, pp. 288-317.

———— (1927). Future of an illusion. In *The Standard Edition of the Complete Psychological Works of Sigmund Freud, vol. 21*, edited by J. Strachey. London: The Hogarth Press, 1962, pp. 18-21.

Fries, J.F. (1980). Aging, natural death, and the compression of morbidity. *New England Journal of Medicine* 303:130-135.

Gubrium, J.F. (1973). Apprehensions of coping incompetence and responses to fear in old age. *International Journal of Aging and Human Development* 4(2):111-125.

Hall, G.S. (1896). Study of fears. *American Journal of Psychology* 8:147-249.

_____ (1915). Thanatophobia and immortality. *American Journal of Psychology* 26:550-613.

Hawley, G.R. (1990). The role of the holistic variable in the attribution of cancer survival. Dissertation Abstracts International [B] 50(11):5369.

Hayflick, L. (1965). The limited in vitro lifetime of human diploid cell strains. *Experimental Cell Research* 37:614-636.

Hinton, J. (1967). *Dying*. Baltimore: Penguin.

Jeffers, F.C., C.R. Nichols, and C. Eisdorfer. (1961). Attitudes of older persons towards death: A preliminary study. *Journal of Gerontology* 16:53-56.

Jung, C.G. (1934). The soul and death. In *The Meaning of Death*, edited by H. Feifel. New York: McGraw-Hill, 1959, pp. 3-15.

Kalish, R.A. (1972). Of social values and the dying: A defense of disengagement. *Family Coordinator* 21:81-84.

Kalish, R.A. (1976). Death and dying in a social context. In *Handbook of Aging and the Social Sciences*, edited by R.H. Binstock and E. Shanas. NY: Van Nostrand Reinhold.

Kalish, R.A., and D.K. Reynolds. (1981). *Death and Ethnicity: A Psychocultural Study*. Farmington, New York: Baywood.

Kastenbaum, R. (1985). Dying and death: A life-span approach. In *Handbook of the Psychology of Aging*, 2nd Ed., edited by J.E. Birren and K.W. Schaie. New York: Van Nostrand Reinhold, pp. 619-643.

a Kempis, T. (1617). *The Imitation of Christ*. Chicago: Moody Press (1980).

Koenig, H.G. (1988). Religion and death anxiety in later life. *Hospice Journal* 4:3-24.

Koenig, H.G., and D.G. Blazer. (1990). Affective disorders. In *Geriatric Medicine*, 2nd edition, edited by J.R. Walsh, C.K. Cassel, L. Sorensen and D. Riesenberg. NY: Springer-Verlag, pp. 473-490.

Koenig, H.G., L.B. Bearon, and R. Dayringer. (1989). Physician perspectives on the role of religion in the physician-older patient relationship. *Journal of Family Practice* 28:441-448.

Koenig, H.G., D.O. Moberg, and J.N. Kvale. (1988). Religious and health characteristics of patients attending a geriatric assessment clinic. *Journal of the American Geriatrics Society* 36:362-374.

Koenig, H.G., L.K. George, D.G. Blazer, J. Pritchett, and K.G. Meador. (1993). The relationship between religion and anxiety in a sample of community-dwelling older adults. *Journal of Geriatric Psychiatry* 26:65-93.

Kubler-Ross, E. (1969). *On Death and Dying*. NY: Macmillan.

_____ (1974). *Questions and Answers on Death and Dying*. NY: Macmillan.

Kurlycheck, R.T. (1976). Level of the belief in afterlife and four categories of fear of death in a sample of 60+ year olds. *Psychological Reports* 38:228-230.

Leming, M.R. (1979-80). Religion and death: A test of Homans' thesis. *Omega Journal of Death and Dying* 10:347-364.

Michaelson, M.G. (1974). Death as a friendly onion. *New York Times Book Review*, 21 July 1974, pp. 6-8.

New American Standard Bible. (1977). New York: Thomas Nelson Publishers.

O'Rourke, W.D. (1977). The relationship between religiousness, purpose-in-life, and fear of death (nursing home patients). *Dissertation Abstracts International* 37(11-A):7046-47.

Osarchuk, M., and S. Tatz. (1973). Effect of induced fear of death on belief in afterlife. *Journal of Personality and Social Psychology* 27:256-60.

Preston, C.E., and R.H. Williams. (1971). Views of the aged on the timing of death. *Gerontologist* 11:300.

Princeton Religion Research Center. (1976). *Religion in America*. Princeton, NJ: The Gallup Poll.

Rawlings, M. (1980). *Before Death Comes*. Nashville: Thomas Nelson.

Rawlings, M. (1987). *Beyond Death's Door*. NY: Bantam Books.

Richardson, V., S. Berman, and M. Piwowarski. (1983). Projective assessment of the relationships between the salience of death, religion, and age among adults in America. *Journal of General Psychology* 109:149-156.

Saunders, C. (1959). Care of the dying: The problem of euthanasia, 1-6. *Nursing Times* 55:960-961, 994-995, 1031-32, 1067-69, 1091-92, 1129-30.

Scott, C.A. (1896). Old age and death. *American Journal of Psychology* 8:67-122.

Smith, D.K., A.M. Nehemkis, and R.A. Charter. (1983-84). Fear of death, death attitudes and religious conviction in the terminally ill. *International Journal of Psychiatry in Medicine* 13:221-232.

Swenson, W.M. (1961). Attitudes toward death in an aged population. *Journal of Gerontology* 16:49-52.

Thorson, J.A., and F.C. Powell. (1989). Death anxiety and religion in an older male sample. *Psychological Reports* 64 (3, Pt. 1):985-986.

_____ (1990). Meanings of death an intrinsic religiosity. *Journal of Clinical Psychology* 46:379-391.

Weissman, A.D. (1972). *On Dying and Denying*. New York: Behavioral Publications.

Williams, R.L., and S. Cole. (1968). Religiosity, generalized anxiety, and apprehension concerning death. *Journal of Social Psychology* 78:111-117.

Wittkowski, J., and I. Baumgartner. (1977). Religiosity and attitude toward death and dying in elderly persons. *Zeitschrift fur Gerontologie* 10(1):61-68.

Yalom, I.D. (1980). *Existential Psychotherapy*. NY: Basic Books.

Chapter 21

Suicide in Later Life

For I know the plans I have for you, says the Lord.
They are plans for good and not evil,
to give you a future and a hope.

–Jeremiah 29:11

The later years can be a time of deep enjoyment and relaxation, as responsibilities lessen and the pursuit of hobbies and interests previously put off becomes possible. As we have seen in previous chapters, however, it can also be a time of loneliness, pain and suffering. In the last chapter, we saw the tremendous drive that humans have to survive and escape death. Indeed, many activities during life are directed at avoiding death or coping with the fear that it arouses. Death anxiety is often so powerful that it can disable a person faced with the reality of their own fragile mortality. Nevertheless, there comes a time and set of circumstances for some individuals when the pain associated with living becomes so great that it exceeds the fear of dying and impels them to pursue their own death with undeterred resolution. The decision to embark on this latter course invariably occurs in a setting of enormous emotional pain or unbearable fear. In older persons, this decision is seldom made on the spur of the moment or after a single painful event; rather, suicide in the elderly is often "a reaction to a total life situation" (Barter 1969). Often these persons have endured months and sometimes years of suffering. Numerous other avenues of relief have often been sought without success. After repeated failures, however, hope diminishes and the will to live disappears.

PREVALENCE

The importance of suicide as a problem in late life is demonstrated by its prevalence (Blazer, Bachar, and Manton 1986). More than 8000 persons over age 60 commit suicide each year in the United States; this figure makes up almost 25% of all suicides, a proportion substantially higher than the percentage of elders in the population (Centers for Disease Control 1988). The suicide rate in the United States for 1983 was 12.1 per 100,000 for the nation as a whole, compared with 19.2 per 100,000 for persons age 65 or over (National Center for Health Statistics 1985). Suicide ranks among the top ten causes of death in the elderly, and is third among causes of death not resulting from medical illness. Of particular concern is that recent reports indicate increasing rates of suicide among older persons in this country. Meehan, Saltzman, and Sattin (1991) calculated age-specific suicide rates for the years 1980 through 1986 from data collected by the National Center for Health Statistics. While rates among the elderly declined from 1933 to 1980, between 1980 and 1986 rates increased by over 20%; the increase among elderly white males was 23% and among elderly Black males was 42%. The reversal in the trend of declining suicide rates in the elderly is poorly understood; however, it underscores the seriousness of the problem in this age group.

RISK FACTORS

Men age 85 or over have the highest risk, with rates ranging from 50 to 61 per 100,000/year; elderly white males age 65 or older have three times the risk of older Black males (46 vs. 16 per 100,000/year) (Meehan, Saltzman, and Sattin 1991). Of even greater concern is that the suicide rate in older white males is increasing (72 per 100,000 in 1988). Compared with aged Blacks or females, older white males in American society apparently suffer more severely from loss of social status, power, money, and role relationships formerly provided by their work (Maris 1969; McIntosh and Santos 1981). The suicide rate in older Black males, however, has tripled since the 1960s for unknown reasons (Koenig and Blazer 1992). Perhaps Blacks are now suffering losses that were once denied, having never been part of their experience in an earlier age. Older women have lower suicide rates than men, and older Black women have the lowest rates (only one to three per 100,000/year between 1980 and 1986) (Meehan, Saltzman, and Sattin 1991). Of particular interest here, is that older Black women are more religiously involved than any other age-race-sex group in America (Princeton Religion Research Center 1982). Religious involvement may contribute to the intense support networks and strong human relationships that characterize the older Black community, which may be protective against suicide (Seiden 1981).

At greatest risk for suicide are elders with mental illnesses such as depression, alcohol dependence, schizophrenia, and all forms of cognitive impairment (chronic or acute). Approximately 15% of all persons with depressive disorders commit suicide to end their life. When depression and other mental disorders (like alcohol abuse) coexist in older men, the risk of suicide increases dramatically. The most common definable precipitants of suicide among the elderly involve some type of loss; less frequent (than in younger persons) are job problems, financial problems, and family relationships. Married persons, regardless of age, have the lowest rates, whereas those who are widowed, divorced, or living alone have the highest (Osgood 1987). Between 1981 and 1986, the suicide rate among divorced elderly men increased from 75 to 110 per 100,000 (Meehan, Saltzman, and Sattin 1991). High income appears to protect against suicide risk, even after controlling for other variables.

Loss of physical health is a major risk factor for suicide in later life (MacKenzie and Popkin 1987). Elders with depression and organic brain syndrome are at high risk, since judgment is impaired and there is more impulsivity. Suicide rates also go up in patients with neurological disorders, disorders associated with pain or dyspnea (shortness of breath), terminal illnesses, and those with other symptoms unresponsive to treatment. Congestive heart failure and chronic obstructive pulmonary disease are primary examples (Frierson 1991). This is sad, because treatments exist today which are capable of relieving even the most distressing of physical symptoms like pain, nausea, and shortness of breath. Seeking appropriate medical treatment, then, in most cases is a better solution than taking one's life (see Chapter 22).

Of particular concern is that rates of suicide in medically ill elders almost certainly underestimate the true prevalence. Medication noncompliance, refusal of life-saving surgical therapies, or neglect of medical care, may result in many intentional deaths which are falsely recorded as due to "natural causes" (Rodin et al. 1981). Because of the strong association between suicide and physical illness, the first line of prevention of elder suicide lies with the primary care physician. It has been reported that as many as 75% of geriatric suicides have visited a physician within one month of death; in fact, one-third to one-half of such elders may have seen a doctor in the past week (Miller 1978; Foster and Burke 1985). Thus, the health professional is often in an ideal position to identify the suicidal elder, provide proper pharmacologic treatment for their condition, and/or assist them in finding social support or economic aid needed to change or adapt to their circumstances. Because of the serious nature by which elders pursue suicide, health care professionals seldom get a second chance at prevention. While the ratio of attempts to completed suicides is 20:1 in the general population, by comparison it is 4:1 in the elderly (Parkin and Stengal 1965).

PSYCHOLOGICAL FACTORS

Explanations for suicide have included psychodynamic, epidemiological, sociological, cultural, and psychological ones. I will now examine psychological factors leading to the decision to commit suicide. Research and clinical experience have uncovered certain psychological factors that are common in the vast majority of suicides (Schneidman 1990). First, suicide is always associated with a problem. The person finds themself in a situation he or she cannot get out of; in other words, the problem is viewed as insoluble. Second, the suicidal person experiences a *flow of consciousness* which is deemed unbearable or unacceptable. There is a violation of the person's ego ideal: "I have Alzheimer's disease and I cannot and will not tolerate this." There is a seemingly impenetrable sense of helplessness and hopelessness. Third, consciousness is constricted and narrowed, so that the person can see only one way out; alternative choices become blurred and inaccessible to reason. The fourth, and perhaps the major, underlying stimulus to suicide is psychological pain. It is this latter problem that I will now address.

Psychological pain involves unmet or frustrated psychological needs. These included the need for achievement, affiliation, aggression, autonomy, dependence, dominance, exhibition, harm-avoidance, shame-avoidance, inviolacy, nurturance, order, play, succor, or understanding. Human character is largely determined by the pattern or relative importance of these psychological needs; indeed, reasons for living are based on them. When the more important of these needs is frustrated, psychological pain intensifies. Psychological pain differs from suffering. While all persons experience pain, not all suffer to the same degree. Suffering increases as hope, meaning, and purposefulness decrease. The ability to tolerate suffering varies from person to person; this ability is closely related to the threshold for suicide.

RELIGION AND SUICIDE

During research and patient care activity, I have had the occasion to ask many hundreds of depressed older persons about suicidal thoughts. I always ask what would prevent them from ending their life. Many give a religious response. Studies that have examined the relationship between suicide or other life-threatening behaviors and religion have likewise found an inverse association. Some of these will now be reviewed.

Over a century ago, in his famous work *Suicide*, Emile Durkheim noted that suicide rates were lowest among persons involved in social groups, particularly religious groups which shared a common identity and tradition (Spaulding and Simpson 1951). Stack (1983) found that countries with the lowest suicide rate were also those which published the most religious books. Martin (1984) examined suicide rates in the United States between 1972 and 1978; he found significantly lower rates of suicide among frequent church attenders. Nelson (1977) examined indirect life-threatening behaviors (pulling out intravenous lines, refusals of medication, and other self-injurious acts) among 58 chronically ill men hospitalized at the Wadsworth VA in Los Angeles. He found an inverse relationship

between these behaviors and intensity of religious belief, concluding that among elders with severe illness, religion provided a source
of comfort unavailable by other means.

Johnson and colleagues (1980) likewise found strength of
religious belief and frequency of church attendance to be inversely
related to both suicide and euthanasia in a cross-national sample of
1,530 Americans of all ages. In this study, persons age 65 or older
were much more likely than younger persons to reject suicide or
euthanasia for persons with incurable illness. Since depression and
alcohol abuse are the two conditions most strongly related to suicide, the inverse relationship between these disorders and religiosity may further explain religion's role in prevention of suicide.

Based on these studies and my clinical experience with patients, I
am convinced that strong religious belief is a major deterrent to
suicide in later life. One reason for this is that religious cognitions
help to diminish the emotional pain driving persons to kill themselves. Even in cases of severe depression, participation in religious
services or reading of scripture may provide a temporary relief. In
addition, strong prohibitions against suicide which exist in both
Christian and Jewish traditions may further discourage elders from
taking this course. According to some early Christians (St. Thomas
Aquinas and St. Augustine), suicide was an unpardonable sin, since
it usurped God's power over man's life and death; furthermore, the
person would not survive to ask forgiveness and thus died unrepen-
tant (Dods 1950). In my opinion, this view is perhaps a bit harsh.
For some religious elders (and their families), however, this act
could mean eternal separation from God and from their loved ones.

For the religious elder, then, it is likely that only the most extreme intolerable pain or mental exhaustion could push him or her
to commit suicide. One might argue that at this level of distress,
normal cognitive functioning becomes disturbed and mental illness
intervenes. The decision to choose death over life, then, because it
is contrary to the most fundamental of human drives and value
systems, is in many cases–perhaps most–an irrational choice.

Studies have shown that 89% to 100% of patients committing
suicide have a psychiatric diagnosis. Reich and Kelly (1976) ana-
lyzed 17 suicides among 70,404 consecutively admitted general
hospital patients; 15 of these patients had concurrent psychiatric

diagnoses. The remaining two patients had cancer; both before committing suicide complained that the staff had given up on them. There is much that health professionals can do to rekindle hope and revive the will to live. And not until all resources–including spiritual ones–are exhausted, does the possibility of a rational suicide exist. Studies have shown that hopelessness is the key linking depression with suicidal behavior (Beck, Kovacs, and Weisman 1975). Because of religion's ability to instill hope, it may help deter this most desperate of all acts.

One possibility not previously considered is that of an ethical suicide or a suicide committed for "higher" reasons. For instance, the dying man with melanoma whose illness will bankrupt his wife's estate and cause her to live for decades in poverty because of the expenses associated with his last month of life, may want to opt for suicide. Even in such circumstances, however, one must be careful about the true motives of the individual. While the last month of life is often the most costly, this is most often due to the use of "high tech" medicine or other expensive treatments that are or should be optional. Patients in such a condition should be allowed to forgo such interventions, and instead choose relatively inexpensive comfort measures that focus on pain relief and meet emotional and spiritual needs in a hospice or at home. My point is that dying does not have to be outrageously expensive, and other options–besides suicide–may accomplish the same aims. Often, however, depression or other psychiatric illness is the true driving force toward suicide and ethical-sounding reasons are given to rationalize and justify the act.

In the situation where a person's motives are truly out of concern for others and no other options exist, it is comprehensible that ethical reasons might underlie a suicide. It is my opinion, however, that such cases are decidedly rare. Careful research needs to be done to determine the frequency of ethical suicides and how to distinguish them from the vastly greater number of suicides driven by reversible depression, pain, fear, anger, and emotional exhaustion.

In a case where mental illness does precipitate suicide, it is difficult to imagine that a merciful and loving God would condemn a person who is incapable of making a rational, responsible decision. This would seem particularly true in cases where the elder has spent most of his or her adult life in religious service (a prime example being Mrs. Smith in Chapter 20). Even our courts of law do not hold incompetent persons responsible for their acts, and may dismiss charges on the grounds of insanity.

Robert Wennberg (1989), professor of philosophy at Westmont College (Santa Barbara, California) and an ordained Presbyterian minister, has written a timely and well-balanced expose on this quite difficult and complex topic (*Terminal Choices*, pp. 39-75). His approach is soundly moral, yet flexible and adaptable to the individual and their unique situation. Wennberg examines the obligation to preserve and protect life, and discusses the circumstances in which living may become so burdensome that one is relieved of this obligation and may legitimately and morally end life (not without some risk, however).

Christian and Jewish Teachings

The Bible is surprisingly silent when it comes to the topic of suicide. Wennberg (1989) notes that suicide was not a serious problem among the Jews. In that society, the idea of suicide as a moral possibility was not even seriously considered, and thus needed no prohibition. Certain scriptures, however, do address the topic even if indirectly. These include the following:

> You shall not murder. (Exodus 20:13 ASV)

> Do you not know that you are a temple of God,
> and that the Spirit of God dwells in you?
> If any man destroys the temple of God,
> God will destroy him, for the temple of God is holy,
> and that is what you are. (1 Corinthians 3:16-17, ASV)

> Or do you not know that your body is a temple of the Holy Spirit who is in you, whom you have from God, and that you are not your own? For you have been bought with a price: therefore glorify God in your body. (1 Corinthians 6:19-20, ASV)

Examples of suicide in scripture typically culminated the lives of persons who had turned away from God. A primary example is

King Saul (1 Samuel 31:3-5; 2 Samuel 1:9; 1 Chronicles 10:4-5). Thus, the overall silence in scripture on the topic should in no way be interpreted as indifference or approval. Perhaps even more explicitly than the Christian Bible, the Jewish Talmud presents strong and clear prohibitions against suicide. A. Cohen (1982) summarizes the attitude expressed in the Talmud by the following statement:

> The time of death is determined by God, and none dare anticipate His decree. Suicide was regarded with the utmost abhorrence and denounced as a heinous sin. . . . Where self-harm ends in suicide all teachers agree that it is forbidden. (p. 75)

Likewise, the great Jewish historian Josephus (37 AD-100 AD), arguing along the same lines as the early Christian theologians, maintained that suicide was contrary to man's natural instinct to preserve life, and that it represented contempt for God's gift of life; because God gave life, he should be the only one to end it (Williamson 1959).

To avoid confusion, the difference between suicide, martyrdom, and taking one's life for religious reasons (Kiddush ha-shem) needs to be clarified. In martyrdom, a person willingly allows others to take his or her life in defense of their beliefs or allegiances. In Kiddush ha-shem ("sanctification of the divine nature"), the Jewish believer is to do everything in his or her power to glorify the name of God, even if this includes taking his or her own life (based on Leviticus 22:31-32). According to Wennberg (1989), when ending one's life in such circumstances, "one affirms in death the values and the commitment to God by which one lived . . . suicide [in such cases] is not a repudiation of those values but an affirmation of them" (pp. 51-52).

In conclusion, then, according to both Christian and Jewish theology, there is little justification for suicide as a way out of life's problems. As Wennberg points out, suicide of this type–in any circumstance–is not without risk from a religious or moral standpoint; in certain situations, however, that risk may be lower than in others.

Suicide and Other World Religions

Research on suicide in religions outside of the Christian or Jewish traditions is scant. Some investigators, however, have examined suicide rates across broad religious groups such as Moslems, Hindus, Protestants, Catholics, and Jews in the Netherlands (Jasperse 1976), Canada (Malla and Hoenig 1979), India (Bhatia et al. 1987; Adityanjee 1986; Sharma and Gopalakrishna 1978), Great Britain (Morphew 1968), Afghanistan (Gobar 1970), Nigeria (Asuni 1962), South Africa (Gangat, Naidoo and Wessels 1987), Israel (Modan, Nissenkorn, and Lewkowski 1970), Japan (Iga 1981; Takahsashi 1989), and other countries (Stack 1983). None, however, have focused exclusively on the elderly.

The findings have varied widely between studies. This is not surprising given the methodological problems with such research. First, different cultures clearly differ in their acceptability of suicide; second, underreporting of suicide is problematic in many underdeveloped countries; third, members of minority groups are nearly always more likely to have higher suicide rates than the general population; and fourth, the inclusion of many inactive members in broad religious categories (up to 80-90% in some groups) renders results virtually meaningless.

Few world religions consider the taking of one's life as acceptable because of overwhelming personal problems. This point is certainly true among Moslem countries, and to a certain extent, is true in Chinese and Japanese cultures as well. As in the case of Judaism, the only exceptions are suicide for religious reasons, for one's "honor," or for one's country in time of war.

SUMMARY

Suicide rates among older persons in this country are rising. Those at greatest risk are white, unmarried, older men with health problems. Suicide is almost invariably associated with preexisting mental illness–most often depression, alcohol abuse, and schizophrenia. The suicidal person's consciousness becomes so severely constricted that he or she cannot see any other way out of their intolerable situation other than to end their life. No society or major religious tradition prescribes suicide as a solution to life's problems. Having a strong religious belief is a deterrent to suicide for many persons. The Judeo-Christian tradition provides a framework by which suffering can have meaning and purpose, and gives a promise of a better life in the next world for those who willingly and courageously bear their crosses in this one.

REFERENCES

Adityanjee (1986). Suicide attempts and suicides in India: Cross-cultural aspects. *International Journal of Social Psychiatry*, 32:64-73.

Asuni, T. (1962). Suicide in Western Nigeria. *British Medical Journal* (October 27):1091-1096.

Barter, J.T. (1969). Self-destructive behavior in adolescents and adults: Similarities and differences. In Suicide Among the American Indians: Two Workshops. U.S. DHEW, PHS Publication No. 1903. Washington, DC: GPO.

Beck, A.T., M. Kovacs, and A. Weisman. (1975). Hopelessness and suicidal behavior. *Journal of the American Medical Association* 234:1146-1149.

Bhatia, S.C., M.H. Khan, R.P. Mediratta, and A. Sharma. (1987). High risk suicide factors across cultures. *International Journal of Social Psychiatry* 33:226-236.

Blazer, D.G., J.R. Bachar, and K.G. Manton. (1986). Suicide in late life: Review and commentary. *Journal of the American Geriatrics Society* 34:519-525.

Centers for Disease Control. (1988). *Suicide Surveillance*. Atlanta, GA: Centers for Disease Control.

Cohen, A. (1982). *Everyman's Talmud*. NY: E.P. Dutton.

Dods, M. (1950). *Augustine, The City of God*. NY: Modern Library (Bk 1:24).

Foster, B.G., and W.J. Burke. (1985). Assessing and treating the suicidal elderly. *Family Practice Recertification* 7(11):33-45.

Frierson, R.L. (1991). Suicide attempts by the old and the very old. *Archives of Internal Medicine* 151:141-144.

Gangat, A.E., L.R. Naidoo, and W.H. Wessels. (1987). Suicide in South African Indians. *South African Medical Journal* 1:169-171.

Gobar, A.H. (1970). Suicide in Afghanistan. *British Journal of Psychiatry* 116:493-496.

Iga, M. (1981). Suicide of Japanese youth. *Suicide and Life-Threatening Behavior* 11:17-31.

Jasperse, C.W.G. (1976). Self-destruction and religion. *Mental Health and Society* 3:154-168.

Johnson, D., S.D. Fitch, J.P. Alston, and W.A. McIntosh. (1980). Acceptance of conditional suicide and euthanasia among adult Americans. *Suicide and Life Threatening Behavior* 10(3):157-165.

Koenig, H.G., and D.G. Blazer. (1992). Mood disorders and suicide. In *Handbook of Mental Health and Aging*, edited by J.E. Birren. NY: Academic Press, pp. 379-407.

MacKenzie, T.B., and M.K. Popkin. (1987). Suicide in the medical patient. *International Journal of Psychiatry in Medicine* 17:3-22.

Malla, A., and J. Hoenig. (1979). Suicide in Newfoundland and Labrador. *Canadian Journal of Psychiatry* 24:139-146.

Maris, R.W. (1969). *Social Forces in Urban Suicide*. NY: Dorsey Press.

Martin, W.T. (1984). Religiosity and United States suicide rates, 1972-1978. *Journal of Clinical Psychology* 40:1166-1169.

McIntosh, J.L., and J.F. Santos. (1981). Suicide among minority elderly: A preliminary investigation. *Suicide and Life Threatening Behavior* 11:151-166.

Meehan, P.J., L.E. Saltzman, and R.W. Sattin. (1991). Suicides among older United States residents: Epidemiologic characteristics and trends. *American Journal of Public Health* 81:1198-1200.

Miller, M. (1978). Geriatric suicide: The Arizona study. *Gerontology* 18:488-492.

Modan, B., I. Nissenkorn, and S.R. Lewkowski. (1970). Suicide in a heterogeneous society. *British Journal of Psychiatry* 116:65-68.

Morphew, J.A. (1968). Religion and attempted suicide. *International Journal of Social Psychiatry* 14:188-192.

National Center for Health Statistics. (1985). Advance report of final mortality statistics, 1983. NCHS Monthly Vital Statistics Report 34 (6, Supplement 2).

Nelson, F.L. (1977). Religiosity and self-destructive crises in the institutionalized elderly. *Suicide and Life Threatening Behavior* 7:67-73.

New American Standard Bible. (1977). New York: Thomas Nelson Publishers.

Osgood, N.J. (1987). Suicide and the elderly. *Generations* 11(3):47-51.

Parkin, D., and E. Stengal. (1965). Incidence of suicide attempts in an urban community. *British Medical Journal* 2:133-134.

Princeton Religion Research Center. (1982). *Religion in America*. Princeton, NJ: Gallup Poll.

Reich, P., and M.J. Kelly. (1976). Suicide attempts by hospitalized medical and surgical patients. *New England Journal of Medicine* 294:298-301.

Rodin, G.M., J. Chmara, J. Ennis, S. Fenton, H. Locking, and K. Steinhouse. (1981). Stopping life-sustaining medical treatment: Psychiatric considerations in the termination of renal dialysis. *Canadian Journal of Psychiatry* 26: 540-44.

Seiden, R. (1981). Mellowing with age: Factors influencing nonwhite suicide rate. *International Journal of Aging and Human Development* 13:265-281.

Sharma, S.D., and R. Gopalakrishna. (1978). Suicide–a retrospective study in a culturally distinct community in India. *International Journal of Social Psychiatry* 24:13-18.

Schneidman, E.S. (1990). Suicide risk in the elderly. Audio-Digest Tape series. *Psychiatry* 19(23).

Spaulding, J.A., and G. Simpson. (1951). *Suicide* (authors' translation of Emile Durkheim, 1897). NY: Free Press.

Stack, S. (1983). The effect of religious commitment on suicide: A cross-national analysis. *Journal of Health and Social Behavior* 24:362-374.

Takahashi, Y. (1989). Mass suicide by members of the Japanese Friend of the Truth Church. *Suicide and Life-Threatening Behavior* 19:289-296.

Wennberg, R.N. (1989). *Terminal Choices: Euthanasia, Suicide, and the Right to Die*. Grand Rapids, MI: Eerdmans Publish Co.

Williamson, G.A. (1959). *Josephus, The Jewish War.* Harmondsworth, England: Penguin Books, pp. 209-210.

Chapter 22

Physician-Assisted Suicide

> I will neither give a deadly drug to anybody if asked for it, nor
> will I make a suggestion to this effect.
>
> *–Hippocratic Oath*

Physician-assisted suicide has become an avidly debated topic in recent years (Callahan 1988; Koenig 1993; Hastings Center Report 1992), and is now coming into even greater focus with the discovery of increasing suicide rates among the elderly (Chapter 21). In the face of a rapidly growing older population, increasing survival of elders with chronic health problems, and escalating costs of health care, there has been talk of limiting health care to conserve resources. Already, serious consideration has been given by America's leading ethicists to a system of rationing services based on age alone (Callahan 1987). Legalizing assisted-suicide might provide an alternative and easy solution to the economic crisis in our health care system that looms ahead.

If decriminalized under guidelines suggested by the majority of its advocates (self-determined, unrelievable suffering, terminal illness), physician assisted-suicide would affect only a small percent of dying persons. The concern, however, is that economic and societal pressures in the near future may expand its use to a much larger group that includes defective newborns, comatose and other incompetent patients, the demented elderly, and the mentally handicapped. These are not exaggerated concerns, and are currently under active consideration by the Royal Dutch Medical Association (KNMG) (Hastings Center Report 1992).

Assisted-suicide has received much recent publicity by TV specials such as *Last Wish* (the story of NBC News correspondent Betty Rollin's assistance in her mother's suicide) and a short segment on *Current Affair* (the story of Dick Bauer who gave his mother a gun which she used to kill herself the day after she was incorrectly diagnosed with cancer–and later found to have a treatable liver infection). More than any other event, however, the actions of Jack Kevorkian have attracted media attention. In June of 1990, Dr. Kevorkian[1] assisted the suicide of Janet Adkins, an elderly woman who in the past year had been tentatively diagnosed with Alzheimer's disease. Later in October of 1991, defying a court injunction against the use of his machine, Kevorkian assisted two *nonterminally* ill, middle-aged women in taking their lives (43-year-old Sherry Miller with multiple sclerosis and 58-year-old Marjorie Watts with pelvic disease); and in May 1992 did the same for another 54-year-old woman with multiple sclerosis (and others since then).

WHAT IS PHYSICIAN-ASSISTED SUICIDE (PAS)?

First of all, let us examine what PAS is not. It is not pulling plugs to ventilators, removing feeding tubes or intravenous lines, failing to institute life-saving treatments (such as antibiotics, medications, surgery, and so forth), limiting food or water, or any other action or nonaction which allows "nature" to take her course. All of these are examples of "passive euthanasia." PAS involves a person taking their own life (committing suicide) with the active assistance of a physician. In cases of non-physician assisted suicide, the accomplice can be a friend, a relative, or a health care provider (aide, nurse, pharmacist).

In PAS, the "assistance" can take two general forms which are distinct, but closely related: (1) the physician may provide the suicidal person with the means to commit the act (prescribe pills or provide an injectable solution and a device to inject it as in the Kevorkian cases), or (2) the physician may carry out the patient's wish to die by injecting or otherwise administering a lethal medication (also called voluntary active euthanasia). A distinction between

---

1. A pathologist and one-time advocate of using prisoners for scientific experimentation.

these two forms of assistance has been vigorously defended (Watts and Howell 1992). In *theory*, there is a difference between actually committing an act and providing someone else with the means to do that act. In practice, however, the separation blurs. If one can justify giving an actively suicidal patient a lethal dose of medication which he or she then takes to end their life, it becomes difficult to ignore the desperate pleas of a suffering but severely ill patient who wants to die but is unable to swallow medication, is too weak to physically inject the medication him or herself, or simply lacks the emotional fortitude to carry out this act without more active assistance. Certainly, if it is ethical and moral to allow the first form of PAS, it would seem permissible to allow the second. For this reason, in arguments for or against PAS, I will lump these two forms of assisted-suicide into one. This is precisely the approach taken by the KNMG in 1984 in Holland which recommended that the distinction between euthanasia and assisted suicide be abolished on the grounds that the intent in both cases was to bring about the patient's death (de Wachter 1992).

What is the purpose of PAS?

The intention is (1) to relieve severe and intolerable suffering in a patient who will die soon anyway, (2) to maximize the quality of life (versus quantity), (3) to enhance the dignity of dying, and (4) to give the patient ultimate control over their life (maximize autonomy). This topic represents a controversial and complex example of a patient's right to self-determination which some believe includes the right to end one's life by suicide (and seek the assistance of others in doing so).

Who is a potential candidate?

In most arguments for the legalization of PAS, candidates must fulfill certain conditions. The person must have a terminal illness with only a few weeks or months to live, must be in severe pain or experiencing other intolerable and intractable discomforts (shortness of breath, nausea, and so forth), must have intact judgment and reasoning enabling them to make a responsible decision to end their life, and make a voluntary request to a physician for aid in dying. Thus, the conditions are (1) terminal illness, (2) intolerable and intractable suffering, (3) rational (unimpaired reasoning), and (4) voluntary request. In some instances, however, PAS has also been advocated for patients whose death is not imminent (Alzheimer's disease or other chronic illnesses) and even in those who are not rational (the incompetent).

Where is PAS practiced?

PAS (either form) is not legal anywhere in the Western hemisphere. While it is practiced routinely in the Netherlands, it is still against the law–although the law is not enforced. Between 2,000 and 10,000 persons per year are assisted in their dying by Dutch physicians. The Remmelink Committee's report in 1991 indicated that 18% of all deaths in that country resulted from high doses of opiates administered by physicians in an attempt to relieve suffering; 3% of all deaths were a consequence of PAS (Van der Maas et al. 1991). In the United States, regardless of circumstances, PAS is currently against the law; individual states, however, vary in the extent to which they prosecute such cases (Michigan being the most lax in this regard). Initiatives to make PAS legal have recently been voted on in Washington state and California; in both states, they were defeated by an identical slim margin of 54% to 46%. If either initiative had been approved, the United States would have become the first and only place in the world where euthanasia is legal. Neither initiative required evaluation by a mental health professional to rule out treatable depression (the most common cause of a suicide in the general population) before complying with patient wishes. Other initiatives are currently being drafted for the electorate in Florida, Michigan, and New Hampshire. A recent (1990) poll in Michigan by the Detroit Free Press found that 58% of residents there wanted a bill allowing PAS while 42% were opposed (*Psychiatric Times* 1992).

WHO IS IN FAVOR OF PAS?

The Hemlock Society has been campaigning for the legalization of PAS in the United States since 1980, when it was founded by

Englishman Derek Humphry in Los Angeles, California. This organization's membership has grown steadily to a number that in 1992 exceeded 40,000. Humphry recently stepped down as its leader and primary spokesman because of the negative image which has surrounded him since the suicide of his second wife.[2] Humphry claims to have assisted both of his former wives in their suicides and has written several books on the subject, the most recent one being *Final Exit* (1991). Two months after *Newsweek* did a cover story about the book (August 26, 1991), almost 150,000 copies were on order in bookstores where it had sold out; by January 1992, over 500,000 Americans had bought the book. *Final Exit* has been marketed as a "how to do it" manual for those wanting to end their lives.

National surveys indicate that between 50 and 60% of Americans favor legalization of PAS. A recent survey by the Harvard School of Public Health (reported in the Boston Globe), reported that 61% of all Americans indicated that they would vote for the Washington State initiative legalizing PAS (Lawton 1991). Fifty-two percent said they would consider some option to end their life if they had incurable illness with a great deal of pain. Thus, it appears that a majority of the American public wants it. Even more notable is that 49% of "born again" Christians in that survey said that they would vote in favor of the Washington initiative.

Why Are They in Favor?

Reasons given for favoring PAS in the Harvard survey included the following: don't want to be a burden (47%), don't want to live in pain (20%), don't want to be dependent on machines (19%), and don't want to live a restricted life (12%). These responses indicate confusion among the lay public on what PAS really is. When talk-

---

2. While Mr. Humphry has been heralded as a brilliant planner and great leader, serious concerns have been raised about the ethics of his personal life, particularly the treatment of his second wife after her diagnosis of breast cancer. Prior to committing suicide, Ann Humphry left a note saying "You [referring to Derek] have done everything conceivable to precipitate my death" (Editorial 1991). A book has now been published that details this tragic situation: *Deadly Compassion: The Death of Ann Humphry and the Truth About Euthanasia*. NY: William Morrow & Co.

ing with patients and older persons about this issue, I frequently hear responses such as "It makes sense not to keep people artificially alive and prolong their suffering by hooking them up to machines when they should be allowed to die." PAS, as noted earlier, has nothing whatsoever to do with either failing to institute life support measures or the withdrawal of them. Rather, PAS involves a physician actively and willfully either providing a suicidal patient with the means to commit the act him or herself, or involves the physician taking an action that causes the immediate death of the patient. This confusion over terms may at least partly explain the high response rates in favor of PAS reported by the public in the Harvard survey and others.

Among those who understand what PAS involves and approve of it, true compassion and a desire to relieve suffering (or be spared from it themselves) are primary motivations. They argue that "the quality of life is more important than its quantity," that "the right to take one's own life is as important as the right to life," and emphasize "death with dignity" (Palmore 1991). If the essence of being human involves the ability to think, love, and have aesthetic experiences, then when these capacities are lost during terminal illness, the person loses much of what it is to be human. This is a powerful argument and one that is difficult to refute. Nevertheless, there are serious flaws in this line of reasoning.

First of all, there is no way to rationally prove that one has a "right to end one's life." This is simply an opinion, and not an undisputable right. Limits on persons' rights to choose are not uncommon in this society. For instance, we often do not allow persons to swim in areas where a lifeguard is not present. People must pay social security taxes whether they want to or not. Human sacrifice is not permitted as part of religious ceremonies, even in circumstances where all parties have consented; the same goes for pistol dueling. Limited resources, protection of public health, or avoidance of harm to others are frequently reasons given for restricting autonomy. While decisions to limit patient autonomy should be difficult ones, they nevertheless sometimes need to be made.

This is especially true in the case of PAS where the "right" to take one's life impacts not only on the suicidal person, but also on others; as John Donne wrote, "No man is an island." The American Association of Suicidology has determined that every suicide affects the lives of an average of six persons; thus, suicide is an act whose repercussions extend far beyond the individual him or herself. The term "assisted-suicide" itself indicates the involvement of other people. Even if a physician or family member freely agrees to assist, it still places that person in the role of an accomplice to an action which concludes in the direct or indirect taking of a life. Does the suicidal person have a right to place others in a predicament of having to agree or refuse to participate in such an act (and if they agree, face the unpredictable psychological and social consequences that might follow)? What about family members who disagree with the patient's decision to end their life? What about their rights? In such circumstances, it is highly unlikely that all family members will be in uniform agreement on this controversial issue, and deep conflict within the family may result.

In cases of assisted-suicide where a family member acts as the accomplice, there is anecdotal evidence for a negative long-term impact on mental health. While much publicity has been made over Betty Rollin's heroic efforts in assisting her mother's suicide, her mother's death still plagues Betty to the extent that she does not keep a single photograph or other reminder of her mother in her house (six years after her death) (Schneider and Carswell 1992). Studies are needed to examine the long-term impact of assisted suicide on those who participate in this act.

The third issue is "death with dignity." Is it really more dignified to take one's life for fear of suffering or because of an inability to endure a terminal illness? In a time when many of the unpleasant symptoms of dying can be relieved with high quality medical care (as will be discussed below), the notion of suicide as a dignified death becomes less tenable. There was a day when "dignity" meant the ability to tolerate pain, to maintain emotional equilibrium and a positive attitude, to be more concerned about the effects of one's actions on others than on oneself, to be willing to suffer because human life is valuable and worth fighting for. Sufficient credit and recognition is seldom given today to those who choose this more courageous route. Suicide is more an act of desperation and fear than it is a pursuit of dignity. It is understandable, however, that even the most heroic acts of endurance and bravery can become overwhelmed by the exhaustion brought on by chronic suffering and pain in the face of little or no hope for recovery. Nevertheless, the notion that suicide confers "dignity" on the dying process is not beyond debate.

What motivates a person with chronic or terminal illness to choose death over life? Often, such decisions are finalized even before suffering has begun (as in the case of Janet Adkins). Derek Humphry's first wife, Jean, may have killed herself out of fear, since it was never definitely proven that she even had breast cancer. It is *fear*–fear of the suffering that might occur, fear of loss of control, fear of loss of self-esteem, and most importantly fear of abandonment by others and loneliness (Weissman 1972; Becker 1973)–that drives people to this extreme and final act. Proponents of PAS capitalize on these fears by describing worst case scenarios and de-emphasizing available medical, psychological, and social interventions that can help relieve such fears (see below).

In the setting of good hospice care, then, how many terminally ill patients actually suffer so intolerably that they request assistance with dying? Surprisingly, hospice physicians report only a small number of such requests (Parkes 1978; Lynn 1990; Gillett 1988). Joanne Lynn–hospice physician, geriatrician, and leading American ethicist at George Washington University–reports the following:

> One of us (JL) has cared for over 1,000 hospice patients, and only two of these patients seriously and repeatedly requested physician assistance in active euthanasia. Even these two patients did not seek another health care provider when it was explained that their requests could not be honored. (Teno and Lynn 1991, p. 828)

WHO IS AGAINST PAS?

There are five major groups that tend to oppose PAS in the United States: physicians, ethicists, the elderly, advocates of the mentally ill and mentally-retarded, and religious organizations. These are, in fact, the groups most likely to be affected by laws legalizing PAS.

Physicians

Although there is not a great deal of systematically collected information on physicians' attitudes toward PAS, what data do exist suggest that these attitudes are unfavorable. Evidence for physician opposition comes from the state of Washington, where the state medical society voted against Initiative 119 by an overwhelming 114 to 22.

A group of physicians in favor of assisted suicide (Watts, Howell, and Priefer 1992) did a survey of 727 ABIM-certified internist geriatricians on their attitudes toward assisting suicide of dementia patients. Only 14% said Dr. Kevorkians's assistance in Janet Adkins' suicide was morally justifiable. Likewise, only 26% favored easing restrictions on PAS of competent, non-depressed dementia patients and only 21% would themselves consider assisting suicide of such patients.

How many doctors in the United States have actually assisted patients in ending their lives? Surveys of physicians in this country have shown that between 10% and 20% have "deliberately taken action to cause a patient's death" (American Society of Internal Medicine 1992). The results of these surveys, however, must be interpreted cautiously because many physicians who admit to such actions have done so not with the intention of ending life, but rather with a primary goal of relieving suffering. The intent to relieve suffering is very different from PAS, where the explicit and immediate intention of the physician is to actively assist in the termination of a life. This distinction is not a matter of semantics. In PAS, *intent* is everything. A primary and indisputable calling of the physician is to relieve suffering. Attempts to relieve suffering by administering morphine, sedatives, or other analgesics may inadvertently result in the shortening or ending of a frail, terminal patient's life. This is quite different, however, from intentionally acting as an accomplice in the patient's death.

Physicians in America and abroad have spoken out strongly against PAS. Richard Fenigsen (1990), a Dutch cardiologist who has witnessed the progress of assisted suicide in the Netherlands for the previous 18 years, observes the following:

I happen to live in a country where doctors do, in fact, 'listen to old people who express the wish to die,' where euthanasia is practiced regularly and–in most cases–without retribution. And I am convinced that, far from viewing this practice as a humane and benevolent service, many older people in Holland feel frightened of their physicians, of the very people who should be dedicated to preserving their lives. Moreover, I believe that these fears have a basis in reality. (p. 52)

Robert Butler (1990), chairman of the Department of Geriatrics and Adult Development at Mount Sinai Medical Center (NY) and first chief of the National Institute on Aging, responds to the Kevorkian case of physician-assisted suicide in following editorial published in *Geriatrics*:

We must distinguish between this case of "physician-assisted suicide" and our very real need to develop appropriate "therapies of dying" in cases where the prolongation of life would be against the patient's wishes, ineffective, and painful. By any reasonable measure, Dr. Kevorkian's role in Mrs. Adkins' death was wrong. Physicians whose role is to preserve life, should not be empowered to end it as well. The doctor-patient relationship depends on trust, and that essential bond would be gravely compromised if doctors were given license to function as executioners. Furthermore, we have to be careful not to fuel the fires of today's over-zealous cost cutters, who might welcome assisted suicide as a remedy for the expense of treating the very ill. (p. 13)

Perhaps the most solid evidence for strong physician opposition to the legalization of PAS in the United States comes from the published policies of professional medical organizations concerning this issue. Both the American Medical Association and the American Geriatrics Society have been outspoken in their opinions that physicians should not be allowed to actively assist patients in prematurely ending their lives (AMA Judicial Council 1983; President's Commission 1983; American Geriatrics Society 1991; Teno and Lynn 1991). These policies make no distinction between forms of physician-assisted suicide (e.g., whether the patient or the physician actually carries out the act). This is clear from the recent position statement by the American Geriatrics Society (1991):

> The current legal prohibition of physician assistance in active voluntary euthanasia and suicide should not be changed (p. 826)

One question which needs to be addressed is why *physicians* should be involved in the first place? Why not a pharmacist, a judge or other legally appointed non-health care provider? The judicial system is currently the only body during peacetime that is authorized to kill (as in the case of capital punishment). An alternative system might work as follows. The physician could write out something that states that the patient has a terminal condition and is experiencing discomfort that is difficult to relieve apart from total elimination of consciousness. Others could then decide on whether to give the patient assistance in taking their life. This leaves the physician in the traditional role of assessor, healer, and preserver of life.

Medical Ethicists

Many of America's most renowned medical ethicists have joined the medical community in denouncing PAS (Sprung 1990; Callahan 1989; Wolf 1989; Singer and Siegler 1990; Gaylin 1988; Foot 1977; Kamisar 1978). Even Daniel Callahan, author of *Setting Limits* (1987) and proponent of limiting health care to persons on the basis of age, has advised against this practice. Callahan, director of the Hastings Center and America's foremost medical ethicist, warns that unintended symbolic messages may be delivered to certain population groups in a society where PAS is accepted and practiced. Elders may come to feel that "old age can have no meaning and significance if accompanied by decline, pain and despair" and that young persons may come to believe "that pain is not to be endured, that community cannot be found for the old, and that a life that is not marked by good health, by hope and vitality, is not a life worth living" (pp. 193-197). Callahan's strong opposition to PAS is explicit in a statement made at the December 1990 meeting of international experts on euthanasia at the Institute for Bioethics in Maastricht, the Netherlands:

> To legitimize active euthanasia is to add a new category of killing. It is to add indeed the worst category of killing, namely private, self-determined killing between people, not for the sake of protecting the nation (as in war), not for the sake of justice (as in capital punishment), and not for the sake of saving a life (as in self-defense), but rather to satisfy private wants and desires (de Wachter 1992, p. 29).

The Elderly

Age has a strong impact on the percentage of Americans who favor PAS. In the Harvard Public Health survey, 79% of 18 to 34 year old's were in favor of doctors assisting patients to commit suicide, compared with only 53% of those over age 50. Thus, the elderly–those most likely to be affected by such policy–are least in favor of it. Proponents of assisted suicide target the elderly as a group where this practice may have special application, especially for those suffering from bereavement (or even before bereavement, as in the "double-suicides" described in *Final Exit*, pp. 100-102).

Advocates of the Mentally Retarded/Mentally Ill

The Association for Retarded Citizens of Washington, the state's oldest organization of parents and other advocates of people with mental retardation, was solidly opposed to the legalization of PAS in their state for a number of reasons. First, they felt that PAS demeaned the dignity of people with disabilities and fostered the attitude that life in a wheelchair or with the need of mechanical supports is intolerable. Second, they were concerned over the possibility of abuse of the voluntary nature of such requests; mentally retarded persons often willingly yield to authority figures when they are confused or do not fully understand a situation. Third, they were concerned over who would determine the competency of mentally retarded persons in making such decisions. Overall, PAS is viewed as a direct threat to the lives and well-being of retarded Americans.

Mental health professionals are also concerned that legalizing PAS may adversely affect the care of persons with chronic mental illness, particularly during a time of increasing rates of illness and limited mental health resources. Eliot Slater, founder of the World Federation of Neurology, and others before him have argued that PAS should be extended to the incurably mentally ill (Alvarez 1972; Williams 1975; Slater 1980). Referring to patients with psychotic illness that is difficult to treat, Slater notes:

> What is the value of saving the life, say, even of a suicidal recurrent depressive, if it is only to force him to face again, in a few weeks or months, the same predicament. How can we be sure that the impulsive psychopath, who has opted for death, is not really doing his best, both for himself and everybody else. (p. 202)

This notion goes against a very basic responsibility of a civilized society to protect its most vulnerable members, including those who have a mental illness that impairs judgment and strips them of their ability to make free and competent decisions. To suddenly turn around and support or assist such persons in carrying out their impulsive gestures is to shirk that protective role.

Religious Organizations

Thus far, only a single mainline denomination (United Church of Christ) has come out in favor of PAS. Most religious organizations in America promote the sanctity of human life and the authority of God in deciding when death is to occur. The notion that spiritual growth and maturation can and often do occur during the final days of life and even during times of suffering is firmly imbedded in Judeo-Christian theology. This is balanced, however, by a strong emphasis on mercy and provision of comfort, hope, and a sense of purpose.

> When you are in distress and all these things have come upon you, in the latter days, you will return to the Lord your God and listen to His voice. For the Lord your God is a compassionate God; He will not fail you nor destroy you nor forget

the covenant with your fathers which He swore to them. (Deuteronomy 4:30-31, ASV)

Religious arguments, however, cannot be used against legalizing
PAS, since this would entail forcing beliefs on nonreligious persons
and thus infringing on their rights. A relevant point, nevertheless, is
that religion can help *make suffering tolerable* because of its ability
to enhance coping and infuse hope (Koenig et al. 1992). Religious
organizations are often involved in providing alternatives to PAS
such as high quality nursing home care, adult day-care, and hospice
programs. Proponents of PAS tend to reject both hospice and
religion for precisely this reason. Describing the "friendly" alliance
between the Hemlock Society and hospice, Derek Humphry (1991)
notes the following:

> This liaison has always been strongest on the West Coast.
> From what I have observed this is probably because hospice
> groups there are more likely to be in the hands of people with
> purely humanitarian motives. On the East Coast, hospices are
> more likely–but not exclusively–to be founded by religious
> people. (p. 35)

The Judeo-Christian scriptures are relatively silent on the topic of
suicide; however, much can be learned about the Jewish attitude in
1 Samuel. In that book, King Saul commits suicide by falling on his
own sword during a battle with the Philistines (1 Samuel 31:4). This
occurred after Saul had fallen out of God's favor and after he had
been afflicted by a "tormenting" spirit (1 Samuel 16:14). The act of
Saul's suicide, then, occurs in a setting of being out of God's will
and in a setting of preexisting mental illness. Nowhere in scripture
is there justification for terminating a human life–either one's own
or another's–except in time of war or for punishment.

Wennberg (1989) provides a balanced discussion of the pros and
cons for assisted suicide from a Christian perspective which is both
moral and practical. What is the reasoning behind the Judeo-Christian prohibition against suicide? According to Wennberg,

> . . . the fear is that in ending life we may prematurely end not
> only a journey ordained by God but a journey whose purpose

has yet to be fully achieved, there still being meaningful life to be lived even if under difficult circumstances. It is respect for that journey, ordained as it is by God and filled with eternal significance that renders the Christian cautious about either terminating it or failing to promote its continuation. (p. 96)

On the other hand, I agree with Wennberg that the final act of a desperate, suffering, and questionably competent person is unlikely to cancel out a lifetime of service to God (i.e., "unforgivable sin"). To say there is absolutely no moral risk, however, is not easily done either.

WHY NOT LEGALIZE PHYSICIAN-ASSISTED SUICIDE?

There is little doubt that there are cases where PAS could be considered an ethical alternative. As noted earlier, one example might be an "ethical suicide" where the person takes their life to preserve a better life for others or for a religious cause (e.g., martyrdom). Another might be a terminally ill person with severe, prolonged, unrelievable suffering and no access to adequate hospice care or appropriate symptom relief. Nevertheless, it is one thing to justify an act and quite a different thing to justify a general practice (AMA 1983; President's Commission 1983). There are numerous reasons why PAS should not be legalized (Figure 22.1).

Ambiguous Indications

Most persons agree that the conditions necessary to justify PAS are the following: (1) intolerable and intractable suffering, (2) terminal illness, and (3) a request by a competent patient (i.e., unimpaired decision-making capacity). None of these conditions, however, are easily established. First of all, what is *intolerable and intractable* suffering? Suffering involves more than pain or other physical sensations; psychological factors are invariably operative–fear, hopelessness, discouragement, fatigue, anger, and feelings of entrapment. It is difficult to determine exactly how much of suffering might be reversible, given adequate pain relief, support and nurturance from others, and maximization of autonomy by providing the person with some control over their care. The request for assistance with dying often involves unspoken elements and interpersonal issues–a fear of loneliness and abandonment, a cry for affirmation that their life is indeed valuable and worth fighting for. If their personal physician then agrees to assist the patient commit suicide, this acquiescence may represent proof to the patient that life is indeed without value and thus expendable (Teno and Lynn 1991; Montalvo 1991).

Second, is the establishment of a *terminal illness*. Not only is the accuracy of physician diagnoses quite poor for many diseases, even when the diagnosis is correct, the ability to predict the exact timing of death is notably poor. Examples include both Alzheimer's disease and cancer. After a comprehensive clinical evaluation, psychological testing, and organic workup (including brain scan and blood tests), the diagnosis of Alzheimer's disease is correct in only about 70 to 80% of cases (McKhann et al. 1984). This means that up to a quarter of persons given this diagnosis may not have the disease. Was Janet Adkins one of these? Even in cases where the diagnosis of Alzheimer's is accurate, the clinical course is highly variable with rates of survival ranging from 2 to 15 years. Much of the psychological suffering in that disorder occurs only in the early stages of the disease; in middle and later stages, insight is often lost and feelings of anxiety and dysphoria lessen.

Likewise, cancer diagnoses can be difficult to establish in certain cases, even with biopsies. Prognosis is also indefinite for many cancers, given the development of more effective treatments with fewer side-effects. Finally, spontaneous remission is not rare and may occur in as many as 5% of some cancers.

The third condition necessary to justify PAS is that the patient be *rational* and have *unimpaired judgment*. This is undoubtedly the most difficult of the three conditions to establish. For a person to make a truly free and autonomous decision, he or she must not have a mental illness that impairs his or her judgment–in other words, they must be rational. The possibility of a rational suicide has been argued (Moody 1991), but by no means proven. Indeed, some psychiatrists contend that suicide by definition is an irrational act. David Spiegel, head of the research team from Stanford University that showed increased survival rates in breast cancer patients following psychosocial interventions, has called "rational suicide" an oxymoron and argued that no rational person wants to die (Spiegel et al. 1989; Spiegel 1992). The will to live is so strongly imbedded within the human psyche that loss of rationality may be required to deter this drive in most cases. Again, the only exception to this may be the rare cases of ethical suicide where a person concludes that there are certain values that are higher than life itself. Studies have shown that at least 95% (range 89% to 100%) of suicides occur in persons with preexisting mental illness (Kaplan and Sadock 1988; Conwell 1992), strongly suggesting that a suicidal state is evidence for irrationality in the vast majority of cases.

In order to determine whether or not a mental illness is driving a chronically or terminally person to commit suicide, the physician must be able to distinguish physical from mental symptoms. Geriatric psychiatrists point out that in many such cases, this is not easily done (Conwell and Caine 1991). The symptoms of chronic and/or terminal illness are often inseparable from those of psychological disorder. Chronic pain, for example, is invariably accompanied by insomnia, fatigue, decreased concentration, and other physiological symptoms that tend to blend together with psychological ones. The symptoms of chronic pain and depression are almost identical. This is unfortunate since depression is the most common treatable psychiatric disorder that leads to suicide. A high prevalence of depression (as high as 45%) has been repeatedly documented among older persons with chronic medical illness, disability, pain or dyspnea (Koenig et al. 1988a; 1991).

The issue becomes even more confusing when depression presents not with a sad mood but rather with somatic symptoms (so called "masked" depression) (Hesse 1983). Physical complaints are often more acceptable to elders than emotional complaints, which may be viewed with shame and felt to reflect a weak character. Consequently, many elders deny depression. Ruling out a reversible depression in this setting, then, is a challenge for even the best clinician. Consequently, as many as 75% to 90% of depressed elders with medical illness are not recognized by primary care physicians (Rapp et al. 1988; Koenig et al. 1988b). Thus, it is difficult to ensure that a dying or chronically ill patient who makes a request for assisted-suicide is truly free of reversible emotional disturbance.

Personal Biases of the Physician

For this reason, the determination of reversible mental disorder in a suicidal patient ends up depending heavily on the judgment (and personal biases) of the doctor. If a physician feels that the patient lacks "quality of life," that physician will more readily concur with the patient's decision to end life. Some doctors believe that when a patient is older and has many chronic illnesses and functional impairments, there is good reason for him or her to be depressed. Treatment, then, may be considered unnecessary. The presence of a reason for depression, however, is not a good reason to ignore it (Fawcett 1972).

When a physician is called on to determine whether a sick patient is mentally competent to decide to end his or her life, many personal factors on the doctor's part come into play—the physician's anxiety about death, moral values, experience with members of his or her own family, and perhaps, the strain of caring for the patient. Furthermore, family members who are experiencing emotional suffering and/or financial hardships of their own may pressure the physician one way or the other and thus influence his or her objectivity. Leaving the physician as the sole person responsible for determining the competency of a patient requesting PAS, then, can be fraught with problems.

While establishing a hospital ethics committee to deal with such issues theoretically removes the final decision-making responsibility from any one physician, it does not solve the problem. In the end, such committees are likely to rely heavily on the opinion of the patient's personal physician anyway. In addition, other sticky issues would have to be dealt with. Who would be chosen to make up such committees and how might political/economic forces influence their decisions? What if a patient is costing the hospital great amounts of money to keep him or her alive; there may be subtle and not-so-subtle pressures on such committees to take care of the problem. It is not at all clear how such committees would be regulated to ensure that guidelines are being followed in both small and large, urban and rural hospitals alike. Private hospitals may foster ethics committees that are more supportive of assisted suicide in order to attract patients during these hard economic times. Other safeguards against abuse, such as requiring consultation from one or more other physicians before proceeding, likewise seems a charade when concurring opinion can regularly be sought and obtained from physicians known to be sympathetic to PAS.

The Slippery Slope

One cannot deny the existence of isolated cases of intolerable suffering from inadequate pain control or irreversible mental anguish during terminal illness. However, the legalization of PAS would not only affect the isolated case but would also open up the practice more generally. The gradual widening of circumstances in which this practice might be considered appropriate has become known as the "slippery slope" concept (Steinbrook and Lo 1988). If one can justify PAS as a solution to the suffering experienced during the terminal phase of illness, then it is even easier to defend the practice for intractable suffering in nonterminal patients with chronic illness, since even greater benefits might be accrued in the latter case.

The current situation in Holland, where PAS has been practiced since 1973, exemplifies this trend. "Mercy killing" in that country has now been extended from terminally ill cancer patients to patients with paraplegia, multiple sclerosis, and "gross physical deterioration at advanced age" (Pence 1988; Fenigsen 1989). The three incidents involving Jack Kevorkian in 1990-1991 prove that such things can happen here in America too. The danger is even greater in the United States than in Holland, where there is essentially unlimited access to health care and ample supportive services for the dying (Rigter 1989); in the United States, the cost of caring for such patients often falls on relatives or on other agencies who, in some circumstances, may be powerfully motivated to rid themselves of this burden.

As indicated by Robert Butler, there are many powerful social and political forces which can and will influence the circumstances in which PAS might be carried out if it were legalized. As the cost of health care spirals upward and the pressures of cost-containment escalate, there will be an increasing tendency to limit health care resources to that element of the population which is less valued, less productive, or seen as benefiting least from such resources (Callahan 1987). Persons most likely to be affected by such policies are the poor and those without health insurance–individuals who cannot afford to pay for their own health care. Because high-quality hospice care is not uniformly available in the United States, legalizing PAS may have unpredictable consequences for the treatment of socioeconomically disadvantaged patients who are chronically or terminally ill.

Generation Effect

Wennberg (1989, p. 202) notes that while it is very hard to introduce for the first time a practice that has long conflicted with moral, social, and legal standards, it is easier to do so the second time. This is particularly true as the current generation passes on and the next and then following generations come into power. While we might consider PAS for cognitively or physically impaired elders reprehensible, our great grandchildren may not see it that way–especially when they have been raised in a society where assisted suicide for people suffering from chronic or terminal illnesses has become the norm.

Currently there are between two and four million persons in the United States with Alzheimer's disease; in 2010, this figure is expected to jump to as high as 15 to 20 million. The estimated cost of care for these patients and lost productivity due to illness has been set at nearly 1000 billion dollars (Sunderland 1992). If legalized, PAS would provide a quick, easy, and inexpensive solution to this problem. In such cases, perhaps "substituted judgments" by either the physician or family member might be called upon to justify such acts.

How accurate are doctors and relatives in predicting patients' feelings about life-and-death issues? The accuracy of "proxy predictions" has been challenged by recent research that indicates as low as 59% agreement between elderly patients and their relatives or physicians concerning cardiopulmonary resuscitation decisions in case of severe cognitive impairment. After such a study, Seckler and colleagues (1991) concluded the following:

The resuscitation preferences of these elderly clinic outpatients were not adequately understood by either of their logical proxy decision makers. On the basis of the kappa statistic, physicians did no better than chance alone in predicting the wishes of their patients and, although the concordance of a family members' predictions achieved statistical significance, the kappas (0.27 and 0.30) did not achieve even the moderate strength of agreement (Kappa > 0.4) that should be required of surrogates making life-and-death decisions on behalf of patients under the substituted judgment standard. (p. 95)

Thus, if the wishes of patients and their surrogate decision makers are discordant for even simple decisions regarding cardiopulmonary resuscitation, it is clear that decisions on active, purposeful assistance in life termination may also conflict. PAS in cases of mental incompetence, then, is difficult to justify and dangerous to consider.

While proponents of assisted suicide argue that this would never happen to incompetent patients or to patients against their will, the situation in Holland speaks loudly otherwise. Van der Maas and colleagues' (1991) recent survey of PAS in that country indicate that about 2.9% of all deaths are currently attributable to this practice. However, nearly 28% of these cases (n = 1000/yr) were performed "without an explicit and persistent request" on the part of the patient. Careful review of the data from this report further indicate that if one includes cases of physicians withdrawing or withholding treatment with the intention of causing death *without the consent of the patient or their surrogate*, the figure of 1000 non-consenting deaths/year expands to nearly 8000/year (Have and Welie 1992). Thus, such abuses can and do happen.

Failure to Follow Guidelines

There is also concern that once PAS is legalized, American physicians may not follow the strict guidelines likely to accompany this law. Again, the Holland experience may be prophetic. Review of deaths by a coroner is the only safeguard in Holland to ensure that guidelines are being followed. While 2000 to 10,000 deaths per year occur as a consequence of PAS, only about 200 cases per year are reported to coroners (a requirement by law). If PAS were legalized in the United States, what guarantee do we have that physicians here would be any more likely than those in the Netherlands to follow guidelines? The ability of society to monitor cases of PAS (public accountability) is severely hampered by the nearly uniform desire to maintain privacy (as indicated by the wording of PAS initiatives in California and other states). The absence of investigations of under-reporting in the Netherlands, then, is understandable and inevitable in the United States should PAS be decriminalized. The absence of monitoring increases the risk of abuse.

Impact on Medical Practice

The legalization of PAS in the United States would have a major impact on the care of the dying. Murphy and Lynn (1990) emphasize that both the quality of care received by these patients and the morale of their physician caretakers would probably decline. The traditional goals of the physician have been to cure and comfort. Allowing doctors to assist their patients in killing themselves as a means of providing comfort may have widespread repercussion in terms of loss of trust and confidence in physicians (Teno and Lynn 1991).

Most importantly, legalizing PAS would weaken societal resolve to provide better supportive care and would relieve the pressure on medical researchers to improve the efficacy and safety of treatments for physical and emotional discomforts associated with chronic and terminal illness. Such research is determined by funding decisions, and funding decisions are determined by societal needs. While the number of people in this country potentially affected by legalizing PAS under current guidelines is theoretically small, if extended to chronically ill or demented elders, impaired newborns, and those who are mentally retarded and severely mentally ill, the number of people affected grows much larger and is likely to impact funding decisions.

ALTERNATIVES

When a chronically or terminally ill person becomes suicidal, it means that his or her life has become so intolerable or, because of fear of future suffering, has become so overwhelming that no other way out besides death is even conceivable. It is known that in the suicidal state, a person's consciousness becomes constricted to the point that he or she becomes unable to consider alternative solutions. Severe disability, admission to a nursing home, abandonment by loved ones, progression of chronic illness, or a painful and protracted terminal illness are situations that may initiate a constriction of consciousness and thus precipitate suicidal yearnings. The most expedient and least costly solution to this problem is to go ahead and allow the person to end their life. The more prolonged, costly, and courageous course, however, is to work with the person to help them to see alternative solutions to their problems.

Most persons who request euthanasia are saying "I'd rather be dead than be _____" (lonely, abandoned, disabled, suffering, in pain, in a nursing home). Rather than provide them with the means of killing themselves, it might be best to *provide companionship* to relieve loneliness, *mobilize family members* to dispel the patient's sense of abandonment, *provide assistive devices* to help limit disability and maximize autonomy and self-care, *make nursing homes more desirable* places to live, *provide adequate psychological and spiritual care* to help relieve emotional discomfort, *provide better medical care and analgesia* to relieve pain and other physical symptoms. All of these actions require effort, money, and time–but they ultimately preserve our respect for human life and are tangible proofs that disabled, suffering, and/or elderly persons are worthy and valuable to society, regardless of their level of productivity or apparent burden.

Relieve Symptoms

Hospice providers have shown that most terminal patients can be made quite comfortable, even in the setting of intractable pain (Saunders 1982). In fact, practically all pain can be relieved today using appropriate pharmacotherapy. Even the 5-10% of terminal cancer patients who cannot avoid pain in the waking state can be treated with continuous anesthesia with high doses of narcotics–administered either by patient-controlled infusion devices or by continuous drip IV techniques monitored by health-care providers. Some patients may choose to tolerate pain if they wish to remain conscious and take care of business; those who do not wish this may have their consciousness obliterated and all supportive therapy withdrawn. In such circumstances, especially when food and water are not forced, death quickly ensues in a matter of a few days. Most of the time, this can be arranged in the patient's own home, thus avoiding the $500-$5000/day expense to the patient and family involved in hospitalization.

Just as pain can be relieved by the appropriate use of narcotics, feelings of isolation, dysphoria, and anxiety can be counteracted and self-esteem enhanced by a close and intimate relationship with another person, supportive counseling by staff, chaplains or mental health professionals, and sometimes, by the use of antidepressants, tranquilizers, or electroconvulsive therapy in cases of severe anxiety or depression. Control can be turned back to the patient by allowing him or her to participate in decisions about his or her medical and nursing care. Thus, under the best of medical, spiritual, and psychological care, there are not many patients who experience intolerable suffering (Murphy and Lynn 1990).

As noted earlier, the prohibition of PAS in this country has forced policymakers to devote research dollars to improve the quality of care that dying patients receive, to develop better treatments for cancer and better drugs to relieve associated physical symptoms (pain, nausea and other gastrointestinal disturbances, breathlessness, excessive secretions, and side-effects from anti-neoplastic drugs). If PAS were allowed, it is likely that meticulous attention to symptom control and psychosocial needs would be compromised, given the easier and less expensive option of assisted-suicide.

High Quality Care for the Dying

Part of humane care to the dying includes a recognition of when care and comfort must take precedence over attempts to cure. A great deal of the public cry for PAS has arisen because of a lack of communication between patients, physicians, and families about decisions concerning the adequate relief of symptoms during chronic and terminal illness and the appropriate forgoing of extraordinary life-sustaining technologies. More advisable than authorization of assisted suicide is the implementation of high quality care for the dying that is now being accomplished through hospice principles (Saunders 1982; Volicer et al. 1986).

It seems reasonable to allow nature to take its course in elders who have terminal illness with only a few days or weeks to live, those in severe pain or experiencing other intractable discomforts that rob life of its meaning, and those who are severely and irreversibly demented, comatose, or exist in a persistent vegetative state, once provision has been made to relieve suffering. Family members and friends should be encouraged to visit and spend time with the patient at this time. If the patient, family, and other concerned staff members all agree, then the physician may proceed to make every effort to relieve symptoms and provide comfort–even at the risk of hastening death. This plan should be clearly documented in the chart. Advanced directives may guide family and health care providers in making such decisions for incompetent patients. If significant depression or anxiety is suspected in a conscious patient, then psychiatric consultation should be obtained and efforts made to treat these symptoms.

Once significant mental disorder has been ruled out or maximally treated, and the patient and family agree to no further intervention, then tubes should be removed and both routine and heroic treatments to prolong life should be discontinued and not restarted. As noted earlier, consideration may even be given to limiting the administration of food and water in some instances where death is imminent and suffering is severe or the patient is unconscious. Research has shown that limiting fluids decreases incontinence, minimizes excessive secretions that interfere with respirations, and causes little discomfort to the patient (Billings 1985; Editorial 1986). Likewise, when food intake is completely stopped, hunger diminishes and the experience of pain from terminal disease may lessen (Hamm and Lyeth 1984; Hamm et al. 1985). When both fluids and food are restricted in the terminally ill elder, death usually ensues quickly.

All efforts by health care providers at this time should be directed at simple comfort measures–maintenance of good skin and oral care, keeping the environment clean and fresh, and vigorously treating physical symptoms such as pain, nausea, or dyspnea with the most effective and powerful medications available. In treating symptoms of unbearable pain or suffocation, a dose of morphine may be needed which in some cases inadvertently hastens or causes the death of the patient. This is unavoidable. The intention of the physician, in this author's opinion, must always be to relieve suffering by *identifying and treating the underlying cause* or *by relieving symptoms*–not by facilitating the premature death of the patient.

SUMMARY

The topic of physician-assisted suicide has been considered. Physicians, medical ethicists, advocates of the mentally-retarded and mentally ill, the elderly, and the vast majority of religious groups in the United States tend to oppose it. The request for assisted suicide is often a cry for help, a cry of fear, a cry of desperation. Rather than support and assist the patient in ending their life, physicians must identify those factors that underlie the suffering (psychological and physical) and do everything they can to relieve them.

Like most moral laws, the law prohibiting assisted suicide applies correctly to the vast majority of persons; however, for extreme cases the law appears in some instances to lose its validity. Consequently, the current law does disservice to a small number of persons who are experiencing intractable and intolerable suffering, have terminal illness, and are rational. Nevertheless, legalizing PAS would establish a new moral law–and like the old law, it too will operate poorly at the extremes, perhaps needlessly allowing the deaths of many persons with reversible mental or physical illness and months or years of potentially meaningful life remaining. It is often during the final days of life, when a person can no longer deny their mortality, that much important work and healing goes on. Family members forgive each other and may express love for the first time in their lives. It is at this time that priorities may finally come into line. If successful aging depends on the completion of such work, and I believe it does, then allowing physicians to cut this time short by assisting the death of their patients, may be a big mistake.

Legalizing PAS may set a precedent that could create problems far worse than exist today, and there will be less societal pressure to correct those problems since dead persons are seldom a very influential or vocal group; those who are suffering, on the other hand, present a formidable problem for our society, which will be forced to improve the quality of care to these persons through research and advances in health care delivery. While there will always be rare cases and exceptions to the rule, the provision of high quality medical, psychological, and spiritual care to those who are chronically or terminally ill should go a long way toward eliminating the need for physician assisted-suicide and ensuring a "good death."

REFERENCES

Alvarez, W. (1972). The right to die. In *Humanistic Perspectives in Medical Ethics*, edited by M.B. Visscher. Buffalo, NY: Prometheus Books, pp. 67-68.

American Geriatrics Society. (1991). Voluntary active euthanasia. *Journal of the American Geriatrics Society* 39:826.

American Medical Association Judicial Council. (1983). *Opinions of the Judicial Council*, 1982. Reprinted in President's Commission for the Study of Ethical Problems in medicine and Biomedical and Behavioral Research, Deciding to Forego Life-Sustaining Treatment. Washington, DC: US Government Printing Office, pp. 299-300.

American Society of Internal Medicine. (1992). Survey of 402 physicians published in the society's magazine. *The Internist* (March).

Becker, E. (1973). *The Denial of Death*. NY: The Free Press.

Billings, J.A. (1985). Comfort measures for the terminally ill: Is dehydration painful. *Journal of the American Geriatrics Society* 33:808-810.

Butler, R.N. (1990). Physician-assisted suicide: The wrong way to go. *Geriatrics* 45(8):13-14.

Callahan, D. (1987). *Setting Limits: Medical Goals in an Aging Society.* NY: Simon and Schuster.

_____ (1988). Vital distinctions, mortal questions: Debating euthanasia and health-care costs. *Commonwealth* (July 15):397-404.

_____ (1989). Can we return to death to disease? *Hastings Center Report* 19(suppl.):4-6.

Conwell, Y. (1992). Suicide in the elderly. Presentation at Annual Meeting of the American Association for Geriatric Psychiatry, February 17, San Francisco.

Conwell, Y., and E.D. Caine. (1991). Rational suicide and the right to die. *New England Journal of Medicine* 325:1100-1103.

Editorial. (1986). Terminal dehydration. *Lancet* 1:306.

Editorial. (1991). Hemlock Society: Built on a myth? *Christianity Today* 35 (15):51.

Fawcett, J. (1972). Suicidal depression and physical illness. *Journal of the American Medical Association* 219:1303-1310.

Fenigsen, R. (1989). A case against Dutch euthanasia. *Hastings Center Report* 19 (Jan./Feb. special supplement):22-30.

————— (1990). Euthanasia: A breach of trust. *Senior Patient* (July 1990):52-54.

Foot, P. (1977). Euthanasia. *Philosophy and Public Affairs* 6:85-112.

Gaylin, W. (1988). Doctors must not kill. *Journal of the American Medical Association* 259:2139-2140.

Gillett, G. (1988). Euthanasia, letting die and the pause. *Journal of Medical Ethics* 14:61-68.

Hamm, R.J., and B.G. Lyeth. (1984). Nociceptive thresholds following food restriction and return to free-feeding. *Physiology and Behavior* 33:499-501.

Hamm, R.J., J.S. Knisely, A. Watson, B.G. Lyeth, and F.B. Bossut. (1985). Hormonal mediation of the analgesia produced by food deprivation. *Physiology and Behavior* 35:879-882.

Hastings Center Report. (1992). Dying well? A colloquy on euthanasia and assisted suicide. *Hastings Center Report* 22(2):6-55.

Have, H., and J. Welie. (1992). Euthanasia: Normal medical practice? *Hastings Center Report* 22(2):34-38.

Hesse, S. (1983). The masked depression syndrome. *American Journal of Psychotherapy* 37:456-475.

Humphry, D. (1991). *Final Exit: The Practicalities of Self-Deliverance and Assisted Suicide for the Dying.* Eugene, OR: The Hemlock Society.

Kamisar, Y. (1978). Euthanasia legislation: Some nonreligious objections. In T.L. Beauchamp, and S. Perlin (eds.), *Ethical Issues in Death and Dying*, Englewood Cliffs, NJ: Prentice-Hall, pp. 220-232.

Kaplan, H.I., and B.J. Sadock. (1988). *Synopsis of Psychiatry.* Baltimore: Williams and Wilkins, p. 453.

Koenig, H.G. (1993). Physician-assisted suicide: Some comments and concerns. *Journal of Family Practice* (in press).

Koenig, H.G., K.G. Meador, H.J. Cohen, and D.G. Blazer. (1988a). Depression in elderly men hospitalized with medical illness. *Archives of Internal Medicine* 148:1929-1936.

————— (1988b). Detection and treatment of major depression in older medically ill hospitalized patients. *International Journal of Psychiatry in Medicine* 18: 17-31.

Koenig, H.G., K.G. Meador, F. Shelp, V. Goli, H.J. Cohen, and D.G. Blazer. (1991). Major depressive disorder in hospitalized medical inpatients: An examination of young and elderly veterans. *Journal of the American Geriatrics Society* 39:881-890.

Koenig, H.G., H.J. Cohen, D.G. Blazer, C. Pieper, K.G. Meador, F. Shelp, V. Goli, and R. DiPasquale. (1992). Religious coping and depression in hospitalized elderly medically ill men. *American Journal of Psychiatry* 149:1693-1700.

Lawton, K. (1991). The doctor as executioner. *Christianity Today* (December 16):50-52.

Lynn, J. (1990). Euthanasia–not in America. *The Washington Post*, April 19, p. A-26.

McKhann, G., D. Drachman, M. Folstein, R. Katzman, D. Price, and E. Stadlan. (1984). Clinical diagnosis of Alzheimer's disease: Report of the NINCDS-ADRDA work group under the auspices of Department of Health and Human Services task force on Alzheimer's disease. *Neurology* 34:939-944.

Montalvo, B. (1991). The patient chose to die: Why? *Gerontologist* 31:700-703.

Moody, H.R. (1991). "Rational Suicide" on grounds of old age? *Journal of Geriatric Psychiatry* 24:261-276.

Murphy, D.J., and J. Lynn. (1990). Care near the end of life. In *Geriatric Medicine,* edited by C.K. Cassel, D.E. Reisenberg, L.B. Sorensen, and J.R. Walsh. New York: Springer-Verlag, pp. 607-614.

Palmore, E. (1991). Should assisted suicide be legalized? *Fifty Plus* (October).

Parkes, C.M. (1978). Psychological aspects. In *The Management of Terminal Disease,* edited by C.M. Saunders. London: Edward Arnold Publishers, Ltd., p. 56.

Pence, G.E. (1988). Do not go slowly into that dark night: Mercy killing in Holland. *American Journal of Medicine* 84:139-141.

President's Commission. (1983). *Deciding to Forego Life-Sustaining Treatment.* Washington DC: US Government Printing Office, p. 72.

Psychiatric Times. (1992). Michigan physician, charged with murder, proposes euthanasia medical specialty. *The Psychiatric Times* 9 (April).

Rapp, S.R., D.A. Walsh, S.A. Parisi, and C.E. Wallace. (1988). Detecting depression in elderly medical inpatients. *Journal of Consulting and Clinical Psychology* 56:509-513.

Rigter, H. (1989). Euthanasia in the Netherlands: Distinguishing facts from fiction. *Hastings Center Report* 19 (suppl.):31.

Saunders, C. (1982). Principles of symptom control in terminal care. In *The Medical Clinics of North America: Clinical Pharmacology of Symptom Control,* edited by M.M. Reidenberg. Philadelphia: WB Saunders Co., pp. 1169-1183.

Schneider, K.S., and S. Carswell. (1992). Love unto death. *People magazine* (January 20), pp. 57-63.

Seckler, A.B., D.E. Meier, M. Mulvihill, and B.E. Cammer-Paris. (1991). Substituted judgment: How accurate are proxy predictions? *Annals of Internal Medicine* 115:92-98.

Singer, P.A., and M. Siegler. (1990). Euthanasia: A critique. *New England Journal of Medicine* 322:1881-1883.

Slater, E. (1980). Choosing the time to die. *In Suicide: The Philosophical Issues,* edited by M.P. Battin and D.J. May. NY: St. Martin's Press, p. 202.

Spiegel, D. (1992). *Psychiatry Grand Rounds,* Duke University Medical Center, Durham, NC (April 9).

Spiegel, D., J.R. Bloom, H.C. Kraemer, and E. Gottheil. (1989). Effect of psychosocial treatment on survival of patients with metastatic breast cancer. *Lancet* 2(8668): 888-891.

Sprung, C.L. (1990). Changing attitudes and practices in foregoing life-sustaining treatments. *Journal of the American Medical Association* 263:2211-2215.

Steinbrook, R., and B. Lo. (1988). Artificial feeing: Solid ground, not a slippery slope. *New England Journal of Medicine* 318:286-290.

Sunderland, T. (1992). *Psychiatry Grand Rounds*, Duke University Medical Center, Durham, NC (February 27).

Teno, J., and J. Lynn. (1991). Voluntary active euthanasia: The individual case and public policy. *Journal of the American Geriatrics Society* 39:827-830.

Van der Maas, P.J., J.J. Van Delden, L. Pinenborg, and C.W.N. Looman. (1991). Euthanasia and other medical decisions concerning the end of life. *Lancet* 338:669-674.

Volicer, L., Y. Rheume, J. Brown, Y. Rheaume, J. Brown, K.J. Fabiszewski, and R. Brady. (1986). Hospice approach to the treatment of patients with advanced dementia of the Alzheimer type. *Journal of the American Medical Association* 256:2210-2213.

de Wachter, M. (1992). Euthanasia in the Netherlands. *Hastings Center Report* 22(2):23-30.

Watts, D.T., and T. Howell. (1992). Assisted suicide is not voluntary active euthanasia. *Journal of the American Geriatrics Society* 40:1043-1046.

Watts, D.T., T. Howell, and B.A. Priefer. (1992). Geriatricians' attitudes toward assisting suicide of dementia patients. *Journal of the American Geriatrics Society* 40:878-885.

Weissman, A.D. (1972). *On Dying and Denying*. NY: Behavioral Publications.

Wennberg, R.N. (1989). *Terminal Choices: Euthanasia, Suicide, and the Right to Die*. Grand Rapids, MI: Eerdmans Publish Co.

Williams, G. (1975). Euthanasia and the physician. In *Beneficent Euthanasia*, edited by M. Kohl. Buffalo, NY: Prometheus Books, pp. 161.

Wolf, S. (1989). Holding the line on euthanasia. *Hastings Center Report* 19 suppl.:13-15.

Chapter 23

Final Comments

Aging is often associated with chronic illness and physical disability. Along with these physical conditions comes emotional distress as the person's sense of control and self-determination are threatened. Hence, depression and anxiety are common among elders with physical illness, whether living in the community or institutionalized in acute or chronic hospital settings. Other mental disorders associated with organic brain impairments such as Alzheimer's disease, multiple strokes, or the effects of chronic alcohol abuse are also common in later life and may adversely impact the quality of life both for elders and their families.

Advances in the medical and psychological sciences, improvement of health care delivery systems, and love and support from family and friends go a long way toward enhancing quality of life and lessening the suffering associated with chronic physical and mental illness. However, much of the burden must be shouldered by the older person him or herself. In addition to providing a community of believers to help carry this burden, religion, through its belief system and rituals, offers the aging person a powerful and enduring source of comfort. It provides an opportunity to start life over again with a new meaning and purpose which is not age-limited, and may infuse even the most pain-filled and dismal life with a sense of hope and future. Religion can enable the elder to transcend circumstances that cannot be altered, and may teach truths about life which can be understood only by those who have experienced loss and suffering, yet have survived.

It has been the premise of this book that successful aging is possible regardless of the circumstances humans find themselves, and that religion can facilitate this process. The comfort that religious beliefs provide is immediately available regardless of physical state, social predicament, or living situation–as long as there remains a capacity to believe and have faith. This ability–the capacity to trust–is the first psychosocial task learned at the beginning of life by the growing infant. It is also one of the last abilities to go at life's end.

Given the current and future mental health needs of aging Americans, and the limited governmental resources being made available, there is great opportunity (and responsibility) for the religious community to demonstrate their own faith and trust by supporting and ministering to the emotional, spiritual, and sometimes physical needs of this population. Both the clergy and religious laypersons will need to work closely with mental health professionals in this regard, referring patients for specialized services when indicated and encouraging compliance with medical or psychological prescriptions that follow. Mental health professionals, on the other hand, need the religious community to provide the necessary psychological and social support that they by themselves cannot provide. Health professionals must listen to, learn from, inform, and encourage religious professionals in these areas. Only a cooperative effort can hope to meet the mental and spiritual needs of our aging population. These efforts will invariably determine the successful aging and mental health of us all.

Acknowledgement

I would like to express my sincere thanks and appreciation to Fred Hine, Lewis King, John Pritchett, and Bill Wilson for their helpful comments and enthusiastic ideas for this book.

Subject Index

Page numbers in *italics* indicate figures; page number followed by "t" indicate tables.

Personality types and religion, 59
Persuasion and Healing (Frank),
    48-49
Phobias, 42
Physical illness
  anxiety and religion, 267-268
  in cognitive and moral
      development, 74
  dependence and loss of control,
      309-310
  and depression
    antidepressants, 151-152
    Durham VA Mental Health
        Survey, 144-151,148t
    prevalence of, 142-143
    psychotherapy, 153-154
    risk factors for, 152-153
  depression and religious coping
    age in, *228*
    changes over time, 227
    cognitive functioning, *232*
    community studies, 236-238
    denomination, 223-224
    Durham VA Mental Health
        Survey, 221-223
    factors in, 224-227,225t,226t
    in medical inpatients, 235-236
    mixed-age studies, 238-239
    psychiatric history in, *230*
    race in, *229*
    relationship of, 234-235,
        239-241
    social support network, *231*
    sociodemographic factors,
        233t
  in grief, 408-409
  in integrity and despair, 75-76
  and mature faith, 130
  pain relief, 498-502
  physician-assisted suicide
    negative impacts, 491-498
    opposition to, 485-491
    reasons for, 481-484
  and religion, 57-59
  and religious coping, 162

  case studies, 190-212
  changes over time, 170-171,
      172t-173t,*174*,175t,181-184
  factors in, 165-169,166t,170t,
      176-179
  older and younger men,
      174-176
  profile of coper, 179-181,
      212-216,214t-215t
  Religious Coping Index,
      163-165,*164*
  and self-worth, 310
  and spiritual nature, 112
  spiritual needs in, 283-294
  and suicide, 465-466
  whole person care (Cassem),
      311-317
Physician-assisted suicide. *See*
    Suicide
Physicians
  assistance in suicides
    failure to follow guidelines,
        497-498
    impact on care, 498
    misinterpretation of patients'
        wishes, 496-497
    opposition to, 485-487
    personal biases in, 494-495
    role in, 478-480
  chaplains, attitudes toward,
      305-307,306t
  dying, care of, 500-502
  Medicare reimbursements,
      297-298
  misdiagnosis, 492
  in nursing homes, 356
  pain relief, 499-500
  personal bias of, 37-38
  prayers for patients, 319
  religious coping, awareness of,
      176
Piaget, Jean
  cognitive development, 73
  Fowler's stages of faith
      development, 88-90

Name Index